FINAL
NEGOTIATIONS

In the series

HEALTH, SOCIETY, AND POLICY,

edited by Sheryl Ruzek and Irving Kenneth Zola

Final Negotiations

A Story of Love, Loss, and
Chronic Illness

CAROLYN ELLIS

TEMPLE UNIVERSITY PRESS

Philadelphia

Temple University Press, Philadelphia 19122
Copyright © 1995 by Temple University. All rights reserved
Published 1995
Printed in the United States of America

The paper used in this publication meets the minimum requirements of
American National Standard for Information Sciences—Permanence
of Paper for Printed Library Materials,
ANSI Z39.48-1984 ∞

Library of Congress Cataloging-in-Publication Data

Ellis, Carolyn, 1950–
    Final negotiations : a story of love, loss, and chronic illness / Carolyn Ellis.
        p.   cm.—(Health, society, and policy)
    Includes bibliographical references and index.
    ISBN 1-56639-270-5.—ISBN 1-56639-271-3 (pbk.)
    1. Weinstein, Gene, d. 1985—Health.   2. Emphysema, Pulmonary—Patients—
United States—Biography.   3. Ellis, Carolyn, 1950–   .   4. Chronically ill—Family
relationships.   5. Social medicine.   I. Title.   II. Series.
RC776.E5W454   1995
362.1′96248′0092—dc20
[B]   94-13912

CONTENTS

PART V
NEGOTIATING THE STORY   301

PART VI
ENDINGS   325

ACKNOWLEDGMENTS

I am grateful to the many friends and colleagues who participated significantly in the last days of Gene's life, cared for me while I grieved, and sustained me when I needed to feel my work could make a difference. My debt to so many people reinforces my strong belief in the social character of storytelling.

From the first field note, Doug McAdam provided unfailing encouragement for this project. Thank you, Doug, for twenty years of friendship, engaging conversations about the human condition, and tons of laughter. Judy Tanur was Gene's closest friend; she became my dear friend as well, and now she and I share happy times, good memories, and life stories. Thank you, Judy, for your loving and compassionate assistance during the last months of Gene's life. John McCarthy was Gene's closest male friend, and he and Sharon McCarthy were our favorite couple. Thanks, John and Sharon, for the wonderful meals, conversation, and helping hands.

The Weinsteins—Beth, Ruth, Paul, and Jerry—became family, and my continued contact with them brings me the joy of extended connection to Gene. Thank you, Beth, for taking part in the day-to-day caretaking of Gene during the most trying times. Without your deep love for Gene and your giving and forgiving spirit, my caretaker role would have been much more difficult than it was. Thank you, Ruth, for raising such a fun-loving, smart, and creative kid, and for providing loving support.

The Stony Brook Sociology Department offered a place where Gene and I felt at home and where we could always return (and frequently did). Thanks to the department for showing us that institutions can have heart and soul. In particular, I want to mention Joan Atwood, Michelle Caplette, Lewis Coser, Rose Coser, Norman Goodman, Michael Schwartz, and the secretarial staff, especially Carole Roland and Veronica Abjornson. Gladys Rothbell and Naomi Rosenthal deserve special recognition for their love, concern, and nurturing. Thanks, Naomi, for stepping in when I was not around, and especially for the chicken soup. Thanks, Gladys, for the midnight sessions, laughter in the face of agony, and your generosity.

Many friends in Tampa sustained me while I lived through and wrote about this experience. I met Jim Sperry nine months after Gene's death, during a very difficult period. With Jim, my hope was renewed that life might once again be happy and meaningful. What would I have done without the gentle love, total acceptance, strong shoulders, and zest for life that Jim provided? Thank you, Jim, my dear friend. Thanks also go to Ruth Anderson, Sheryle Baker, Gerard Brandmeyer, Sunne Brandmeyer, Etta Bender Breit, Diane Cutler, Nancy Hewitt, Kitty Klein, Steven Lawson, Helen Levine, Marilyn Myerson, Suzanne Nickeson, Barbara Ogur, and Ray Wheeler.

I greatly appreciate the colleagues who paved the way for this work. In particular, Laurel Richardson has been an inspiration, a wonderful friend and colleague, and an insightful critic for many years. Norman Denzin always pops up at the critical time to review my work, putting his finger immediately on the crucial point. Early in this project, Patricia Adler, Peter Adler, and David Franks offered spirited encouragement. As colleagues and caring friends, Ruth Linden, Doyle McCarthy, and Mark Neumann read the entire manuscript and responded intellectually and personally with penetrating honesty. Mitch Allen probably has no idea how great I felt when I heard the exuberant message he left on my phone the day after he "stayed up all night" reading my manuscript. Soon after, John Johnson provided an enthusiastic and insightful reading. After that, my confidence never wavered.

Many other people stimulated my ideas or read parts of this manuscript and offered important responses. They include Betsy Amster, Candace Clark, Jerome Crouch, Gary Fine, Michael Flaherty, Bruce Gronbeck, Bill Gronfein, Douglas Harper, Arlie Hochschild, Sherryl Kleinman, Richard Koffler, Lyn Lofland, David Maines, Gary Marx, Doug Mitchell, Virginia Olesen, Bill Rawlins, Carol Rambo Ronai, Allen Shelton, Lynn Smith-Lovin, and Arthur Vidich. Most respondents enthusiastically embraced the goals of my project, providing support just when I needed it. The few who did not share my purpose still provided valuable feedback that pushed me to develop my position more forcefully. Reactions that challenged my commitment to connecting social science and humanities merely strengthened my resolve to fashion sociology as a human search for meaning in spite of the difficulties in doing so.

At the University of South Florida, Dean Rollin Richmond has been particularly important in creating a supportive climate for work that diverges from the orthodoxy. The Institute for Interpretive Human Studies has brought together interpretive scholars from around the campus and across the country. The greatest joy in my career has come from working with graduate students on their writing projects and participating in lively and challenging class discussions. The students' willingness (indeed, eagerness) to try new approaches, their passion for learning and writing about lived experience (including their own), and their excellent work, all enliven me to continue to pursue my "calling" and take risks in the work I do. Thanks go to Janet Andrews, Judy Perry, and Sheree Wood for reading this manuscript; thanks go to all my students for sharing their experiences so creatively.

It has been a delight to work with the staff at Temple University Press. I applaud the Press's receptivity to interpretive social science. I especially thank Irving Zola, who identified personally with my work, shepherding it enthusiastically into Temple University Press. I also thank Janet Francendese for appreciating the goal of evoking the reader's experience, for making me feel my work was important, and for making helpful editorial suggestions.

I have learned much about loss and attachment in the last dozen years. I dedicate this book to the memory of family members whose deaths compelled me to come to grips with and give meaning to loss: my father, Arthur; my brother Rex; my aunt Florence; my dog Poogie; and, of course, Gene. I thank my family, especially my mother, who loved me and supported my goals even though many of my life choices must have seemed peculiar. Without the unconditional love, kisses, and frequent visits from Ande, Likker, Martina, and Traf while I worked, I never would have had the endurance to finish this book. Their "here and now" orientation often transported me back to day-to-day experience, reminding me of its importance and providing relief from my absorption in the past, the future, and analytic discourse. Now that this project is finished, I promise to take more walks in the park and play more catch on the beach.

Last, I acknowledge my partner, Art Bochner. Art is my best friend; my favorite coauthor and colleague; my relentless and untiring editor; my coconspirator of the heart, soul, and mind; and a gentle, kind, and loving mate. Many of the ideas for this book and much of my understanding of communication and relationships in general have developed in conversations with him. Thanks, Art, for appreciating that people come with histories and for being so wholeheartedly supportive of this project. Thanks for understanding that this book needed to occupy a place in our relationship. Thanks for showing me that relationships do not have to be guided primarily by the metaphors of power and exchange. Thanks for creating with me a partnership that balances adventure and contentment, commitment and freedom. Thanks for sharing in the co-construction of our stories. I'm sure glad we found each other.

PART I

Beginning

FINAL NEGOTIATIONS tells a story within a story. The central narrative gives a detailed account of attachment, chronic illness, and loss in my nine-year relationship with Gene Weinstein, a sociologist who died in 1985 from emphysema. The framing story chronicles the process of writing the personal narrative and contextualizes its meanings. The result is a multilayered, intertextual case study that integrates private and social experience and ties autobiographical to sociological writing (Broyard 1992; Butler and Rosenblum 1991; Frank 1991; Haskell 1990; Krieger 1991; Linden 1993; Mairs 1989; Murphy 1987; Paget 1993; Quinney 1991; Ronai 1992; Roth 1991; Yalom 1989; and Zola 1982a).

My goal in this and related work (Ellis 1993, in press; Ellis and Bochner 1992) is to make sociology an intimate conversation about the intricacies of feeling, relating, and working. Some friends and colleagues have reacted to the intimate quality of the text by asking why I would "risk" divulging personal details about my life that show my flaws, disappointments, and bad decisions as well as my strengths, achievements, and good judgments. Although I appreciate the significance of these risks, I have not been swayed from my conviction that the sociological imagination can touch on the complexities, ironies, and ambiguities of living *only* by showing the bad as well as the good, what has been private and confidential as well as what is public and openly accessible, what makes us uncomfortable as well as what makes us comfortable.

Written as "experimental ethnography" (Marcus and Fischer 1986), *Final Negotiations* intersects two recent burgeoning interests in human studies research—autobiography (for example, see Bateson 1989; Berger 1990; Friedman 1990; Goetting and Fenstermaker 1995; Heilbrun 1988; Higgins and Johnson 1988; Jackson 1989; Merton 1988; Okely and Callaway 1992; Personal Narratives Group 1989; Rosenwald and Ochberg 1992; Stanley and Morgan 1993; Steedman 1986; Williams 1991; Women's Studies

3

International Forum 1987) and narrative (for example, see Bruner 1986b, 1990; Coles 1989; Gergen and Gergen 1993; Josselson and Lieblich 1993; Kleinman 1988; Kreiswirth 1992; Maines 1993; McCabe 1993; McCloskey 1990; Parry 1991; Polkinghorne 1988; Richardson 1990a; Riessman 1993; Rosenwald and Ochberg 1992; Sarbin 1986; and Turner and Bruner 1986), bringing social science closer to literature (Benson 1993). Consequently, this work takes an unorthodox form for social-science research in its narrative structure, its self-conscious focus on emotional experience, and the reflexive position I assume as both narrator and a main character of the story. As with all narrative accounts, mine is partial, historically situated, and mediated (Bruner 1986a; Clifford 1986). I try to show this experience as I remember it, as a life being lived in a particular moment, place, and culture, rather than as a model for how life should be lived everywhere by everybody.

"The beauty of a good story is its openness," as Robert Coles (1989, p. 47) says, how you take it in and use it for yourself. How you, as a reader, respond to my story as you read and feel it is an important part of this work. I coax you to be open to your feelings as you take this narrative journey. Some of you may prefer to feel with me, as in watching a true-to-life movie; some may be reminded of and feel for the parallels in your own relation-ships, as in reading an engaging novel; some may prefer cognitively processing the feelings expressed, closer to a traditional social-science reading. My goal is to engage you in aspects of relationships that usually are neglected or overlooked in social-science inquiry. It is my assumption that this kind of "knowledge" comes from actively getting close to the text, rather than from being a passive spectator observing from a distance (Dewey 1980; Jackson 1989).

Although scholars who study personal relationships say it is important to understand the dynamic qualities of intimate bonds, most research "freeze[s] the fluid motion of relational processes" and "transforms the passionate process of 'falling in love' into a cooler, more rational state of being that substitutes product for process" (Bochner 1990, p. 3; Shotter 1987, p. 245). These researchers usually operate under the tacit assumption that it is more important to be true to the practices of rigorous social science than to the practices of lived relationships. Conversely, I have chosen to examine my own relationship in-depth in order to show a thickly detailed chronicle of how people get together and manage attachments or pull apart, and how they feel during these processes. This strategy moves closer to lived particulars of what happens in relationships than the traditional social-science research practices that categorize, generalize, and abstract from snippets of the experiences of others. My story provides enacted episodes of the dialectics of close relationships; that is, it shows how the contradictory pulls of private and public life, adventure and security, instrumentality and affection, independence and interdependence, expressiveness and protectiveness, and attachment and loss are played out in ordinary and extraordinary circumstances (Bochner 1984; Rawlins 1992). The relationship story shows the ambiguous, complex, and contradictory aspects of my connection to Gene as we interacted in our day-to-day lives, confronted epiphanies, managed attachment and loss, and struggled to make our life together meaningful. The result is a narrative that attempts to be true to the practices of relationships, taking the reader inside our experience as if it were happening now, instead of using our life mainly as "data" for preexisting sociological hypotheses.

Final Negotiations is addressed to social scientists interested in narrative research, medical sociology, and relational processes, as well as readers engaged by the complexities of attachment, chronic illness, and loss. Medical and social workers seeking to comprehend the experience of chronic illness for patients and caregivers, as well as those who want mainly to understand relationships, may want to turn now to the relationship story in Parts II, III, and IV. Interpretive social scientists and ethnographers will find a discussion of methodological and contextual issues of how this story was constructed in Part V, which may be read in sequence or at any point after reading Part I.

Contextualizing My Project

Why have I chosen to tell a personal story to sociologists and other students of relationships who in this century have not encouraged the idea that personal experience or narrative prose is a way of "knowing"? Certainly I did not learn this way of investigating lived experience from the academic model of social science I endured, first as a graduate student in sociology and later as a professor. To make the shift in my research orientation understandable, I will describe events in my work and personal life that led to the writing of *Final Negotiations.*

In 1974, after completing my undergraduate education, I spent a year as a social worker. My work was with abused and homeless children and adults unable to hold their families together. What I learned upon returning to school as a graduate student in 1975, however, seemed to have little to do with my experience in the public world. I had gone into sociology as an undergraduate because I was drawn to writers like Erving Goffman (1959,

1971), who excelled in opening readers' eyes to the world in which they lived. I had hoped to continue the same study in graduate school and learn more about my life and the social world around me.

In search of a real-world connection, I worked on a comparative study of two isolated fishing communities in the Chesapeake Bay (Ellis 1986), which allowed me to live with the people I studied and to participate in, observe, and describe their day-to-day lives. This seemed preferable to a library project or a secondary data analysis, where I would not meet the people I studied or be involved in their lived experience.

While in the communities, however, I often experienced conflict between remaining uninvolved and distant, as I had been trained, and participating fully; between recording only my "objective" observations of fisher folks' actions and speech and noting my sense of their emotional lives, a process that required my engagement. Often distance won out over involvement because of my concern about meeting the requirements I had learned for being a neutral social scientist.

When I returned to the university to write my dissertation, I struggled with the constraints of detached social-science prose and the demand to write in an authoritative and uninvolved voice. Though I worked hard to follow these principles, professors I admired still reprimanded me for having "gone native" and for being too sympathetic toward my subjects.

My dissertation was organized around "legitimate" sociological topics—social structure, family, work, and social change. Within this framework, I discussed "hard" sociological concepts, such as personal attachment, locus of social control, reciprocity, public conformity, civic status, individualism, communitarianism, center, and periphery. Yet, it was difficult to capture the complexity of the lives of the fisher folk using these categories, and I often felt unsure of the distinctions I was forced to make. To me, these theoretical concepts seemed as vague, subjective, and ethereal as emotional experience. I wish now that I had placed more emphasis on how the people felt, which was my primary interest.

I also wish now that I had been more present in my writing about the fishing communities. Mostly, I describe "them," the fisher folk, interacting with each other, as though I am off in the corner, invisible. In reality, most of what I learned came through my interactions with the people, especially their reactions to me. But those exchanges and the effects my presence might have had on what the fisher folk said and did took a back seat. I anguished over speaking in the first person, having been told it was "unprofessional" and that readers would then conclude I had not been neutral and distant (see Krieger 1991).

And, I wish that I had talked about how I felt, instead of being reluctant to admit how much my own emotional experiences in the communities influenced what I saw and even the theoretical framework of my book. The modes of writing and abstract terms I had been taught to use in my education as a sociologist inhibited me from communicating my own emotional and aesthetic experiences as well as those of the community members.

Even during this research, however, I was drawn to stories for conveying lived experience and insisted on inserting vignettes showing specific incidents. In these stories, I could occasionally be present, though I rarely got to speak and almost never got to feel. But I knew, even then, that I wanted readers to hear the participants' voices and see them acting. The vignettes breathed life into my more passive telling and categorizing of the fisher folk.

Informally, my primary mentor in graduate school was Gene Weinstein, who is a main character in *Final Negotiations*. Before the idea was fashionable, Gene said his goal in sociology was to bring emotion into our rational studies of human behavior. Still he advised me not to stray too far from the "realist" model of social research and its category systems and to keep my work within the boundaries of social science. "Your eye," he said to me once, "you're so perceptive about what people are feeling, thinking, and their hidden motivations. Too bad there isn't a way to turn that into sociology" (which for him meant abstraction). "Yes, too bad," I remember thinking wistfully, yet somewhat puzzled.

Not surprisingly, my next sociology project involved a direct examination of emotions. In the early 1980s, Gene and I wrote a paper on jealousy. Although we administered a survey about jealousy experience, our main source of information consisted of our own episodes of jealousy buttressed by friends' descriptions of their experiences. In our essay, Gene and I played down our introspective method and emphasized instead informal interviews and written descriptions we had collected from students. The reviewers rejected our paper saying we needed numerical data. When we inserted a few statistics from our survey, the article was published (Ellis and Weinstein 1986).

Why did introspective data have to be hidden in our social-science studies? After all, I knew some things from my own jealousy experiences' that I would never know from surveys or interviews of others, such as what it felt like when the jealousy flash took me over in spite of my most rational intentions.

Why did social science have to be written in such a way that detailed, lived experience was secondary to abstraction? Even though our jealousy paper was based on peoples' stories, the final version was written abstractly so that peoples' everyday experiences were camouflaged. Wasn't there something worthy about showing lived experience in and of itself? Wasn't there something valuable about evocative detail? simile and metaphor? Didn't "like a dentist's drill hitting a nerve" tell readers more about the jealous flash and get more reaction than "extreme, intense pain" or "blended emotion" (Ellis and Weinstein 1986)? Wasn't there something valuable in readers' seeing themselves in our work and reacting with feeling to what we wrote?

Several events happened in my life during the next few years to impact my work. First, my younger brother was killed in 1982 in an airplane crash on his way to visit me (see Ellis 1993). At the same time, Gene entered the final stages of chronic emphysema. Mocking my fears and hopes, flashbacks of live TV footage of passengers from my brother's plane floundering in the Potomac River were interrupted in real life by Gene choking and yelling for me to untangle his oxygen hose. Suddenly, the scientifically respectable survey of jealousy I was working on seemed insignificant (cf. Krieger 1991).

Instead, I wanted to understand and cope with the intense emotion I felt about the sudden loss of my brother and the excruciating pain I experienced as Gene deteriorated. My presentation of self as a cheerful optimist was challenged. What was happening to our relationship—to Gene, to me—as we reversed roles, as our world narrowed, as our identities were called into question, and as our human condition threatened every shred of meaning we had constructed as a couple in love?

In early 1985 I was promoted to associate professor, meaning my work had passed the standards set by colleagues in social science. Now I could better afford to challenge the boundaries of what counted as legitimate sociology, an endeavor that became a passion after Gene died a few weeks later. Then, with the advent of a section in the American Sociological Association called "Sociology of Emotions," many sociologists began to consider emotions a proper arena of research. Nevertheless, it was disappointing to see many of them fall into the same trap as "rational-actor" sociologists, as they busily handed out surveys, counted and predicted emotions, observed facial muscles contracting on videotapes, categorized people, and abstracted from lived experience. I feared that emotion was in danger of becoming simply another variable to add to rational models of social life. What about emotion as lived experience and interaction? I vowed to resist the rationalist tendency to portray people exclusively as spiritless, empty husks with programmed, managed, predictable, and patterned emotions.

The Writing of the Relationship Story

The writing of the relationship story began in 1984 during the last year of Gene's life when I started to keep daily field notes about our personal relationship. My narrative about writing this story continued until the manuscript was accepted for publication in 1993, ironically duplicating approximately the length of my relationship with Gene—nine years. This metastory, begun here and taken up again in "Negotiating the Story" and in "Endings," represents my encounters with the process of writing the text, a text that I constructed and that, in turn, constructed me.

The notes that I kept for eight months prior to Gene's death and for two years afterward included thoughts and feelings; verbatim conversations between Gene and me concerning meaning and death; day-to-day descriptions and analyses of events; stories of contacts with physicians, support staff, and friends; and details of grief and grief work. My goals in making these notes were to document my feelings, thoughts, and interpretations as the events occurred and to write eventually about my experiences. As an ethnographer, I followed the rules for keeping ethnographic field notes and tried to be rigorous and systematic.

As soon as I began to write from the notes, I realized that I could not talk about loss without showing attachment. This led to recreating through memory my chronological history with Gene by first recording major events during the relationship and then connecting them. Interviews with family and friends; physicians' records and nurses' notes; tape recordings of conversations; diaries, calendars, and travel logs contributed to my systematic recollection of this period. I also had the advantage of many years of interactive sociological introspection with Gene about the illness process (Ellis 1991a).

I felt I had to write about this experience. Not only did these notes and recollections serve as an anchor preventing me from being swept away by this epiphanic event, but it also seemed important to describe and bring meaning to this experience for me as a person who will lose other loved ones and for others who will go through similar losses. As a sociologist, I thought it was imperative to personalize and humanize sociology and try to deal with the complexities of relationships as we live them.

I knew this would be a difficult task, but I had no idea how difficult. It was complex enough that, once again, I became an ethnographer of my own experience, keeping notes on the details of the actual construction of the text. Thus, after the relationship story, I used these notes to tell the writing story, emphasizing how the text was conceived and reconceived—initially as science and then as interpretation, first as realist ethnography and then as an evocative narrative.

Part VII brings the stories of the relationship and the writing together. Here, I integrate the two stories, examining in particular the dialectical tensions of "endings." Finally, I discuss this work as an identity- and meaning-making project, circling back to the initial inspiration for the book.

The Relationship Story

The relationship story is divided into three parts. The first two chapters show Gene and me negotiating our attachment through a maze of jealousy, attraction, love, and arguments. Chapters 3 through 8 reveal a rocky period of negotiating stability and change as Gene's health grows worse, our relationship becomes stronger, and we change roles. The bulk of the relationship story is contained in Chapters 9 through 16, as we come to accept Gene's demise yet try to work out how to live a full life in spite of it and struggle not to define Gene as "dying."

I present the relationship story primarily in the present tense, which invites the reader to share in the immediacy and intensity of the interaction, dialogue, and emotionality. Seeking to provide perspective for readers to analyze my experience and contemplate their own, I express my personal reflections, sociological observations, and general descriptions in past tense. Chapter 1 starts with my first meeting with Gene, where the complex process of attachment begins as we enter into our first negotiation.

PART II

Negotiating Attachment

1

"HI, I'M CAROLYN ELLIS, a first-year graduate student here."

Revealing his weakness for women—especially young ones, Gene looks up with a gleam in his eye. "Oh, you did come. Ed told me about you."

Wondering if it was my intellectual ability he had heard about from my former professor at William and Mary, I reply, "He told me about you too. So did Gina."

"Ah, yes, Gina," Gene says wistfully.

"But they didn't tell me you were so good-looking," I continue, ignoring his response to Gina, to whom I knew he had been engaged, and displaying openness to more than a mentor-student relationship.

Gene's face brightens as he takes my hand and says seductively, "Sit down and tell me about yourself." His style of asking questions, listening to answers, and following up on details makes me feel interesting, and I become animated.

Seeming not to mind that we are the only people at the Sociology Department party engaged in an illegal activity, Gene passes me a marijuana joint. After a few tokes, he suggests a walk to a nearby dock. On the way there, he holds my hand lightly. The sounds of his labored breathing, silenced only slightly by the spraying of his oral nebulizer, are masked by my racing pulse and the aura of marijuana.

"You should know that I am here with another woman, but we're no longer a couple. I'm free to do what I please."

Amid conversation, he quietly kisses me, softly, undemanding. The lack of desperation coupled with the intensity I feel are like experiencing a storm at its center from inside a safe enclosure. Gene would later admit to similar feelings: "My life had been crazy since my son died. Joyce and I had broken up. And there you were—attractive, soft, telling me I was good looking. The electricity that came from running my hands along your bare sides made me want to stay there forever, doing what we were doing."

That was not to be. Suddenly, "Gene, Gene, I need your keys," commands a voice from the darkness. Joan, a colleague and close friend of Gene's and one of my professors, steps into view. As we quickly move apart, she says to Gene, "I have to take your date home." I am forgotten as they argue heatedly about the virtue of Joan's intrusion. Tears of humiliation stream down my face as I slip away unnoticed.

■   ■   ■

I met Gene in 1975 at the end of my first year in graduate school. I was a twenty-four-year-old graduate student in a sociology Ph.D. program in New York; he was a forty-four-year-old professor there. I had gone to SUNY at Stony Brook specifically to study strategies of interpersonal negotiation and control with Gene, but he had been on sabbatical when I arrived. Although I then worked on a study of isolated communities with another professor, I knew my academic talents and personal interests intersected with Gene Weinstein's social-psychological approach to human interaction, and I eagerly looked forward to working with him later on.

Gene made quite an impression when I finally met him. I found him good looking, although not in the traditional, magazine-cover way. A tall six-foot, one-inch frame, wide shoulders supported by an iron-rod straight posture, and a barrel chest made him look much bigger than his 160 pounds. The touch of gray in his thick, naturally Afro hair called attention to the generous size of his head, face, ears, lips, and nose. Set off from his nose by two deeply indented triangular lines, his rounded, puffy cheeks presented a moon face that glowed with expression. His crooked, decidedly Jewish nose interrupted the symmetry. Lines danced around his deep-set eyes, more piercing still because of the bushy eyebrows that curved around them and, in the middle of each eye, rose to a point. The eyebrows questioned while the eyes penetrated. Immediately I felt I could keep no secrets from him.

From having read Gene's work, I had an inkling of his intelligence; from listening to other professors, I sensed he occupied an important, mediating position in the Sociology Department; from student rumors, I suspected his adventurous but kind spirit; from the "energy" between us, I assumed his reputation as a "womanizer" who dated students was accurate. Given the commonness of such relationships in 1975 and my own history of friendships with professors, this image made Gene more, not less, attractive. I craved the exhilaration that came in learning in an intimate relationship, and rose to the challenge of being considered an equal. I was not concerned then about using my appearance and youthful exuberance as currencies of exchange, since they seemed to be valuable bargaining chips for a woman. Attractiveness got me an audition, a chance to play and hone my intellectual role. At the time I met Gene, the script was already in place. I did not consciously calculate or plan this exchange. But much of how we act, I know now, becomes routinized; our motives are hidden, even from ourselves; our reactions become automatic, scripted. Whatever the case, my anxieties about "measuring up" interpersonally and intellectually created heightened emotion that I translated easily into romantic attraction.

■　■　■

"Hello, this is Gene. I hope it's OK to call. I'm so sorry I put you in that embarrassing situation."

Since meeting Gene two days before, I have fantasized about him continuously, alternately glowing with excitement and wincing from embarrassment. How did he get my parents' telephone number, I wonder as I respond, "Everything is OK now."

"Is it?" he asks softly. "I was concerned. You were crying when you left."

"I was worried about what Joan thought, and crying from confusion and guilt."

"You shouldn't have felt guilty. You didn't do anything wrong. I'd like to take you to dinner to make up for that evening."

"But you're in New York and I'm in Virginia. That's over 400 miles."

"I don't mind driving."

We made plans to meet two days later in Washington, D.C., on the steps of the Lincoln Memorial. Although I had never driven in a big city, I found the Memorial and waited with my small terrier, Poogie, for Gene to arrive. When he walked toward me, my feelings of excitement were muted by how much older he looked than I remembered. His out-of-style leisure suit— baggy in the seat and emphasizing his lack of rear—hung loosely. What am I doing here?

Later, Gene would confess to a similar reaction: "You were dressed in a tacky outfit that was too tight. That and your little dog made you look like a kid. I thought 'she's so much younger than I remember. And a lot heavier too.' "

Awkward at first, we discuss how to spend our time. "How about a walk in the park while we talk?" Gene asks, taking Poogie's leash. I nod. The dog scampers one way, then the other, wrapping Gene in bow-tie fashion. I acknowledge that Poogie is accustomed to running freely, and pay only slight attention to Gene's shortness of breath.

"We could have a picnic," he offers. "I have wine and cheese in the car. Or go to a museum."

"A picnic would be nice," I say, wanting us to be alone.

"Can you stay in Washington tonight?" I shake my head yes as he continues, "No obligation now. I'll understand if you want to have the afternoon together and then go your way."

We spent the afternoon in a hotel, laughing, and sharing stories about our lives. Making love was tender, yet passionate, and the intensity of my excitement and the attention he paid to me were new. Later, when we went to a French restaurant, the menu was unfamiliar and expensive, and after a short lesson in French cuisine, Gene ordered for us.

Back in our room, he says apologetically, "I need to treat my lungs. It's not a pretty process, so I'll do it in the bathroom." As I undress, the continuous humming of a motor provides background for periodic spraying and hissing sounds.

Afterward, we talk about his disease for the first time. "I have emphysema, and I have to 'pump out' my lungs each night with an electric nebulizer filled with normal saline and a bronchial dilator."

"The emphysema makes you cough and short of breath?" I ask, acknowledging that I have noticed these symptoms. His illness appears to be minor, and intrudes little into my fantasy.

As Gene prepares to leave the next morning, I say, "I'll miss you, and I hope to see you again." I am concerned that I won't see him until I return to graduate school after summer vacation four months later.

"Think of our time together as a gift from life," he replies, ignoring my implied question.

"I will." Then I try again. "I might be coming to New York in the middle of summer to look for a place to live."

"I'll be in England for a month. I'm traveling with a friend, part of my 'foreign empire.' "

The phrase "foreign empire" grates on me and I wonder if I am now included. Was last night just a one-time fling to make up for our initial meeting? If so, surely he feels different after our time together.

"Let's have our picnic before we part," Gene suggests.

■ ■ ■

"Welcome back. It's good to see you," Gene says as he hugs me. It's the third day of the fall semester and I've run into Gene in the Sociology mail room. When he doesn't linger, I am disappointed, but, since he asks about my old boyfriend, I assume our hesitant communication comes from my acknowledgment that Rick has moved to Stony Brook with me.

Like a high-school girl with a crush, I try to run into Gene at school. Usually surrounded by students or with his friend Joan, he is pleasant but distant. I am assigned randomly along with five other graduate students as

Gene's teaching assistant. Attending his classes and constructing and grading his exams provide chances for interaction, but our conversations are brief and task oriented.

■ ■ ■

"The German nation is divided into East and West Germany," Gene says in a thick German accent as I come into his first undergraduate class. What is going on? Obviously, some of the undergraduate students wonder too as they shuffle in their seats. A few calmly take notes. Finally, one brave student raises a hand and says, "Isn't this a sociology class?"

"Oh, so je vant sociology?" Gene switches accents and starts talking about the sociological perspective. Continuing his performance, he explains sociological concepts of "working consensus" and "definition of the situation," pointing out that in every interaction we have to agree about what reality will be honored and answer for ourselves the question, What's going on here?

■ ■ ■

"I want to talk to you," I say to Gene as I enter his office. "Rick has gone and I want to see you."

"What happened?" he asks. "He's only been here a month."

"Our friendship wasn't enough to sustain our relationship."

Rolling his desk chair to where I sit, he takes my hands in a fatherly fashion and says, "No, this is not a good idea."

Surprised, I ask, "Why not?"

"It wouldn't be fair. First, I'm seeing someone else in New York City every weekend. Second, I'm twenty years older than you."

"Nineteen and a half," I kiddingly remind him.

"And third," he continues, without being amused, "I'm a professor and you're a student and that's sure to make problems."

I calmly respond, "I don't care if you're seeing someone else, I'm not asking you to marry me. I don't have a problem with age. And I don't think the status difference will be an obstacle, if we don't let it. I've dated professors before."

He is silent, thinking, still holding my hands. Since he doesn't seem convinced, I prepare to argue my case. Then, quietly, he says, "Why don't you come over tonight and we'll talk about it." I smile.

His speech that night about needing to have no strings if he continued seeing me did not interfere with the champagne and lovemaking that began the most intense romance of my life, and the most problematic one.

■ ■ ■

"Why don't you like group conversations?" Gene asks.

"Because they take on the character of least common denominator. You end up talking in a superficial way about what most people know about, or a few people hog the conversation."

"I like group conversations."

"Of course, that's because your style is to 'hold forth,' for which you need an audience. I like to dig deeply into what I'm interested in, and you can do that only in one-on-one conversation. Or in large groups, because there you can break into pairs."

We spent most evenings in such discussions—foreplay for the lovemaking that followed. Gene said he found my insights as fascinating as I found his, and he liked what he called "my eye," which was the ability to pick apart the most common interpersonal episode and talk on different levels about "what is really going on here."

We loved talking about group process and interpersonal relationships, and other people's emotions, motives, and strategies. But addressing these aspects of ourselves provided our favorite topic. His interest peaked when I told him how people perceived him and why.

"You intimidate students," I say.

"Really, I don't think of myself as intimidating."

"Well, you are. Your voice is loud and overpowering and sometimes you make them feel stupid. Remember when you were talking to Cathy and she asked you how to determine class?"

"Yes. Why?"

"You said to her 'that's a really complicated question. You don't realize how difficult.'"

"Yeah, I was trying to tell her she shouldn't feel bad for not knowing."

"But, instead, she felt stupid because you indicated that she didn't even know how complicated the question was. It's your tone, sort of all-knowing, that's intimidating, as well as your booming voice."

Perhaps this was a way to tell Gene that his aggressive manner sometimes intimidated me too, especially whenever the topic veered from interpersonal relationships to historical or more macrosociological issues. I wanted to learn from him, yet was afraid to admit to what I didn't know. Would I be less valuable if he thought I was not "smart enough?"

Given my background, my apprehension was understandable. I had grown up in a Protestant, rural, working-class area in the Blue Ridge Mountains. The intellectual, metropolitan, Jewish-influenced culture I confronted at Stony Brook presented a formidable but exciting challenge. Since Gene epitomized this world, I was more than willing initially to let him play Pygmalion and mold me into his version of a "cultured sociologist.'' Gradually, through talking about my insecurities, I became comfortable with our teacher-student exchanges, and I learned more formal sociology around the kitchen table than I encountered in classes. Gene didn't seem to mind that it was one-sided. "Nor," he assured me, after my confession, "do I think you are dumb."

Gene intimidated many people, even some who loved him, but the same elements that intimidated also drew people to him—his self-assurance, comfort in any situation, and ability to talk intelligently about most topics. Always ready for a good discussion and intellectual argument, he took up a lot of space—both physically and psychically. He earned attention and validation for his intelligence by listening closely and asking probing questions, allowing others to proclaim their wisdom. Challenging every statement with his darting, alert eyes, he was in control, directing the story even when someone else spoke. His ability to frame and analyze intellectual and practical problems meant that many, even some who were put off by his aggressiveness and need for power and control, sought him out.

As I did. I became intellectually dependent on Gene, my toughest critic, needing his approval of my ideas. If he said my work was good, I believed him. If he didn't, I worked until he approved. This feedback offered an invaluable push then; later I would see it as holding me back.

■ ■ ■

"Hi, Gene, this is Carolyn. Could we have dinner tonight?"

"Sorry, but I'm tied up."

Two weeks later, I call again. "Just to talk," I say.

"Sorry, I have company."

I resented Gene's control over when we got together and what we did. Although he acted as fascinated by our relationship as I, he never asked to see me more than one night a week, and I always accepted his invitation.

"Hi, would you like to have dinner tonight?" he asks at 6:00 P.M.

"I would love to," I say, putting my half-eaten dinner into the refrigerator.

■ ■ ■

I could not understand Gene's need to control the expression of his feelings. Even in bed, he would not say he loved me. Yet, he seemed to crave our lovemaking and relished that I was having new experiences. "Have you ever felt this way before?" he asks.

"No, I've never experienced loss of the boundaries of my body before. I soar into another reality, where there's only blackness and energy, over and over."

"Do you experience this with other men now?" he asks hesitantly.

"Not quite like with you," I reply, "but sex in general is different from before." I wonder, but don't ask, what it is like for him, the "teacher."

"One of the things I really like about you is that you're so undemanding. You don't ask for more. You just seem to enjoy what we have. I've never had that before," Gene says, repeating sentiments he has expressed previously. "You're gravy."

I smile, but feel uneasy that these characteristics are so important, and resent that he is trying to reinforce my behavior. Yet I am delighted that my ease about the relationship is drawing him to me. I know that one rarely, if ever, gets more in a relationship by demanding it—especially not over the long haul. "Don't ask for more time," I admonish myself. Instead, I say casually, "I like my freedom and I enjoy seeing other men." Does he flinch? I don't tell him that there are others only because I can't have more time with him. Besides, making myself look valuable, independent, and attractive to others is a good strategy. Soon Gene starts seeing me two nights a week.

■   ■   ■

"Look at the individual petals," Gene says, as we lie in the grass amid the blooms. "Each flower is different, delicate."

"Yes, the field unfolds in blended color," I reply, as I lay back with my eyes shut. "The sun shining on my body makes me feel like I am having multiple orgasms."

"You are," he says, leaning over to kiss my eyes.

■   ■   ■

"In the throes of romance, love is a high-arousal and high-interpretation emotion," Gene says, as he lectures to our graduate class in social psychology. "It is unclear whether we experience symptoms as consequences of the definition or define ourselves as being in love because of the symptoms."

"Love may not be the same for everyone or the same for each person all the time. But in each situation, we label feelings as love because it makes sense to do so. Enough of the details fit the love frame."

"At times we may be more willing or needful to define ourselves as in love. But it is hard to know sometimes whether we are in love with the role (in love with love) or the person. Is our claim to being in love valid? Are we loving just to get love back?"

"Love provides new mirrors for our sense of self. We narrow the gap between what we are and what we want to be by falling in love with a person who can reflect back to us an image of ourselves we value, or get us further away from one we devalue."

■   ■   ■

"I will not evaluate your exams in my class," Gene declares when I meet him at his house after class. "Two other professors have agreed to do it. Nor will I be on your Ph.D. committee or evaluate you in any way."

I understood, but was disappointed with the B I received in his seminar, my favorite graduate class, especially given the work I put into it and the anxiety I experienced from wanting to impress him.

■   ■   ■

"So you're leaving your toothbrush here now," Gene teases with a half-smile on his face. Although he pretends to be joking, the hidden message is that I do not live in his house.

"Oh, I'll be sure to take it home," I reply, and then don't.

■   ■   ■

Most of the time Gene's actions belied his words concerning my place in his life. Although he verbally held me at arms' length, he now invited me to his house on weekends and most evenings.

I never had felt so connected to anyone, and a piece of my heart wanted more. Or, more accurately, I wanted him to want more. Was this to validate my worth? Was this because the love I wished for was not obtainable and therefore more desirable? Or did I want to change the power imbalance, which I found infuriating and exhilarating at the same time?

On the other hand, I was worried about the consequences of getting more. Having some idea now of the extent of Gene's illness, I was hesitant about becoming more involved with this older, sick man. What did I want? Sometimes I questioned the value of the relationship in exchange terms—I was getting a great deal now, but wouldn't there be diminishing returns in the future?

Confronting the cold economic model of relationships made me flee to the romantic notion of pure love. Then I compromised, telling myself I had the best of both worlds: intensity and love, yet no future demands or commitments. I felt better then, for a little while. In spite of my feelings for Gene, I was caught up in the ideology of the sixties that considered commitment and monogamy to be bad words. People should stay together only as long as they both wanted. This simplistic thought would haunt me much later.

■   ■   ■

"Get a cart," Gene commands, the first time we enter a grocery store together.

"We don't need a cart for a few items," I reply.

"Well, we might get more than that."

It soon became apparent that leaning on a cart made walking easier for Gene. Sometimes I felt impatient and even embarrassed to be seen with a much older man who appeared sick and short-of-breath. At the same time, I argued with myself that age and health discrepancy should say nothing about my self-worth—or his.

■ ■ ■

From a distance, I see Gene on his way to class, moving more quickly than usual, chest heaving, his face betraying the struggle of the short but slightly uphill walk. His destination is a wall at the half-way mark, approximately a block from his classroom. Once there, he leans over, resting on his elbows, a position that, I learn later, makes it easier to breathe. I want to approach him, but I am unsure if, in that condition, he will be glad to see me. What will I say to him? I feel envious of the students who easily stop to talk to him as he sits on the wall to rest. His expression changes quickly from agonized to animated as his breathing slows and he holds court for the students who surround him.

Although there were 600 people in his introductory sociology class, Gene managed to elicit discussions that played off the provocative lectures he gave spontaneously, without notes. He became my role model for the kind of teacher I hoped to be. In Gene's classes, I was able, unobserved, to watch him for fifty minutes, three times a week, and slide into fantasies about the time we had spent together.

Yet, even here my fantasies confronted a contradictory reality. Projecting his voice without a microphone to 600 people took energy and sometimes required that he stop for deep breaths or to cough. Spraying his inhaler sometimes helped and other times seemed like a prop or a pause between paragraphs. After one particularly rough day, another assistant said to me, "I wish he would just die and get it over with." Her comments forced me to come face-to-face with how bad his disease appeared to others.

■ ■ ■

"Maybe you should pull over," I say to Gene, who is coughing uncontrollably while driving. My calm voice belies my fear.

"No, I'll be OK in a minute."

He must know what he's doing. But he's choking, and now turning gray. Pull over, goddamn it, I scream silently.

"It's a 'clump,' a mucus plug," he explains between coughs from deep in his gut. "It'll come up and then I'll be OK."

The car weaves into the oncoming lane. "Maybe I should drive," I suggest, controlling my alarm.

"No, I'll be fine."

The coughing continues, the mucus that thwarts his breathing rattles. He works—cough, cough, clear the throat, gag—and finally, five minutes later, he swallows the loosened mucus. I, too, almost gag, before my anxiety turns to relief.

Exhausted, he still manages a smile. "See, I'm fine now."

"Do you get those often?"

"Just once in a while. But they're sons-of-bitches."

I learn much about clumping the next few months. Because of constant inflammation, Gene's lungs produced a flood of mucus to combat irritation. That and the pus from the infections he got sometimes covered the air sacs and membranes of his lungs. Then, because of the buildup of carbon dioxide, he felt like he was suffocating and drowning, and he coughed furiously to get the mucus to release, which would allow him to breathe comfortably again. If he were "well," the clumping might happen once every two or three times I was with him, and be minor. If he had an infection, he could have six or seven a night, or, during a serious infection, the clumping sometimes went on continuously.

Since panic restricted Gene's breathing further, it was important that he stay calm during these episodes, preparing for the violent coughing that finally forced the mucus into his mouth. Sometimes he worked as long as ten minutes on a plug before it loosened and allowed his pale gray color to change immediately to pink.

Initially, I grew numb as I waited for the emergency to be over. Once I understood the process, I joined in the fight. "Relax, baby, it'll release soon. OK, give it a try. No, not this time. OK, rest. Deep breaths. OK, maybe now. We'll get through this." I hold his hand, rub his back. Imagining what it must feel like, I hold my breath, letting it go only when his mucus plug is displaced. His struggle becomes my struggle too, and feels better than numbness. Later, when he is worse, I will welcome the numbness.

"I think the time has come," Gene says when he can breathe freely, "for me to show you what to do in case I don't come out of one of these."

"See this needle and vial of adrenalin?" he instructs. "I always keep one in the car and one in the bathroom medicine cabinet. If I ever seem to be suffocating, stick me with this." He could die, I realize, feeling both close when he talks openly about his disease and fearful of the meaning of the information.

■ ■ ■

"I'm going to Alaska," Gene announces when I arrive at his house. "To see my daughter, Beth. We'll go from Seattle to Alaska on a ferry and sleep in sleeping bags on the deck. Then travel hippy-style around Fairbanks and Mt. McKinley National Park."

"Are you sure you'll be OK?"

When he says, "Of course," I wonder if he always knows his limits.

He returned from his trip ecstatic about his adventure but with a cold that made him sicker than I had ever seen him. His coughing rattled with never-ending mucus plugs. Later, I would define this as the first drop in his health that I witnessed firsthand. Neither of us was prepared.

I stand by helplessly, on alert, regretting that I have gone ahead with this surprise birthday and welcome-home party. After opening each present, Gene chugs codeine cough syrup in hopes of silencing his rattling cough. We ignore the fact that codeine will stop the expectorating of built-up mucus, perhaps causing more damage. As he had said earlier in the evening, "The codeine might get me through the night and that's all that matters right now." This was my first experience with weighing long-term difficulty against short-term problem solving.

"Oh, a wine stein, I get it," he says, laughing and appreciating the pun of the present. The laughter renews his cough.

"Bad cold, huh Gene?"

"Yeah, a bad one," Gene responds, pointing to his chest. But Gene's attempts to normalize the situation fail to cover the sorrowful, tense feeling in the room as people realize the extent of his problem yet try to act normally.

For the first time, Gene and I function publicly as a team, trying to carry off the charade together. "God, I feel awful," he says quietly to me. "Should I take more cough syrup?"

"Yes, here," I say, and then turn to explain cheerfully to someone that Gene caught a cold from sleeping outside on the ship to Alaska. This training for learning to grab the moments between agony and fear would come in handy later.

I alternated between embarrassment, caring and concern, and numbness. When my fear took over, I was glad we were not in a committed relationship. Was this a glimpse of what was to come?

"I can't let anyone see me like this again," Gene says forcefully when we arrive home. "Do you have any idea what it does to the image people have of me? They don't see me as a whole person when I'm this sick."

"Come on, Gene. These are your friends." I flinch at his anger and want to assure him no damage has been done. "They worry about you, but this hasn't changed the way they see you."

"How can they see me as an influential person at work when I'm this sick? I have to hide it."

"Tonight didn't look as bad as you think," I respond. "People see you as having a cold, it's something you'll get over. Everyone is sick sometime." As I try to convince him and myself, Gene continues to insist that he will not let this slipup in identity maintenance happen again.

Gene faced one set of identity concerns while I faced another. He said he wanted to be seen as a "whole" person; the irony was that he really only wanted to be seen in terms of the healthy and robust part. I couldn't help but wonder how our friends had seen me. On the one hand, I liked being seen as a caring person. On the other, I wondered whether people thought Gene was using me as a caretaker. Was I seen as a love-struck young woman? What about my identity as a student and professional? Did acquaintances wonder why I was with someone who was "not a good catch"? Did it lower my value in their eyes? Gene's deteriorating health had raised a new problem: how to preserve our identities in the outside world while coping with the disease and our relationship.

Gene continues getting worse, and I stay with him the next few days, until he says, "Don't come over today."

"But who will take care of you? You need someone."

"I'll be fine. I have to be able to take care of myself. I'm worried about all the time we're spending together and I don't want to need you like this."

You'll be sorry, you bastard, I think angrily. Then I feel some relief that I am not yet fully responsible for his care. But what if he gets into real trouble?

After only one day, Gene asks me to come back. When he opens the door, he looks like my picture of a tuberculosis patient—bent over, weak, skinny, pale gray. "I feel better when you're here," he admits quietly.

I fix something to eat and then get his medicines. "Look, when you're better, we can cut down on time. But not now. I want to be with you and help you. Just accept it. No strings."

During the next two weeks, Gene rarely slept at night and spent days kneeling on the floor, leaning over a chair. "I can breathe better that way," he explains, as I ration the cough syrup and marijuana that provided relief, with a cost.

Gene readily admitted that no one could care for him the way I did. I tried to let him make decisions for himself, yet be available if he got into a jam. I never had felt such giving love before. We grew closer, and I trusted

Gene's looks of love, even without the words. Sometimes it upset me that for Gene our increased closeness might come out of need. But maybe love always comes from need. What makes this particular need any different? Becoming more and more involved in this relationship, I experienced the complexity in being drawn to his vulnerability.

Although amazed at how much I wanted to help him, I was scared, more than ever, of this disease and its potential. Where did our relationship go from here? I reassured myself that this deteriorated state was temporary. Unaware of how little power I had in combating the disease, I was determined it was not going to control our relationship, or me.

Finally, the crisis passed, leaving Gene a little shaken, more breathless, and less mobile. Most people probably failed to notice his deterioration, but we couldn't ignore it. Our lovemaking was less varied; more and more the top position became mine. When Gene failed to return to his condition prior to the Alaska trip, we were forced to come face-to-face with the "progression" of the disease. "I have a progressive disease," he laughs cynically. "Progressive—what an absurd way to describe it."

The power margin in the relationship was narrowing, but the costs of equilibrium ironically exceeded its rewards.

2

"I WON'T HAVE TIME to see you during the meeting," Gene announces. "I'll be busy with old friends." The meeting he referred to was the annual American Sociological Association conference, which provided an occasion for sociologists to give papers, talk about their research, and renew friendships.

Since Gene and I had been seeing each other every night for several months, his proclamation surprised me. At first, I rationalized that our relationship wasn't going to work anyway; I didn't want a long-term relationship with a sick person. That I was free to see other people, however, failed to cheer me. Why did I live my life waiting to be with him?

Then I released the anger I had stored during the last few months. "I no longer accept that you control when we are together and when we aren't. I am not your toy to toss aside whenever you feel like it."

"But I've always said I need my freedom."

"And I need more consideration."

"What kind of consideration?"

"I mean the way you treat me in public. Like just another person or another student. I am not just another person."

"But you have no right to be angry. I never promised you anything. Don't you get a lot out of this relationship?"

"And don't you?"

"Yes, but there are other people in my life. You get your time."

"Well, 'my time' is no longer enough."

■ ■ ■

The day after the conference, Gene called, as though nothing was different, and invited me to his house. I went, but I showed little enthusiasm. During the next few weeks, he worked hard to please me, buying presents, calling more than usual, and being loving and considerate when we were together. He invited me to drop by his office, a place that had felt

27

off-limits because that was where he spent time with Joan, his cowriter and best friend. I acted reserved, hoping that it would make him redefine our relationship and, if not, that I could will myself out of love. Although being out of control and in love were wonderful sensations, feeling unfulfilled and less than special were not. I withdrew to a "safe" place, emotionally contained yet with enough enthusiasm to maintain Gene's interest.

■ ■ ■

"Are you coming over tonight?" Gene asks.

"No, I have other plans," I respond.

"But we usually get together on Tuesday nights."

"But we had no specific plan."

"I really wanted to see you," he says. "Do you have a date?"

When I say yes, he replies, "Oh, there must be someone new," and I don't answer.

My defense of seeing other men when I periodically felt myself getting too needy now made Gene more jealous than before. "Did you have a good time?" he asks when we get back together.

"Yes."

"Who did you go out with?"

"Jack."

"But I have to work with him. How could you do that?"

"Who gives you the right to make the rules?" Putting him on the defensive makes me feel powerful.

"I don't like it when you go out with people I know."

"Too bad," I say, laughing. "I don't like it when you go out with people I don't know. My goodness, I think you're jealous."

"I know I shouldn't be. But I am," he admits for the first time, taking my hands in his. "I don't want to lose my special place in your life."

Sometimes I reassured him, but this time I don't. "Well, you might. Jack is great to talk to and the sex is wonderful."

"As good as with us?"

"Not yet."

Gene tried to woo me back in love by making the evening the best he could. But then nothing else changed. In spite of his illness, Gene continued attracting and being involved with several women. I tried to understand his decision, made after two marriages and many serious relationships, to live the rest of his life with friendships and romance from various sources, but I still was uncomfortable with the amount of distance he seemed to need. He argued that it was not fair to me to get involved with a sick, older man. But I wondered if that was just an excuse to hold me at arm's length. Although I was as committed to the ideology of "open relationships" as he, I was less committed to the practice. To be honest, our dedication to an open relationship wavered for each of us depending on the availability of threat.

■   ■   ■

"Is it painful when you lose your breath?" I ask.

"Not really pain. Hold your nose until you can't stand it," he directs. "Now was that pain?"

"Not exactly. But it was horrible."

"Well, that's what it feels like."

I shudder.

■   ■   ■

"Look at all the lights across the inlet. Each one represents a house, a family, people. Think how insignificant you are," Gene says. When I am horrified, he continues, "Look at the ant hill. Think how important you are." I laugh at his play with multiple realities.

"How do you know your feelings are real?" Gene asks. "If we shed all our masks, will there be anything under them?"

We have taken LSD—my first time—and are lying in a secluded place on a private beach, huddled close together for warmth. For the third time in our year-long relationship, I say "I love you." For the third time, Gene says nothing, his silence contradicting the intensity of his passion, the emotion in his eyes, and the tenderness of his touch. My mind is spinning, the strength of my feelings out of control. I cannot deal with the discrepancy. Later he will admit to mouthing the words "I love you" as he kissed me. "I was sure you 'heard,' " he will say. Because I didn't 'hear,' I retreated again, consciously deciding that this relationship was worth the problems and the pain only from a distance. Yet, I still wanted him to fall hopelessly in love with me.

■   ■   ■

"Let's go to Puerto Rico for Thanksgiving."

"But Thanksgiving is only ten days away," I say.

"So?" Gene replies, picking up the phone to make a reservation, and I am reminded of why I am never bored with him.

■   ■   ■

"I find you very attractive," the young man says.

"I like the way you look too," I respond during the New Year's Eve party Gene and I are hosting in 1976. This is fun. Who cares if Gene is jealous. Just look at him over there flirting with first one and then the other. He's not even aware I'm here.

As soon as the last guest leaves, Gene yells, "How could you do that?"

"What? Oh, you mean flirt with the psychology professor? What do you care? You hold me at a distance. You can't also decide when I can be attracted to other people." My laugh ends with a self-righteous scream.

"But why under my nose? With all my friends here?"

"Because that's when the opportunity arose," I reply coldly.

"Are you going to see him again?"

"We have a date next week."

"You hurt me," he says, beginning an argument that will last most of the night.

"How can I hurt you? You don't even love me."

"You never think you can hurt me, but you do."

I had him going now and I wasn't going to stop. "How do I hurt you?"

"By not considering my feelings."

"What do you want? Who am I to you?"

"I don't know. I just know I care about you."

"I'm not getting enough in this relationship. I need to distance myself more. I need love in my life."

To this, Gene yells out, "All right. I do love you. I have tried not to, but I can't help it. I love you."

"Do you really?"

"Yes. I love you. I really do love you."

As though a flood had started, he woke me up every few minutes with kisses and words of love. I had won a victory; now we stood on the same side of the war, still to be fought. I was too elated to pay attention.

■ ■ ■

"Hello, I love you."

"I love you too," I respond. Seemingly, there is no boundary now to Gene's feelings and his desire to please me. I become more trusting. Somehow we will figure out a way to deal with this disease.

I passed my comprehensive exams for my Ph.D. in February 1977. Since Gene was feeling relatively healthy and we had learned to deal with the clumping and restricted exercise tolerance, we ignored his illness as much as possible, thinking about it only in emergencies. Then the pill changed our lives.

■ ■ ■

"It's the pill," Gene says. "I can't breathe. Oh, god. Help me."

"What can I do?" I ask, hoping he doesn't die. I feel selfish when I don't want to make the effort to go to the hospital. At times he can barely breathe. It is the most acute panic situation either of us has encountered. Then my feelings shut down. He is disgusting. I hate him.

We have gone to Florida in my camper-pickup truck, a cozy and romantic place to sleep. It is difficult for Gene to climb in and out of the back, and he has to have access to electricity to pump out his lungs. But Gene's enthusiasm for camping along the panhandle of Florida is childlike and unbridled. We are kids together on the beach, sociologists at work while driving, adults in love at night.

One night in a campground a pill lodges in his lungs when he swallows. For hours, Gene crouches on his hands and knees in the camper trying to cough it up. When he defecates from the effort, I calmly collect his feces in a paper bag.

Is this real? I am numb, but give him encouragement, and then suggest going to the hospital. "They'll kill me," he says, refusing. Finally, he falls asleep from the effort, and I, alone, think about my situation. I am immersed in a bathtub of whipped cream, but it is turning to liquid, as it eventually must, and I will drown.

The next morning Gene coughs up some of the pill. From that day on, he will complain about "the spot," and I will increasingly withdraw from his pain.

■ ■ ■

Reaching for my second doughnut, I hear screeching, feel the car lurch sideways, and then the sensation of rolling over, suspended in space, tumbling in slow motion. We crawl out the broken window. The truck is upside down; the passenger cabin is smashed in. "Are you all right?" we yell at the same moment. "Yes," we scream together. Blood streaming down her face, my dog staggers toward us. "I don't believe we are alive," I say, as we hug her and each other. In that moment, facing loss of each other, our love is all that matters.

Our accident took place in a small South Carolina town on the way back from Florida. Being stranded with no transportation reminded us how sick Gene was. When the only town taxi was unavailable, we walked, but Gene's breathing now was further restricted by the lodged pill. My small-town upbringing made me aware of how strange we appeared to the locals, who watched our discrepant pairing with suspicious glances as we struggled down the street. Gene huffed and sprayed adrenalin into his mouth and stopped each block to catch his breath; I stood silently by his side. We bought an old "clunker," a 1953 Ford, to drive back to New York.

■ ■ ■

"If we go half way, we might as well come back from the other direction," Gene says with glee.

"Go around the world?" I am incredulous.

"Why not?" he responds with a grin, as we look through a book on the Himalayan mountains that I bought him for Christmas. Although we don't have much extra money, we agree that it is unclear how much longer he will be able to make a trip of this magnitude. With $6,000 from Gene's savings account and my $1,500 educational loan, we buy our tickets and a miniature world globe. We are learning to live in the present.

"What will we do if you really get sick?"

"I'll just kick ass," he says, using his expression for pushing himself past his physical limit and enduring the acute distress he felt when he lost his breath. But even now I can see his health gradually deteriorating. We don't walk much anymore. I am becoming "his legs."

■ ■ ■

"Labor is part of my contribution to the relationship, Gene. You finance most of our activities."

"But I want to pull my own weight," Gene says, as he continues vacuuming. "Even though it takes me twice the time and energy it takes you, it gives me a lot of satisfaction. I don't want to be dependent, nor take advantage of you."

"It's not Pareto optimal," I say, using one of Gene's favorite sociological concepts to indicate that we could increase efficiency without increasing proportionate cost. I wonder if his action is a distance-maintaining mechanism.

■ ■ ■

"I have presents for you," Gene says when I arrive at his house. The box contains a beautiful, handcrafted silver necklace. "That's not all. Look in the refrigerator."

"Truffles. My favorite. How did you get those?"

"I asked Tim to bring them from the City."

■ ■ ■

We spend most of our evenings at home around the dinner table. Preparing our meal together occupies the first part of the evening. Eating it course by course with a bottle of wine and conversation provides foreplay for lovemaking. Our evenings at home alone contrasted with evenings with other people. At home, Gene was attentive and loving; out in the world, he was the center of attention. Often, I sat silently, left to fend for myself, unable to find a place to enter the conversation. Gene did not address questions to me then, as he concentrated on showing off his "smarts." In private, when I complained, he would promise to do better, but then forget.

Sometimes it wasn't his fault. My southern, small-town, working-class background had not prepared me for competitive repartee among north-eastern Jewish intellectuals. My soft style meant that even when I commented, what I said often went unnoticed. And, sometimes, I did not have enough knowledge to address the historical and political issues about which the others spoke so intently. In other contexts, I continued as an outgoing, vivacious person; in this one, I was an apprentice learning the ropes.

■　■　■

"What did you do last night?"

"Just the usual." The contrast with Gene's normally detailed descriptions makes me silently question his answer. Becoming a spy, I check the stereo while he's in the bathroom, but the record we played two nights before is still on top of the stack. What is he hiding? I already know he occasionally sees other women. What else can it be? It must not be anything. Or he would have slipped up by now.

■　■　■

I approach Gene's house nervously. He has a visitor, the woman with whom he had been seriously involved before he moved to New York. He refers to Linda as "the first love of my life." Now she lives in Washington, but she comes to New York frequently on business trips. He sees her whenever he goes through Washington, and occasionally he meets her in New York City or she visits him in Stony Brook. "It's not sexual," he assures me. "She's like family." But since I have never arrived at Gene's house unannounced before, I feel cautious.

I knock and turn the knob. My sigh of relief when the door opens is jerked short by the chain lock snapping taut. My heart races. Gene never locks his door. Never. The bedroom window curtains move aside as someone peers out. Music is playing, the music we make love by. I walk quickly to my car, hyperventilating. I no longer care about the groceries I had planned to leave at his house before my afternoon tennis lesson. Now it all makes sense. The strict allocation of time. The silence concerning what he is doing sometimes when I am not with him. How could I have been so duped? He has been having another relationship all along.

It is Gene's birthday and I have planned a celebration that evening at his house. I want to cancel the party, but not as much as I want to confront him. Let him sweat through dinner. The key lime pie, Gene's favorite, I make that afternoon tastes awful.

After everyone leaves the party, Gene puts his hands on my shoulders and says, "It wasn't your time."

The nerve. "Go to hell, you lying bastard," I reply and pick up my coat.

"I'm sorry. I promised Linda I wouldn't tell anyone because I didn't want to endanger her marriage. I wanted to tell you. My relationship with her wasn't going anywhere, anyway. It was just for now. We had tried in Nashville to make it work and it didn't. But I still love her." I walk toward the door. "You aren't going, are you?" he asks incredulously.

"Of course I am," I respond coldly and continue walking. When he hugs me, I pull away. "Don't touch me," I hiss at him.

"Don't go," he pleads. "I care about you. I love you too."

"Bullshit," I reply, with hate in my voice.

"Please don't go," I hear him say again as I slam the door. I feel liberated and heartbroken.

For several days, I ignore Gene's phone calls. Much of the time I spend alone working on hating him or, at least, loving him less. In that short time, I pull back from him more than ever before. When I finally answer the phone and he says he misses me, the ice melts a little. But when he tries to explain his strong feelings for Linda, I am not understanding. "Flings are one thing," I yell. "A serious relationship, I will not tolerate." I hang up on him, determined more than ever to get him out of my heart. At the same time, I hope he will continue calling back until I talk to him.

Lying violates the definition of who we are to each other, I tell myself. We have gotten through many difficult situations by openly working out problems. Although I am miserable without him, this time he has gone too far. Does he care at all? I know he does, but now I need him to care in the same way I do, especially if I am going to consider staying in this relationship and facing his deterioration in the future. I will not be just his nursemaid, I tell myself in my angriest mood, delighted by how much that thought would hurt him. But please let this not be the end, I plead to no one in particular.

We are scheduled to leave for our trip around the world in less than a month and I'm not even talking to him.

■ ■ ■

It was only later, when Gene and I wrote analytically about our experiences as part of our work on jealousy, that I began to comprehend the meaning behind these interactions.

It seems more useful to view what is being threatened in jealousy not as possession of resources but . . . as control. The basis of control is the attachment with . . . the person who embodies the resource. Identification is the psychological root of that bond. By identification, we mean breaking down the cognitive boundary between the self and another person or persons in some arena so that self and other(s) constitute a transactional unit. The newly-formed unit is then experienced as part of the self in the relevant arena.

Exclusion of others from the unit is central because control is, by its very nature, structured in zero-sum terms. Since the bond between people forms the basis of control, jealousy is rooted in the threat from outsiders' intrusions on that bond. . . .

We often represent the uniqueness of this attachment . . . through symbols that imply sexual exclusivity. We institutionalize our attachment . . . and incorporate it into our public identity as in marriage ceremonies and announcements of "going steady.". . .

Without these particular ritualized symbols, however, others arise to denote uniqueness in relationships. . . . Rules for swinging couples, and for all non-institutional relationships without built-in symbols of attachment, become so important because attachment is so intangible. . . . The credibility of attachment (trust) can become a problem that self-vouching, so easily faked, cannot readily cure. How does one prove that the statement "I love you more than anyone" is true? (Ellis and Weinstein 1986, pp. 342–344)

■ ■ ■

"Will you come with me to "The Garden Terrace?" Gene asks over the phone.

"I don't know," I respond, tempted by dinner at our favorite romantic restaurant.

"At least let's talk. Don't just throw it all away."

"Why not?"

"Because we have something special."

"Had," I correct.

"Well, I want it back."

Feeling he has groveled sufficiently, I say, "OK, what time?"

On the ride to the restaurant, Gene showers me with loving glances and complimentary words, but I am unresponsive, and conversation is difficult. Once seated, he says, "Let's order a nice bottle of wine. No reason not to have a good time now, no matter what happens later."

"I guess you're right," I agree, relaxing and feeling strangely romantic—a blend of attraction, excitement, and hope.

"I have missed you, more than I thought I would. I love you. I know it'll be difficult, but I want to work out our problems."

Although I want to give in, how will I ever trust him again? "Well then," I respond, "start explaining."

We talk about our relationship, the deception, my feelings. I vacillate between experiencing our mutual love and reminding myself that he has deceived me and loves another woman. "I swear it doesn't take away from what I feel for you," he offers.

"But how is that possible?"

"I compartmentalize my feelings."

"How can you do that if you really love me?"

"Don't you do it too?"

"No, there is always a piece of you with me no matter who I'm with or what I'm doing." Even though my answer challenges his argument, he seems pleased with my response.

"I'm sorry, baby, sorry for deceiving you. I understand the impact of lying on a relationship. I don't want to lose you." I believed that he didn't. "It isn't that you don't measure up," he assures me. "I care for you more than I ever thought possible. But Linda was here before you. We have a history."

"So what? Are you still in love with her?"

"Yes, I am," he says hesitantly. "I'm sorry. But the truth is, I am." A knife surges through my heart, and, all at once, I feel the wildly conflicting emotions of jealousy—hate, love, rejection, resignation, and fight.

"What about our trip around the world?" Gene asks. "I want us to go."

How can I give up our dream trip? Yet, in spite of all the planning, I respond, "I refuse to commit to going on our trip unless we can work out our relationship to my satisfaction. I understand you can't change your feelings for Linda, but your relationship with her better not interfere with us."

"The only solution for me," I continue coldly, my rationality now providing a hiding place for my contradictory emotions, "is to become even more adept at getting the most from our relationship without wanting more. This means investing even less of myself in it than before. Then I also will feel less fear about your physical problems because they will not be my responsibility. We'll both gain. And I will just be another person in your life, which is what you seem to want."

Quietly, he responds, "That's not what I want. I have never wanted you to feel responsibility for my physical problems, but I don't want our relationship to change. I like the intensity of what we have. I like being in love with you."

"But I am responsible for your physical problems, whether you want it or not, just by virtue of our relationship," I say, wanting him to feel like a burden. "What would I do if suddenly you got sicker? Leave you? No, I would want to help you. Now I feel the responsibility because of our tie, yet I am not getting what I need from you. I don't want to feel that way, and I won't anymore. Surely you understand."

Gene responds sadly, "Of course, do what you must. But don't take away more than you have to."

Because I was willing to contain my love, even to leave the relationship, the power balance was changing. Now the burden shifted to Gene to work harder and demonstrate more involvement to keep the relationship going. Gene seemed willing to do anything to make us work, short of giving up Linda.

Gene cared, but did he care enough? What I still hoped for and didn't say was that I wanted to be reassured that I was the most important. But at least now the boundaries he had constructed made some sense. Maybe I could treat our relationship as an open marriage now that I knew what was going on.

■ ■ ■

"How do people go about the business of getting others to do, think or feel what they want them to?" Gene asked in an article entitled "Toward a Theory of Interpersonal Tactics." He answered:

> In Goffman's terms, the working consensus is a tacit agreement as to whose claims to what issues will be temporarily honored. It is an agreement as to . . . the definition of the situation jointly subscribed to (although not necessarily believed in) by participants in the encounter. . . .
>
> Any actor has a double problem in interaction. He has his interpersonal tasks. But he is involved with other actors, each with their own purposes and associated preference orderings which, in all likelihood, are somewhat different from his. . . . The actor, in seeking to achieve his own goals in the encounter, must also keep the others bound in the relationship. . . . Of particular importance . . . is maintaining the acceptability of the identities of the participants, his own included. (Weinstein 1966, pp. 395–396)

He studies interpersonal manipulation—maybe I have been duped all along.

■ ■ ■

After many discussions, I decided not to pass up our trip. While taking care of last-minute details, I fluctuated between being moody, short-tempered, and distant and being loving, excited, and understanding, between being physically close and emotionally unreachable. Patiently, Gene tried to respond to my sudden mood swings; finally, we called a truce. "This trip is an event of a lifetime. One that shouldn't be intruded upon. Let's crawl back into our bubble," Gene pleads, "and be together on this trip. There will be time for problem-solving when we return."

I agree, relieved to have a reason to stop arguing, one that didn't look like I had given in or forgiven him.

On July 15, 1977, we left for Spain, then Greece, India, Turkey, Egypt, Nepal, Malaysia, Japan, and Alaska. I pulled a large suitcase on wheels filled with Gene's medicines and pumper, and minimal clothes; he carried a small backpack loaded with other essentials. If necessary, I could carry it for him.

During the next seven weeks, our experience bound us together and more than met the expectations we had of experiencing other cultures. The trip was strenuous, and even I was sometimes exhausted, overstimulated, and plagued by the usual traveling diseases. In fact, tourist maladies took their toll on me more than on Gene, and often he lovingly took on the caretaker role. "I am glad to reciprocate," he says.

A few times during the trip, Gene stayed behind while I explored, and the rest of the time, he limited himself. For example, in the Egyptian pyramids, he had to climb up rudimentary ladders and then maneuver through small openings. Since a crouched position made breathing difficult, he saw only the first few rooms. Often I scouted ahead to see if the view was worth his effort.

This routine worked fine until I told him that an Egyptian tour guide had made sexual overtures toward me while I was alone. "I can't even protect you. I am not a whole man." I kidded him about his "old-fashioned" protective attitude. "But this is the way men in this culture think," he notes. "And given that, it's dangerous for a woman to be alone." I felt sympathy knowing that his physical disability threatened his manhood. "If ever you don't return in thirty minutes, I'll come looking for you or I'll send someone to find you."

Reading through my day-to-day notes from the trip, I was surprised that we walked many hours every day. A year later, we would have been unable to make the trip.

■ ■ ■

"Yes, madam, I assure you. The rain will stop. You will see the mountains," the tour guide says as he drives up the mountain.

"Are you sure?"

"Yes, yes, sure. A beautiful view."

The rain kept pouring. And at the top of the peak, all we saw were children with outstretched hands, saying, "Capital of California, Sacramento. Bakshish," which meant they wanted a tip.

"Will it stop raining?" we ask the children, assuming their knowledge of such events is greater than ours.

"Oh, yes. The mountains, very beautiful. You'll see." When they told us what we wanted to hear, we tipped them well.

But the rain continued to pour. "Gene, it's no use. Let's go back to Katmandu."

Finally we had arrived in Nepal, but we couldn't find the mountains. Only twenty-five miles away, the Himalayas were covered by fog, clouds, and rain. Although we had planned our trip well, we had underestimated the impact of the monsoons. We tried all the avenues usually open to tourists to see the mountains. But our flight to a small town in the foothills was in vain, and the $35 airplane rides into the high peaks were canceled for the season.

After ten days of bad weather and no mountains, we went to the airport to change our reservations to leave Katmandu the next day. Gene left me waiting in line, "I'll be back in a few minutes."

When he returns an hour later, beaming, holding up two miniature tickets, I lash out, "Where have you been?"

"We're going on a helicopter ride," he explains, ignoring my question. "What?"

"Just you and me. To see the mountains."

"But how?" I ask. "How much does it cost?"

"Well," he says, matter-of-factly, "it's $375 an hour. They even fly to Mt. Everest."

"How long does that take?"

"Two hours to get there." Gulping for air, I start calculating: two hours there, two hours back, and some time looking at the mountains. Was he crazy?

But," he continues, still beaming, "they can't guarantee ahead of time that we actually will be able to see Mt. Everest."

"Hundreds of dollars and we can't even be sure to see the mountain? Gene, have you lost your mind?"

Again ignoring my question, he continues, "So I booked a flight to another mountain closer by. It will take an hour total and they can tell us by four o'clock tomorrow morning if we will be able to see the mountain."

That sounds better. But, still, $375? "How many can go in the helicopter?" I ask.

"There's room for five."

"Great, let's find some other people to go with us. Then it won't cost so much." I start off in pursuit of passengers.

"Wait. No," he says calmly, grabbing my arm. "Just you and me. It will be romantic. I don't want to share. Three-hundred-seventy-five or two-hundred-fifty. It's all crazy." I smile at the Gene with whom I had fallen in love.

"You're right," I say. "Let's do it. After all, we came to see the mountains."

Next morning the phone rings at four o'clock. When Gene is told the trip is on, he swallows a tab of LSD and hands a half to me. "Don't worry," he says. "It'll take an hour to come on and then we'll be in the helicopter."

Reluctantly but excitedly, I swallow mine, then give Gene a shot of adrenalin. "I want to feel my best," he says. "This is the high point of my life." We take a taxi to the airport and silently climb into the helicopter. One start. Two starts. We hold our breath. Three starts. Then the engine roars and the helicopter rises into the air.

It is difficult to capture the experience of soaring in and out of the mountain ranges, stopping in midair to observe the Sherpa villagers and yak pastures in the isolated valleys below, hovering near the glaciers and waterfalls so close I want to reach out and touch them. Gene wrote in our diary: "Twenty-five thousand foot Himalchauli flanked the quadruple peaks of Ganesh Himal like vanilla ice cream cones glistening in the sun. Sheer mystery was etched onto our synapses." But that and the pictures I took through the tinted green windows could only hint at the experience we had.

We returned to New York feeling closer than ever, but continued living in separate houses. When Gene picked up where he had left off with Linda, I was hurt and lonely even though I had expected it. After being with Gene for seven weeks, I was once again back to allotted time. Even though we saw each other often, I grew irate when he was inaccessible, and I interpreted his absence and my feeling about it as a symbol that I was not the most important person to him. Not only did he spend some weekends with Linda, he worked on research projects with his best friend, Joan, several afternoons a week. Even that was a relationship I was not privy to. How could he do this after our spiritual experience in the Himalayas? He had a best friend and a lover. So who was I? Once again, I concentrated on trying to live my life when I was not with him as though we did not have the connection we had.

■ ■ ■

"Quit sleeping with Linda," I demand, "and I will be willing to talk about changing the nature of our relationship."

When he says, "No," I shrug and say, "So you want me to stop seeing other people while you do what you want?"

Sensing that I enjoy spending time with David, and that the usual reasons for my seeing others—to appear more valuable to and less obsessed with Gene—have become less salient, Gene continues, "No, this one just bothers me. I don't like that you are so close. Look, I know it's a double standard. I can't help it."

"Do you feel threatened that David is so smart? That he might take your place?"

"Maybe, I don't know. It's just painful. Now I have to pull away." What a soap opera we were living. "I've made a date with Joyce, my old girlfriend," he says. How juvenile and absurd, I think, as I recall that she's the person he had brought to the party when I met him.

"Go ahead, what difference does one more make? You will not control my actions while you continue to do whatever you want. You're acting like a child." Our relationship was volatile and deteriorating.

■ ■ ■

"Liberalization of relationship rules," Gene and I wrote in our article on jealousy, "presents an inherent problem in inhibiting jealousy. Even if some details would no longer signify an intrusion or violation of trust, the extended access permitted by the liberalized rules creates more chances to distrust and greater opportunities for loss of control by either partner. Thus, in open relationships, in contradiction to the 'official' feeling rules, the actual structure of preference often aggregates to a mutual double standard. Each partner would like access restricted, but only for partner and not for self" (Ellis and Weinstein 1986, p. 351).

■ ■ ■

"Could you come to my house?"

"I have a date," I answer, surprised to hear from Gene, who is supposed to be with Joyce.

"It's real important," he announces. "Can't you postpone it?"

"No, but I can come over tomorrow," I say, showing interest. "What happened to your latest fling?" I ask sarcastically.

"I canceled it," he says. "It's not fair to Joyce."

"That was smart."

"I want to marry you," Gene says, when I am seated at his kitchen table the next day. Solemnly he continues, "I want both of us to give up other relationships. I want a chance to have a real relationship, to build something before I die. I don't want to lose you."

His proposal surprises and frightens me. I am in love with him, but I don't want to marry him. After a silence, I say, "I need time to think about this. I have been working to have a full life without you, and I'm succeeding. I have all my friends, some romance, and my dissertation is going well."

"But we're so good together."

"This is such a change. I don't feel as close to you as I have in the past. What about your need for freedom?"

"It's no longer the most important thing," Gene replies.

"What about Linda?"

"She already knows. She's upset, but wishes us well, since she understands I want a long-term monogamous relationship. She knows you make me happy and that she and I would never work out. The same problems are still here—our jobs are in different cities, the incompatibilities, and besides she wants to work on her marriage. Take some time to think. You don't have to tell me now."

So this is how one shows that "I love you more than anyone" is true. Finally I had gotten what I wanted (and more) and instead of feeling happy, I was confused and scared. I liked my identity as an independent, single person. What will I do about my career? What will my parents say? What about Gene's age and his health problem? Am I really his first choice? Or just more convenient than Linda?

Gene's face lights up when I arrive back at his house later; it falls when I say, "I don't want to get married. I agree that we should be monogamous. Not because I believe in it, but because the jealousy arguments are destroying our relationship. Can't we just live together?"

Gene considers a minute, and now I am surprised when he says firmly, "No, I won't do that. I want to be married to you. I thought you wanted it too. You've pushed for more. Now I want more too; this time total commitment. I have wanted it for some time, but then there was my decision never to marry again. You have changed all that."

"Is it the illness?" he asks. "Is that the problem?"

"Only a little," I answer, realizing how hard it is to admit those concerns.

"I guess I could understand if it was my health. You're so young. With so much life ahead."

I was still angry because of Gene's deception and attempts to control me while he continued to do what he wanted. Even if his offer had come before the erosion of trust, my answer probably would have been the same. Frightened of his emotional strength, I feared he would succeed at controlling me. I felt two people did not have to be married to have a close relationship, and I worried that marriage was not good for women (see Bernard 1972). I gave little credence then to the importance of rituals, family ties, and commitment.

My parents also played a role in my decision. After not telling them the truth about Gene—they knew of him as a good friend and professor with whom I spent time—it had become even more difficult now to reveal the intensity of our relationship. Camouflaging our relationship had been easy since my parents asked few questions, but I would not be able, nor would I want, to hide a marriage.

In hindsight, my refusal seemed mostly connected to my fear that I could not handle his further deterioration. Although I argued that marriage made no difference in a relationship, I felt I had an "out" as long as we didn't tie the knot.

When Gene refused to commit to monogamy without marriage, we continued our open relationship and jealousy battles—the price I paid for my "freedom."

■ ■ ■

"All right, why don't you move in?" Gene offers in November 1977, three months after his marriage proposal. "You're at my house most of the time anyway," he adds, which takes away some of the romance from his proposition.

"But how will we deal with your seeing Linda?"

"When she is here, we'll get a motel room. If you are away, we might want to use the house."

Feeling generous, I volunteer, "And I can even plan to visit friends occasionally when she comes."

As it happened, I alternated between accommodating to his relationship with Linda and feeling painful jealousy when he went into New York City to meet her or even when she called on the phone. Lack of access was still the hardest part. When I wanted to talk to Gene, I wanted to do it at that moment. It was probably no coincidence that often this need for conversation occurred when Gene was with Linda. That I had the power to make all this different—he was willing to marry me—made me more tolerant, but not accepting, of their intimacy.

Although our relationship was working, it was not without its day-to-day problems. Many times I felt suspicious that Gene was not telling all. How difficult it is to be as open as possible with another person became clearer later in our relationship when I found myself skirting the truth. Then I convinced myself that I was protecting Gene.

■ ■ ■

"So, what did you learn from *The Eclipse of Community*?" Gene asks, as I settle into the driver's seat. We are on our way to Arizona, where Gene will teach for a semester to see if he feels better in that climate. I study for my preliminary exams while he drives. At night I drive, summarize out loud what I have absorbed, and answer his questions. After my oral exams in New York, I will fly to Virginia to do field work in isolated fishing communities for my dissertation research.

Being apart for a semester created a particularly quarrelsome time for us, made worse when we didn't have the hours to discuss our insecurities face-to-face. When the semester ended, Gene left to drive to New York without calling me. He had never let his anger last this long nor had he ever severed communication. Knowing I could not let this relationship end here, I drove 350 miles from my fishing island to New York and was waiting when he arrived from Arizona. We had one of our worst battles then over fairness and rule breaking, justifying our feelings by anything other than admitting we were both insanely jealous.

"Who am I to you anyway?" I yell, picking up on a conversation we had had continuously on the phone. "That you would come back east to see Linda and not see me?"

"But you came to Arizona for three weeks," he responds in a voice just as loud.

"I don't care. She doesn't get equal time with me."

"And you slept with my close friend while I was gone. How could you? He is off-limits."

"That is your rule, not mine," I scream and, outraged at his injustice, I feel my nails scratch across his face. How dare he try to control me? My feelings intensify with my physical outburst, and now I sob. "I only did it after I found out you were going to visit Linda."

"You bitch," he says, wiping the blood from his face, and pushing me to the ground. Stunned at our behavior—I have never been like this before—I sob. I hate him then, but at the same time, my loss of control amplifies the intensity of my love.

"You see other men, then you want to control my behavior."

"You have another emotional relationship, and you put her first."

"I asked you to marry me. What more do you want?"

"To know I'm most important whether we are married or not."

"You have no consideration for me or my feelings."

"Nor you mine, or you would stop seeing Linda."

"You will not control me. I get a lot out of that relationship." This statement once again makes me question my place in his life, and I move from sitting to lying face down on the wooded path on which we're walking. Our relationship seems futile, and, with that thought, my sobbing is renewed.

"Get up," Gene commands angrily, in contrast to his usual softening when I cry. "Someone is coming."

I am torn by my need to be appropriate and my desire to play out my distress—to show Gene how much he has hurt me. Remaining on the ground as people discreetly walk around me, I am delighted that Gene, not I, must deal with the embarrassment.

We fluctuated for a few days between breaking up and renting a house together in Stony Brook. I still wanted exclusivity without marriage, while he would promise exclusivity only with marriage. Both strong willed, we wanted our way and didn't want to give up anything. We had reached a crisis point, but seriously contemplating breaking up once again made us face an incomprehensible loss. So we declared our undying love and moved in together. This time I was not moving into his house; we were renting one together.

"I want to have an exclusive relationship," Gene announces soon after we are settled. "I still prefer marriage, but since you're unwilling, let's just settle in and love each other. We have so much together, I don't want to destroy it."

A certain excitement and unpredictability had been generated by our open relationship. We liked the constant stimulation of living on the edge and not being able to control each other, but we could see now that we were asking a lot to hope our love would always get us through the battles.

Is love a zero-sum game? Most of us seem to experience the receiving of it that way. Can a person love two people at the same time? At some point, resources—time, energy, money, attention, loyalty—are limited. Giving these resources to a third person then can take away from the primary relationship. Part of being partners is having primary access to each other, holding top importance for the other, and sharing unique experiences. When access is limited and loyalties and experiences are shared in a second relationship, the symbols of specialness disappear. To experience romantic love is certainly easier when one feels unique—I am the only one—or at least the most important one.

Finally, we had the pact of uniqueness, and we experienced our next year as our happiest period together. Early each Friday afternoon, we stopped working to prepare for the weekend. We planned menus and shopped together at specialty stores for our favorite foods. Then we closed the door to the world, sometimes staying in bed all day making love and talking. Or we watched sunsets or lightening storms from our porch. Except for Gene's illness, the time was close to perfect. Eventually I would need other outlets; this dream house would be sold before we could arrange to buy it; and Gene's health would deteriorate more. But, for now, we basked in the present.

PART III

Negotiating Stability and Change

PERIODICALLY, WHEN WE felt overwhelmed by disease, we set aside weekends to deal with Gene's deterioration and impending death. Gene took additional steroids, though they increased the rate of deterioration of his muscles, upset his stomach, and caused other less visible, long-term side effects. Our decision to meet short-term needs with long-term costs scared us but gave Gene a sense of strength. For a while, we did not have to deal with the worst effects of the disease—the clumping and severe shortness of breath.

For Gene, the process was one of rational, conscious acceptance of his deteriorating health. Pure will, determination, and pushing hard could not defeat the disease and, in fact, sometimes made it worse. With that recognition, he became more loving and sensitive, gaining a renewed sense of the importance of caring and relationships.

These weekend retreats evoked deep emotions in me that I normally tried desperately to suppress. My immersion in mutual self-revelation, at times uncontrollably passionate, was not without consciousness. I experienced wrenching pain as I sobbed—my entire body shuddering with grief—but still I observed myself. As I tried to gain entrée into Gene's world of anguish, I entered my own, positioned as a third-party observer to a world collapsing around and inside me.

During the first of these weekend retreats, Gene tries to pull me out of my agony. To ease my pain, stop my tears, and lighten my heart, he says, "Think of all the good times, baby. Be happy for our love."

"No, let me feel it. I think it's good for me. Just hold me." The loss of emotional control is the most excruciating sensation of my life. I want to get away, deny it; paradoxically, I crave this emotionally pure, but seductive, experience like a masochist craves the whip. Feelings of being a separate entity, alone in the world, fluctuate with spiritual connection to Gene and the universe.

At first, I don't know what I'm experiencing. Like the power of an intense orgasm, the abyss of agony pulls me in, until I am powerless. But, this feeling is different from the physiological release of orgasm that rushes to emotional release. This sensation simultaneously penetrates body, mind, and emotional being. The painful sobbing, moaning, and, sometimes, at the peak, screaming, go on and on, culminating in the internal explosion of the emotional ball that has been building in my gut and threatening suffocation. Then, like spent fireworks falling to the ground, my agony is diffused and I can breathe freely. Immediately, I feel the fluttering of the surviving sparks converging and struggling to be reproduced. The explosion itself triggers and becomes physical release. I go deep into my self, where I have never been before.

"Tell me what you're going through," Gene says, after my sobbing slows. "I want to share it with you. Please, let me be there for you."

I hesitate. Can he stand it? Can I bear telling him? When he insists, the feelings I try to describe come out in short phrases: "The pain. The human condition. Meaninglessness. The deterioration. It hurts—in my heart. I feel so helpless." When the sobbing renews, his strengthening embrace encourages me to continue. "I have so many unanswered questions. What is life about? Why do people die? Isn't there something we can do?"

He doesn't pull back, giving me confidence now to talk between sobs. "I feel grief for every single thing you have lost—that you have trouble walking, that your lungs will no longer carry your booming voice in class, that you run out of breath when we make love. These are my losses, too. I cry for both of us. For the pain I stifle in my heart when I see you struggling for breath, just to walk. For the love I feel when you suffer. For the numbness that comes over me when my pain becomes too great. And, even for the anger, yes, the anger I feel because we don't have a normal relationship."

"What else? What else are you feeling?"

When I hesitate, he says softly, but strongly, "You're experiencing how you might feel when I die, aren't you?"

Can I admit this? To be thinking about life without him seems disloyal. I let myself picture him as an invalid, then as dying, and, finally, for the first time, as dead. The pain tearing through my body means that, for a while, I exist again only as feeling, sobbing. He's going to die. I'm going to die. This is all there is. I find solace in the warm blackness that surrounds me, but then am drawn back to Gene, holding me tightly, our bodies rocking gently together in a soothing rhythm.

"Hey, open your eyes. I'm still here," Gene says, reminding me of the immediate present. "Touch me. Kiss me. I'm not dead yet. We still have wonderful time together."

I open my eyes to his smile, his strong embrace. I feel relieved; he isn't dead yet. I want to make good all the time we have left. So does he, he says.

He wipes my face. "Do you feel better about my death now?" I shake my head no. "But you just experienced it and you're still functioning. Just like you will when I really die."

"No, I can't imagine it," I say, turning away.

"Yes, you can. Make yourself think about what it will be like," he demands, turning my face back to him. "How will you cope? What will you do after I'm dead? You need to practice this too. Not just death itself." The slow and drawn out act of acceptance now contrasts with the quick, immediate emotional release I just experienced. I can't take any more now.

■ ■ ■

After that first retreat, we agreed that "practicing death and grieving" was good for me; catharsis was therapeutic and instructive. The rehearsal deepened connective pathways of feeling pain and accepting separation. By the time Gene died, we reasoned, I would have routine ways of feeling, and this repetition would dull my experience.

I periodically longed for the relief that came after plunging into the agony, when all the weight, accumulated from suppressing emotions, lifted from my body. After letting go, I was freed from the choke collar that tightened as I struggled to cope with the details of everyday life and once again enjoy the moment.

Later, I proselytize for Gene to have the same depth of experience. "Let go. It'll help to let it out." For me, it is now an article of faith that everyone should "be in touch with their emotions."

"I get release through your pain," he says, and I realize that in helping me confront the reality of his death, he is forced to face it as well.

Silent tears run down his cheeks. He chokes on a singular cry and then moans softly, holding onto me tightly. "Knowing you love me makes it all worthwhile."

"Let go, baby, I'm here for you."

"How do you know it won't make me feel worse?" When I admit I don't, he continues, "Holding in emotion and dealing with it rationally works best for me. I maintain distance from my feelings by talking about them. I'm scared to try anything else."

I understand what he is saying, because that had been my way of coping until my first emotional catharsis. "Maybe it doesn't work the same way for everyone," I finally acknowledge, confronted suddenly by the conflict of wanting to help him, yet not knowing if I can. Anyway, I feel reluctant to relinquish my place on center stage. After all, I take care of him all the time.

"I can't let go the way you do," he continues. "I'm afraid I won't be able to regain control. Besides, sobbing seems like self-pity."

Is he trying to tell me he disapproves of my self-pity? "So what's wrong with that?"

"It just doesn't seem right for me. What's the use anyway? The problem will still be there. There is no answer on the other side." I am shocked by the bluntness of his statement, then realize he is right. I will learn to manage his death, and he will die.

My emotional release and Gene's rational confrontation blend to transform our renewed feelings into tender and passionate lovemaking. Surrendering to the "involuntary" and "unknown" in sexual connection provides additional rehearsal for dying (Keleman 1974). Agony blends with ecstasy for me during orgasm, while Gene seems to experience only the ecstasy. "A gift from life," he says, and smiles. When Gene holds me tightly as I cry, we both are emotionally spent.

We then reenter a rational discussion about how to make our life together meaningful. For the answer, we turn to our connective bond, which means that being alone together, we are not alone, and that life is still worthwhile. Then we talk as two sociologists about the different ways we handle our feelings. Are these differences a matter of socialized gender roles, we ask, or shaped by our locations in the disease process? "Since the deterioration is happening to your body, not mine," I offer, "perhaps I can afford to 'give in' to my emotions and you can't."

"But would the roles be reversed if you were the one with the disease?" Gene quizzes. Although I don't think so, there is no way of knowing. Nevertheless, the conversation gets us "out of ourselves."

Feeling the intensity of our love and the depth of our mutual care enabled me to experience release during these weekends and to accept the vulnerability it implied. I needed to experience his death and lose self-control in a safe situation. That this letting go was a sign to Gene of my love, and not my weakness, made it acceptable to me. In the process, I realized how much pain I had hidden or suppressed, often because Gene's physical distress was more demanding and immediate than my feelings, and I ceased worrying, for then, about his ability to handle his psyche.

He did not doubt the depth of my caring when he experienced those moments. Nor I his. Comforting me made him feel worthy and gave him his best coping mechanism: "See, I am a tough fucker." Desperately needing me to see him as powerful and coping, he also needed to see himself as the strong man comforting his woman. He needed to assume a "worst-case scenario" about his disease and make himself handle it to stay in control.

Sometimes afterward we could even laugh at the human condition. "Life is absurd, isn't it? It's not going to get us down," we agreed. Yet the realization that eventually the disease would defeat us helped Gene and me to be more caring and loving and to face and resolve disagreements more easily. "What can you do?" we asked each other, acknowledging our helplessness, resigned to our fate. Seize the moment and live each second to its fullest. Make love and happiness. Give to each other. I wanted to give him the rest of his life.

After an intensive weekend, Gene was reassured of my love and respect, and I was more patient and loving. For a while I was not preoccupied with fighting his illness, and I accepted it as part of him. Though I still hated his disease, I didn't hate him for having it. Being open to him avoided the dilemma that when I protected myself from feeling the pain of his disease, I also shut off some of my love and openness. It was difficult to suppress one emotion and not another. Was it necessary to be so open to intense pain in order to feel intense joy? It seemed so.

These weekend moratoriums allowed us to hold his disease at bay, at least its psychological consequences, leaving us to deal only with the physical details of the disease. Only? The physical particulars were present everyday. Still, in the cyclical fluctuations between our psychological victories and physical emergencies, we pretended we were living normal lives and became skillful at building and sustaining our illusions.

But eventually the preoccupation with physical infirmities overtook our happiness. As it did, tension and strife between us built until finally we realized that we needed another weekend to recapture love and understanding. The cyclical movement from psychological catharsis to physical emergencies would become more unbalanced over time, until finally Gene no longer would have the physical strength to deal with the intensity demanded during these weekends.

■ ■ ■

Visits to Dr. Silverman, Gene's physician, also provided occasions for confronting and evaluating Gene's illness. The doctor's office was on Park Avenue, yet he made us feel we were being visited by a rural doctor in a horse-drawn carriage. Sentimental and grandfatherly, he held Gene's hand and teared when he had to tell us bad news; but his eyes brightened when immediately afterward he informed us of some new medicine to try or of a success story—a mayor who was working while hooked to a breathing machine—or when telling Gene how far he was above the normal curve given the extent of his emphysema.

"Most people in your condition are home in bed, but look at you, you're traveling around the world," he says to Gene, after hearing about our vacation.

"See, I'm not a wimp," Gene tells me when Dr. Silverman leaves the room.

"Don't you know that I know that?"

Gene needed the validation. Otherwise, how could he be certain how well he was doing? The same was true for me: How else did I know how hard he was trying to cope? Dr. Silverman understood those needs and recognized that his words motivated Gene and supported our illusions.

Dr. Silverman usually was engaged in several activities at the same time—phone calls from patients in other countries, questions from staff—but we never felt shortchanged. Although our appointment took most of a day, we had time to ask questions and hear about the latest findings on emphysema, including the doctor's own research. He responded to Gene as a colleague, not a dying man, asking about his sociological projects and letting Gene take part in the analysis of his disease. Later developing lung cancer himself, Dr. Silverman talked quite candidly to Gene about his own health, quality-of-life concerns, and how to live to the fullest as long as possible.

Still, at every successive visit, Gene was worse. As Dr. Silverman compared the indices of tests measuring breathing rate and lung capacity for us, we could not ignore the downward progression.

During one visit when there is a dramatic drop, Dr. Silverman tries to be optimistic, "But look at what you can still do. And there are some developments; a new drug is being tested in Canada. Let's see if we can figure out a way to obtain it."

Gene listens attentively, hopefully. Then a cloud passes over his face. "But, Doc, it's not a cure, is it?"

"No," the doctor replies, holding eye-to-eye contact with Gene. "There is no cure. Maybe in the future, but not in your lifetime."

Gene's shoulders sag farther into his chair as Dr. Silverman looks away, busying himself with altering Gene's many medications. "I think changing your antibiotic will help. Try taking one, four times a day, instead of two, twice a day."

This isn't real, I say to myself, looking down and holding my breath, thankful that no one is paying attention to me. Yes, it is. Accept it. Be glad the doctor is truthful. Now, you know the score. My mouth is dry, my eyes are wet. How can I feel so numb but like I am exploding at the same time? I suddenly laugh, then cover it with a sigh. What's wrong with me? Nothing. How in hell are you supposed to feel in this situation? There are no rules.

Desolate pain overcomes me, and I want to get away from this disease, which now seems like my disease too. "My god," a voice inside my head screams, "he's going to die. There is nothing I can do. Get me out of here." A calmer voice responds, "You can't leave him. You love him. He needs you and he's doing the best he can."

As we go into the outer office for Gene's new prescriptions, I try to be optimistic. "Maybe these changes will make a difference," I say to Gene.

"Bullshit," is Gene's reply.

Prescriptions in hand, Gene doesn't give me a chance to say anything else hopeful as he breathlessly hurries out of the office before me, pretending for a minute that he doesn't need help to reach the car.

It took only a few visits to realize that new medications and rearrangements of old ones were of little value. We simply substituted one steroid, one adrenalin, for others. The only time the change mattered was when Gene developed an allergy to an ingredient in one medication. Initially, Gene's improved condition gave us false hope that this medication was a panacea, only to let us down again when the allergy disappeared and the labored breathing continued.

Upon leaving the doctor's office, we often argued, sometimes about the shortest way to the car, other times about which errands to run. The visits left Gene emotionally and physically exhausted; they left me scared and withdrawn. We both were defensive and vulnerable. Managing to move around in New York City was physically difficult when Gene was at his best, and next to impossible with our tempers at the surface and our anxieties challenging our usual teamwork.

After this visit, we say little. Gene races through traffic, yelling at bad drivers. "God, I can't stand this traffic," I finally complain, my head throbbing. "And you're driving like a mad man."

"You think you can do better?"

We don't talk then, but my anger quiets when I think of the news we just received. "Why don't we have a late lunch, go somewhere where we can relax?" I ask timidly.

"What about the errands?"

"They can wait. Besides we aren't really going to beat the rush-hour traffic home anyway."

"Will you park the car if it's a long walk?"

I nod.

"I know a great place on the upper east side. You'll love it," he says, suddenly turning the corner. We're on the same team again.

Settling into Maxwell's Plum, the tension dissolves under the influence of champagne and gourmet food. Cost does not concern us. Like new lovers, we hold hands. Like old companions, we talk about death and the shortness of time we have left together. We cry softly as we admit the lowered numbers on pulmonary tests have reaffirmed our worst fears.

Then Gene says angrily, "Why does Silverman pretend there's hope, when there isn't any? Why doesn't he just say so?"

"He does, Gene. He said there was no cure in your lifetime." A pall spreads over our conversation.

"But then he says the shuffling of the medicine will help. It won't," replies Gene, still angry.

"That's true. But think of his position. He wants to be honest, yet not totally depress you or make you feel there's no hope for improvement. So he confronts us with the stark reality of your deterioration, and then gives us a ray of hope to hang on to. It isn't dishonest. He wants to have hope too."

"I guess," Gene replies, softening with resignation. Then, because nothing reminds us of our love in quite the same way as facing the loss of it, Gene connects with my eyes and mouths, "I love you." As the feeling flashes back and forth between us, my fear subsides.

"At least we have each other," he continues, now changing sides. "And who knows. Maybe I'll live longer than anybody thinks. There's always the possibility of a lung transplant."

Sure, I think ironically, but say sincerely, "Anything is possible. I'm just glad to have this time now. I guess our situation is not really worse than others. Everybody will die."

"This champagne is wonderful," Gene says. "Taste it in the back of your throat. It's so full and dry."

So began a tradition of having lunch at Maxwell's Plum after each doctor's visit. Without fully realizing it at the time, the two of us were being socialized into the roles of dying and grieving. I rehearsed how to show Gene love, yet shut out pain and fear; Gene practiced how to face his illness, yet escape living as a dying person.

The doctor's candid opinion, supported by the declining test results, confronted us with the reality of Gene's impending death. We began to relate to the disease much as the doctor had—facing the inevitable and then looking for some reason to be hopeful. Ambivalence as a coping mechanism offered comfort yet left room for reality. These afternoon lunches provided opportunities to integrate hope and reality, a balance that would tip toward reality as the illness took over.

■ ■ ■

During the fall of 1978, Dr. Silverman told Gene it was time to have oxygen at home to use at night. Although Gene had had the prescription for several months, he still had not made arrangements for delivery and, secretly, I was glad. Oxygen? What a scary thought. Would the whole room be oxygenated? Would it affect me? Oxygen? Such a symbol of illness. Old people dying in hospitals take oxygen.

One day I watch him struggle from the car into the house. Would oxygen help? We have to try it, I think, and say to him, "You are being irrational about the oxygen. Why aren't you doing something that might help?"

"After the oxygen, what else is there to do? I like to know there's still something to try."

I understood, yet I wondered how much he also did not want to admit to needing oxygen. So what? I answered myself. Does one always have to face reality?

"How do other people see me? How sick do they think I am?" Gene asks, this time more pointedly seeking details.

So I am more open than usual in my response. "Sicker than you think you portray yourself. But not nearly as sick as you actually are, as you let yourself be around me." His eyes dart from one part of my face to another as he attempts to determine the truthfulness of my response, then fall as he realizes I have no reason to lie. The look on Gene's face tells me his self-image is in question. Amazed at the power of my statement, I vow to be careful with information. Should I always tell him the truth?

Almost immediately Gene struggles to regain control, "I have to remember not to let down so much around you too."

Although I know his harsh words are an attempt to cover the fear that he can no longer handle his situation alone, I angrily respond to the content of his remark and to his distant tone. "Either I am a partner in this, or I'm not. Don't expect me to be there when you need me, and then think you can hide your condition from me." Anger is my attempt to cover my fear that there is nothing I can do.

"You're right," he says in a soft, understanding voice, the one that always grabs my heart. "But I don't want you to see me as handicapped or dying, or less powerful. I want to be net-plus in your life. I don't want you to want to run away."

"Your disease is difficult, but I want to be your teammate, if you let me."

■   ■   ■

In the middle of dinner, Gene begins coughing and I hear the rattle of the mucus plugging his breathing. Please release, I beg silently, as I place my hand on his arm and continue the conversation with our guests. "A little cold,'' Gene explains, pointing to his chest, and then coughs until he chokes and turns bluish-gray.

''What can we do?'' asks our guest.

''Nothing, I'll be fine. Yes, I think the department politically has become more polarized,'' he says, continuing the previous conversation, then coughing again.

''It's OK,'' I say to quizzical looks, and we sit silently. The scenario repeats itself several times before the mucus plug releases, and, finally, I relax. Offering no explanation for what has just happened, Gene continues the conversation.

After our company leaves, I continue to be tense and upset, almost to the point of anger. ''What's wrong?'' Gene asks. ''It's over now.''

''I know, but I hate those situations.''

''I do too. Believe me. I'm the one who's suffering.''

''I know, but I think we could handle them better.'' When he asks how, I explain, ''By telling people ahead of time what to expect.''

''No, I don't want them to know how bad I am.''

''Your friends deserve to understand how sick you are.''

''My friends don't really want to face it. It's too painful.''

''But it's horrible this way. They're concerned, but don't know what to do. And you make them feel helpless when you wave away their help.''

''But they'll feel pity. And they won't want to be with me if they think I'm this sick.''

''That's not true,'' I say, and then wonder if Gene is right. ''Anyway the costs of covering up the extent of your illness are too high. And your friends already know you're sick.''

''But not how sick.''

''Some of them suspect. Anyway this is too hard, for me too.''

''Tell me,'' he says, his voice softening.

''I'm embarrassed and anxious when you can't breathe. You can't help it. But then it's worse because I have to assure other people you're fine and continue to have conversations while you choke. They don't believe me, and it's awkward. Then I worry about you. Is this one an emergency? Should I help? Or will you resent it? On top of this, I have to make sure I don't reveal to anyone how sick you are. Instead, I should pretend that it's normal to punctuate interaction with gagging. I don't want you to lose your identity, but we have to come up with a better plan. This one worked for a while, but now you're sicker.''

''I don't want to cause you unnecessary problems,'' Gene says softly. ''What should we do?''

"Talk about your disease to friends and even to acquaintances in casual conversations when you're feeling well. If they know what to expect, they will more likely be calm in semi-emergency situations," I argue. "Then you won't have to deal with panicked people pleading to know what can be done to help at times when you need all your energy for breathing. This will normalize the state of affairs more successfully than avoidance and denial."

"Will it be better for you too?"

"You bet. I can pay attention to you instead of having to divert others' attention from you or make them feel OK. And I won't be as embarrassed and anxious."

After that conversation, Gene discussed the physiology of emphysema with close friends, made some undisclosing statements about deterioration, and explained what was happening when he was unable to breath. "It looks like I'm dying, I know," he admits. "But it isn't life threatening. There's really nothing you can do except be calm and continue what you're doing. I won't be able to talk at these times and will need all my energy to dislodge the mucus plug. It always comes up. Sometimes it just takes a while and a lot of coughing."

Most close friends asked questions and appreciated knowing what to expect. For them, interacting with Gene became a series of intense conversations punctuated by time-outs while he took care of immediate problems. They grew accustomed to continuing conversations with each other while waiting for the crisis to pass.

A few, unable to face the disease, responded to his confessions with, "Oh, you aren't that sick. You're going to get better." With them, Gene continued to play out his "just a little cold" routine. Sometimes these same people privately asked me about his deterioration, placing me in a bind between telling the truth and respecting Gene's wishes. I verified only for closest friends that deterioration was continuing at a rapid rate and that his life expectancy was limited.

■ ■ ■

In the fall of 1979, Gene's daughter, Beth, came to New York to enter the Fashion Institute of Technology. She attended school in New York City from Monday until Thursday and lived with us the other four nights each week. With her move came all the role confusion and conflicting demands of a reconstituted family. Gone were our flexible and romantic weekends. Now there were three of us, each with separate claims. I frequently went from trying to work out the situation to feeling that this intrusion was the last straw. Life with Gene was too frustrating: First, the constant presence of disease; now Beth.

"Why does Beth have to have dinner with us tonight? Do we have to entertain her every evening?" I ask Gene.

"Why don't you discuss this with her?" Gene responds. "And work out a system."

"I don't want to talk it over with her," I reply angrily. "I just want her to have a life of her own, so we can have time alone."

Beth walks in, her posture indicating anger. She doesn't respond when Gene says, "Hi, honey. What are you doing?" As she stalks around the kitchen fixing a sandwich, her demeanor indicates she has overheard our conversation. I say nothing, then feel guilty for not trying harder.

When Beth leaves, Gene continues, "I don't want to leave her out. She doesn't have friends here anymore." When I ask why she doesn't make some, he responds, "I don't know, but I don't want to tell her she can't have dinner with us."

"Well, you work out a schedule with her then."

"I don't want to be in the middle."

"I don't want to be there either. I didn't choose this situation. Don't you miss our alone time?"

"Sure I do, but I want her to feel welcome. She tries to stay out of your hair."

"She doesn't do a very good job. This is just too frustrating. Our talks, the romantic dinners, and sense of endless time together used to give me strength to deal with your illness."

"But we still have alone time during the week when Beth isn't here."

"But then we have to get up early for school."

"Well, you're going to have to deal with it yourself."

"Fuck you," I say, as I escape out the door, upset that my battle with Beth has now become my battle with Gene. I go to a movie to give myself time to plan leaving him. Instead, I analyze the situation. As Gene's daughter, Beth had claims on him that I could not challenge as I had the role of other women in his life. She, on the other hand, felt direct competition with me for his attention and affection. "I always 'suck hind tit' to your other women," she had accused. Although I wanted to support Gene's attempt to make amends for inattention in her past, my good intentions didn't make the problems I experienced any easier. Who were we to each other? Since Beth and I were almost the same age, I could hardly become her stepmother; we did not have a sibling relationship relative to her father; yet it was not a voluntary friendship.

Seeing the problem as a structural one, and fantasizing life without Gene, made me leave in the middle of the movie for home, even though I couldn't imagine living with this disease and the day-to-day discord much longer. I continued struggling during the next year, fluctuating among understanding, sulking, and lashing out because I couldn't have the world my way.

■ ■ ■

After one particularly dramatic drop in health in late 1979, Gene and I discussed getting oxygen delivered. "It's time," I argue. "It's getting more difficult to do anything physical. It might make life much easier on a day-to-day basis."

"If it makes it easier for you, then OK," he says. But "I can still do without" was the underlying message. "It will only be while sleeping," he says optimistically.

The oxygen actually wasn't as bizarre as I had envisioned. Instead of a mask covering Gene's face, a small and flexible plastic tube fit over his ears, in his nose, and under his chin. Two small openings directed the oxygen flow into his nose. I wondered how I was supposed to feel sexually turned on to someone with a hospital-green oxygen cannula framing his face.

"It bothers you, doesn't it?"

"Not really," I reply, determined to turn that lie into truth. At first, I closed my eyes during lovemaking so I wouldn't see the tube. Still, the steady bubbling sound of the oxygen picking up moisture from the humidifier attached to the four-foot-tall barrel holding the liquid oxygen—also hospital green—reminded me of its presence.

Soon oxygen became, somewhat like glasses or a hearing aid, a normal part of Gene. Because he could now breathe better, sex was more physical. The adrenalin that normally poured out during sexual arousal along with improved breathing meant that sexuality was, even more than before, Gene's primary physical outlet. But a loving embrace often ended up with both of us strangled by the hose. Anything other than the simplest activity meant we were bound up inextricably, the hose lassoed around us in every direction. "Watch the hose" became a phrase we both used. Sometimes Gene yelled in frustration when the hose became a problem; more often we laughed at the absurdity of the picture we created.

In no time, Gene began using oxygen around the house to help in other activities or to "perk him up," especially when he got home from work. By summer 1980, he would call for the hose as soon as he walked into the house. A fifty-foot-long hose made it possible to walk around the house, but it was constantly knotted and intertwined. It wrapped around tables and chairs and pulled blankets off the bed and through the house. We called it "the python." Occasionally, even Poogie got tangled up in it and barked for help. Sometimes, as Gene was walking, his head suddenly snapped back as the hose caught on some object we had not yet moved out of the way. "The python!" he yelled, and I came running. I hated what the hose symbolized. I felt hooked to it myself. Yet I knew it was fast becoming Gene's lifeline.

After a few months, we got out the portable tank the oxygen company had left us. "Let's take it on short weekend trips. Just a little hit now and then," Gene reassures. But soon it was a constant companion in the car. The portable tank was enclosed in a rectangular box about fourteen by eight inches. When we filled it from the larger tank, sometimes a piece of ice lodged in the opening or the valve on the small tank stuck and the oxygen escaped. Trial and error first produced arguments, then simple solutions—using a hair drier to eliminate the ice problem or hitting on the portable tank to open the sticky valve.

Even with the oxygen, our activities continued to slow down and our trips were more difficult and time consuming. There were tough times and embarrassing moments—his yelling for help on a busy street corner; leaning over a trash can because it was the only thing around for support while he caught his breath. Just don't make a scene, I silently pleaded. But more and more, scenes couldn't be helped. Mostly I stood by silently waiting to do whatever was necessary. "Just touch me," he sometimes requested. "Let me know you're with me." I fluctuated between acting like I was not a part of this picture and doing anything to make it better. I could make my eye contact with interested strangers say, "Oh yes, isn't that man over there sad?" Or, "We're doing the best we can, and we love each other."

"Let's buy a 'shooting stick,'" Gene says one day.

"A what?"

"You know, a cane that folds out into a three-legged chair."

"Great idea," I say, surprised by his willingness to use a cane.

Since most of our embarrassing moments revolved around Gene losing his breath when there was no place to sit to "catch up," the cane meant that Gene had a built-in chair. While it looked strange for him to sit on a cane in the middle of sidewalks, now we got less attention than before. People still saw him as a person in distress, but they viewed the problem as a chronic one under control, not an emergency. Thus, they felt less compelled to stop and offer help than when Gene was bending over a trash can gasping for breath. Having the cane meant that he could sit before the problem became acute. Less worried, I could then smile at people going by and indicate that the situation was under control. What a life saver that simple little chair became.

■ ■ ■

Usually Gene and I worked well together, though occasionally we got our signals crossed in tension-filled situations. We tried to suppress arguments during serious emergencies since they compounded our problems. Getting irritated often worsened Gene's breathing and lessened his receptivity to my help. Being angry made me less able to solve problems successfully at the moment we most needed clear heads. Arguments usually began after we had gotten through the crisis. For a few brief moments, stored-up tension flowed. "If you had only not tried to walk all the way into the movie without stopping, you wouldn't have had to yell for me to come help." "If you had listened to me about the shortest route, I wouldn't have run out of breath." As damaging as they were at the moment, these disagreements quickly turned into problem-solving discussions.

But just as we perfected a routine for dealing with the current level of health, the level dropped. The disease stabilized on a plateau for a while, with small peaks and valleys camouflaging the sudden drop that inevitably occurred, often without warning. It took a while to recognize that this was a permanent decline; sometimes we knew and ignored the warning signals. At each new level, we found ourselves arguing, sometimes viciously, about strategies for coping. Often one step behind, playing catch up, we failed to understand why our coping mechanisms, which had functioned so well for a while, had stopped working. It took a time-out weekend to deal with the new reality. A vicious progressive disease!

When the summer of 1980 approached, I felt optimistic. Beth had gone to Alaska for the summer. We were spending three weeks camping in Nova Scotia and the rest of the summer would be at home alone. Even the large oxygen tank on the backseat—in case Gene needed an occasional "toke" while he drove—did not daunt my spirits.

"I can't get the damn tent peg into the ground," I say, frustrated, but determined to make this camping trip work. "I need another pair of hands."

"Are you angry because I can't help?" Gene asks from his chair cane positioned close by.

"No, that's not it. I just want to get this damn tent to work."

"Well, stop pounding and let's think about it logically."

"It's not a logical problem, it's a physical one," I say as I hit the tent peg with enough force to bend it, and feel jubilant when it curls. Since Gene is the only available receptacle for my anger and resentment, I convey with my facial expression, "It's messed up, and it's all your fault because you can't help." When he looks glum, I feel responsible. Knowing there is nothing he can do intensifies my feelings.

"I'm so worthless. You think I'm a burden, don't you?"

"No," I say, but my actions—pursed lips, aggravated tone, furrowed brow—contradict my words. "It's just that everything is so hard."

"Oh, god, I hate this."

"Quit feeling sorry for yourself. I'm the one having the problem here. Why do I now have to deal with your psyche?" I respond, giving into my frustration.

"You're a spoiled brat. I think you enjoy making me feel helpless."

"How can you say that when I'm always so supportive?" I ask angrily. "You are an unappreciative asshole. Put the tent up yourself."

"I can't," he says, and I melt at his vulnerability.

"I can't do all these things by myself," I say, this time in a soft voice.

"I know." He closes his eyes, and an agonizing look appears on his face as he reaches out to hold me. "I'm sorry you have to deal with this. I'm not a whole person."

"You're wonderful. You do so well under the circumstances. I respect you so much. Think of all the wonderful times we have together," I respond. I feel his frustration now; he feels mine. Immediately we are friends again.

Any indication that one of us was trying to see the world through the other's eyes was all it took to get the argument over and love flowing. Then we were ready to talk about what, in addition to two strong temperaments, had contributed to battles. His disease was always the culprit. How to keep these struggles from happening was a constant topic of discussion. In this case, after a few nights, we abandoned camping for the convenience of a motel and sadly realized we would not try it again.

Although Gene's health needed constant monitoring while traveling, we could still "put it away," which meant attending to his needs quickly and returning to our travel cocoon. Our trips were organized around nature— water, mountains, and forests. We tested the limits of his health; I pushed him further, he played cheerleader to my efforts. In Nova Scotia, we made love on an isolated beach, laughing like children at our naughtiness and basking in the joy of spontaneity. Just riding down the road was like watching a nature movie from inside our own private capsule. Even the dull interstate provided hours to talk about ideas and feelings. Sometimes I took notes for a new project while he drove. Then, in an expensive motel at night, we opened a special bottle of wine or a bottle of Tab and "had a party." This meant continuing the discussion from the car, now with each other's full attention and access to physical pleasures not compatible with driving.

. . .

"You have to ask the doctor about marijuana," I say to Gene, "and increased oxygen use." Gene had quickly discovered that turning the dial past the prescribed limit (two liters of oxygen per second at rest; five for activity) made him feel better and permitted more activity.

"Why would increased oxygen hurt? When I turn it up, I feel so much better. And the marijuana doesn't have nicotine."

"Then the doctor will say it's OK." Initially, Gene smoked marijuana for the high and partly as a substitute for cigarettes, which he had given up in 1971. Now he often smoked to open his breathing passageways.

"Marijuana is an excellent bronchial dilator," the doctor says at the next visit in response to our inquiry. Then he cautions, "Although it has positive short-term effects, the long-term effects from the hot smoke are negative. You must do your own cost-benefit analysis."

"Ask him about the oxygen, Gene," I push.

"I can breathe much better at higher numbers and do more, Doc. This isn't a problem, is it?"

"If the oxygen is too high, your lungs might stop working on their own. At the least, it will cause loss of lung capacity."

Shocked, we began constant monitoring of the oxygen flow, turning it up and down depending on the activity in which Gene was engaged. "Turn it down while I'm watching TV. Turn it up while I go to the bathroom." Usually I spontaneously jumped to help him. When Gene needed to assert his independence from me, or didn't want to bother me, he sometimes insisted on changing it himself. Although I was glad not to have to get up, I felt guilty watching him struggle to the oxygen tank in the bedroom, and I hated losing him for the ten minutes it might take for his breathing to return to normal.

Gene reciprocated for my physical labors by taking care of a greater portion of our expenses, reading my work, driving when we traveled, and doing what he could. Still, it was hard to convince him, and sometimes myself, that these contributions evened out the growing burden of my physical labor.

4

GENE WAS ASKED in 1980 to apply for a job in California as chair of a department. "I have a good chance of landing it," he tells me.

"This might solve our dual-career problems."

"Yes, California would give you a better job market than New York."

"And I could work part-time there while I finish my dissertation. I could pursue my career and yet we could be together."

"So why the frown?"

"I just don't want to be in a situation where it's assumed I got a job because I was the chair's girlfriend."

"So you'll try for a job at another university there," Gene replies, looking annoyed and then concerned. "Remember, I'd be giving up a lot too. Stony Brook is my home."

If Gene was willing to leave Stony Brook, I could not hold on to "I have to do this by myself." I felt confident that once I got a foot in the door, I would be able to make my own case.

We talked through the impending interview time and again to figure out how Gene would manage it physically. "You'll have your chair cane," I say.

"But won't that make me look handicapped?"

"Not nearly as much as running out of breath walking across campus."

"I'll ask if they can hold everything in one building. Maybe have people come to me."

"Even so," I remind him, "you'll have to walk to cars and restaurants."

"Oh, geez. I'll take extra steroids before I go."

"Maybe I should go with you, to help."

"Oh, baby, is this going to work?"

In his letter accepting the interview, Gene pointed out that he had a physical problem that would necessitate special consideration but would not keep him from doing a good job. It was after writing the letter that Gene decided to ask his doctor about longevity. "How long will I be able to work, Doc? How long do I have to live? I want to make sure it's not unethical to take this job."

"You know these things can't be accurately predicted," Gene's doctor says, after hearing about our situation.

"We know, but we want your opinion," Gene replies, as we sit on the edge of our seats.

"Emphysema is a plateau disease. As you have experienced, when you drop a level you never come back to where you were before. How long you stay on a plateau depends on many variables, such as whether you get an infection. But I'm going to give you a guess anyway. If you don't catch a bad cold, you'll probably be able to work for three to five years and live from seven to ten."

"OK," Gene says, matter-of-factly, and we are silent. The doctor returns to writing prescriptions, touching Gene's shoulder affectionately as he leaves the room.

Should I be happy or sad? What had I expected? Ten years is a long time, but three seems just around the corner. We don't talk until we are seated in our favorite restaurant. Then, in a depressed voice filled with regret, Gene says, "He's giving me optimum figures. There's no way I won't get a cold. Three years is not a long time. If I can't promise five healthy years to build a program, then I can't take this job."

"I guess you're right," I say, lamenting our lost dream, but feeling relieved. Every time I pictured Gene at an interview trying not to appear sick, my stomach turned queasy. The same thing happened when I imagined him dragging into school every day to run a department. These projected numbers took on a reality and were used to calculate the feasibility of future plans even though we acknowledged that there was no way to predict what actually would happen.

Shortly afterward, we decided to buy the house we were renting. That we could consider this investment when our future—our relationship, his health, my career—was so unpredictable is a tribute to human tolerance for ambiguity, or for denial. But we couldn't bear to surrender the dreams that had been a part of this time together, symbolized by our house. Our landlady accepted our offer two days before we received an eviction notice from her estranged husband who had sold it to another buyer. Was this a bad omen?

■ ■ ■

"I love this one," I say to Gene, admiring the old house located in the middle of a little town called Port Jefferson.

"But it doesn't have a bedroom downstairs," he reminds me.

"It has a bathroom off the kitchen."

"I can't climb the stairs every day."

"I know. But I love the living room. Can you believe it has two fireplaces?"

"Maybe we could look into that automatic chair lift we saw advertised to carry me upstairs."

"Yes," I say excitedly, then think how ugly it will look in our house, and how much about Gene's health it will reveal. "I have another idea," I say. "We'll make the living room the bedroom. Who says a house has to have a living room?"

"But what about when we have company?" Gene asks. Although the tone of his voice indicates my suggestion is unworkable, the impish grin on his face conveys he is getting into the idea.

"Who cares? We usually entertain around the kitchen table anyway. And if we have formal company or a party, we'll make our platform bed into a sitting area."

"Do you think it'll work?"

"Yes, most of our friends will love the arrangement."

"What about the oxygen tanks?" Gene asks. "People will see them."

"We'll cover them with a blanket. Or, when we have company, I'll lug them to the closet."

"What about your back?"

"I'll manage. I want this house."

"Done."

The house worked well. The biggest change was that the oxygen tanks (now there were two) were in full view instead of hidden in the back bedroom. Although we occasionally put them in a closet, most of our friends grew accustomed to the ugly green containers in the corner. Soon it would not matter, because Gene would use oxygen while they were present.

■ ■ ■

In November 1980, I finished my dissertation and was invited for an interview at the University of South Florida in Tampa. As we talked about how to work out our relationship if I got the job, Gene first was shaken, then began to see Florida as a solution to our problem. "I'll have to retire at some point," Gene says. "Winters are getting harder for me. Florida has a good climate."

"I know," I respond. "I see you having trouble breathing in the cold air."

"Yes, it's awful," he says, tears forming. "Like I'm suffocating. My body has gotten so thin and the cold just seems to go right through it. God, I'm so fragile." I hold him, wanting to make his fears go away. "And I worry about catching cold from being chilled. That's what will do me in. But," he says, now sounding cheery, "Florida could solve all that."

As I fantasized about getting this job, I moved from feeling sad about Gene's condition to being excited that we might work this out, and then I felt scared of the responsibility moving together would entail.

Once in Florida for my interview, I felt confident. The faculty reacted favorably to my presentation about change in isolated fishing communities, and one-on-one interactions went well. My southern, polite, and laid-back upbringing came in handy. I camouflaged the aggressiveness I had learned in New York, trying to appear as a pleasant colleague with compatible intellectual strengths, productive but not threatening. When the professor who took me to the airport said, "This job is yours. I can tell," I left feeling on top of the world.

A few days later, I was offered the job starting in January, only six weeks away. Gene tried to be excited for me, though I was certain he felt insecure and neglected. I worked late most evenings finishing my dissertation. He spent time talking to Joan about what he should do with his life, the details of which he did not share. I was glad not to be the only recipient of his emotional distress.

"I don't know if I can trust you to stick it out with me," he says in one of our intimate talks during this period, "or whether it's even fair to place the burden of my health on you."

"That's something you have to decide. I don't know either. All I know is that I'm willing to give it a try. I can't predict what I'll feel like in a few years."

"This would be your chance to escape my disease," Gene offers.

"I hate your disease, but I love you. I don't want to lose you."

"The disease comes with me. Go to Florida and start your life." Was this a test?

"This is my life," I say. "I am living it now. Moment to moment. I'm not waiting for it to happen."

"You should forget about me. You're too young to be dealing with this."

"If you were my counselor, is that what you'd tell me to do?"

"Probably. But it's not what I want you to do. Life is easier with you around."

Changing strategy, he says, "I need to know if I can count on you until the end. It's getting hard to do this by myself. I have to make other arrangements for my life if you aren't going to stay with me."

"I can't promise that anything is forever," I say, touched by his admission. "But right now I want it to work." I knew I had not adequately responded to his fears. I was caught between my belief that two people stayed together out of desire, not some agreed upon commitment, and my recognition that he needed to prepare for his future. Gene felt that commitment would enhance our relationship. Why had he changed positions so drastically from when I first met him? How much of it had to do with his greater need now?

"Call the university and ask to start work in April, the third quarter, instead of January," Gene demands.

"But it might jeopardize my job."

"You don't want to wait, do you?" he accuses.

"It's not that. I'm just scared they'll think I don't really want the job."

"You think they're going to take away your job because you ask to start a quarter later? The administration will be glad they don't have to pay anyone for that quarter. They offered you the job, didn't they? They see you as the best candidate. I would like you to help me through the worst part of winter before you go," he adds reluctantly.

Although I feel needed and appreciated, I hate that what he says is true. He continues, "It would mean that we would only be apart for ten weeks. Then we would have the summer together. Then we would be apart for one semester and after that I have a sabbatical and could come down there. Then maybe you could take a leave of absence and come to New York for a semester. By that time I might be ready to retire. If you leave now for six months, we're probably doomed."

A burden lifted off my shoulders as I realized this was a plan that would allow us to be together, yet still give me full flexibility to pursue my career. It wasn't foolproof, but I felt hopeful. "You are losing your escape hatch," the little voice reminded me. "I am getting everything I want," another voice replied.

After I made arrangements to start teaching the end of March 1981, Gene and I took a vacation in Florida, where I set up a talk for him at the University of South Florida. It would be important for him to have a role in my department, we both thought, so that I was not his only connection.

Would he have trouble getting to the department? Would he look sick? In New York, people had known Gene when he was healthy. His position and popularity among faculty and students there meant that people accorded him status regardless of his illness, and continued to treat him like the old Gene. Being attached to Gene there reflected back to me a positive image. In Tampa, his physical disability would be a more compelling source of identification than it had been in Stony Brook. I hoped Gene would so dazzle my colleagues with his talk that his disability would seem insignificant.

"I want to go into the department alone first," I say to Gene when we arrive in Tampa.

He looks hurt, then says, "OK, I understand. I'll pump out my lungs and work on my talk while you're gone."

When I return, I meet with the assistant dean in the bar of the hotel. "Did you drive down alone?" she asks.

"No. A friend came with me."

"Oh, where is he?"

"Back in our room."

"Why didn't you bring him to have a drink? I would have liked to meet him."

The truthful answer was that I did not want her to see me as part of a disabled couple nor did I want to worry about Gene's illness while I tried to make a good impression. What I say is, "Oh, he is preparing a lecture." Should I invite her to our room now? If I do, how will I explain the oxygen tank?

When I insisted on maintaining an identity apart from him, Gene felt shoved aside. "I want to know you're still proud to be with me, in spite of my disability. I want to know you still see me as a worthwhile person," he says that night when we get into bed.

"Can't we have this conversation another time?" I ask, feigning exhaustion.

The next day, I scout ahead to find an elevator and the easiest route to the second floor, where Gene will speak. "It will be a difficult hike," I announce when I return to the car. "Two long halls and some steps."

Taking a deep breath, Gene dashes thirty steps before stopping to sit on the chair cane I carry. I hope we can make it to the room without anyone I know seeing us. Once seated in the room, it will be harder to tell how sick Gene is, in spite of his labored breathing and adrenalin spraying.

"Are you sure this is the shortest way?" Gene angrily asks after the second dash.

"I told you it was." How dare he be angry when I'm suffering too and trying to help. But scared to risk an argument now, I substitute numb hope for my anger. Just get me through this, I plead.

My numbness spins into charm as one of my colleagues approaches, and I hope my charm covers my nervousness. "Hi, Ben, good to see you," I say. "Gene, you remember Ben."

Sitting, catching his breath, Gene smiles and shakes hands. "Oh, yes, I remember you from Tennessee." His labored breathing makes it difficult to say more.

"Hi, Gene. Great to see you again," Ben says.

"He's having some trouble breathing—from the walk," I explain to normalize the situation.

"Let me walk upstairs with you and show you the room where you'll talk," Ben offers.

When Gene's eyes convey that he does not want this pressure, I say, "No, go ahead. It'll take us a while."

"I'm in no hurry." We are caught, and now are forced to "cover" the extent of Gene's disability in order to keep the stigma "from looming large" (Goffman 1963, p. 102).

Gene changes his strategy to one he hopes will make him look less ill. Walking very slowly, he gets into a rhythm, like in a wedding march. Now he is not as winded when he stops every thirty feet to sit on his chair, but his progress is slower. I talk to Ben as we walk; Gene picks up the conversation when he is seated. Sensing we would rather do this alone, Ben finally goes ahead.

On the second floor, where the Sociology Department is located, Gene moves slowly, stopping more often to rest, so that he is able to talk to colleagues who approach to be introduced. My clashing worlds make me feel tied up in knots, but I negotiate the situation, remembering everyone's name while monitoring Gene. When we finally make it to the lecture room, I relax. Gene seems more composed once seated.

Gene's presentation went well, although not as smoothly as I had hoped. His nervousness stemmed from realizing how important this audience was to us. When I distanced myself to watch him as though I did not know him, his breathing looked labored. When he sprayed his inhaler often, I was aware of its intrusiveness in a way I had never been before. But people responded positively to what he said. Relieved that we were making it through this one, I thought how good Gene would be for the department. Little did I know how negative some of the reaction to him would be.

I thought of how this experience must be for Gene, who had always been so good at meeting and talking with people. Being met as a "disabled person" was new. So was having to sit back while I got wrapped up in my new job.

It was a difficult but, to some extent, welcomed role reversal for me. I had grown used to looking up to Gene and depending on him intellectually. Yet that strong part of my personality that wanted more recognition sometimes had felt stifled.

After we returned to Stony Brook, we had three months before I had to move to Florida. Caring times alternated with tense ones. Gene was supportive as I edited the final version of my dissertation. "I'm waiting," he says. "My turn to be taken care of is next."

It was a hard winter for Gene, and I was glad I was there. The quaint house we had rented was drafty. When the landlord insisted on turning off the heat at night, Gene caught several colds, and his day-to-day deterioration was visible. His morning ritual now took more than two hours and he often wondered how he would get to work. Although he said talking in class took all his breath, he never missed a day. The department scheduled small classes for him, so he wouldn't have to talk loudly, in rooms near his office, so he wouldn't have to walk far.

Still, he often arrived home from work exhausted and fell in the door desperate for oxygen. Although he now relied more on oxygen at home and used the portable tank in the car on the way to work, he refused to take it into school. "Why not?" I ask, wondering whom he was trying to kid now.

"People shouldn't think I'm that sick," he replies, a line I had heard many times. "What would that do to my ability to influence decisions?" And what about your survival and my peace of mind?

When I thought about the future and what was to come, a voice inside me screamed, I can't handle this. When the situation was too overwhelming, I stopped thinking about it. Sometimes I grew angry, his demanding tone disgusting me. Then I looked at his suffering—his vulnerability—and relented. He could be so kind, sensitive, and understanding of my emotional pain about his disease that I cried for him. Then I loved him with a fierce passion. Still I questioned whether I could survive this and continue being good for him and myself. Would he drag me down with his illness? Secretly, I was glad I was going to Florida alone for a semester so that I could think about what I was doing.

■ ■ ■

"So you'll drive to Florida with me," I say, "and spend the week of your spring break. You can help me find a place to live. Some time on the beach will do you good. Then you'll fly back."

"Then in May," Gene continues, "I'll be finished with my semester and I'll come down while you teach for another three weeks. Six weeks apart—that's nothing."

As I try on what used to be my favorite outfit, I interrupt to ask, "What about this one?"

"Oh, god, throw it away. That's what you were wearing when I met you. It's awful."

"It was expensive," I say, hesitantly throwing it on the growing yard-sale pile.

"I'll buy you another."

"OK, look at these pants on me."

"Have you worn them in the last two years?"

When I say no, he replies, "On the pile."

"Too big."

"Out of style."

Left with a few tops and two pairs of pants, I say, "What a wardrobe to take to Florida," but I feel liberated to be rid of clothes I had lugged around since high school.

In the same manner, we boxed up unnecessary kitchenwares. Gene bought a microwave oven, so he could fix frozen dinners while he lived alone. We rearranged the kitchen so it was convenient for him, and placed items he used on top shelves and near the front of cabinets and the refrigerator.

Our fear and insecurities showed in our incessant talk about how it was all going to work out. But we were having more private conversations in our heads than usual. Now Gene seldom spoke about his fears of losing me, although I assumed they were on his mind, and I didn't always show the excitement I felt about my new adventure.

How would it be without him? He had become a large part of my life. Would I like being alone? In the middle of my thoughts, I glimpse Gene bent over a table trying to catch his breath, and I think about the freedom of not facing his pain everyday. Then he turns to me and says, "Let's have a party. Enough work. Let's talk."

We talked about my anxieties about my new job, and how he would manage without me. But I did not mention my yearning for freedom from taking care of him. Instead, we planned where we would travel during the summer. Then we cuddled in bed, content for the moment in our love.

■ ■ ■

We drove to Florida without taking oxygen since Gene would be flying back to New York. Nor did we make arrangements to have it delivered, since we were staying at a colleague's house. More concerned about my transition than Gene's, I refused to think about the chance we were taking.

Once in Florida, Gene complained constantly about feeling bad. This isn't fair, I thought, when there are so many things I have to do. "I can't help it," Gene yells. "You might think I'm whiny, but I can't breathe." It was a case of both of us feeling needy at the same time, which framed the other as self-centered and set the scene for some of our worst times.

He had just supported me through the completion of my dissertation, and now, because ordinarily we took turns being supportive, he felt it was his turn.

"Just let me get through this one," I plead, realizing Gene's health soon would not allow for my turn.

We spent a day at the beach, hoping the warm sunshine would make him feel better. When he was too sick to enjoy it, I felt sympathetic, but it was hard to feel love for someone who was complaining, short-tempered, and depressed, especially when I was so goal-oriented and excited. I made myself numb to his pain and concentrated on the tasks at hand; he retreated into his shell and suffered silently.

Finally, we had to acknowledge that he no longer could function without oxygen. And the reality of the change we faced as well as his inability to deal with the demands of a new world made him frustrated and depressed and less able to boost his shallow breath. My insisting on freedom to explore other relationships while we were apart added to the tension. We both were relieved when the week was over.

When we returned to the airport, I persuaded Gene to use a wheelchair. Resisting at first, he finally let his weak body slump into the chair to be pushed to the gate.

"We are now boarding anyone with small children and those needing assistance," the voice calls over the loudspeaker.

"That's us," I say in surprise, and then cry as the airline official pushes Gene onto the plane. When he turns in the chair, blows me a kiss, and mouths the words "I love you," I choke back more tears. I am alone, empty, and don't want him to go. I now understand the expression "I thought my heart would break."

Driving back to my new apartment, bare except for the few pieces of ugly rented furniture, I recalled the first and only other time he had used a wheelchair, a year before in New York, an event I had repressed.

We had gone with friends to a Picasso exhibit at the Metropolitan Museum. Guards refused to allow Gene's chair cane in the museum. Desperately, he demanded, "But I have to have it," and we both argued with them.

"Too many people," they said. "It is an absolute rule. The traffic must flow smoothly," and then they rolled up a wheelchair, which seemed a much bigger obstacle to me.

"No way," Gene responded.

Our friends left us alone so we could decide what to do. "Come on, baby," I pleaded. "It doesn't mean anything."

"No. You don't understand. It will affect my identity. I'm not ready for it yet."

"But it's just their bureaucratic solution. It's this or we can't go."

His mouth set firmly, he reconsidered, and tears glistened in his eyes. "OK," he said calmly. "But just this time." He plopped down, relieved to be sitting.

I breathed a sigh. Easy for me. My identity wasn't on the line. Or was it? Who was this person pushing a wheelchair? I wondered when I caught a glimpse of myself in a mirror.

It was much more pleasant to be able to concentrate on what we were seeing rather than on Gene's breathing and where he would sit next. Going to museums had been one of our favorite activities, but we hadn't done much of it for a while because of Gene's lack of mobility. What freedom. But pushing the chair put me in control of his movements.

"I'm not through with this picture yet," he said, putting his foot on the floor to stop the forward motion and almost causing a spill.

"But those people had to get by."

"I don't care. I don't like your deciding when I have to move to the next picture."

Ignoring his irritated tone that usually set me off, I offered a solution, "You direct and I'll push. If I see a hazard I'll tell you about it—before I change direction." I would have done anything to make this experience less crushing to his ego.

"Deal," he said.

We took on a new identity together, as one person, with me being the part with whom people dealt. The crowd was courteous, almost too courteous. I had more eye contact than usual with individuals as they looked for a clue as to where I was headed so that they could get out of our way. When, from a distance, I noticed people looking at us curiously, at first I pretended to be a dutiful daughter taking care of her ailing father. I caught myself being less affectionate with Gene so that others would not know I was intimate with a man in a wheelchair. Then, since I knew Gene needed me now, I closed out the world and bent over to kiss him while he discussed a painting in the insightful way I admired.

When we became more comfortable, we talked about the change of identity brought on by the wheelchair. "They either stare or refuse to look at me," Gene said.

"We have a live social-psychology laboratory," I giggled. "Let's stare back and see what happens." When he tried staring at people looking at us, they immediately turned away, refusing to make eye contact. "It's as though

I'm not here," he said sadly, "except as a curiosity. I'm a 'nonperson' "
(Goffman 1963).

"They aren't acting that differently toward you," I said, trying to placate
Gene.

"OK, you try it then," he said, standing up. I recoiled, but had no choice
other than to sit. Instantly, I felt helpless.

"You're right," I admitted after a few minutes. "Nobody looks directly
at me. Only children, who are then quickly pulled away by parents."

My thoughts returned to the present. We had called ahead so that a
wheelchair and assistant would be waiting for Gene when he landed in New
York. Crossing this boundary upset both of us; yet we also were relieved.
Trips to airports had become gut wrenching. Even arriving at the airport
several hours early did not ensure that Gene could make it to the gate
without misfortune. Although I understood Gene's need for physical
mastery, there was a better way of doing this and I wanted to use it, now.

Gene had postponed using a wheelchair in order to maintain his
identity as a fully functioning person, but also for the same reason that he
had waited to use oxygen. "There is nothing left after this," he said. Oh,
how wrong he was. Thankfully, we could not anticipate all the horrors and
technological devices yet to come.

As I unpacked in my apartment, I worried about Gene, alone on the
plane. "There is absolutely nothing I can do about it," I said out loud,
realizing how much of my time was spent thinking about how to make it
easier for him to manage. The boundary between being available when
Gene needed me and hovering changed continuously as he needed me
more, and the conflict over my proper positioning demanded constant
negotiation as Gene's health deteriorated.

I shook my head free from these thoughts. It was time now to think
about my life. Most of my energy in the next few weeks was directed toward
my career and adjusting to my new job. Gene and I talked on the phone
often, which eased my loneliness. Although he missed me, he had his Stony
Brook world, and his daughter had arrived to take care of him. Ironically, it
occurred to me that Gene was much happier than I was with my new-found
freedom.

I enjoyed teaching classes, but found it difficult to concentrate on my
research. Since it was hard to make friends at the end of a school year, most
of the time I spent alone, thinking, reading, enjoying the sun, exploring the
region, or talking on the phone. I fantasized occasionally about meeting
someone. But my focus was on my future and the large hole in my life
caused by Gene's absence. I missed our talks, our laughter, our love, the

attachment, but I didn't miss the deterioration. What is it going to be like when he needs me even more? The sense of obligation I felt was a small part; a more important issue was that I could not imagine his being in the world and not being with him. My world was not right when he was not with me. Somehow we would work it out. Somehow I would manage.

. . .

"You had to get an upstairs apartment, didn't you?" Gene yells, as he sits on the steps to catch his breath. "Even though I asked you not to."

"I'm sorry," I say. "It was just, well, this was available, and it was so cheap."

"I would have paid the extra."

"It's only for a few weeks."

Taking a deep breath, he rose and rushed the last few steps. "Open the door," he demands angrily.

Gene had come to Tampa in mid-May after he finished teaching. As usual, our time together vacillated between ecstatic comfort and overbearing angst and frustration.

"Let's have a party," he says, after catching his breath. "Give me the phone book. I'll bet we can find gourmet goodies, even in Tampa." Off in the car we go, with Gene driving and paying, and me running in and out of stores. We arrived home, our arms loaded with the best delicacies in town.

After opening champagne and basking in being together, Gene says, "OK. Let's talk about our trip." We had planned a month-long driving trip to the Canadian Rockies after I finished teaching in June. We would travel for a month and then settle back into our house in Stony Brook for six weeks. After that, I would return to Tampa to teach while Gene taught at Stony Brook. Starting January 1982, he would spend his four-month sabbatical in Tampa. We would travel that next summer and then I would take a leave of absence and go to Stony Brook for a semester, which would get us to January 1983.

"If it works," Gene says, "we'll have been apart less than five months, and we won't be forced to make any decisions about your career or my retirement."

Still I knew I had to make some decisions at this point. After six weeks apart, Gene's struggle to make it on his own was more obvious. He shouldn't have to worry about whether he could count on me as well. I had already practiced my new feelings, without saying anything to Gene. I am committed to being with him, I had started to repeat silently a few weeks before. It felt right. Now, weeks later, I still didn't want to renege, and felt sure enough of my commitment to discuss it with him.

"Gene, I want to commit to you until you die. You can count on me."

His eyes light up. "Do you mean it?" Although I say yes, he replies, "I don't dare trust it."

"I'll show you."

"Oh, god, I'm so happy. I didn't dare hope."

"I know that things can change. But I want to give this relationship my all."

Gene says, "What about all the times you said you didn't believe in commitment, that you couldn't stand to watch my deterioration?"

"I feel different now. It would have been great if the ideology of 'staying together as long as it is good' had worked, but other factors intruded. You need to know whether I will be with you when you can't make it alone. I will. You'll see. And at some point you'll come to trust me."

"I haven't trusted you."

"I know that."

"Other people reinforced that. Beth once told me that since you couldn't be counted on, she was planning to come and take care of me when I couldn't."

"Yeah, but can you trust that? She was supposed to stay with you next semester, but she has already reneged." Gene shrugs, and I continue, "Even my friend Gina said that I was too self-absorbed to give myself to this task, but I don't feel I've been any different than anyone else, just more honest about my ambivalences and less willing to make commitments I wasn't sure I could keep."

"I want to lie beside you, hold you," Gene says.

In bed I thought about how fearful I felt. Yet, I was sure I was going to live up to my commitment, unless doing so was out of my control. I valued keeping it under my control, "but who knows," said the little voice, "it might drive you crazy." "I'm willing to take the risk," another voice answered.

How had I made this decision? I added up all the factors, played them and replayed them through my mind. On one hand, there was the pain of staying and living with the deterioration; on the other, the pain of leaving and accepting an identity that included deserting Gene when he needed me most. On one hand, there was the joy of his love and companionship; on the other, loneliness and other opportunities. Either way there'd be loss. Was it a rational cost-benefit decision? More likely, I manipulated the factors in favor of my heart, which wanted to stay with Gene.

We made love that night without reserve. On my side, passion was kindled by the danger of promises I spoke. On his, abandon more likely came from security symbolized by promises he heard.

We turned to getting ready for our summer vacation. Although we loved to plan trips and always worked well together, this one was more difficult than usual. We fought over where we would go, when, and who should do what in the division of labor. I could not recall this happening before. While apart from Gene, I had become more independent, while he had taken on even more need to control his shrinking world. Perhaps I also felt that along with my increased commitment should come more control. And, with Gene's mounting health problems, our plans needed to be much more organized now, which gave rise to more arenas for dissension.

On this trip, we were taking a rental wheelchair "as a safeguard." The oxygen tank Gene arranged to bring would have to be filled every four or five days, which meant planning to be near major cities that had liquid oxygen. When Gene failed to schedule all the oxygen stops and held up our planning, I yelled, "You want control, but you often neglect to make phone calls and get information." When I began to make calls, he yelled that I was "controlling."

Eventually, the trip was planned, and once it started, we relaxed into our day-to-day experiences. We stopped at Bellengraf Gardens, a favorite spot of Gene's. I convinced him to let me push him in a wooden wheelchair, quaint enough to negate any stigma. Gene loved it until I got stuck several times in the garden and called workmen to help. I wanted to give him this experience; he got angry at my bad judgment. I wished he could be easier in these situations, and was glad when he apologized. We went to the Tetons, Yellowstone, Canadian Rockies, Banff, and Jasper. We rented a cabin in the mountains in Banff and made love in front of a roaring fire. We had a picnic on a lake in the Tetons—now I didn't mind doing all the work—took naps in fields of wildflowers, and had magical dinners in wooded resorts.

Sometimes I became irritated when my back hurt from lugging the seventy-pound oxygen tank in and out of motels, but then I felt recognized for my efforts when Gene apologized for the inconvenience. Sometimes I complained when filling the tank every few days meant going 100 miles out of our way. We adapted by devising interesting side trips and staying several nights in cities where we were able to get oxygen.

For the first time, we became aware of facilities with disability access and occasionally used our rented wheelchair on paved trails. Although sometimes we ran into difficulties, other times Gene was able to see scenery otherwise impossible. Occasionally, Gene would insist on walking with his cane instead.

"No, you don't feel well enough," I say at one juncture.

"I'll decide how I feel."

"But then I suffer the consequences."

"Too bad. I'm in charge of how to do this."

I walk quietly beside him then, but when he offers his hand, I take it.

I felt a certain freedom and security just having the chair with us, and when Gene said at the vacation's end in New York, "Let's buy the chair, just for trips," I was greatly relieved.

◾ ◾ ◾

"I think we should be monogamous while we're apart," Gene says, as we near the New York airport for my return flight to Florida. "Let's not take any risks." I had hoped to avoid this conversation, but Gene was not a person who left loose ends dangling.

"Things are going well for us. I want to keep it that way," he continues.

"I would like the freedom to see others," I say hesitantly, hoping he won't blow up and destroy the good feeling we have. "I probably won't act on it." I wanted to keep an escape hatch open, no matter how temporary or superficial, especially now that I was in this relationship for the long haul.

"I really don't want this," he says. "But if you insist, then you know that I might see others too."

"I know. The thought of your being with other women makes me crazy, but. . . ."

"This is dumb," Gene interrupts, "plain dumb."

"Maybe when we get together next semester, I'll be ready for monogamy. Just think, I'll fly up for a week in October and then you'll drive down for a week at Thanksgiving. Then I'll fly up at Christmas and drive back down to Florida with you. There won't be much time apart at all," I say, wanting him to feel better.

"Then why is it so important to have your freedom?"

"I don't know. It just is."

Soon Gene began seeing a former student. Delighted to attract an interesting person in spite of the oxygen hoses and labored breathing, he talked to me about strategies to deal with his physical restrictions around her. I knew this relationship was no threat to our partnership and it was good for Gene's ego. I would have continued feeling fine about it if my life had been going well.

It wasn't. I was lonely, needy, and insecure. For Gene, talking on the phone was an addition to his full life. For me, it was much more important. I worked hard on my courses and submitted papers for publication that too often were rejected. Although I had friends, I still did not feel integrated into the Tampa community. With few exceptions, my colleagues did little to make me feel a part; they had lives of their own. It was strange to be dealing with the world as a single person. I told people about Gene, but he wasn't a reality to them. I dated a few times; it was exciting initially, but the men bored me after one or two evenings. What conflicting feelings! When I pretended there was no Gene and that this was my life, it made me unhappy. The freedom of not having to deal with Gene's health did not make up for this emptiness.

In this context, I became jealous of Gene's new adventure. One weekend, I was unable to reach him. Since it was too hard for him to go away for a whole weekend with the oxygen, pumper, and medications, I assumed he was at home and not answering the phone. Maybe there is more to this relationship than he is telling me, I thought, and at the same time knew I was overreacting. The thought of his being with another woman and not responding to me reminded me of lack of access in the past. When he finally answered after thirty minutes of ringing, I exploded, "How dare you worry me like that!"

"I'm sorry," he said, "but I was busy."

"How important is this woman to you anyway?" Gene alternately laughed and tried to soothe me. I shifted between feeling angry and knowing I was being ridiculous. Yet when Gene suggested monogamy as a solution, I refused. In spite of his fling, he said he wanted it; in spite of my jealousy, I said I didn't. Gene's attraction to someone else, as difficult as it was, still gave me the illusion that I was less responsible for him, somehow less attached to his illness. His attraction for and attractiveness to someone else made him seem more valuable, stronger, and more powerful. Jealousy was the price I paid. I felt out of control then. As much as I hated that feeling and fought it, I liked that it helped rekindle my passion. It was more interesting and exciting to wonder where I stood with Gene than to see him exclusively as deteriorating, dependent, and sick.

■ ■ ■

This time when Gene came to visit, I had oxygen delivered before he arrived and met him with a wheelchair at the airport. "I couldn't breathe on the plane," he says, introducing a new problem, one that made my jealousy seem minor. "Even going to the bathroom was almost more than I could manage."

"Maybe you shouldn't fly anymore," I respond, noting his gray, sickly look.

I am shocked when he gives in so easily, "That's what I'm afraid of," and with that Gene lost another level of independence, and so did I.

Although I wanted him to come to Tampa to make my world complete again, his many problems also meant my world immediately got reorganized. It revolved around how he was feeling, how well he was breathing, whether the oxygen tank was working, where the hose was. No matter how much I prepared myself, the transition was always a rude awakening.

Excited to see me and lose himself in our love, he arrived ready to let down and be taken care of, to be relieved of dealing with his health on a full-time basis. Initially, I tensed up when he had problems. He sensed my reluctance, and we bickered about details. He wanted to control how I helped him. I felt that if I was doing a lot of the physical labor, then I should have some say. He reacted by pulling back, refusing to let himself be dependent on me, which then gave me justification for pulling back. And off we went again.

"How are you going to handle all this in the future when I'm worse, if you can't handle it now?" he asks several days into the visit.

"I am handling it now, and I'll handle it then. Maybe not exactly like you think I should, but I'll manage in my own way." Added to the stress that had built up from being apart, this tension was almost too much to bear. Yet at some point the love and goodwill broke through and we were once again best friends. This time it happened after a near tragedy.

To provide an atmosphere for problem solving, we decided to have a "party" and were smoking marijuana. Because of our concern about fire in the presence of oxygen, I took the oxygen hose into another room whenever we smoked, which required constantly getting up and down. One time, to save a trip, Gene removed the cannula from his face and laid it in his lap before lighting the joint. Because the oxygen was turned up higher than usual, the stream flowing freely into the air from his lap made contact with the match flame and the oxygen ignited. The fire skipped quickly down the plastic hose burning the carpet wherever it came into contact. Although I was able to turn off the oxygen before the flame reached the tank, we had come close to a real emergency. Responding to the terror opened us to each other's feelings.

"My illness is very painful for you, isn't it? Sometimes I forget," Gene says.

"Yes," I respond, crying. "I'm frightened and don't know how to deal with the deterioration. I want to help you. But I don't know how. All I see is loss when I look at you. And you feel so bad and are so out of sorts, we can't even talk about it."

"Oh, baby, I want to help you. It's just so hard when I feel this way. And I'm scared you'll turn away from it."

"I won't. Trust me. But I need your help. You're feeling worse, aren't you?"

"Yes, but I haven't wanted to admit it."

"Oh, god," I say, realizing that his engrossment with his pain and my absorption with mine had once again set the stage for a fight. No longer a sign that I didn't love him, my fear was intelligible to him in this caring context, and he wanted to understand what I was experiencing. He let me cry and comforted me, after which I could focus on his anxieties, hear about his pain, and take care of him with the love and patience that he required. Then we were problem-solving partners again, lovers, and friends.

Leaving each other at the end of the week to go back to our different worlds was difficult after this emotionally wrenching togetherness. Would it have been easier if I had stayed withdrawn? Yes, but then I wouldn't have had this release or felt this love. But I had to open up to my pain to get to it.

In this context, I necessarily defined caretaking—both his and mine—as a gift, a symbol of our special relationship, and a solution to the problem of a quickly changing kind of attachment. So I was convinced I couldn't wait for him to move to Florida in January, just two months away.

5

NOW IT WOULD be happening, a few seconds after takeoff. There is the bridge the plane hit. Here is how his head snapped forward. Boom. I let my head fall into the seat in front of me. The vivid picture of the gash in Rex's head helps me reenact the scene.

I am flying back from attending the funeral of my younger brother in my hometown of Luray, Virginia (see Ellis 1993). Rex died in a commercial airplane crash on his way to visit me on January 13, 1982. Death now is even more the enemy. It isn't just happening to Gene; it can happen to anyone at anytime. Death, you win.

When Gene picks me up at the Tampa airport, I fall into his arms, overwhelmed by my love and need. Then I shudder when I feel his frail body and hear his labored breathing, realizing that one day I will be experiencing his death too. I hold onto him tightly. He and Rex were the two most important people in my world. Is sudden loss harder to get over than a lingering dying? I will find out.

I am glad that Gene is living with me now. I need him as I never have before. Yet I hold him at arm's length because I do not have the emotional energy for closeness. Sometimes a veil hangs between me and interaction with him, between me and everything, even sights and sounds. For the most part, I listlessly do what is expected. I know I must adjust to my new job and publish articles. With only four years before my tenure review, I have no time to waste.

"I miss the energy and excitement you usually generate about life," Gene says.

"I can't help it," I reply, feeling nothing, and speaking in a flat monotone.

"I sympathize about the loss of your brother, but you have to shake out of this."

When I say I can't, Gene asks, "What about me? It's getting harder to take care of myself and, without a job, I am losing my identity."

"I know. I feel for you too. But I don't have the emotional energy to help. Getting you through physical crises is all I can do."

The struggles with Gene's health remind me daily of my brother's death, which then reminds me that I will lose Gene too. I cannot let myself think about or feel what's happening to Gene, but I try to be sympathetic to his needs. After all, it is supposed to be "his turn."

"Let's go car shopping," Gene suggests to cheer me. When we do, he buys a Datsun 280Z, the car I want, and not his fifth Trans-Am, as he had planned. He had bought a new car after his son died in 1974. A car would be his last demand before his own death.

■ ■ ■

"Somebody loves you. I wonder who. I wonder who it could be." Although it is the middle of the night, I listen for the verse Gene will add this time to our favorite song. "Somebody loves you. I wonder who. Why it's the wandering Jew. Who loves you." I laugh and curl up closer.

Little gifts—a special pair of earrings, a fancy dessert, tickets to a concert—sometimes awaited me when I arrived home from school. Given the level of effort it took, they were especially significant, and I responded to Gene's attempts to lift my spirits after my brother's death.

■ ■ ■

Gene's appointment as "courtesy professor" at South Florida provided office space, but he came into the department only once a month because it was difficult to walk that far. He tutored graduate students at our house each week, "to make me feel useful," he explains.

"What happened at the university?" Gene asks as soon as I arrive home. While I am at school, Gene watches TV, reads bridge magazines, or talks long distance to friends. Our roles have reversed from our last few years at Stony Brook where I worked at home on my dissertation and eagerly awaited Gene's arrival and news about people and activities.

"I'm not being productive," Gene complains after I tell him about my day.

"Yes, you are," I reply. "You give me feedback on my papers and work on dissertations with graduate students at Stony Brook. You tutor students here and help my colleagues."

"But I need someone to work with me," he explains, ignoring my praise. "I've always had someone."

When I offer to try, he replies, "You help, but you have your own work to do. I'm doing a lot of thinking, but I don't have a new idea."

"Sit and write and maybe one will develop. That's what I do."

"It doesn't happen that way for me," he says. "So, why should I waste trees? I don't need another line on my vita." Revealing his unresolved conflict, he adds, "I could have been even more successful if I had worked harder."

"The curse of the academic ego," I reply. "One is never successful enough."

In April, we went to the Southern Sociological Society meetings in Memphis. I flew and met Gene, who was driving there alone. This saved me time, let him visit old friends along the way, and meant he did not have to be in an airplane.

"How did it go?" I ask when he picks me up at the Memphis airport.

"Old friends just don't know how to cope with this level of illness," he says, "or how to help with the technology. It's too hard traveling without you." Another warning flag went up: now he couldn't drive alone. My thoughts turn quickly to the transition that lay immediately ahead—getting into our room at the conference hotel.

"No, no, not like that. It must be upright," Gene screams at the bellman who has tilted the oxygen tank on its side as he drags it out of the van.

"Gene, how are you?" an old friend asks as he approaches Gene, who, from the exertion of yelling, is now gasping for air. I want to hide; instead I help with the tank while Gene catches his breath on the cane chair. Confused, the friend says, "I'll talk to you later."

For the first time, we have taken oxygen to a professional meeting. "I'll only use it in the room," Gene had said earlier, "and we'll hide the barrel in the closet when we have visitors." When I had asked how we would get it and him into the hotel, he had responded, "Don't worry, I'll organize it all. You stay out of it. You don't have to do anything."

After we finally are settled, Gene plants his cane chair in the middle of the busiest corridor in the hotel and then "holds court," providing a central place for people to gather. I watch him sometimes from a distance, and sense a return of the animated person I had met in 1974.

■ ■ ■

"It's like a small golf cart," Gene says, telling me about the battery-operated wheelchair advertised on TV as we dash out of the apartment to see it.

"Even though I have multiple sclerosis, it's effortless," the saleswoman says while demonstrating the Amigo. "Try it."

The Amigo operated simply. Gradually pushing down a lever on the handlebars propelled it forward from one to four miles per hour. The

Amigo slowed to a stop when the lever was released. Pushing down on the alternate side of the lever for reverse provided a quick stop and then backward movement.

Fantasizing about the freedom it would give, I wanted to buy one on the spot. "We can go to the shopping malls," I say. "You can ride it into the movies."

Gene's eyes light up at my enthusiasm, the first he has seen in a while, but then he frowns. "I want to think about whether the Amigo can do what I need it to. Eighteen hundred dollars is a lot of money."

"I don't care," I respond, since this one is important enough to nag. "Check with your insurance. They bought your other chair."

"They won't buy this kind," he says, irritated by the pressure to decide.

In spite of my pleas, Gene refused to buy the Amigo even when he found out the insurance would pay. The message was that he, not I, was in control of decisions affecting his life. Not until several months later did he return to the Amigo distributor.

This time Gene practices going up and down ramps. "The main thing," says the saleswoman, "is to approach hills at a direct angle so the machine won't tip. Keep one foot ready to plant on the ground for stability."

"How do you handle curbs?" Gene asks.

"Someone must lift up the front, then the back. It's easier if you get off, but a strong companion can do it while you're sitting."

Disappointed, Gene responds, "That means I can't use it in New York City by myself."

"I'll be with you. I can lift it," I interject enthusiastically. "And think of all the places you can go alone."

"How do we get it in and out of the car?" Gene asks, ignoring my comment.

"There are several ways, the easiest with a van and lift, but that's quite expensive."

"How much?" I ask.

"A good lift will cost four thousand dollars plus the van. You ride onto the lift, which can be raised by pushing a button. If you take out the driver's seat, you can even wheel the Amigo into driving position."

"Oh, we don't need that," Gene quickly inserts. "I can walk. It's just for long distances."

"Well, then, you have two choices. Let me show you what I do. Since I still have upper-body strength, I've installed a lift in place of the backseat in my car. You attach the Amigo to the lift and then swing the whole contraption into the car."

"I have the strength for that," says Gene, attaching the Amigo and giving it a push as we watch, expectantly, and then he gasps, "but unfortunately not the breath."

"The other solution," continues the woman without hesitation, "is to take it apart and put it into the trunk of your car."

"Will it fit into our Datsun?" Gene asks.

"I think so."

"Will I be able to do it?" Now Gene is enthusiastic again.

"Let's try it."

The saleswoman instructs Gene to separate the Amigo into its four parts. When he has difficulty pulling the handlebars from the base, and I, automatically, try to help, he pushes me away, saying, "I have to be able to do this alone." He struggles to lift the largest section, the forty-pound platform, over the eight-inch lip in the trunk of our car. Although it fits, Gene frowns and, after he catches his breath, says, "I might be able to do it on a good day, but if I'm not feeling well, it'll be impossible."

"I can do it," I say, nudging my way in, taking the Amigo piece by piece out of the car and then putting it back in, glad that I have been lifting weights for the last eighteen months.

"Is it easy for you?" Gene asks.

"No, but I can do it with a little effort." Don't back out, I silently plead. "We could get a van with a lift so you could do it by yourself," I say hopefully.

"Not yet," and I know this time not to push.

Then, smiling, he says, "Let's take it home. If you're willing to help, we can do it together."

"Yippee," I reply, feeling like a little girl who has finally gotten her first bicycle.

The Amigo opened up new worlds. Gene took visiting students to Disney World. He rode beside me while I jogged on campus, and we walked on paved paths in local parks. The shopping malls provided a favorite dragstrip. In contrast to the pitying glances Gene felt while being pushed in a regular wheelchair, we relished attention when we sped through the mall on the Amigo in pursuit of a good buy. With me in front, Gene holding around my waist, and oxygen flowing, we wove in and out of traffic, laughing hilariously amid an occasional "beep, beep, excuse us, please."

Sometimes, though, the laughter made him cough. And, when we ran into friends, Gene, in an attempt to look closer to normal, quickly removed the oxygen from his nose. But the Amigo, with the oxygen tank displayed in its basket, still was as intrusive as the boom boxes of teenagers passing by, and, along with Gene's shaky hands and heaving body, conspired to betray his presentation as a healthy person.

The Amigo was by no means trouble free. While lifting it in and out of our car seemed relatively easy at first, it became onerous when added to day-to-day stresses and strains. A few times, I tore the vinyl in the trunk; occasionally, I pulled my back from the awkward movement. "Let me help," Gene insists.

"I would rather do it myself than wait an extra ten minutes for your breath to return," I say. "And I don't like to see you suffer," I add softly.

"But it's worth the pain to feel useful."

Sometimes I encouraged Gene to accompany me on the slightest errand, gladly taking out the Amigo. Grocery shopping and planning meals had been a favorite activity of Gene's before his health deteriorated. Now he zipped around the grocery store to retrieve forgotten items, which he put in the basket attached to the Amigo. "See, I am helping and actually we get this done faster when I come in with you, don't we?"

"Yes, it's great," I reply, choking back the tears that came from realizing that getting a few items had grown into such a big deal. "I have a love on you," I would say then, using our favorite expression.

"Me you too," he would reply in sign language.

In the same day, I could go from these love highs to deep lows about Gene's disease, experiencing each problem as more proof that "life sucks," a new attitude I'd developed since my brother's death. These fluctuations showed in my response to the Amigo. Sometimes I asked Gene to wait in the car while I quickly did the shopping. "I don't want to deal with the Amigo for a quart of milk," I say. Sometimes I argued from the opposite direction. Especially at first, Gene insisted that we use the Amigo only to cover long distances. "I don't want to quit walking," he says. "My muscles will deteriorate and I'll get too dependent on the Amigo." Sometimes he rejected my offer to fill the portable oxygen tank and take out the Amigo for a trip to the movies. Then, if he had trouble walking, which increasingly happened, the "I told you so" on my face made the situation worse.

Sometimes we argued about the issue at hand; just as often, a particular situation, such as whether to use the Amigo, provided an outlet for the frustrations that built up as emphysema took more and more of our lives. The inconvenience of the Amigo allowed me to be bitchy, when I really wanted to scream; it gave Gene a reason to get angry or sulk, when he really wanted to cry. Then, at home around the table, we reminded each other that most of the time I was patient and he was understanding, that most of these situations worked out, and that usually we negotiated successfully. In this context, I ask, "What about the van? It would solve our problems."

"Not yet," he replies, and I know the issue is closed.

■ ■ ■

"Let's go to Hawaii. I've never been," Gene says.

"But what about your trouble breathing on planes?"

"It's risky, but I want to do it. Are you willing?"

"Let's go for it," I say, thinking this might get us out of the doldrums left over from my brother's death. "Let's find a place in Maui to stay for two weeks. It'll be too strenuous to move around, and anyway it'll be fun to be settled."

"I guess, although I like to be on the move. Let's stop in San Diego going out, and see Beth in Portland on the way back."

This trip was considerably more difficult than the last. Only a few companies in Hawaii handled the liquid oxygen we needed to pick up every few days. Since we were not allowed to take our oxygen on planes, we also were concerned about the lag time between boarding the plane in San Diego and arriving in Hawaii, flying to another island, and only then, six to eight hours later, actually getting to the oxygen company, which might be closed.

Since this plan held too many risks, we decided instead to rent an electric machine that extracted oxygen from the air. Although the tank weighed fifty pounds, it was small enough to take as baggage on planes and for me to handle. "But don't worry, we'll use porters," says Gene. We were told that the machine was "maintenance free." Still, we needed to have access to electricity and to find a portable system allowing us to carry oxygen outside our motel room. To solve that problem, we rented a gas cylinder, about two-feet high, four inches in diameter, weighing about twenty pounds. We could have it filled at any welding-supply house, we were told.

We also found out that each airplane had its own emergency oxygen supply that we could arrange in advance to use for $40 per leg of our journey. Since breathing oxygen on a plane indicates a level of illness for which I am not yet prepared, I am glad when Gene says, "I really don't need it."

What a traveling caravan we made with suitcases, oxygen compressor, portable oxygen tank, cane chair, and regular wheelchair, which was versatile on different terrains and easier to transport than the Amigo. We checked everything as baggage and arranged for an airport wheelchair to take Gene to each plane and to pick him up at each stop. Our cumbersome equipment reminded us of the risks we were taking.

"I can't catch up," Gene says, turning gray soon after the plane takes off from New York to Chicago. "It feels like I just ran a race." He gulps for air, but reacts as though someone is holding his nose as he breathes out. Later, his doctor would explain that cabins are usually pressurized to 8,000 feet, comparable to being on top of a mountain. For Gene, the shallow air created the sensation of drowning.

Gone were romantic plane rides, when we drank champagne and talked about ideas and the trip that lay ahead. Now, every minute is consumed by his health. I try not to show my resentment, and I want to make it easier for him, and for me too. God, I shudder, please, I just want to make it.

"I have to go to the bathroom," Gene says, panic in his eyes. I walk behind him and sit in an empty seat nearby. Suddenly, the bathroom door bolts open, revealing Gene sitting on the toilet seat, lid down, and moaning loudly as he gasps for breath. My body goes numb, while my brain works furiously to take in the situation and act.

Rushing to him, I lay my hand on his shoulder. At least his pants are zipped, I think, and am distressed that even in a crisis I am embarrassed. And I had been afraid that using oxygen would call attention to us, I think ironically. My thoughts stop in the flurry of activity as several flight attendants appear. "What's wrong?" one asks.

"He has emphysema," I reply, then kneel in front of him, taking both his hands in mine. "He just needs to sit here for a while." I feel less embarrassed now that the flight attendants are involved.

"Does he need oxygen?"

"Do you?" I ask Gene, thankful to know we have the option.

"No," he heaves from his chest, shaking his head. "I'm getting better now [gasp] with the door [gasp] open. I felt claustrophobic [gasp]. There's less air in here," he continues apologetically, his face slowly changing to pale pink.

Taking a deep breath, he dashes to his seat. When he does not recover from the move, I ask, "Are you sure you don't need oxygen? It's available even though we didn't reserve it."

"Won't it embarrass you?"

"No, don't think about that," I respond, ashamed that that should be his concern now when he can't breathe. "I just want you to be OK."

"I think I'm OK now," he says finally, his breathing slowing. "But that was awful. I couldn't help it," he says with agony on his face and tears in his eyes.

"I know. Believe me, I know you couldn't," I say, hiding my eyes on his shoulder and crying.

Comforting me now, he says forcefully, "We're going to make it through this trip."

"Damn right we are," I say, smiling between tears. "Let's plan how to take care of this problem."

Before we reached home, we still had five more flights on this continent and several between the islands in Hawaii. "I'll take fewer steroids. They make me pee. Next time we'll request seats next to the bathroom so I don't have to walk very far," Gene says.

"And I'll stand at the door near you, keeping it open a bit so I can help with the claustrophobia from the shallow breathing."

"Thank you," Gene says, looking lovingly into my eyes. "Thank you for helping me."

"I'm glad I'm with you," I say, meaning it although this is one of the most difficult situations I have ever been in.

While the situation is calm, I close my eyes to rest. Who knows what emergency will happen next. I have never seen him as panicked as he was in the bathroom, nor as breathless as when he walked the twenty feet to his seat. The voices in my head speak, "Get out while you can. You aren't going to be able to stand this. Already he can't travel. His world is narrowing and yours with it. You are only thirty-two years old, too young to be so old." Resentment toward Gene ricocheted through me, but was quickly contained by waves of love, empathy, and pity. What would he do without me?

During the flight from Chicago to San Diego, Gene once again has trouble breathing. "Do you want to watch the movie?" I ask, thinking that might take his mind off breathing.

"What is it?"

"You won't believe this," I say, reading from the magazine. "*Whose Life Is It Anyway?* The one about the quadriplegic who wanted to be allowed to die. I know it's crazy, but I want to watch it." I think I might learn something useful about what it feels like to be or take care of an invalid.

"Why not?" Gene says. "How much worse than our life can it be?" We hold hands and wipe tears through the movie, both of us identifying with the plight of the main character. "I don't want to live like that, you know," Gene says, breaking the silence.

Periodically, suicide had been a topic of conversation. Gene maintained that when the disease got to be too painful or restrictive, he wanted to kill himself. "It would be the brave thing to do," he says, stimulated by the movie. "I don't want to be a vegetable, nor do I want to be a burden to you or anyone. I have codeine stored up for when the time comes."

This wasn't what I wanted to think about now. I still wasn't sure we would make it to Hawaii. What if we get stuck in California unable to take a plane to Hawaii and unable to get back to New York? We can always drive. But what if we are stranded in Hawaii? Cross your fingers and hope, I say to myself, as I envision stretchers and emergency planes.

We got to San Diego without any more acute incidents and settled into a motel. As soon as Gene was attached to his oxygen compressor, he felt better. Now we had some time, desperately needed, to talk over our feelings about the new level of problems experienced on the plane.

"Let's open a bottle of champagne to celebrate making it this far," I suggest.

"And talk about what happened on the plane. I really loved you when you were so patient and loving."

"And, I loved you when I saw you in such pain."

"Did it embarrass you when I threw open the bathroom door?"

"Yes, but then I didn't care anymore. I just wanted you to be OK."

"I felt that. Your attitude helped me get through the crisis."

"I'm so glad I still have you."

Our kiss is interrupted suddenly as Gene pulls the hose from his nose and blows against the air flow. "Oh, god, no, give us a break," he pleads. Without asking, I know that our "maintenance-free" oxygen machine has quit working.

"Don't panic. We'll get it fixed," I say, desperately needing to hold onto the tranquil, loving atmosphere we have just entered, the one dissolving in front of me. Our anxiety returns as we check the machine. "It's plugged in," I say.

"Is it turned on?"

"Yes, and nothing seems jammed."

"Try another plug," Gene instructs, already breathless.

"No, still not working, and I don't know anything else to try," I respond, too frightened to be upset. Unfortunately, "maintenance-free" technology comes with no instructions.

It was six o'clock on the Saturday evening of Labor Day weekend, and we were scheduled to leave San Diego by plane early Tuesday morning. A more immediate consideration was that Gene had no oxygen now when he desperately needed it after the long period without any. What was to keep this from happening in Hawaii? Where were we going to get this fixed now? How were we ever going to have a working system by Tuesday morning?

Even if we could get a later flight to Hawaii on Tuesday, we would miss our connecting flight in Oahu.

"Calm down," I say gently, trying to organize my thoughts. Fear and anxiety increased Gene's breathing difficulties, and I felt I had to be in control. "Let's take this step by step. The most important thing is to get oxygen for you now. Right?"

When he says yes, I respond more confidently than I feel, "OK, I'll take care of it. You relax." Since we have no phone, I call oxygen companies from a phone booth outside the motel. Several do not answer, then I get a recording. Then, "I'm sorry but we only deliver to our regular customers." Finally, I locate a company that, for double the normal price, agrees to bring a large cylinder (about six feet tall and twelve inches in diameter) at eight o'clock that night.

"I don't care about price," I say. "This is an emergency."

Gene and I hold vigil, anxiously awaiting the oxygen. By ten o'clock, I am pacing and Gene is on the verge of panicking, so I call another company.

When two rival oxygen companies arrive simultaneously at our door, Gene pays both of them their doubled fees and sends one away. For $80 we had oxygen for the night and a promise that the company would try to fix our compressor by Tuesday.

The machine needed a simple adjustment that had been thrown off by moving it around. The repairman showed us what to do in case it happened again—it did frequently—and didn't charge us. On Sunday, we were able to fill our small portable cylinder, which would last two hours, and I wheeled Gene around the San Diego Zoo with friends. It was great fun, but I choked back the tears at the picture he made: a fragile, aging man in a wheelchair with an oxygen canister attached to his nose.

Even with all the health problems, Gene continued to resist technological devices. Later, when we find he has to climb stairs up to an airplane, I want to use the airport's system of raising him in the wheelchair with a lift powered by a motorized tractor. When Gene protests, I plead, "Please, babe, let's use their system. It's easier than creating one of our own. They've dealt with this before." When he still resists, I continue, "Forget your ego now. We can go back to other strategies later. Let's just concentrate on getting there now, the easiest way we can."

"Agreed," he says, smiling, responding to the intensity on my face. "You're in this too, so you should have some say." Because we were in a loving space with both of us willing to do anything to make the world work, this negotiation proved easy.

Gene was more willing now than ever to let me take over planning how to get us from place to place. He watched our luggage from his wheelchair while I picked up and dropped off rental cars. He arranged for cars from his wheelchair while I dealt with checking the luggage.

The first time I leave him in line, he says when I return, "No one would pay attention to me until I was real assertive." From then on, being treated like a person in spite of the chair became his challenge. It came from his acceptance that the chair was now more than a rare assist, and carried over from his experience of independence on the Amigo.

On this trip, Gene increasingly had to deal with people who treated him as though he was retarded. Even when he asked a question, people frequently turned to me to respond. "People don't mean any harm, Gene. They just don't know how to treat a person in a wheelchair."

"It's the 'is he cold?' phenomenon," Gene says, referring to a question an attendant had asked me. "Being in a chair doesn't mean I'm mentally retarded. I'm going to educate them." And he did. Sometimes he asked people to sit down when they talked to him so he could face them instead of looking up. He insisted on talking to airline employees. "I can talk and I'm going to United," he responds when they ask me where he is going.

In the process, Gene changed from bent-over and old when he first got into this wheelchair to proud, head-held-high. My attitude changed along with his. Gene pointed out how I assumed control of all decisions. "You're right," I admit. "I do. And people rarely touch or look at you, or start conversations with you," I say, echoing what we had experienced before.

"You don't touch me either," Gene accuses, taking me now to a new level of awareness. Ashamed, I worked hard to overcome the stigma, and, in the process, noted that I too felt treated differently. Nobody dared flirt with or pay undue attention to the partner of a man in a wheelchair. I felt less attractive. Was I losing my appeal to his disease? Did they pity both of us?

After renting a car on Maui, we went immediately to an oxygen company to fill our small canister. The first company didn't fill medical oxygen tanks and the second didn't have the proper connectors, so we rented a second small tank. When it took a day and a half to solve this problem, I gained more empathy for the struggle Gene had gone through in planning this and previous trips. "The trouble is," I say, "that few people travel on oxygen. We get bad information because many companies have never dealt with the problems we present."

"You're right," says Gene. "How many people have you ever seen using portable oxygen at all?"

"Only a few," I say, realizing how uncommon a sight we were.

Once we got all the kinks worked out, the two weeks in Maui were wonderful. We stayed in a lovely, romantic room on the beach and watched the sun set each night between two outer islands. We spent every other day in our house or on the beach. On the alternate days we went out for leisurely dinners and sightseeing, driving twenty miles out of our way each time to get oxygen.

■ ■ ■

"I want to go snorkeling," Gene insists.

Reluctantly, I go along, but say, "It's too strenuous."

"I have a plan. You stay near me. Hold the portable tank while I snorkel in shallow water with the hose in my nose."

I want it for him, but what will people think? It looks weird, and, besides, it's dangerous. What if he can't breathe? Why is he making me do this?

Moody and less than cooperative, I want Gene to be discouraged quickly. As soon as he puts his nose under water, he panics. But then he wants to try again. "You aren't being helpful enough," he accuses.

"You're crazy to be trying this."

"OK," he says, defeated, and I am relieved, then sorry that I have been so harsh.

"I'm sorry that I wasn't more helpful. The water scares me."

"I know. It's just that my world has shrunk so much. I didn't want it to be true. And I don't know where the line is between pushing and being crazy."

"Snorkeling is crazy."

■ ■ ■

When we arrived back in New York to start our semester there, Gene reluctantly says, "I guess I won't fly anymore."

"It doesn't look like it," I reply, grieving for yet another loss.

■ ■ ■

At first, we took the Amigo to New York City, but getting off each time I lifted it up or down from a curb tested Gene's endurance and wore my patience. Gene solved the problem by riding in the street, but that created a distance between us and was unsafe. And, unlike the standard chair, the Amigo couldn't just be folded up and put into a taxi. More than ever, I became aware of barriers for disabled people.

We began taking the regular wheelchair to the City. To negotiate the curbs, Gene decided whether I should push him forward or tilt the chair backward. When Gene said that the distance we had to go would be too strenuous, I took it as a challenge. "Thirty blocks? Who cares? I'll pretend I'm jogging." I sometimes jumped on the back of the chair to ride down hills. Gene did not have to worry about his breathing or about being a burden, and I could talk to him as we moved along, dashing into stores for a spontaneous splurge. If there was not enough room in the store, he sat patiently on the sidewalk holding our packages and watching people pass by until I came outside to model or bring him an item that caught my attention. Then, like two best girlfriends, we discussed the pros and cons of each purchase.

One day as we are waiting to go into the theater in New York, we hear, "Gene. Gene Weinstein."

"Well, my goodness, Fred Bernstein. It's been ten years." When Gene stands up from the wheelchair to shake hands, Fred hesitates, then steps forward, shakes hands, stutters a hello, and moves back quickly.

"How are you doing, Gene?" Fred finally asks, looking sympathetic.

"Fine, but there's not enough oxygen in the air," Gene says, patting his chest, which seems an understatement as his chest heaves from the effort of standing. "But fine."

"Great," says Fred, looking bewildered. "Hope to see you again." Was he more surprised that Gene was in a wheelchair or that he had stood up?

"That was strange," I say. "He didn't know how to react to your getting up. Were you a disabled person or not?"

"Well, I didn't want him to think I was an invalid."

■　■　■

Gene refused to use either of his wheelchairs in Stony Brook, and he still would not take his portable oxygen to the university even though his doctor thought he needed an occasional boost during the day. To compensate, Gene came home early in the afternoon for oxygen. Occasionally, he used the hose while he worked there with students. By this time, we had stopped hiding the tanks in the closet when we had company. But Gene still insisted on covering them, so "the tanks won't be such a presence and so we don't force other people to deal with them," he explains.

Often, by the time company left, Gene was exhausted from his need for oxygen that came from exerting himself conversationally. "The hose," he yells, as soon as the last person is out the door. "What's taking so long? I can't breathe. Now!" Usually I rushed, but sometimes, resenting that his need to appear well to others resulted in my dealing with his irritability, I took my time.

During the semester, it became too difficult, even with the chair cane, for Gene to make it to class without oxygen. At first, he carried the portable box closed, strap over his shoulder and hose hidden in the rectangular case, and used it only in his office. Then he began putting the hose in his nose as he walked. Later, I carried the box with the hose connected to his nose. It would not be long before he rode the Amigo into school, but he couldn't get it in and out of the car. Would he then be totally dependent on me for his mobility?

"I've decided to trade in my 1974 car for a van," I announce.

"But I don't need a van," Gene says.

"Fine," I reply, "but I've wanted to trade my car for a while. And I've always thought a van would be fun. Then, later, you can use it if you need to."

"I'm afraid I'll have trouble driving it," he says, acknowledging my ploy. "It's hard to use mirrors and it takes too much breath to turn to look out the back. Anyway, it won't be fun to drive."

"I'll drive it," I respond. "But we'll fix it up for camping and install a generator to run your pumper. We'll make a place for oxygen tanks so I don't have to lug them in and out of hotels. Traveling will be much easier."

"How do we do this financially?" Gene asks.

"With the fifteen hundred dollars I can get from my old car and my savings, I'll have six thousand dollars to spend on the van."

Gene says quickly, "I can pay the rest."

"Do you want to put in a lift now?"

"Why not? It's probably easier." I am astounded by how easily he gives in.

The van was big and awkward. Because we had not anticipated that Gene would have problems breathing in a bent-over position, we had not raised the roof. Now Gene had trouble getting from the driver's seat to the Amigo. When he was finally on the Amigo, he opened the doors with a power switch and then extended the lift from a vertical closed position to a horizontal one extending out the open doors. Maneuvering the Amigo onto the lift in limited space meant Gene had to drive it forward and backward several times, keeping his head down to clear. Since it was hard to turn his body to look backward, he ran into walls, sometimes got stuck in a corner, and came close to backing off the edge of the lift, saved only by a six-inch protective lip. Once on the lift, he pushed a lever to be lowered to the ground. Then he drove to the rear of the van where he used other controls to close the lift, then the doors.

Although this was the best system available, and Gene could manage it, he preferred to have me with him. Sometimes I volunteered to bring the Amigo to his side of the van. Then he could step out and sit down on it. But often he refused my help. "I have to be able to do this myself. That's the idea of the van." Then he huffed and puffed and cursed getting the Amigo out while I sat there, often impatiently, watching to make sure he managed.

Sometimes I got angry at his dependence, but more often now I got angry at his fighting the dependence, which made life miserable for both of us. Where was the line between healthy resistance and giving in to the disease?

■ ■ ■

"Why did you leave the Amigo and oxygen outside the doctor's office?" I ask Gene, as I enter Dr. Silverman's examination room. "Of all places, I would think you'd feel OK with it here."

"No, there's an atmosphere of wellness and recovery here," Gene explains. "The Amigo would be out of place." So, instead, he tries to look cheerful as he struggles to breathe.

"The numbers have gone way down," Gene informs me about his breathing tests.

Before I can respond, Dr. Silverman returns. "I'm moving to Florida to be with Carolyn," Gene tells the doctor.

"That's great. It's time to get away from cold. The Gulf coast is an excellent place—warm, not too humid, not too dry. I know a good doctor at the university."

"I have to tell you something," he continues, in a very solemn voice. "I've found a spot on my lung. It looks like the beginning stages of lung cancer."

"I'm sorry," says Gene. "What will you do?"

"The same as you. Keep working as long as I can. Quality of life, that's the issue. But back to you. What else can I do for you?"

Gene asks several questions about the doctor's health before requesting, "Would you be willing to talk to Carolyn alone? I want her to know what she's getting in to."

"Certainly," he responds. "But there's nothing I don't tell you."

"I know, but I want to give her the opportunity to ask questions without my being there."

"I can do it now." Gene nods and leaves the room.

Although Gene and I have discussed what I might ask, I think about fleeing or saying I have no questions. As these thoughts soar through my head, I hear myself ask quickly in a voice that sounds like I am not getting enough air, "I know you can't be sure, but what can I expect from here on? What will the deterioration be like? And the end? How will he die?"

Taking a deep breath, Dr. Silverman's eyes focus directly on mine. With piercing intensity, he says, "It won't be pleasant. He'll continue much like in the past. More and more he'll be unable to move around, and will probably just sit in a comfortable position. What you have to watch out for are his blood gases. If he ever gets groggy and confused, get him to the hospital immediately."

The lump in my stomach grows. Mental confusion? It could happen now? "His brain will go?" I ask timidly, grabbing onto my seat. My chest feels expanded and hollow.

"Thankfully, the brain is the last thing to deteriorate," he replies, and I relax. "He'll probably be mentally active way after his mobility goes. But at some point, his body won't be able to get rid of carbon dioxide and it will impair him mentally. It could happen any time, but it will be temporary. As soon as doctors regulate his blood gases, his mental faculties will come back one hundred per cent."

I finally breathe, and then ask, "How will they do that?"

"They'll probably hospitalize him to control oxygen intake and give him high levels of steroids, which at some point will cause bone deterioration."

"What about a respirator?" I ask. This had been a topic of speculation for Gene and me on several occasions. "Can that help?"

"Yes," he responds, and then studies my face quizzically, "but the issue is quality of life."

"Can he talk on it?"

"Yes, there'd be a hole in his throat that he would cover when he spoke. He would speak slowly between breaths."

"Could he come home with it?"

"He could," he replies slowly. I shake my head to get rid of the image of Gene in bed with a machine hooked to a hole in his throat.

"Is there anything else I should know?" I ask.

"I don't think so. But feel free to call if you have other questions," he says in a more professional tone, then extends his hand and continues more softly, "Good luck. Keep in touch."

On the way to our favorite restaurant, Gene and I hold hands as I walk beside the Amigo. Glad for the quiet, we talk only when necessary, pointing out which street to take or the driveway that permits Gene to drive onto the sidewalk without assistance. The expansion in my chest has now risen to my throat, and I am aware of every swallow. The sighs and wails of grief are being pushed up by the love I feel, but my fear of losing control convinces me to hold it all inside.

"Do you want to tell me what you and Dr. Silverman talked about before I arrived?" I ask, as soon as we are seated.

"Yeah, sure, a new procedure. The latest thing is to cut a hole into the trachea to let oxygen flow in directly. It's more efficient; the oxygen goes straight to the lungs. We could carry it in smaller amounts and it would be less obvious."

"Would it help more than breathing oxygen through your nose?"

"He thinks it would. Some people have improved."

"Could you talk with a hole in your throat?" I ask.

"Yes, but it would be difficult. I don't quite understand."

"Me neither," I say. "Is this the same as what they do when they attach a respirator?" Gene isn't sure. "Do you want to know what I talked to the doctor about?"

"Only if you want to tell me. It was your private conversation."

I tell him what he already knows about gradual deterioration, loss of mobility, and the problem with steroids. My head is spinning. Should I tell him everything? How will he handle information about mental deterioration? That at some point he will not be able to think clearly? Dr. Silverman had told him previously that his brain would be the last organ to be affected, and Gene thought it would happen, if at all, only at the very end. Until this discussion, so had I. But now it sounds like the confusion will come and go. I think about the slight bewilderment that accompanied Gene's last change in medication. "I can't think, can't focus," he had said irritably. "My body is speeding." Is that what it would be like?

Gene interrupts my thoughts, "I know all that. Did you ask about the respirator?" When I repeat what the doctor said, Gene replies, "It doesn't sound as good as I thought. I guess it will be hard to talk."

"Would you want to live like that?" I ask, wanting him to say no and then fearing that he will.

"If I could talk and still work with graduate students, I think so. But would you want it?"

"I don't know. I would want you to live as long as you could, as long as you wanted to. But it's hard to imagine what it would be like. Would you be in an institution or at home?"

"I don't know."

"If you were home, who would take care of you all the time? Could you go out with the respirator? Could we still have conversations?" I feel claustrophobic as I imagine caring for an invalid. I hope he doesn't notice my head and shoulders trembling involuntarily. It all seems hopeless and confusing.

"Maybe I could handle being in bed all the time," Gene responds, addressing his own concerns. "But when I can't read and think clearly anymore, I'll want to kill myself."

"We have to get more information."

"But not yet," he replies. "We have enough to think about. This isn't happening now. No decisions have to be made. I want to think about how much I love you." I smile and take his hand. We talk about the treats we will buy at Zabar's delicatessen, another ritual stop after a doctor's visit.

■ ■ ■

We spend more and more time at home now. To compensate, we often invite people for dinner. Now Gene gets out of the van only for the long supermarket stops. When we are close and loving, he lets me take out the Amigo. Or, when we are close and loving, I am willing to stand by and cheer him on while he struggles with it. When no technical foul-ups occur, the van makes the time seem like the old days when shopping together was fun and romantic.

Gene does all the chopping, grating, and peeling for dinner, the tasks I enjoy least. "Show me a piece," he says, when I tell him to chop. "I don't know the difference between chopping and dicing. How big do I make them?"

"Think about eating the food," I say. "How big do you want the pieces to be in your mouth?"

"Oh, I get the principle," he replies, delighted to have a concept. As taster, he tells me what ingredient the dish needs. In spite of the occasional arguments over details when we're both trying to supervise, cooking often is as much fun as the dinner party that follows.

Three nights or more a week we cook dinner for the two of us and spend the evening talking about our relationship. More and more, the conversation focuses on our future.

"I'm thinking seriously," Gene says, "about moving to Tampa at the end of this term—furniture and all." I am surprised and quiet, as he continues what seems to be a rehearsed speech. "I could take sick leave. But I still wonder if your love is strong enough to get us through. You'll be my only source of support. I'll be leaving my students and colleagues, who are there if I need them, my job, everything that I know. Are you willing to do this? Can you? You know that I am going to get sicker and sicker."

"I made a commitment to you a year ago," I answer. "I still mean it." I think of him without his work and friends, waiting for me to come home at night. The oxygen, the pain, the limits on mobility. Being tied to him. "Help," the voice inside my head screams, but I know I will not leave him. It is time to deal with his anxieties and problems, not mine.

I say, "We'll have each other. We can work together, and you can tutor at school. Your friends can come to visit. Maybe you'll join a bridge club."

"It's not too late. You can still get out, go back to Tampa, and I'll get someone to live with me. We'll call and visit."

"No," I reply. "I don't want to be without you. We still have so much together. Besides, you need to get out of the cold weather."

The cold weather was the clincher. Breathing in the cold air was painful, even lugging around a heavy winter coat impeded Gene's breathing, and he always got at least one cold each winter.

"I just want to feel that you want me, that you aren't looking for a way out. I talk to Joan sometimes about setting you free. You're too young to have these responsibilities."

"What does Joan say?"

"That I should let you make your own decisions."

"That's right. I'm surprised you're willing to leave your world, especially your job."

Gene admits it's hard. "But I won't be able to work long anyway, maybe another year or two. So if I'm going to leave, it might as well be now, instead of dragging myself into work another winter. And what for? This way we won't have to be apart."

What conflicting feelings I had in these conversations. Sometimes I was haunted with fear. Maybe I did want another semester apart, time to be sure I was doing the right thing, to have more fun before I had full responsibility, to postpone the beginning of the end. Then, inevitably, the feelings of intense love and dedication to making this work washed over me.

As the move drew closer, Gene became more irritable and needy. Mostly, I tried to be understanding about the agony of the decisions he weighed, knowing he was grieving already for this part of his life that he would never have again. In some ways I was the enemy, pulling him away from everything he knew and loved. And he wasn't even sure he could trust me. Yet in his loving moments he appreciated that I was a part of his life and willing to take on his problem. So we had close times amid arguments and irritation, an intense microcosm of what our relationship had always been.

"My bottom line," I say, repeating what I had said a year before," is that I don't know if I can handle your deterioration. But I am committed to trying and to being with you until you die. I value living up to that commitment, but I guess there are ways you could be that would cause me to violate that promise."

"Like what?"

"Like being constantly irritable to the point that I get nothing out of the relationship and feel you aren't taking my needs into account." I hesitate. Then, "No, even then I would still try to make it work. All I can say is that I will do my best. And, yes, I am scared of failing. I would be an idiot or insincere if I said I wasn't."

"I feel like you're trying to be honest."

"I am. I want to make this transition as easy for you as I can. It's your turn now."

6

"SINCE GENE is retiring," a student announces during the Sociology Department Christmas party at the end of the semester, "we have collected poetry from his friends." "Retiring"—the word jolts me.

Written in calligraphy on beautiful, large sheets of parchment paper, the poems were funny, full of love and multiple meanings, and portrayed Gene as a kind and caring intellectual. One read:

> Once ego and alter, they met for a chat
> They talked about this, they talked about that.
> The problem they had concerned what to do
> This damned Ph.D. program, could they really get through?
>
> They spoke of their problem for a night and a day,
> 'Til one of them said, "Let's go to Weinstein, E. A."
> So off to Gene's office they marched very fast
> The site, so they'd heard, of a clear altercast.
>
> Gene looked at them both with a smile in his eye,
> "Now tell me," said he, "which is me, who is I?"
> Who is acting this play, who is acted upon?
> Who wants to stay here, who wants to be gone?
>
> He helped them to separate their selves from their scene
> To get their work done, they sought out Weinstein, Eugene.
> Gene tailored his talk to the looks 'neath their faces
> His kindness and genius has left many traces.
>
> So now alter and ego, who often still talk,
> Can we get this work done, should we just take a walk?
> But when they're in doubt, how to write, what to say,
> They just give a shout down to Weinstein, E. A.
>
> Bill

■ ■ ■

Gene and I drove to Florida and sent his furniture by moving van. On the way, he dropped me off to spend Christmas with my parents. Refusing to stay at my parents' house, he visited friends in Washington. "I have to pretend there just to be your friend, the professor, and I don't like it," he says. "On top of that, I have to worry about how my health looks to them." I understood, but how could I tell my parents that this was the man I loved—someone twenty years older than I who was able to breathe only with a hose in his nose. My father didn't say much about Gene, just looked at him curiously; my mother always wondered why he didn't stay longer. Although they suspected more, all I told them was that he was my friend.

My parents' home had the feel of a funeral parlor. Although on previous Christmases, my mother had decorated the house, this year she refused to symbolize the holiday. Because of my brother's death, she had decided never to celebrate Christmas again. I gave some unwrapped books to my parents, hoping not to violate her wish.

Our conversations during the vacation revolved around my brother's death. My mother told the same story over and over about the last time she saw him. She couldn't control that memory, nor did she want to, and she hoped each time for a different ending. I encouraged her to keep telling the story, hoping one day she would accept the final ending, just as I was struggling to do.

I hated the memories churned up by being home. How horrible it must be for my parents to be reminded of Rex everyday—his office was a block away, the cemetery was down the street, Rex's wall hangings and knick-knacks were enshrined in a special room. Did my resemblance to Rex make it worse for them when I was home? Added to the memories and the choking feeling that stayed in my throat, I also was reminded of my loss of an important tie to my family. Rex was the only family member who knew the nature of my relationship with Gene. I had changed a great deal since I left home; without Rex, I had no one to bridge our differences.

Whenever I had time alone, my thoughts turned to my life with Gene. I feared losing someone I loved again. This time I would have to watch and deal with the deterioration, only I would be able to say what I needed to say and be the kind of person for Gene I wanted to be. To have no regrets became my goal.

Loss permeated my life now, constantly threatening to wear me down and make me long for the innocence of childhood. In place of long-term illusions that everything would be OK, I substituted living in and for the moment.

■ ■ ■

"I'll take the oxygen with me," Gene says.

"What about the Amigo?"

"No, I don't want to be seen as any weirder than I have to."

"Riding on the Amigo seems less weird to me than having oxygen in your nose," I respond.

"But the Amigo makes it look like I can't walk."

"That's true," I reply, "but wheelchairs are familiar. Oxygen isn't, and it makes you look like you can't breathe."

"I never thought of it that way."

Back in Tampa, Gene and I now had to negotiate new routines. In New York, I had urged him to ride his Amigo and use his oxygen. In my world, I wanted him to look as normal as possible.

Gene rode the Amigo to the Sociology Department. And, before long, he brought the oxygen along. Soon he put the hose into his nose as he rode to give him more breath to maneuver hills, turns, and doors, but he removed the hose when he came near the department.

"The department needs diversity," I hear Gene say in his passionate, debating voice.

"Not if it doesn't meet our standards," comes the retort.

I stop grading papers to listen from my office. "But Black role models are important, even if they don't have long vitae," Gene continues.

"Fine, but we had no say in the matter," says the voice.

Gene is having what he thinks is an academic debate with one of my colleagues. But I know this interaction will be interpreted as Gene interfering in department business.

Even without oxygen, Gene was viewed as "different," threatening, and too aggressive by several of my senior colleagues, who made it clear to the chair that they did not want an outsider formally involved in the department. Although the chair and junior members genuinely liked Gene, enjoyed talking with him, and appreciated his help on their projects, the physical and psychic costs of going to the department often outweighed the benefits for Gene.

I felt that animosity also was directed toward me as Gene's girlfriend. And, I often wondered if some of my colleagues were disappointed that the nice, single, Southern girl they thought they had hired had turned out to be an independent woman openly living with a "loud-mouthed Jew" boyfriend.

■ ■ ■

Looking out the apartment window, I see Gene returning from his bridge game. I watch him closely now, because the fifteen-yard walk to the apartment is sometimes too much, even when he carries oxygen, and there are too many curbs to use the Amigo. It occurs to me that he never goes anywhere now without the hose. When did that happen? We had reached another plateau without either of us noticing it.

Suddenly, his hose is caught by the slamming van door, which cuts off Gene's oxygen supply and makes it impossible to move. Practically in tears, he screams an almost bloodcurdling call, "Carolyn, help!" and at the same time drops his small bag of groceries. I am angry that I am made to feel embarrassment as our neighbors pull aside their curtains. Why did he have to get groceries?

I rush out to untangle the hose, hopelessly caught in the door and through the seat belt. Then, when the emergency passes, I choke back a sob, and, as usual, feel compassion for Gene's anguish.

The van had not made Gene as independent as we had hoped, since, like all our technological devices, it was not dependable. Several times we had to take the lift for repair. When it continued to malfunction, I learned to fix it with a simple manual adjustment, but one that required more breath than Gene could count on. We both feared that trouble would arise when he was out alone, but we also resisted the loss of his independence.

■ ■ ■

"Stay with me until I get the Amigo out," Gene requests.

"But it'll take you fifteen minutes. I could be in the store shopping. Let me help you."

"No, I need to do it so that, when you aren't here, I won't have gotten dependent on you."

"Gene, you know you can do it if you have to, so let me do it now and save time and your energy."

"No," he says, this time forcefully. "I need to make mistakes and get myself out of them." What about me? I wanted to yell and didn't, although I charged him for his control by sulking. What could possibly go wrong now? How was this different from his being out alone?

When he's seated on the Amigo inside the van, I say, "I'm going into the store now."

When Gene does not appear after twenty minutes, I walk to the entrance. Suddenly he comes rolling through the door. Angry, he says triumphantly and pathetically, "The lift wouldn't open. See, I told you, it breaks. I do need you around. I had to get out of the van, walk around it, open the lift from outside, then walk back around the van, get in through the driver's side, and lower the lift."

"I'm sorry," I reply guiltily. "You made your point." After that I stayed with him, sometimes impatiently waiting while he drove the Amigo out, sometimes suggesting better and quicker solutions, even though he didn't want to hear them.

"I want to figure it out myself. Just be here," he demands then, "in case I need you." Fuck you, I think, hating his control, but standing silently at his side.

Finally, when the tension got to be too much, we sat down to talk. "I have to be able to go out alone," he says. "My world can't be that narrow. And I can't do that to you."

"Let's work this out," I reply in my best problem-solving voice. As a team, using our intellect and common sense, we experimented with the lift until we figured out systematically what caused the problems. Sometimes a wire came loose when the lift was lowered, but the more frequent problem occurred only when we closed the lift either too quickly or raised and closed it in the wrong order.

"I can handle this," Gene says. "And if, at some point, I can't, I'll drive directly to the repair shop."

"What if you are out of the van?" I ask, feeling protective.

"I'll call you. You're almost always at home or in your office. If I can't reach you, I'll wait until I can. Anyway, I have never had a problem—so far—when I was out of the van. But you still have to check every few days to make sure the Amigo battery is charged and the oxygen tanks are working, and fill my portable tank if I'm not feeling well."

"It's a deal," I say, relieved that he still is willing to leave the house without me, and proud that we have worked out a solution. We have the best equipment available. Surely I don't have to be with him all the time!

■　■　■

"Wouldn't it be nice, Gene? To have a garden, flowers, and a hot tub? We could build a fence, and go naked outside."

"I don't want to tie up my money in a house," Gene responds hesitantly. "Money gives me freedom and independence from you. It allows me to fly my friends in from New York whenever I want. And if things don't work out with us, I want to be able to go back to New York."

"But it would be a good investment," I say, hurt that he still doesn't trust our relationship, yet relieved that maybe there is a way he could work out his life without me.

"For you, yes. But I can't think about the future. I need security now."

I persist, "Isn't there a way you can have your security, yet I can also have my house?"

"No way," he says.

"But, look, we could pay just five percent down. And the monthly payment, after an income tax break, would be only slightly more than we pay for rent."

He argues against it. "There will be repairs, yard maintenance, moving expenses, all kinds of things."

"But I want to move on with life, at least pretend we have a normal relationship, and do things other people do."

Because Gene wanted to make me happy and the idea of a house and a hot tub appealed to him too, he finally consented. I was excited, yet nervous about forming another tie.

Many discussions ensued about his financial independence as we looked at houses. Finally, I grew angry enough to say I wasn't sure I wanted to be financially attached to him either. Then we calmed down and looked at houses, carrying our battles into the search. I would get enthusiastic about a certain house; he would find fault. We would come home and fight about the house and then about our relationship: how much each cared, how much each contributed, and who did what to whom. We both knew what was happening, but we felt powerless to stop it.

"I am sick of this," I yell, during a fight over a house I particularly liked. "I can't stand what's happening. You are so irritable, all the time. I just want to buy a house. A normal thing. Nothing is normal about this relationship."

"That's right," he shouts back, "and that's the way it is. Take it or leave it. You could move out, you know."

Gene felt hemmed in and out of control when he acknowledged how much he depended on me. He needed reassurance, but at the same time I caught his rage against his disease. He was rarely his happy, loving, sensitive self now. I responded in kind, out of my own insecurity and tension. I didn't know what to do about our deteriorating relationship. At times I questioned whether I wanted to do anything. We had never had fights like this before without making up. Now sometimes we had three or four without reconciliation. I could remember and sometimes feel the love we shared; yet he was so hard to get along with now. This was only going to get worse as he got sicker. I escaped the bickering by going to school. If he continued like this, I hoped that he got upset enough to leave me. Sometimes I wished he would get even more irritable so I would have a legitimate reason to leave him. Perhaps I even egged him on.

On top of it all, Gene's health was going through another transition. Nauseous, he was always nauseous. And complaining of an upset stomach. Sometimes he could barely eat. Too much was happening too quickly.

Finally, we just stopped house hunting. What a strain it had put on us, bringing to the forefront all the problems in our relationship and all the insecurities we both felt.

■　■　■

"The oxygen," Gene says, "it's out. What am I going to do?"

We have taken a trip to visit friends in a cabin in the backwoods near Nashville. Until now, one tank of oxygen had been sufficient as long as we filled it every four days.

"Let's drive right now to Nashville and get oxygen."

"I'll go alone," he offers. "I don't want to spoil your time."

It would be fun to visit these friends without Gene's illness putting a damper on the atmosphere. But he can't drive two hours without oxygen. "No, I'll go."

"Thanks," he says, out of breath from just getting into the car. "I really appreciate it." Knowing how bad he feels, both emotionally and physically, I swallow my resentment and offer to drive.

"Perhaps we should carry two tanks from now on," Gene says, and another plateau is reached.

When we got back to the cabin, our friend, Jim, gave me a lecture about poor planning. "I leave these kinds of decisions to Gene," I explain.

"Fine," he says, "but it affects you when they go wrong, so you need to pay more attention. Gene doesn't always plan ahead." Jim, and everyone else, had no notion of how much was planned ahead. Nor did they always understand the progressive nature of the disease. Until this moment, one tank had been plenty. Experiencing a disaster often was the first obvious indication that we needed to change strategy. Anticipating each decline would have occupied every waking moment. We tried to forget about the illness as much as we could, but it was getting harder to do, and becoming more costly when we did.

"Even when we plan ahead," I say to Jim, "the equipment breaks down."

"Then you have to have back-up systems all the time."

"Sometimes there aren't any," I reply, and am jarred by the seriousness of my acknowledgment.

"Manufacturers don't make this equipment with people like Gene in mind. They make it for dependent people, who will always have someone around to help, and who spend most of their time in bed. No one is as active as Gene in his condition. Technological props are made for people who live disabled lives, not people who try to do things like normal people."

"Exactly," I say, feeling vindicated. "So, do we continue as we have, risking breakdowns and disasters but living full lives? Or does Gene go to bed and play the role properly?"

I resist Jim's reply, "You take over the planning."

This incident resulted in increased closeness between Gene and me. When I felt for Gene's limits, I didn't quit resenting his illness, but I often quit resenting him. The discussion with Jim also made me feel like Gene's coconspirator, proud that we accomplished so much in spite of his disease, and defensive that no one understood the effort.

■ ■ ■

"Why do you need to be alone with your friends?" asks Gene, in a hurt voice, as we plan our drive to Arizona and California.

"I need time away from your illness and time to talk about you and us."

"Why? When you can talk to me?"

"It's different. Besides this will give you time away from me. And you can talk with Beth about me," I say, deciding to take another approach. "We'll appreciate each other more when we get back together."

We drove together to Arizona. Then while Gene traveled with Beth, I stayed with David and Donna. The three of us had great fun—laughing, dancing, eating, and hiking. David was one of the few, maybe the only, person to whom I could reveal the details of my conflicting feelings about Gene—my fears and need to stay with him, the love and hatred I felt, the admiration and disgust that got played out. We discussed what was best for me. People who were friends with Gene usually thought about what was best for the relationship, which often meant what was best for Gene. My new friends in Tampa didn't understand Gene or our history well enough to give advice. They had trouble understanding why I was in this situation in the first place.

"It takes so much energy to take care of Gene," Beth says, when we meet. "I had to be 'on' all the time. The energy needed to always be available and alert was draining. Then the physical energy of taking care of him. Just setting up the bed in the van meant taking out all the wheelchairs and suitcases to unfold it. Then there's the fetching. He always needs something."

"I know," I say quietly, feeling close to Beth and appreciating her validation that this was hard. "And he can't change any of it. The one night we camped, Gene had trouble moving around in the van, and the lift made it difficult to get in and out the door. Do you believe—one large liquid oxygen tank, two portables, an electric one, an Amigo wheelchair, and a standard wheelchair? It's too much."

We giggle at the absurdity. Then Beth says, "But I don't know how you do this all the time." Reluctantly, I agree that sleeping in the van is more trouble than it's worth.

Beth flew back to Portland, and Gene and I drove to the wine country. We had missed each other and were glad to be together again. I felt refreshed and patient; he felt loving and appreciative. We stayed in a cabin overlooking the Pacific Ocean. Since Gene couldn't walk to the beach, I went alone. He was glad for my enjoyment; I was glad for the solitude.

One day we felt close enough to take LSD again. What would we find out about ourselves? What would we find out about our relationship? On acid, it would be difficult to hide feelings. Facing up to his current level of deterioration might be too much for us. "Maybe the love we once had isn't here anymore," Gene says, putting our fears into words. But we couldn't go on like before. We needed a time-out period.

Once the acid took effect we were best friends again and romantic, sexual, and emotional lovers. What came out was that we both were in tremendous pain. There it was again. Whenever we both were needy, we had problems. Often the need and pain were associated with Gene's health dropping a level. On acid, we could no longer deny the massive deterioration of the last few months. Just look at the equipment we now carried. Just think about how much less he could do now than on the last trip. Just look at how difficult moving around had become. Just consider how much more he needed me. Just feel how much of our time his disease occupied. If we weren't dealing with his illness directly, we were thinking about it, or planning how to cope with it at some later date.

No wonder we argued. He had been overwhelmed by his problems and insecurities, and I had been absorbed by mine. He was facing helplessness, body deterioration, and loss of self. And, it hurt me to watch. To be old at thirty-two, with most of my waking thoughts concerned about death and chronic illness. To be embarrassed by oxygen hoses and wheelchairs. To find his irritability impossible. To know that the situation could only get worse. To think about being without him. And, at the same time, to be grieving for my brother, my counterpart; the person in the world most like me. I was absorbed by self-pity. What happened to my youth? My joy? My laughter? My idealism?

Now, finally, I listened to how the world appeared through his eyes, and then I understood his irritability and anger at me. Where else did he have to put it? When I listened, Gene relaxed and focused on my pain. "I forget your pain in all this," he says. "I get so self-centered. I forget how much effort it requires to take care of me. Beth reminded me. Let me hold you.

Talk to me. Let me understand you. Let me help you deal with my deterioration and death."

I start to cry, then become tense. It has been a long time. Can he still comfort me? His arms surround me. When I close my eyes, his body feels healthy; his shoulders are broad; his emphysemic, expanded, barrel chest feels sturdy, hard, and strong. His mesmerizing and kind voice tells me about the love in his heart. Hungry for feeling, I take it in and return it.

The dam breaks, and my feelings are set free from their safe. I surrender to his love and my love for him, and, along with the love, I feel the pain of loss. Love and pain, loss and attachment fill up the same space. I cannot feel one without the other. This is the wonderful and horrible state I fear and long for at the same time. This fear and the day-to-day realities of the disease have blocked my love. I sob—for him, for me, the loss of my brother, and the inevitable loss of Gene. I wallow in the pain, which is nothing more than the pain of the human condition and nothing less than a search for meaning. Everyone feels it at some time, in some way, at some place, but I am not comforted by company.

"I can't stand the pain alone," I say. "I need a safe context in which to feel it. I haven't had that for a long time. I am afraid to feel. I am fucking afraid to feel."

"Let it go. Let it all go," he encourages, and holds me while I cry. "I'm here for you now."

Then he says, joyfully, "It's still there," and I wonder what he means. "The love is still there. Yours. And mine. I have been afraid too. So much loss. And I didn't know if you were still with me. I have felt so alone. I can deal with this if you're with me. If not, it's not worth it. It hurts too much."

"I'm with you," I say simply and am impassioned by the truthfulness of the words. "Oh, god, am I ever with you."

We immerse ourselves in feelings then, believing they have been let through because of, not created by, the drug. As we hold on to each other, the feeling is spiritual. I may never have a more meaningful moment. Aloneness is, for now, held at bay. Our love and our struggle to participate in dying together make life meaningful. I lose track of time.

Then the rational part of me wants to be expressed. "It's harder and harder to talk to you about my feelings. The sicker you get, the more I don't want to place the burden of my pain on you. And the less I think you can handle."

"No," he insists softly, "you must let me help you. It makes me feel close to you. I need to feel I give you something too. That I'm still a plus in your life and not just a burden."

"But sometimes now it's easier to talk to someone else about your death and deterioration. If you are feeling good, I don't want to get you down."

"How much have I deteriorated?" he asks.

"There's been a big drop. Just look at all our equipment," I say, waving my hands.

There is silence for a moment, then, "Still, no one can help you deal with my condition like I do." He is right, of course. Even now, I love that he is sure of his self-worth. I lounge for a while in the thought that Gene will get me through this. Then I am struck by the contradiction. At some point he will be too sick to comfort me. Eventually he will die; be no more. Then what? He will not be here to help me. There is no happy ending.

"I'm not sure," I say, "that dealing with reality now is always the best approach. I would welcome a little fantasy."

Wanting to dissuade me from my position, he argues that things aren't that bad and can be worked out, but finally he says, "Maybe you're right, but don't shut me out. I need you to see me as a tough fucker. I know I whine and complain, but often I don't tell you how bad I feel."

"I know that," I say.

"And sometimes you're so impatient," he continues, "it makes me feel like a piece of dirt. That you don't respect me, that you really can't stand me and my disease. You take your frustrations out on me."

Knowing his remarks are true, I am about to apologize when he smiles and says with a twinkle, "But mostly you're incredible. I don't know how you do it. Thank you. I love you."

For a while, we exist together as feeling, swept up in our love. I have missed it, longed for it. Now there is no question on either side. We are as together as two people can be. If I never feel love again, I will have had this moment. I will have known meaning. Love gives us meaning. Other than our selves, it is all we have to fight the battles. It must be nurtured. Life can never be the same without him.

My thoughts have pulled me away from the near-pure emotion I experience. The same happens to Gene. I focus on my own thoughts; he on his. I rarely deal with my pain; his seems so much more immediate and important, while mine is secondary. He not only has psychological distress; he also has physical pain. I have to find a way to make my anguish primary without intruding upon him. The plain truth is that sometimes he can't handle my agony. There already have been occasions where our discussions about what I am feeling are interrupted by a clump that has to be dealt with immediately. Or when he feels too dizzy to concentrate on our conversation. Or he is temperamental and irritable. He can't always give me what I need. He can't always provide a secure place for me to break down. We are at the mercy of his body.

And, on the other side, he will die alone. At some point, we will separate. I don't have to say this. He knows it. At the moment, he wishes to deny it, or at least avoid it, and so do I. We choose unconsciously for the first time not to turn over every stone.

Instead, we move to the physical expression of our love as a replica of our emotionality. I am lost in our passionate kiss. With each motion, we lash out at death, yet move toward it. Our bodies integrated, we create energy to work toward the final plunge. The grief inside me, its protective structure, breaks apart, causing the boundaries of my body to disintegrate. Our energies soar off into the universe, intricately intertwined. Then we are in the darkness. This must be what death is like. Only more. With my sobs, I am released.

We join together in total, committed love in a way that we haven't for a while. Aloneness is not here. We are inside each other. There are no bodies. No boundaries. Our orgasm occurs in our heads, our hearts, and spirits. We cry during and after, happy to be alive. All the pain that I have held back is, for now, dissipated. Our love in all its aspects has escaped from its rationally contained cage and remains as strong as ever. Outside of this moment, we recognize our relationship cannot be perfect. The disease still is eating away at his body, and we cannot continue being all things to each other. Day-to-day concerns will make us forget our love. Momentarily. But we will try to remember that our love can be called on when we need it.

I will never forget the little cabin that looked out over the rugged and beautiful Pacific coast. The waves pounding the craggy cliff reminded me of our lives. We could not resist the excitement of riding them, the seduction of catching a wave at its peak and soaring onto shore. Eventually we knew we would fall into the ocean, maybe before others who chose to walk safely along the beach. Maybe our fall would be harder. But the ride was worth the risk.

■ ■ ■

"I want to be your equal, not your secretary or student," I say, as Gene and I work on a paper on jealousy after arriving back in Tampa. "I don't want to just comment on what you say, or write while you dictate."

"OK, write the next paragraph then," Gene responds, folding his hands, and moving back from the table.

"Just like that? That's not the way I write. I need to be by myself, surrounded by reference books, writing and rewriting, organizing and reorganizing. Why can't each of us write sections alone, then put them together and edit?"

"I can't work by myself. I like to bat ideas off someone. Besides, my hands shake too much to form letters. So sit with me while I talk, ask me questions, and put our ideas into sentences. Then, if you still want to write sections alone, that's fine," Gene says.

"I don't have time to work with you and write apart. I have to teach and work on my book." So we compromised. He wrote some alone; I worked on the literature review, sought out references, edited his material, and sometimes still worked beside him. Although I never felt he treated me as a colleague and he probably never thought I quite deserved the status of one, writing the paper gave Gene structured work to do and made him feel intellectually active.

"Don't you want to work on your other papers?" I ask.

"Why bother?" he responds.

■ ■ ■

Oxygen tanks. Cane chair. Pill boxes. Inhalers. Antacid. Amigo batteries. Wheelchair lifts. And pills. Now there were more. Prednisone—a steroid, tetracycline to prevent colds, brethine and theodore for breathing, vitamin C, and aspirin. The codeine he had taken daily for some time relieved pain and opened up his breathing. But he suffered even more when it wore off. He rarely smoked marijuana now because the aftereffects were costly—greater shortness of breath, no energy, and sometimes more-than-usual clumping. Gas and upset stomach, byproducts of the buildup of carbon dioxide, were more common, and food, once one of our greatest pleasures, was less enjoyable.

During early fall, Gene developed another symptom. All at once he would get light-headed and dizzy, sometimes so unbalanced that he had to sit. Since often he felt worse after eating, we thought his condition was connected to food. Was he allergic to something? Did the digestion of food take most of his energy? How would we deal with this one too?

I wanted to scream, but instead I made an appointment with a psychologist. "What do I have to lose?" I ask Gene. "My insurance will cover the visits."

"I don't like it. Why do you need to go to a psychologist?" he asks. "What will he know that I don't? I'm much better for you to talk to than he'll be."

Since Gene's ego is at stake, I try to be gentle in my explanation. "It has gotten more difficult to talk to you, to complain about how much trouble I'm having with your illness. Or to get sympathy. You are occupied with your own psychological and physical distress."

"I can't help it," he says defensively.

"I'm not attacking you," I reply. "I know you can't. But that still doesn't help me. I start to talk and you have an emergency we have to deal with. I need someone outside the relationship who can focus on my pain, to admit that I have a problem too and make time for it independent from yours." When he closes his eyes and looks defeated, I say, softly, "Gene, I feel like I'm going crazy." Then I hold his hands in mine, kissing them to convey my need and care. It is important that we be on the same side.

"OK, maybe it'll be good for you." I am relieved, but I would have gone, no matter what he said.

On the first visit, the therapist, Ken, a gay male in his late thirties, asks me what I hope to get out of therapy. I respond, "I might just want a place to cry every week. Maybe that's all." Ken does not respond to my "plea" and moist eyes, moving instead immediately to "the problem." Still, what a luxury to talk about my life. I paid Ken to concentrate on my problems for fifty minutes, and only occasionally did he connect my issues to his life ("Yeah, that reminds me of the time . . ."), or did I worry that I was boring someone, or wonder whether this person really wanted to hear about my agony.

Driving back and forth to therapy provided a time to think about myself. Once in Ken's office, it was helpful to hear myself talk. Whenever I felt tears welling up, Ken handed me a Kleenex box and quickly retreated to his safe corner of the room to ask rational questions sure to stop my crying. "What are you going to do now?" "Why do you think this is upsetting you?" "What items of business do you need to take care of?"

After a few sessions, we turned to an exploration of my past life, in particular sexual experiences. This was somewhat insightful, a turn on, and certainly a relief from the day-to-day heaviness of Gene's illness. When we talked about my pattern of getting involved with older, powerful men, Ken says, "You know you're running out of men more powerful than you."

"So I've noticed," I respond, thinking of the men I had met in the last few years. Maybe they weren't any different; maybe I was.

"Most of the men you meet now," he continues, "will have less or equal power to you. You'll have to learn to have relationships where you are in the powerful, teaching position."

"I have that in my work," I say, "why would I want it in my intimate friendships?" But, for the first time I thought beyond Gene to relationships I might have after he died. I also wondered about the crush I now had on Ken. Was it simply because he was in a power position? Had this been my pattern?

Feeling a change in my orientation, after my third session, Gene accuses, "You and Ken form a coalition against me. That man has only your best interests in mind, not our relationship, and certainly not my interests. He is turning you against me."

"Well, go with me then," I reply, although I don't really want to share my time. When Gene declines, I say, "Then go to Ken alone."

He refuses again, explaining, "He can't do anything for me that I can't do for myself. What is there to accomplish? He can't take away my illness, and that is my problem."

"Perhaps he could help you accept it," I try.

"Accept it? I don't want to accept it. I want to fight it."

"But you need someone to talk to," I try again. "You need to talk about me as well as to me."

"I have friends for that," he retorts, but more and more he talked only to me.

I wasn't getting everything I needed from Ken, but my pain was validated. The visits also provided a time where I could admit and talk about all my negative feelings—not being sexually turned on to Gene, Gene's irritability, my growing older, hating Gene sometimes, my resentment. I didn't want to tell other people about these feelings. But, they were as real as the love, commitment, and caring I also felt. Expressing negative feelings in therapy helped free up positive ones and meant that sometimes I was more loving and patient as a result. Basically Gene was right. Therapy encouraged a "me" orientation. As a result, I thought more about what was good for me, and I planned my future after Gene.

After a few months, I no longer felt I was benefiting from therapy. The exploration of my past had stopped helping with the present or future. Ken's rational problem-solving approach, quite useful in the beginning, soon became a repeat of what I had already figured out. How could he in a fifty-minute period every two weeks come up with problems or solutions that I had not thought about in my lived experience every single day? I quit seeing Ken the end of March 1984 after sixteen visits and didn't go back until the middle of the summer, this time to deal with my own deterioration.

In spite of disagreeing about therapy, Gene and I were getting along well. I was more tolerant; he was less reactive. We were more accepting of his restricted health and relished the short trips we continued to take.

By this time, we both felt that Tampa was home and enjoyed being included in activities there. Parties provided opportunities for Gene to meet new people. But there was always the problem of what to do with the oxygen tank he now had to carry with him. We tried making light of it. Once Gene and I went to a costume party dressed as a computer. He had a sign on his back that read "mainframe"; he was connected to the portable oxygen tank, labeled "modem." Designated the "printer," I carried the modem so that its hose connected me to the mainframe as well. People laughed hilariously at first, then suddenly became silent as they realized the oxygen tank was not just a costume prop.

After this fiasco, we devised a system to make ourselves and others more comfortable about the presence of oxygen. When Gene first started a conversation, he took the oxygen hose out of his nose. He felt that if he communicated without it interfering, people might find him interesting enough not to be put off by his disease. My task then was to check constantly to see how Gene was doing.

This watchful and controlled attitude carried over into our bedroom. More and more, Gene's breathing difficulties affected our lovemaking. While we still had loving, caring sex, rarely did we have abandoned or playful, giggly sex. There was too much to think about and too much that might go wrong. We missed it, but waking up curled like spoons and holding each other provided good compensation.

■ ■ ■

"You'll never be able to make it by 8:00 A.M.," I say, trying to convince Gene not to attend the fifteen-kilometer race I'm running. "Anyway, I don't want to have to think about whether you're OK. I'll be too busy."

"I understand," he says sadly. "I'll watch it on television."

It was hard to admit even to myself that I was embarrassed to let my athletic friends see me with Gene. Health was status in that world, and it was an understatement to say that Gene was not a picture of good health. Still, when he told me he saw me on TV, I choked back a sob of regret that he had not been there to share my accomplishment.

■ ■ ■

"It's out of oxygen," Gene says, as he attempts to fill the portable tank from the unit in the van.

"Then we must go home," I reply. We have spent the day with two friends and are on our way into a movie.

"But home is twenty-five minutes away," Gene says. "We'll miss the movie."

"We can go to a late movie," I say, irritated.

"No, we've been out all day and I'm tired. Let's try to make it through this one."

Although I don't like taking the risk, neither do I want to drive home and back. "OK," I say, "but ride your Amigo into the theater, just to be safe."

"No," he replies, in a tone leaving no room for negotiation. "I want to manage without that." I respond with angry silence. "I have to push myself to walk," he explains. "And the Amigo is sometimes more trouble than walking. There's never a place in the theater to put it."

This time I want it my way, and ask him again, softly, to ride his Amigo. "At least you'll be sitting down if you get into trouble," I say. "I'm worried about the oxygen."

"No, I want to walk. Just stay near me and carry the cane chair and oxygen tank, if I need you to."

I didn't want to be a part of his oddity, but, having no alternative, I went ahead to purchase tickets and Gene walked directly into the theater and sat down. Sighing in relief, I sat down next to him. Once Gene caught his breath, he began complaining about the low oxygen flow. I tensed and tried not to listen. We can't even go to a movie, I say angrily to myself. How relaxing this is, I think facetiously. When I do not respond to his complaints, Gene stops talking and retracts his body. In the middle of the movie, I timidly rub his hand. Seeming relieved, he squeezes my hand and holds it tightly for the rest of the film.

When the show is over, Gene still has a little oxygen in his portable tank, but the flow is weak. Feeling how tense he is, I offer to get the Amigo. "No, I can make it," he says. On the way out of the theater, he carries the oxygen and I take the cane chair. My friends stop to talk to acquaintances. When they introduce me, I glance at Gene, breathing heavily, walking methodically ahead of us, then I turn back to the introduction. I'll stop a minute, I decide quickly, resentful that I can't greet people in a normal way. If Gene had ridden the Amigo, this would not be such a problem. I forget Gene as I say hello, but the conversation is interrupted by a loud voice yelling, "Carolyn, help!" Embarrassed and angry, I rush to Gene. "The chair. I need the chair," he gasps, pointing to the cane. I unfold it and he sits down quickly in the middle of the lobby. I narrow my shoulders and look to the floor, trying to make myself invisible as people walk around us.

When he says between gasps in a loud voice filled with hatred, "You castrating bitch," I storm out of the theater, not waiting to see if he is OK. I don't care. I hate him.

Determined to take control, I get into the driver's seat and let Gene struggle alone into the passenger's side. Sensing a problem, our two friends take their time coming to the van. No one talks. Driving faster than normal, I am out of control.

I drop my friends off at their home, and immediately I explode. "You disgust me," I yell. "You make bad decisions and I suffer. I come to help after you yell in a public place. Then you scream complimentary terms like 'castrating bitch'. I've had it. I can't live like this anymore. I want out."

Although I have had these thoughts before, and we've discussed the pros and cons of separating, I have never threatened in anger to leave him. Normally I could not get past his pain to say hurtful things.

"You were angry at me the whole evening and then you punished me by not staying beside me with the cane like I asked you."

"I wasn't punishing you," I interrupt. "I was being introduced to people. What was I supposed to do?"

"Then when I yelled for you," he continues as though he hasn't heard me, "you still waited before you came to help. You are a castrating bitch."

His words get me going again. "Go to hell," I say. "I've had it." I jerk the van to the side of the road and open the door to get out.

The urgency of my action calms his anger, and he pleads, "Please don't leave me." I soften at his tone, which reveals how much he needs me. My god, I am caught, the voice inside screams as I clutch the steering wheel, trying to figure out what to do. It doesn't matter how irritable he is, I can't leave him.

He puts his hand on mine and says softly, "Come home. Let's talk about it."

"OK," I reply. By then my explosion has passed and I calm down, but I don't hold back feelings. "It's hard not to live a normal life. Not even to be able to meet people. To have to think about you all the time."

When he says softly, "I know, and I'm sorry it's this way," my heart opens to him.

I close the door, and we drive home in silence. I wait beside him as he catches his breath before the final plunge into the apartment. Gently I place my hand on his shoulder, open the door, and get the oxygen hose. "We need to talk," I say, taking my place at the table.

"Yes, please."

"I admit that I felt resentment in the theater," I begin, "and that I was not thinking of you when I stopped to meet those people. But I was not trying to punish you. I would never intentionally hurt you. How could you think that?"

"I'm sorry," he says again. "But this is hard for me too." I embrace him then and we both cry. "I feel so much anger toward this disease," he says, "so helpless. I don't want to lose you. I'm sorry. I know it's hard for you too. I'll try not to be explosive. Don't leave me."

"I won't," I say, and mean it. "And I'll try to be more thoughtful. I don't want you to be scared and in pain." I cringe at what the experience must have been like for him.

"You know what the real problem is?" I ask, and Gene looks to me expectantly. "You've dropped another level. You need to use the Amigo now for a movie. You can't walk that distance any more, even with oxygen."

"No," he says, at first not wanting to hear. Then, "I guess you're right," he admits, swallowing hard, eyes cast down, his head shaking no at the same time. "It's happening so fast."

It seems that we would have learned by now that when we had trouble to first look to the disease as the cause. But we always wanted to deny that Gene was worse. Those were hard drops to acknowledge, but they were harder still when we didn't.

As usual when we attempted to understand each other, our love drew us together. Yet I felt emotionally drained and knew that these episodes also did irreparable damage. I would never forget the words "castrating bitch"; Gene would never forget feeling alone and scared as he panicked in the lobby.

We talked about how to prevent this kind of incident from happening again. "I would feel more comfortable," I say, "if we took the Amigo in all these situations."

"But the Amigo's a problem too," he replies.

"Then let me help you with it when you're not feeling well. Let me get it out of the van. Save your energy. When you don't, we both suffer."

"I still want to push, kick ass," he says. "That is the way I've managed so far. No matter how painful it is, I've always been able to keep going knowing that the pain and breathlessness would go away."

Tenderly, I say, "I'm not sure this is a good strategy anymore. You often seem to suffer the day after exerting yourself."

When he claims this isn't true, I reply, "Yes, it is. Think about it." When I see the sadness on his face, I desperately want my revelation to be wrong.

"I guess you're right," he admits.

These conversations were painful, but important. We anticipated problems and were ready with solutions the next time they arose. Things would then work smoothly for a while, until the level of the disease dropped once again.

7

"GENE, IT HAS a downstairs bedroom," I yell excitedly.

"We'll take it," Gene says on his way through the front door. What a change from his previous reluctant attitude. We had found the perfect house—a modern, angular, two-story with cathedral ceiling and fireplace, in our price range, and only two miles from the university.

Later, around the kitchen table, Gene says, "Buying a house is a big move. Can I trust you?"

"We're still together, aren't we? And, you know I care about you?" When he says he feels it, I ask playfully, "So what other evidence do you want?"

"How about a kiss?"

After several kisses, Gene's tone is serious as he says, "There's another issue I want to raise. Why don't you buy the house without my name on the title? Then I'll pay you rent."

"What will that accomplish?"

"It'll give me freedom in case I want to split. But don't worry, I'd still help you financially," he reassures. "And your part of my pension will cover your mortgage payments after I die."

I agree to his plan. Although I don't believe that he will leave, I understand the illusion of control that keeping options open creates, and I pretend that this plan might give me options as well.

This discussion makes Gene's eventual death real. Although I tell myself death is in the indefinite future, I also know that one day I will be dealing with his pension, disposing the body, learning to live without him. "Don't do this to yourself," an inner voice screams. "You don't have to handle this now." But the voices continue to argue. "Maybe there will be a miracle." The chances of that are slim to nonexistent. We've already decided against a lung transplant, because of the danger and poor quality of life that would result. "Gene could stabilize and live a long time, but look at his deterioration in the time you have known him. Face up to the reality. It's not going to be long. Maybe three years if you're lucky." Three years—that's nothing. "Remember what the doctor said in 1981, three years ago? Three to five years to walk, seven to ten to live—under the best of circumstances with no bad infections." Yes. "Well, he has already had colds since then, hasn't he?" I can't bear it.

"Gene, let's celebrate with a nice dinner. Then come home, open a bottle of wine, and make love."

"Good idea," he responds. Did he need to get away from the same thoughts as I? Usually these celebration times got us into the bubble of intensity where we wanted to deal with our pain and agony. This time we chose to push it away. More and more, that would become our modus operandi.

Later, in bed, the wave of pain washed through me again as I experienced orgasm. What a beautiful, yet agonizing and unprotected moment. The pain and ecstasy, intertwined in the same knot, exploded in sex. Gene holds me tightly as I sob, "I don't want to lose you."

"You'll be OK," he says, caressing my face. "I love it when you cry. I don't want you to feel pain, but it lets me know you love me." We cling to each other as though it is the last time our bodies—and souls—will meet. We don't talk any more about the future. What is there to say?

After I cried, the knot of pain and grief was replaced with emptiness. These intense experiences were still necessary, but less of an escape now; for Gene as well, I assume. Afterward, it was hard to convince myself, even for the moment, that all was well. I watched Gene as he slept. He now weighed only 148 pounds, not much for his six-foot, one-inch frame. But less weight made it easier to breathe and was better for his heart. His shoulders rose up and down, in a labored way, and the chalky color was there most of the time now. I thought about how he often complained of feeling dizzy and spacey.

Then a bell went off as I remembered my private discussion with Gene's New York doctor. "If Gene gets light-headed or is not making sense," he had warned, "get him immediately to the hospital. It will mean his blood gases are out of whack." He was often light-headed; sometimes he had trouble concentrating. This is what the doctor was talking about. I've been ignoring the symptoms. But Gene always makes sense, I think with relief. So that isn't what's happening. And he has improved now that he has reduced his oxygen intake.

He's OK. Isn't he?

■ ■ ■

"You're not embarrassed?" Gene asks, as people stare at him floating in the gulf, connected by a fifty-foot hose to his portable oxygen tank on shore.

"No, I'm just happy you can do it," I say, standing guard beside him. Like a little boy, he is overjoyed. On the one hand, I am like a mother, proud of her child's accomplishments and pleasure, and, on the other, I giggle with him, like we are kids getting away with something. "If only Dr. Silverman could see me now," he says, his fingers locked together and resting on his chest. His overinflated lungs support his body abnormally high in the waves.

We were spending a week on Sanibel Island, three hours south of Tampa. We read novels, cooked dinner together, and talked as we drank champagne on our cabin porch and watched the sun set. Walking the few yards to the water required several rest periods, evidence that Gene's health was worse.

The sicker Gene became, the more I concentrated on physical health and exercise. I jogged every day on the beach with my dog and exercised in the cabin. This routine gave me something to do during the two hours Gene needed to accomplish his morning routine.

First the pumper. The steady hum of the machine changed to a hiss every thirty seconds as Gene removed his finger from the opening to force the mist deep into his lungs. When the hiss stopped or occurred sporadically, I knew he was playing out a bridge hand in his magazine and forgetting to spray. Next he had to take his morning medications and organize the day's pills in his plastic pill box, a recent substitute for the many expensive, decorated ones he had lost. Getting dressed required a rest between putting on his pants and shirt. He shaved sitting down with an electric razor, bought as soon as we noticed that standing cost breath. After another rest, he filled his portable oxygen tank.

Finally, Gene would be ready for breakfast. Sometimes he was so worn out by then that he needed to rest before having his cookies and milk. Because digestive problems occurred as soon as he finished, and worsened the more he consumed, he ate little. The antacid we carried usually relieved his distress.

If Gene asked, I assisted. When I tried to help to speed things up for my convenience, he criticized me for hovering and thinking only of myself. But usually we dealt with problems quickly and efficiently in order to make time for enjoyment whenever Gene had enough energy and health to participate. Sometimes it all seemed too much for me, or he got into a bad mood.

If one of us was understanding, we got out of the negative frame quickly. When both of us were short-tempered, we argued.

We had learned to cope with each other's different conflict styles: Gene was quick to anger, flaring into a rage over something that seemed small to me; then, once released, his anger would end as quickly as it had come. I was slow to anger, but when I yielded to it, I thought the world was ending and, even when it didn't, I simmered a long time, often withdrawing emotionally and sometimes physically. "You are the only person I know who can go to sleep in the middle of an argument," Gene says.

"A just punishment," I respond, "for someone who yells."

I convinced Gene that yelling, no matter how short its duration, violated our relationship. "But it's not directed toward you," Gene says defensively.

"But it pollutes the environment I'm in and makes me angry," I counter.

"OK, I see your point. I'll try, but it flares before I know it."

Likewise, Gene convinced me that withdrawing was just as nonproductive. "It means," he says, "that there is no opportunity to make things right."

"But I need time to cool down, to work things out in my own mind," I rationalize, before finally admitting that most of my withdrawal is to punish.

I shake my head in agreement when he says, "It's always more fun to be together and loving than to be angry and morally indignant. It's better to be happy than to be right. We're responsible," he continues, "for getting us back to that state. The sooner the better. We have to trust each other's goodwill and believe that is what the other person wants as well."

I finally stopped trying to hold onto anger as long as I could, a technique I had learned from my mother, who used to get mad at my father and not speak to any of us for weeks. I stayed withdrawn a shorter time, and often argued without withdrawing at all. Sometimes, when I listened to our yelling battles, I had to worry that I had gone to the opposite extreme.

Gene worked hard at controlling his temper. Though he never conquered his flare-ups, now they came less often and were less fierce. Being sick actually helped, once he admitted his rages against his illness caused him to feel worse and made whatever situation he was in more problematic.

One of the few positive effects of Gene's illness was his increasing serenity. The Gene I was with in 1984 was less domineering, more sensitive and vulnerable, than the Gene I had known in the early years of our relationship. While I liked the change, sometimes I missed the adventure and excitement generated before. Sometimes I picked fights with him if we had been sailing along too long without them. Fighting put us on more equal footing—it was hard to feel sorry for someone arguing with me. As much as I hated to fight, it energized me and made me feel I had a challenge, someone to bang heads against. Our fights cleared the air and usually ended with intense passion. Since anger signified potential loss, we ended up clinging to each other, trying desperately to understand what was going on. I used the surge to get me away from feeling fatigued and restricted by the seriousness of Gene's illness.

■ ■ ■

"So why don't you drive to New York this summer and stay for the month of July? I'll stay here and work, then visit friends out west, and then meet you at the ASA [American Sociological Association meetings] in San Antonio."

"I'm afraid to drive by myself. I can't stand this," Gene says, banging his fist on the table. "I was never fearful."

"I can't stand it either," I respond. "What if I drive to New York with you and stay a couple of weeks in the house you've rented? Then I'll fly to California to visit friends and then fly back to drive to San Antonio with you. Or, if someone from Stony Brook will ride with you, then I'll meet you in San Antonio."

"Maybe we should just forget the whole thing."

"No, we have to deliver our paper on jealousy at the conference in San Antonio. Come on. We can work this out."

"I guess I could manage in New York as long as you go with me to help set up. I don't want to keep you from doing what you want, so I'll pay students to help after that."

That Gene could no longer drive to New York by himself, something he had done just six months before, took on symbolic meaning. Another iron door slammed shut. No longer could I ignore this restriction, which had been coming for a while. He was dependent on me in a way I never wanted anyone to be. Most of the time I refused to think about what it meant.

Then my body gave out.

■ ■ ■

At the end of May 1984, I went with friends to a Woman's Music Festival in Georgia. The first day there I hurt my knee playing basketball and was unable to walk. How ironic. I had gone away to have a break from Gene's illness, to play sports and go places without worrying how he would get there. Now people had to bring my meals and carry me to music events. What agony I experienced just maneuvering around the muddy hills in the constant rain on borrowed crutches.

The doctors at the festival thought I had pulled a ligament. "But, see a doctor when you get home," they instructed, "since there is really no way to tell." I was sure I just needed time to heal.

Feeling depressed when I got home, I called Gene, who was visiting his mother in Miami. "I'll be there in five hours," he says, when I tell him the news.

"There's no need to cut your trip short," I say. But I'm glad when he insists.

When he arrives, he says, "Sit down, and let me bring you what you need." Sadly, I watch his struggle to get a glass of water before falling into a chair, exhausted. "I can do nothing for you," he says, defeated. "I want to take care of you."

"You do," I reply. "You love me and care about me and hold me and comfort me. And you edit my manuscript and ease my anxieties." But he wanted to be strong for me in the heroic male way he had learned.

Three weeks later my knee still hurt and we had less than a week to pack and move into our new house. I could walk, as long as I didn't put full weight on my left leg. I packed what I could, friends came to help, and Gene hired a former student. A company moved our furniture while we watched.

∎ ∎ ∎

I place the ladder into the opening to the attic over the garage to put away empty boxes. Before stepping on it, I ask Gene to check the positioning. "Sure, but wait until I fill up my tank."

"Oh, it's not that important. I don't know why I need the reassurance. I guess I feel vulnerable and almost superstitious from the knee injury."

"If you bring out a chair, I can do it without the oxygen," Gene says, and he walks breathlessly to the garage. Gene examines the extension ladder I have hooked over the molding around the opening into the attic, and says, "It looks fine."

Just as I climb to the top of the ladder, the molding pulls loose and I fall face down onto the cement floor ten feet below, still holding onto the ladder. I hear myself moaning. I see blood. I turn onto my back and hold my knee. Time moves slowly. "My knee. My knee. I fucked up."

"What hurts, baby?" Gene asks, rushing toward me.

"My knee." Do I really feel pain in my knee? A deep gash in my hand makes me wonder what else I have done. "My face," I say. "Gene, what have I done to my face?" My hand reaches for my teeth, then hunts for my glasses.

"There's some blood on your nose and your lip is swelling, but it doesn't look serious."

Although I feel a pounding sensation in my knee, I can walk when I get up. I examine the deep, inch-and-a-half-long gash in my right hand and feel a few nicks on my face. My left wrist shoots with pain.

Gene wraps a towel around my bleeding hand. "I'll fill the oxygen and take you to an emergency clinic." I start to help him, then relax into being taken care of.

As soon as Gene and I are in the car, we hug and tears glisten in his eyes as he says, "I'm so sorry. I thought the ladder was safe."

"Me too," I say. "But I shouldn't have hooked it over the molding."

"The molding was the worst place," Gene agrees. "I should have known that. It's just soft board nailed into a plywood ceiling. It was bound to pull loose."

Choking back tears, Gene continues, "I can't believe how I felt when I saw you fall. I was afraid you were really hurt. I don't know what I would do without you. I'd want to die too. I mean it." I reach out to him and, similar to after our car accident, I experience the fragility of life and body.

Moving into the house should have been wonderful. Why were all these bad things happening? What was next?

The gash in my right hand was sewn with ten stitches. But the most aggravating problem was my left wrist, which I had either sprained or broken when I fell. I couldn't bend my wrist nor hold anything weighing more than a few ounces. What a way to move into a house. Gene was having trouble with mobility and breathing, while I was limited in walking and carrying.

But with hired help, soon the blinds and pictures were hung, the spa and privacy fence installed, and we were moved in. We frequently sat on our private patio sharing conversation as the sun set, and we found it almost as nice as looking at the water and woods from our back porch in Stony Brook. Sometimes it was hard for Gene to get in and out of the spa and the steam bothered his breathing. Still, he enjoyed occasionally relaxing in the water with oxygen in his nose, and he loved my enjoying it. In a few weeks the stitches came out of my hand, and my knee and sprained wrist had improved somewhat. We began to feel optimistic, in spite of the bad omens.

■　■　■

"I need to go to a dentist to take care of my temporary cap. It finally fell off after all these years. But I might have trouble getting there," Gene says. "Go with me."

"Do I have to go to every doctor or dentist visit?" I ask fearfully.

"It's just that I don't know what this one will be like."

"What if I scout out the office to see if it will be difficult getting there?"

"I'd rather you just went with me."

"Let's try my plan first. If it's too problematic, I'll go."

When I discovered that reaching this office demanded a long walk down a corridor and up a flight of stairs, I asked Gene if he wanted to cancel the appointment. When he said no, I reluctantly accompanied him.

At his appointment, Gene tells the dentist, "I only want another temporary cap and a cleaning."

"Your mouth is a disaster," the dentist responds. "You have broken teeth, you need a root canal, you have gum problems. About four thousand dollars of problems."

Gene responds, "It doesn't make sense to do all that work. I'm not going to live long."

"It's up to you," the dentist says uncomfortably, after a long pause.

Gene decided to have one-half the work done. The physical exertion of getting to the dentist's office and the unpredictability of the reaction of his body to medication made it necessary for me to accompany him. "We need to hire a companion for you," I argue after the third visit. "I can't continually take off work."

"You're being selfish," Gene complains, and I sulk, as much from my own physical problems as from his accusation.

■ ■ ■

I still felt pain in my wrist and knee. Occasionally, my knee buckled when I walked. At the end of June, I tried jogging a half mile. Compared to the six to ten miles I was accustomed to running, this brief exercise made me aware that I still had a problem. I made an appointment with an athletic trainer at the university, who told me I had torn cartilage and advised me to see a knee specialist as soon as possible since the cartilage might tear further.

I rushed home to tell Gene, my thoughts racing, my body numb. He'll know what to do. Maybe the trainer is wrong. But he sees these problems all the time. "This will ruin our vacation," I say, after telling Gene the news.

Gene replies calmly, "Make an appointment. Let's not panic until we have more information."

At the knee clinic the next day, Dr. Tension x-rays my knee and wrist. As he manipulates my leg roughly, he says little, other than to give commands gruffly. After studying my X rays, he reports, "I have good news and bad news. Which do you want first?"

"The bad."

"You do not have broken bones in your wrist," he replies, giving me the good news anyway. "It's just a bad sprain and will be fine."

"The bad news is you have torn cartilage in your knee. We'll do arthroscopic surgery, insert a tiny knife into a small incision and observe the inside on a TV monitor placed in another small incision. It's fairly painless and minor. Once we're in the knee, we can see if there's any other damage. I don't think so, but we can't be sure."

In a daze, I ask about recovery. "You mean will your knee be normal? No it won't," he says bluntly. My body quivers involuntarily. "A knee with something cut out of it will, by definition, never be normal. But you should be able to jog again," he continues, "with a custom-made knee brace. As for other activities, we'll have to wait and see."

I explain that I have planned to leave on a six-week vacation in two weeks and would like to wait until I return before having surgery. "Up to you," he says flippantly. "If it were my knee, I wouldn't wait. Schedule an appointment for whenever you want it." He walks out of the room.

Gene had driven me to the doctor and was waiting for me. His presence comforted me, and when I felt guilty that I didn't like accompanying him to the doctors, I rationalized that mine was a one-time problem. With him, pain was a constant. And he didn't have a full-time job. My excuses didn't make me feel better. I thought how often I was faced with making decisions that both protected my own freedom and showed caring and concern for Gene. How much did I have a right to expect for myself?

"Find out if you can have surgery this week," Gene says. "And recovery time. Maybe we can still leave in three weeks and take a three-week vacation." The nurse informed me that the next available time for surgery was three weeks away, on July 25, and that recovery usually required six weeks, during which I would be expected to see a physical therapist five times a week.

Since it was risky to wait and because I did not feel safe traveling in this condition, especially carrying Gene's seventy-pound oxygen tanks, we decided I should have surgery as soon as possible. We planned a short trip that could be canceled if necessary. A month after my surgery, Gene would go to New York, accompanied by a student. I would fly to San Francisco from Tampa to visit my friends. Gene and I would meet two weeks later in San Antonio.

While waiting for the surgery, I felt overwhelmed by our problems and began writing the notes that would form the basis for the rest of this book. My brother's death. Gene's illness. And now my body. There was nothing to count on anymore. My life felt like clashing cymbals. The notes I wrote provided the only possibility of muffling the clamor.

My first set of notes, on July 14, 1984, forced me to face up to my worst fears as I described Gene's alarm about going to New York without me. I acknowledged that my situation was as bad as I imagined.

My fears and anger centered on the "human condition." "Life has a lot of pain," I wrote. "I am an optimist, always have been, but it's getting harder. How does one find fulfillment with the pain?" Concluding that there was nothing unique about our situation, and that it was just one of life's possible scenarios, prevented me from being angry at Gene. Seeing myself as one among many fellow sufferers made me feel I was not alone in my pain and kept me from asking, "Why me?" "Why not me?" seemed just as appropriate.

I wrote stream-of-consciousness thoughts about my feelings—embarrassment, love, jealousy, commitment, martyrdom. I realized more fully that *Gene and I had switched roles.* Now I was the more powerful—advancing a career, making friends, in demand, healthy, while he was needy, demanding, dependent on me, and unhealthy.

Yet, writing also made me realize that I was being engulfed by Gene's tragedy. When I tell him how I feel, he responds, "Nothing will ever take you over. You are too strong." Then he points out all the ways I am in control: "I moved here to be with you. We bought a house, which was your idea. We take separate vacations, which you want. The list is endless."

He was right, but I still wanted to scream, "I can't take it anymore. Won't someone please listen?" No one wanted to hear about this tragedy with no happy ending, and presenting myself as a tragic figure didn't fit my image as a person who made others feel good. Although Gene read my notes and tried to help me with my feelings, I needed to talk to someone else. So, once again, I paid a therapist to listen, anything to regain some control over my world, which seemed to be running amok.

This time I went to therapy mainly to deal with my first midlife crisis. A few days before my first visit, I wrote: "I fear for my body. It has never given out before. I have never had to say, 'I can't do that anymore or I am too old for something.' I may not be able to play basketball again. It wasn't even that important. Yet, it is a loss. My knee may never be the same. At this moment, I have physically peaked or ended my peak. From now on there will be deterioration. So this is middle years."

Ken, the therapist, and I talk about aging and deterioration. "You know," he says bluntly, "at some point you'll have to figure out ways to get attention other than your appearance and physical ability."

We talk about my knee injury and the helplessness and vulnerability I feel. Ken asks, "Does this help you understand how Gene might be feeling?"

"Oh, yes, I think it's a big part of why I've been so easy and loving toward him recently. I've quit being mad about his illness, an anger which unfortunately got directed toward him. Now I feel only sadness and compassion."

Going to a therapist felt like pampering myself in a meaningful way. It meant I took my pain seriously enough to structure time to deal with it. In my physically vulnerable condition, Gene's illness seemed less manageable as well. When the therapist asked about Gene's health, I cried.

I tell Ken, "It's killing me to watch Gene deteriorate. Everyday he seems sicker, weaker. It's hard to say out loud that he is deteriorating. That's what I can't say to Gene. I don't want him to know I see it. I don't want to validate for him that it is actually happening. I don't want to force him to deal with his own deterioration and death. Nor do I want to help him cope with his demise." As difficult as it was to say this, I felt relieved, and I realized why I needed someone besides Gene to talk to.

"So what are you going to do for yourself?" Ken asks, handing me a Kleenex.

With that, it seemed reasonable to collude with Ken about making my own life better. With this session, I began to concentrate more fully on living on dual tracks. One track dealt with my relationship with Gene and centered on his illness and my response to it; the other focused on my life apart from Gene—taking care of myself, relationships after Gene died, my career, and my individual needs.

■ ■ ■

"What do people ask you about my health?" Gene asks, and continues when I don't respond, "Because I'm so sick, people don't ask me questions anymore. They ask you and now you don't tell me."

"Not many people say things to me about your health. Remember, I'm in this drama too. It would be in poor taste for people to ask too much. Anyway, I wonder if it might not be better if you don't know how others see you."

"What do you mean?" he asks, his eyebrows tensing together.

"You say that if others know your condition, it influences how they see you. Well, don't you think your knowing their questions and perceptions would influence how you present yourself?"

Even though it is a tough discussion, he grins. "Go on," he commands.

"For example, what if Ann [a friend and student whom Gene had paid to run errands] asked you if you were dying and how long you had to live? Then you saw in her eyes 'poor Gene.' How would that influence your interaction with her?"

"Well, what did you tell her?"

"No, this is hypothetical," I insist, hiding the truth.

"Well, what would you reply if she did?" he responds, playing the game.

"Most people," I hedge, "perceive you based on the information they get from the few friends I have confided in."

"What have you told them?" he asks, not letting me off the hook. "Do you tell them I'm dying?"

"I never tell anyone you're dying," I say, "because I understand that acknowledgment would make it more difficult for you. I tell them it's impossible to know."

"Yeah," he says, "if you tell them I'm dying, they'll feel they shouldn't get too close, because after all they don't know how long I'll be around."

"Besides that," I add, finding abstraction much easier, "what does saying you're dying mean anyhow? At what point do we define someone as dying? We're all dying."

"I guess you're right. But somehow this seems more real. And we're reminded of it every day."

I want to disagree, because it would make both of us feel better to define our situation as not different from others, but I don't. "The constant presence. It is different," I admit. "Having to plan for it. Not just by buying a cemetery plot, or making a will, but constantly calculating. And seeing the deterioration. But, it doesn't make sense to live life as a dying person."

"It doesn't, does it?" Gene responds. "At least not now. That's why we can't tell people I'm dying."

"Or even let ourselves believe it."

"Do you watch me? Do you look for little signs of deterioration?"

"Sometimes. I can't help it. I want to know how you're doing."

"Do you see them? The edema, the shakes, nodding off?" I tell him I do. Although he knows it already, his hurt expression makes me want to lie. Instead, I use his questions as an opening to remind him to be careful about his personal appearance. "Right now, for example, you have snot running out of your nose."

When he is embarrassed, I wonder why I am so honest. I just want him to be more careful in taking care of those things he can, I rationalize.

We talk about Gene's recent visit to the doctor, and Gene tells me Dr. Townson is surprised that he is able to come by himself. "See," he says to me, "I am still a tough fucker." Noticing how important validation is, I make a mental note to tell him how well he does. Then I am saddened by what a feat going alone to the doctor has become.

"He really doesn't tell me anything," Gene says, showing anger. "It frustrates me. Maybe he doesn't know anything. But he's seen people at this stage before. I want the whole truth."

Does he really?

I remember the time recently when Gene asked Dr. Townson how long he had. The doctor flippantly had replied, "It's possible you could still be like this in ten years. Some people are. Or you could die tomorrow." It was encouraging to pretend Gene might live for ten years. Maybe it was better to be lied to. We ignored "tomorrow."

■ ■ ■

First, there is the needle in my veins. Then, the two-hour wait for surgery during which I think of Gene's deterioration. I am glad for the Valium daze.

After the surgery, I sit in a chair in the recovery cubicle, wanting to sleep. My throat hurts. My knee throbs. I feel drugged. The next time I open my eyes, Gene and Ann are there. Feeling comforted, I smile, and immediately go back to sleep. A nurse wakes me again and tells me to put on my clothes and walk. I think she is kidding, but suddenly I am stumbling on crutches to the car. At home, I cling to the security of Gene's body beside me during the night.

The next day Gene drives me to the doctor. Since I don't want to deal with his problems getting there on his Amigo or have to explain to the doctor who he is, I do not ask him to come into the examining room. A twinge of guilt ricochets through me as I concentrate on getting myself to the examining room.

The doctor tells me they discovered a torn ligament while doing the surgery. "That complicates matters," he says. "This ligament, the cruciate, keeps your knee stable. You might continue to have problems. And you'll probably need a knee brace to jog. If it bothers you too much, you'll have to have major surgery."

When I tell Gene about the ligament, he embraces me for a minute in the waiting room, and says, "We'll work it out together." In the night, when I cry, Gene holds me and says, "Go ahead and cry for yourself. It's all right, you deserve it." I feel self-indulgent, then I sob, letting myself melt into his strong-feeling chest.

During the next few days, I try to be appreciative of what Gene does for me without making him feel he should do more, but his disability frustrates both of us. In the hours when no one is around to help, Gene and I are depressed about our conditions. It is unclear exactly who at this point should be taking care of whom. For the first time, I realize how many steps it takes to put together a meal already prepared and waiting in the refrigerator. Now I understand why Gene likes me to fix his meals. It is apparent now how much of the physical labor I normally do.

One day, when everything seems to go wrong, I tell Gene, "If you weren't here, friends would come to take care of me. With you here, they don't come and you can't help me."

"You're right," he says quietly. "I'm useless."

Why am I so cruel? "Come, let me hold you," I say tenderly, and he falls silently into my caress.

■ ■ ■

"No, we're doing fine," Gene says to my friend Becky, who has come by and offered to help. "Can I get you something to drink?"

As soon as Becky leaves, I lash out, "Why don't you let people help? You wait on them, and then you have no energy after they leave."

"I don't want to be seen as helpless," he says.

He understands my point and I realize how important it is for him to deny the severity of his limitation, growing more apparent the longer I depend physically on him. What I didn't understand then was that being an invalid was not part of my identity, while Gene was fighting being a man who couldn't take care of his sick partner.

Four days after surgery, we go out to dinner, since it seems easier than trying to prepare food. However, it is hard to shake my embarrassment as people stare at Gene's oxygen tank and my crutches, much more than they did when I looked normal and Gene was attached to oxygen. What a pair.

Much later, I viewed these feelings as representing a pattern. Why did I usually leave Gene to wheel out his Amigo, while I went into the grocery store alone? Was it really to save myself five or ten minutes, as I said? Or did I want to disassociate myself from the bizarre? Why did I get angry and resentful when he wanted me to carry his oxygen while it was attached to his nose? It wasn't that inconvenient. No, it directly connected me to the oddity. How much even then I cared about what other people thought. Being with Gene now made me feel that others saw me as part of a permanently disabled pair. We were freaks. No wonder I was so uncomfortable. No wonder we were irritable during dinner.

■ ■ ■

It is near 100 degrees and our air conditioner is broken. Gene sits while I walk on crutches to bring food. Why doesn't he set our places after I bring everything to him? That doesn't take breath. When I explode, he silently places the silverware, and immediately knocks over the sugar bowl. Cleaning it up takes all his energy. When I see sugar still on the table, I reprimand, "Look, there's still more there."

"I'll wash it off when I feel like it," he replies nastily. I start to cry and hobble to my bedroom—it's hard to stalk off on crutches. The sugar is just a symbol of life—one wrong move, and it is spilled and wasted, the sweetness gone. As usual, Gene comes in to comfort me.

Later that evening, we are watching a movie when he says he is nauseated. What more can happen? Gene wants a drink of seltzer to help release built-up gas from the retained carbon dioxide. Our refrigerator system—the top shelves are for items that he might need—has broken down. While trying to get the seltzer from the bottom shelf, he gets so distressed that he just sits down and moans, then yells, "Please, god. Seltzer." I know this is his way of psyching himself. But because I want to be angry, I respond as though he is asking me to get it for him. I feel numbness, disgust, and pity; he is a wounded animal. I turn off the sexually arousing movie we were watching on TV. As soon as Gene catches his breath, he says, "Sometimes you are so punishing. I can't help this."

I respond angrily, "I'm not trying to punish you." Am I? Maybe I am. It is hard to sleep when we don't talk or touch all night.

■ ■ ■

On Tuesday my doctor says I have developed phlebitis and must keep my leg elevated and wrapped in hot towels for three days. For the next few days, friends mysteriously arrive to take care of us. We hire a nurse's aid who fixes breakfast, cleans up, and prepares something simple for dinner, placing it near the front of the refrigerator. Now that the crisis is unambiguous, Gene seems willing to accept more help. I can't get up, so he either has to do what is needed when we are alone or it doesn't get done.

The phlebitis clears up and physical therapy begins. Gene insists on driving me to therapy each day and waiting, even though I can drive myself. Together we fight to regain control of our lives. I respond to feeling out of control by reasserting my will in every arena I can. I manage my temper to make life easier for us. I diet, thinking how pleased I will be at the end of this to be thinner. Since I can't go upstairs to my computer, I read novels, assuring myself that this will relax and ready me to work harder when I can get up. I begin to understand why control becomes more important to Gene the more his resources shrink.

Wrapped up in my own health, I am unaware of how much Gene goes downhill in those few months after my surgery. The only mention of any deterioration appears in notes I wrote on August 7, 1984: "My illness is pointing out to both of us how sick Gene really is. He seems to need more sleep now, and gets tired toward evening. The drugs—increased adrenalin—occasionally make him somewhat short. 'It won't leave me alone,' he says. Having students' dissertations to read keeps him from being so down."

Because I improve rapidly during the next ten days from daily physical therapy, I make reservations to go to San Francisco, as Gene and I had planned. Gene arranges for a student to fly to Tampa and accompany him to Stony Brook. After five days in Stony Brook, we will meet in San Antonio to deliver our paper on jealousy.

"Are you sure you won't go with me?" Gene asks. "I'm worried."

"I need to get away from your physical condition," I tell him. "I want to go to San Francisco to get nourishment from my friend."

The thought of having fun is a strong pull. I'm tired of the irritability—Gene's and mine. I'm tired of health problems—his and mine. I'm tired of identity crises—his and mine. Being away from each other would be good—at least for me. I rationalized that these "times away" helped me to deal with Gene's health as well as I did.

■ ■ ■

David, who has been my best friend since graduate school, picks me up at the San Francisco airport, and we spend the afternoon picnicking. Closely following my relationship with Gene, he has counseled me continuously over the years, pointing out options and possible outcomes. Gene probably is right when he says David's advice, much like my therapist's, deals only with my perspective and does not consider the "us"—him and me—as the most important unit.

Giving an account of Gene's condition, I describe how difficult it is to deal with the "new level," the first time I have acknowledged a new plateau. I think how difficult it must be for Gene to go through this crisis alone, without my support. "Do you want to explore how you feel about all this?" David asks.

"I don't think so," I respond. "I'd rather have a good time. I don't want to talk about my knee or Gene's deterioration." Sharing my sentiment, David also foregoes the opportunity to dissect his recent divorce. Instead, we discuss sociology and enjoy the scenery.

To be away from the stress of the last month is exhilarating. When David is busy, I enjoy casual conversations and sexual flirtations with other old friends. For a while now, sexual feelings have not been able to push through my pain and insecurities. This reminds me of how Gene, with his permanent disability, must feel. Sex has taken a backseat in our lives. My knee adds to the difficulty now. By the time we find a comfortable position—where Gene can breathe and I can extend my leg—the mood is gone. I recall how important sex had been initially.

Because I fear holding up other people, I walk faster than I can comfortably in San Francisco, sometimes going beyond my limits. Just like Gene does, I realize, surprised at the similarity. Often I walk the streets of Berkeley alone, feeling safe in spite of—no, because of—my disability. I do not think anyone will see me—a woman walking with a cane—as a sex object.

■ ■ ■

"Peter," I yell, "is that you?"

"Is that Carolyn?" the man asks, peering closely.

"What are you doing with a cane?" we both ask simultaneously, then discuss our mutual knee problems.

Peter is an old friend of Gene's. When he asks how Gene is doing, I reply that he is deteriorating. "I can't ask Gene, but I guess I can ask you. What's the prognosis? How long does he have?"

In a detached voice, I answer, "It's unclear. He's not going to die soon unless he gets a respiratory infection. He'll probably be around for a long time. Unfortunately, there is a big possibility that part of this time he'll be in bed on a respirator."

"This is a silly question, but how are his spirits?"

"Good. Unbelievably good. He wants to go out fighting."

"Beautiful, that's beautiful," Peter replies. Although I don't know what "go out fighting" means in practice, I know it will not be beautiful.

After this conversation, I feel uncomfortable with how I have portrayed Gene. Would Gene have wanted me to say he is doing great? But I can't tell a blatant lie. Have I said too much? Will Gene be upset? But I haven't said he is dying. Maybe I need to tell more of the truth than Gene wants. Sometimes I want sympathy for how bad he is doing (and by definition how well I am doing). I want to grieve with others who also feel the pain. Sometimes I get tired of carrying so much of this burden alone.

Later, I tell Gene about this conversation, thinking he will be pleased that I haven't revealed he is dying. "That was probably the worst thing you could have said," he responds. "I would rather be seen as 'could die any time' than as an 'invalid around for a long time needing to be taken care of.'" My jaws clench to prevent crying. How do I know what I am "supposed" to say? What is the "best" image anyway?

PART IV

Negotiating Loss

8

"I BARELY MADE IT through the proposal hearing," Gene tells me, sadly, when I phone him after three days apart.

"Let's talk about why you might be feeling so poorly," I offer. "Maybe there's something you can do. You're doing a lot physically?"

When he acknowledges that this is the price of staying alone, I tentatively suggest, "Maybe you should get help."

"There is mold in the house."

"Maybe you should move to another location."

"I don't want to impose on anyone. I feel dizzy, my head is swimming."

Tension fills my body and I want to believe Gene is making a big deal out of nothing. I hope that working with a student that afternoon will get his mind off his illness. "I'll call you tomorrow to see how you're doing."

In a forced but cheery voice, he replies, "Oh, don't do that. Just enjoy yourself. I'll be OK."

What if he doesn't pull out of this? Nonsense. He has been this bad before and it always lets loose. Often we don't know why, but he gets better. "Do you have people to call if you need them?"

"Yes, don't worry. I can call Joan. And Nora has been checking on me. I love you. Bye, bye. I'm OK."

■ ■ ■

"I'm in trouble," Gene says, when I call the next morning. "Real trouble."

My stomach knots as the panic in his voice alerts me that this is not just distress about a passing problem. Then my "how to deal with this" voice takes over. "What's going on?"

"I'm dizzy, exhausted. I can hardly walk. The oxygen debts [deficiencies] won't stop and I can barely breathe. My mind sometimes won't think clearly."

"Are you alone?"

"No, Robin is here. We're working together."

"How's that going?" I ask, relieved he isn't alone. How bad can he be if he's working? "Are you able to think with her?"

"Sometimes, I do fine. I'm brilliant, actually, aren't I, Robin?" I hear "yes" from the background. "Then my head clouds. I don't know what it is. Carolyn, it won't go away," he says, desperately.

Oh, no, he isn't even trying to hide his fear from Robin. Calm down, I say to my racing heart. He needs my help.

"I'm afraid I have congestive heart failure. Maybe my lungs are filling with water."

Is he serious? Or is he being overly dramatic? What should I do? "Gene, you have to go to a doctor," I say sternly. "Get Robin to take you."

"No, they'll kill me. Besides Robin has to leave in a while." Then, in a calmer voice, he says, "Maybe it's just carbon-dioxide poisoning. Not heart failure." Then panic again, "But I've never felt this way before."

"Don't let Robin leave," I plead. Calm down, Carolyn, I tell myself. The desperation in your voice will make him panic. I say more calmly, "If Robin leaves, promise you'll call Joan or Nora or someone."

"OK," he says softly, and I wonder if he means it.

"God, I love you," I say passionately.

"I love you, too."

"Don't you dare die on me, or I'll never forgive you." I hope I am joking.

He laughs lightly, "It's good to have contact with you. I'm not going to die. And we are going to make it to San Antonio."

Once I am off the phone, I write between tears: "I don't want him to die! I feel alternately numb and ready to scream. Calmness sets in after each piece of bad news."

A few hours later, I call Gene back. Sometimes lapsing from clarity into disorientation and confusion, he tells me what is happening. "I can't think straight," he says. When, in the silence, I hear his labored breathing and feel his distress, I breathe with him. A big gasp on intake. I don't hear the air come out. Then in again. Each time it sounds like there is less room for oxygen to enter his lungs. I hold my nose to imagine what suffocation must feel like. Stop it, Carolyn. Concentrate on problem solving. "I can't talk now," he says in exhaustion.

"OK, baby, I'll call back later."

■ ■ ■

"What's going on?" I ask John, Nora's husband, and wonder why he has answered Gene's phone.

"Gene's in the hospital," he responds. "Nora went with him. The doctors insisted on admitting him. I was told to wait here for Gene's oxygen delivery. That's all I know."

Desperate, I ring the switch board at University Hospital and ask for the emergency room. Assuming they won't tell me anything, I am determined to push. "Yes, Dr. Weinstein is here. He's resting comfortably. Just a minute and I'll let you speak to the person with him."

I cry at my success when Nora cheerfully says, "Hello." In a reassuring tone, she continues, "Everything's OK. They're giving him medications through his veins. It's helping. We're waiting for an available room and eating Chinese food."

"Is he really bad?"

"He was. He was having trouble breathing and was a little disoriented. Robin said he would be fine for a while when he was helping her and then he would have trouble."

"That's exactly what he told me," I say, exuberant that he is in touch enough to describe accurately what is going on. "Tell him I love him."

"I will. Now don't worry. It all seems under control. Maybe he just needs some rest. I'll call you if there's news."

"Thanks, Nora. And thanks for being there."

■ ■ ■

"Hi, baby," Gene says cheerfully when I answer the phone. It's 11:30 P.M., which is 2:30 A.M. his time. I choke back sobs. Is he being cheerful just for me? Who cares? At least he's able to fake it. "Don't worry," he says, "I'm going to be OK." He is coherent and seems rested and relaxed. I sense the "old Gene" when he says with pride, "They were shocked I had never been in the hospital before. See, I'm not a wimp."

"I know you aren't darling," I say, hearing love in my voice.

"I don't know how to think about this. Am I being dramatic? Maybe I'm just exhausted," he says, as though that explains it all. "And it caused a buildup of carbon dioxide. I, too, am a casualty of your basketball injury."

I swallow my defensive retort and say, "I guess we didn't pay much attention to your health the last month, since we were so busy taking care of me."

Gene says, "In a few days, I'll be fine, and I'm still going to meet you in San Antonio."

"That's asking too much of your body. But," I add, so he will feel in control, "that's for you to decide." We talk of the intensity of our feelings for each other. "I have never loved you more," I say.

"Yeah, fear of loss—it's amazing how it makes us appreciate what we have."

I ask him about the events leading to hospitalization. "After talking to you the last time," he explains, "I called Joan and we talked for over an hour about what I should do. I decided that I should at least go to the emergency room to be checked out, so I asked Nora to ride with me. I told her it was no emergency, but I wanted to see if they could give me something to make me feel better."

"You drove?"

"Yes, I insisted."

"I guess I know the rest," I say, still wanting more clues to his condition.

I sleep lightly that night and, hoping for improvement, call Gene at 7:30 the next morning. Out of breath and distressed, he sounds much worse than the night before. "I went to the bathroom," he says. "And I could barely get back. I had a huge oxygen debt. I feel so spacey. Like I've been poisoned."

"Gene, darling, I'm coming there."

"No," he replies, emphatically. "Don't come. Wait and go to San Antonio on Saturday like you planned and then come here afterward on Wednesday if you must. It'll do me good to relax and be taken care of for a few days. I'll be OK. Plenty of people are checking on me."

"We'll talk about it."

I hang up and cry. He is less loving this morning and doesn't want me to come there. Doesn't he love me? Of course, but he is trying to be strong and not disrupt my plans. In the shower, I have trouble thinking clearly. He seemed so good last night, but so bad this morning. I have to go there.

Nora calls at 9:00 A.M. from the hospital. "He's better now," she says. "His color is back and he seems more comfortable."

"Do you think I should come?"

"I don't know. It's unclear how bad he is." But unless a miracle takes place in the next hour, I already know I'm going.

At eleven, Joan calls to tell me she has talked to Gene's doctor, but he has told her little. When she informed the doctor about my relationship with Gene, he questioned our marital status and then asked for the name of a relative. "What should I tell him?" Joan asks.

"Oh, my, we don't want them calling his mother."

Joan agrees.

"Why do they need a relative's name now?" I ask, fearing they think he might die.

"There's some talk of a respirator. They will need a relative to make the decision."

"You mean I can't?" My world closes in. "A respirator? Now? Would that be permanent?" I ask, trying to remember what I know about respirators and inhalators.

Joan responds, "It's unclear. I asked them whether it would be permanent, but I'm not sure of the answer. I've made an appointment with the doctor for you to call at three o'clock today. I think he'll tell you more than he will the rest of us."

Joan continues, "Nora just saw him and called me. She's scared because sometimes he loses touch with reality." She says the last part softly.

"Loses touch?" I ask. "He hasn't done that with me. He was coherent over the phone. And he just worked with Robin yesterday and supposedly that went OK. And Nora said he was quite helpful even though Robin said he was slow at times. But that's all, Joan, just slow. Maybe she said disoriented, but there was no mention of losing touch with reality."

Joan says, "I'm going there. Nora shouldn't have to handle all this."

After I hang up, my head pounds. Not married? Somebody has to decide about a respirator. I'm not his wife. I can't decide. Why can't he make the decision? It's his life. Losing touch with reality. Maybe he's incapable of making it. Oh, my god. It's much worse than I thought. I've got to get there. Why didn't Nora tell me this? Maybe she didn't know it this morning. Or maybe he got worse after that. Are they keeping things from me? Or maybe it's easier to let Joan tell me. No, they seem to be telling all. And I just talked to him.

Between my outbursts of sobbing, I tell David, who has arrived, what is happening. I have no desire, or ability, to control the tears. Please don't die. Memories of my brother and death soar through my head.

David comforts me while I cry. "It's too soon for this stage," I tell him.

"I know," he says, switching into a rational mode. "I think this is temporary, but it doesn't matter because even if it is, it foreshadows the future. So even if it isn't as bad as you think now, it will be."

I let this sink in a little and say, "I guess it will always seem too soon, won't it?"

David makes a list as he encourages me to think about what I have to do. Call the travel agency, pack, call the doctor from airport, call Joan back. Between tears, plans are made.

■ ■ ■

"I'm coming, baby. I want to be there with you," I say when I call Gene. I take a deep breath and try not to sound worried.

"Why are you panicking? I'm getting better."

Doesn't he realize the seriousness of this? "I just want to be there with you."

"What about our paper? You have to deliver the paper."

I answer calmly, "If necessary, I can fly to San Antonio from New York to give the paper."

"If you have to come, come tomorrow," he pleads. "I don't want you to see me like this," he blurts out, now close to tears.

Shocked that he is hiding his condition from me, now I must face that he is as bad as everyone is saying. "Why the show for me? Baby, let me be your partner in this," I plead, lovingly.

"OK, come," he yells with relief and love in his voice.

I smile and release the breath I didn't know I was holding. "I'll be there before you know it."

Then he backs off again. "What can you do here?"

"Take control and take care of you."

"Lots of people are taking care of me."

"But not like I can. If you won't let me do it for you, let me do it for me. I need to be there." I know he wants me to come, but he doesn't want to admit it. Is he still trying to give me an out?

"OK," he says finally in a gentle, loving voice.

"You're going to like my being there," I say softly.

■ ■ ■

After getting a seat assignment, I spend a few minutes at the airport writing down questions to ask the doctor. Then, ignoring my queasy stomach, I take a deep breath and dial. Be in control, I say to myself. To get information, I have to handle this properly—ask the right questions, not break down, not let my anxiety show. This is like gearing up to give a public presentation. I ask the female voice who answers to page Gene's doctor, noting to her that this has been prearranged.

After a five minute wait and introductions, the doctor begins, "It is unbelievable that he has not been in a hospital before. His CO_2 level is so high that it is poisonous."

"What's causing it?"

"Part of the problem might be allergens. The ragweed is bad here right now."

"What are the possible courses of action?" I ask, using doctor talk.

"If I can stabilize him in twenty-four hours, we will continue giving him steroids and other medications through his veins. Otherwise," he hesitates, "we'll have to intubate him."

"Is this permanent?"

"No, people can get off the machine. But I don't like to intubate until we have to, because once lung muscles relax, they tend to give up more easily the next time."

"How would he be connected?"

"The tube can go down his throat or his nose."

"How does this differ from being on a respirator?"

"A respirator would require a tracheotomy, cutting a hole in his throat." I cringe. It sounds like an understatement when he continues, "It's not aesthetically pleasing."

"Would he still be able to talk?"

"The hole must be covered to talk. Of course, then he can't breathe while he is speaking. But he might want to have a tracheotomy anyway so he can then be plugged into a respirator when necessary."

When I try to imagine it, I feel nauseated and say to myself, "There will be plenty of time to draw pictures. Clear your mind. Think about what you need to ask."

"Are there dangers?"

"Infections can occur."

I'm glad he answers my questions honestly. I don't want to add figuring out the truth to my already overloaded agenda.

The doctor continues, "I will proceed then with radical treatment. Do you agree?"

Everything is happening too quickly. "I will want to discuss it with Gene," I say. "We make decisions together."

"I see," he says hesitantly. Does his response mean we don't have time? Or does it indicate that I won't be the one making decisions?

Before I lose my confidence, I rush into the next topic. "It was mentioned to you that Gene and I are not legally married. But we do have a marital relationship, and we've been together for eight years."

"We'll need the name of another relative then."

"I want to be the person who makes the decision," I say, "with him, I mean. His closest relative is his seventy-seven-year-old mother."

"I really should refer this to the hospital social workers, but they won't be available over the weekend." I hear urgency in his voice. "Let's see. In New York, seven years is a common-law marriage." Silence. Then, "I will consider you his wife. You can give consent."

I finally breathe. "Thank you. Could you get me connected to Gene's room?" He says he'll try.

When I suddenly hear Gene say, "Social Science Annex," I laugh. When he sounds much better than I had imagined, I experience several realities simultaneously. Gene tells me he feels better and that his friends Joan and Gina are with him.

"I'm on my way, baby," I say. "I'm at the San Francisco airport."

"Joan will pick you up. You can stay at her house." At least he's well enough to organize things.

"I talked to your doctor," I say, and then wonder how I will respond to Gene's questions. I don't want to hide anything if he seems well enough to deal with the information.

When he asks what was said, I respond, "He's optimistic," and I say it twice to give myself time to think. "But if in twenty-four hours you're not better, we have decisions to make."

"You mean intubation?"

"Yes. I told the doctor that we would make any decisions together. He considers me your wife."

"I don't want this to happen here," he says in a fearful voice. "I want to get back to Florida."

"We'll get you there," I say, glad he feels this way.

"I love you so much," Gene says, and I know he means it.

"I love you so much too. When I get there, I want the biggest kiss I've ever had."

"You'll get it."

I ask to talk to Joan, and am aware that my tone changes. "There is a chance of a respirator," I say.

"Oh, no," Joan responds quietly, trying to cover up her alarm, while Gene talks to a nurse.

We built a facade to some extent, pretending to tell Gene everything; we smoothed out rough edges to make his condition seem better than the messages we received. I rationalized this stance: When I arrive there and can figure out how much he can handle, I want to be as honest with him as he can stand. But knowing so little about his physical or mental state, we need to exercise a little caution now. At the same time, I felt disloyal when I remembered we were dealing with his body, his life. Feeling cut off from him this way was strange since we were used to sharing almost everything.

Gene returns to the phone. "I'm another casualty of basketball," he says, for the second time. "See, I told you I was bad off."

"I believe you," I say, resisting the impulse to question the basketball connection. "I did then, too. But I have always wanted to push you, even knowing that one day we would push too far. I hope you aren't sorry."

"No, you were wonderful. The best. I can't wait to see you," he says, like a little kid being promised a present.

After I hang up, I feel no guilt about the basketball injury. It couldn't be helped then. And it can't be changed now. At some point, Gene would have gotten worse, basketball injury or not. Who knows what actually has caused his deterioration. This might be the "natural progression" of the disease.

I feel overwhelmed by my love for him. We are in this together. And, I am resolved to see it to the end. When I remember the problems associated with not being legally married, I make a note to think through how to solve these. Then I write: "I want to be his wife, to have been his wife. Right now I want it desperately."

I am shocked by my thoughts. Then I am not. I continue writing: "Talking to the doctor, facing that he might die, may be the low point of my entire life."

■   ■   ■

Flying from San Francisco to New York gives me time to examine my life. What Gene and I have dreaded for so long is finally happening. "No, it's not," I whisper. "This is a false alarm." But the fear in my gut alerts me that this time, more than any other, I'm not sure. I feel nervous, then hollow and numb, as I anticipate disaster. How can I stand this?

Grabbing a pen and paper, I write down events of the last twenty-four hours. It has helped before. Anything. Anything, I think, that will focus my thoughts, calm my emotions. I write all the way across the continent, on note pads, the back of deposit slips, and then borrow paper from the people next to me. I am obsessed with documenting my feelings and thoughts.

Gene and I have talked about and planned for The End. But now? August 1984. It can't be happening now. "So what makes this time sacred?" I ask myself. "Nothing," I answer. "So face it, Carolyn. Maybe now is the time." My gut sinks lower; my stomach feels more hollow. All my internal systems are in battle, some slowing, others speeding, all needing release from stress. Oh, god, I shouldn't have let him go to Long Island alone.

I record and then refuse to think about my feelings. Instead, I return to writing the details of what has occurred so far, an exercise that helps sort out what I know from what I guess and distances me from the experience. It seems sensible to make a project out of this, to pretend that something positive is happening. Writing soothes me. Recording the events frees my mind and body to relax. Knowing that the details are recorded keeps me from going over and over them, to see if I can force a different outcome. Reliving what happened just makes the situation appear worse, and then the panic returns. I do not have enough information to be sure of anything, I assure myself. I still hope for a miracle, to wake up from a dream, or to find that this is a morbid joke.

When I arrive in New York at midnight, Joan and I embrace a long time without saying much. Then we put down her convertible top and drive the sixty miles to Stony Brook.

Joan has figured out how to get into the hospital at any hour. I leave my cane in the car so as not to draw attention to us. We walk confidently through the only open door.

As I walk down the long corridor, fear of how Gene will have changed slows down my bodily processes and my breathing becomes shallow. When I enter his room, he looks weak and sick surrounded by IVs and oxygen tubes, but his eyes sparkle when he sees me. As we kiss and I hold his hand, he says he is glad I am there. Only then do I greet Gina, who has been reading while Gene sleeps. Is it a death watch? Gene dozes off and on, tossing his head, waking to smile at me standing beside his bed. Show me you're OK, I want to yell. His breathing is even more labored than usual, and he doesn't have enough energy to talk. Is he worse? Or, just not pretending now?

When he starts to sleep more soundly around 3:00 A.M., we go to Gina's for a drink. We talk about things, saying little about Gene. I want to talk about him, but there isn't much to say.

I am glad when Joan stays with me at Gina's house. "I don't want him to die," I say to her, crying.

"This is so unfair. You're too young to be dealing with death of a partner," Joan says, comforting me. I appreciate her concern, and I want to care for her in return, but I lack the strength and am glad she does not seem to need it. We find the other's presence and our mutual love for Gene comforting. I don't feel alone now, but I feel numb—a state I will feel often in the next seven months.

■ ■ ■

The next morning, Joan and I go early to the hospital. Knowing that soon I will be in charge, I watch Joan's routines. She keeps juice and special foods for Gene in the staff refrigerator across the hall and uses their stove to heat his food.

Gene is used to a flow of five to eight liters of oxygen when he moves around; he is getting only 1.5 liters. The doctors now say the high CO_2 that results from high oxygen intake is the source of his problem. A nurse reminds us, "Absolutely do not turn up the oxygen."

But he is always uncomfortable. His breathing is shallow, he feels he is suffocating. "Check the oxygen," he demands over and over. "Something is wrong. I'm not getting any," he moans. We take the tubes off his face and blow into the nose piece, feeling the resistance of the flow. When we learn to put the nose piece in water, the bubbles dancing from the opening make him feel secure.

Urinating is an adventure. Attached to a pole carrying his IV bottles, Gene walks across the room to the bathroom. Joan pushes the pole, attempting to stay near him. I carry the oxygen hose, at first reverently, as though it is a bridal train. But the mood is lost as the hose snags on the bed table, then the corner of the bed, and finally, victoriously, pulls the plant off the window ledge. Next, Gene gets tangled in the cords extending in every direction from the pole, and his head jerks back. Then, the slack between his IVs and the pole carrying the dripping bags pulls taut, and the IV-needles bulge, threatening to erupt out of the purple blotches on his arm. The bridal party becomes more like a comedy act; then, I shudder, like a funeral procession. Gasping for air, Gene yells, "You're not doing it right. Help." We do not take his rage personally, and, quickly, he begs forgiveness. We sneak up the oxygen flow; otherwise, he will not make it back to bed.

How will I get him home?

■ ■ ■

"I am cautiously optimistic," Dr. Simpson says, after examining Gene. "Your CO_2 levels are down a little, but you still are exchanging almost no air. You will be in here at least a week," he says in response to Gene's question. In the hall, he tells me quietly, "He's not out of the woods yet." I assume that means that he still might die.

There is constant activity with RNs and LPNs who check the oxygen, IVs, and temperature, and give medication. Gene looks forward to the respiratory therapists who arrive every four hours to give nebulizer treatments and to gauge his exchange of air. He feels better immediately after a treatment, but blowing into a peak-flow meter to see if the oral treatment of bronchial dilator has opened up passageways exhausts him. Soon his breathing is again shallow, and a nauseous feeling accompanies his everpresent headache.

When visitors come, he perks up to present his situation optimistically. "Just not enough air in the air," he says, and laughs. "I needed a little rest." But it is too hard to put on a front for long, and he grows weary, sometimes dozing off during the attempt.

When Gene is distressed, signaled by moans and groans or silence, I engage visitors in conversation. I resent then that I can't give Gene my full attention. I crave more time alone with him and grow tired of being on stage. But since Gene seems to like company, I encourage people to come. I want him to feel that people care. When I ask if he enjoys the company, he says, "Not always. I feel horrible when I can't be cheerful. Sometimes making them comfortable takes too much energy."

After twelve hours, Gene encourages me to go and enjoy myself. But my visit with friends feels like a wake and I am glad to return to Gina's house. I can't write, because I fear writing will reduce the welcomed distance between me and my feelings. A few days later, when I finally record the events of these days, I write: "Even now, I can't express my feelings. I can only record events." The sole state of feeling that I mention is numbness.

■ ■ ■

Gene cannot get into a comfortable position the next day. What if he is always uncomfortable? What if he never gets better? Or gets worse? He is going to get worse. I am shaken from my thoughts by Gene's panicked yell as the oxygen tube falls from his nose. I can't think about the future now.

"I can't breathe," Gene says over and over. I move his pillow, adjust his bed, raise his feet, lower them, raise his head, lower it. Nothing seems to make him feel better for long. He is a grouch, then he apologizes. I help him into a chair. Then I do my knee exercises on his bed.

Looking forward to his "treatment," he monitors his watch. With rare exceptions, our conversations deal with his health—how he feels or how long it is before the respiratory therapist will come. Each time a nurse enters, we ask about his latest carbon dioxide and oxygen readings, measured through blood samples several times a day, but the levels change little. Today he can't even get the peak-flow meter to register before the treatment. When he blows as hard as he can into the device afterward, he watches the technician expectantly. Since she is turned toward the light, only I see the alarm on her face. "Rest for a little and try again," she encourages. Disappointment breaks through on Gene's face. When the needle barely moves the second time, I am glad when she fibs, "It's a better reading this time." Even so, he is disappointed that the fake reading she tells him is not as good as the reading the day before. The treatments are doing little to get any movement of air through his lungs.

Following the exhaustion after the peak-flow test, the evening meal comes. Gene pushes the food away after a few bites. "It takes too much energy to eat," he apologizes. But when I get the chicken soup Nora had made for him, his face brightens and he eats hungrily. It tastes good and requires no chewing. I feed him because it takes less of his energy, and because the contact makes us feel close. I want to sob, but this is not the time or the place. When my throat contracts, I swallow. When contractions occur in my stomach, I take deep breaths. Instead of crying, I eat the food on his tray. I am losing weight, but not nearly as fast as Gene who has dropped ten pounds, now weighing a scrawny 138. I watch Gene's thin body toss and tumble, then doze.

Occasionally, we have a close moment when we aren't consumed by the illness. I touch and caress him then, and I am delighted when in the middle of his agony he has an erection and an orgasm. I get into bed with him afterward, unconcerned finally about what the nurses will think.

"I love this," he says. "You make the struggle worth it."

"Me, you, too. In fact, I have been thinking I want to marry you," I say, trying out what I wrote in my notes in the San Francisco airport, unsure if I mean it or just want to make him feel good.

The pleasure on his face belies his response, "I'm too sick now. Why do you want to marry a sick man?"

"Because I love you. Thinking of losing you has made me realize how much."

He kisses me gently, "It just doesn't seem right. Then I'd be your responsibility. And you'd have to bury me. But I like that you think about it."

We move to more immediate issues. "My health has been going downhill for three months," he says.

"And I didn't see it—couldn't," I reply. "Gene, I'm so sorry. Maybe there was something we could have done."

He silences my lips with his finger. "And maybe not."

"What about when we get home? We're going to need help."

"I guess so. Someone to come in a few afternoons a week."

"I guess we should see what your insurance will cover," I say. "I'll do that."

I try not to raise too many problems at once, since he concentrates mostly on the moment at hand. It is my job to get him to Florida and figure out how to manage once we are there. My head goes in all directions, seeking information. But I must wait to see how he recovers. My mind skips over "if."

▪ ▪ ▪

The next day, Gene's doctors talk to us about respirators and inhalators. The difference, they say, is that an inhalator is usually temporary and requires a tube down the nose or mouth through the vocal cords, meaning that the person cannot talk. Or the tube can go in through a tracheotomy, which then must be covered to talk. A more permanent device, a respirator, can be plugged in through this opening. Gene's regular supply of oxygen also can enter through the tracheotomy. Repeating what Dr. Silverman told us, the doctors say this is much more efficient than oxygen administered through his nostrils.

When the doctors leave, Gene says, "I don't want the tracheotomy if I can help it."

"I agree. You don't need this now."

When I leave that night, Gene still has not "broken through." His CO_2 has decreased, but not enough. Tracheotomies, inhalators, anything is still possible. I sleep soundly that night, an exhausted sleep, and awake with a start that comes from waking up into a nightmare.

Our days become routinized. I arrive at the hospital and help him eat breakfast, wash up, walk to the bathroom, and put on a clean gown. Today we wash his hair, while he leans back in a chair.

Uncharacteristically, Gene gets irritable with hospital staff and refuses to take any more exhausting peak flows even when a respiratory therapist tells him he must. The next day, he says no to a chest X ray, "Because," he explains, "I cannot get from bed to table and back again."

That afternoon I experience the first of many therapeutic buying sprees. What difference does it make? People die. I deserve it. I call Gene, who delights in helping me decide on gifts for people who have helped him. Then I tell Gene about some soothing chimes. "Buy them. I'll pay," he says, and then he encourages me to spend more. "What are we waiting for?" he asks. While we have never been tight with money, we don't usually spend this freely. For a few minutes during and after my purchase, I feel joyous and forget about our problems.

I eat a bagel and discover that starchy foods, especially bland ones, have a soothing effect. I begin to listen closely to my body.

■　■　■

Back at the hospital, Gene and I talk about the seriousness of our situation, our love, the possibility of not having much more time together. "What will we do about the paper we are supposed to give?" I ask.

"I still think you should fly there on Tuesday, give it on Wednesday, and then fly back here. Or better yet," he says after thinking a while, "fly on to Florida. Then I'll join you when I can. That way I won't have been any real trouble for you."

"Do you really think that's what I should do?" I ask, hopefully.

When he says yes, I check on flights to San Antonio, but in the middle of a conversation, I hang up. "I don't want to leave you." He smiles and sighs, but doesn't resist.

Because his CO_2 has gone down a little, the nurse increases his oxygen from 1.5 to 2.5 liters. Immediately, he is less light-headed. Dare I be optimistic? This has happened many times already, followed by a downhill battle. Then a nurse sticks Gene with a needle several times to find a vein big enough to get more blood. "Is it worth it?" he asks me, halting my optimism.

Later that evening Gene records a temperature of 99.8 degrees. "Perhaps an infection has caused all this," he says encouragingly, and I wish it were that simple. The nurse comes in and, without saying anything, turns the oxygen down to 1.5. It is her job; it is Gene's life. "His CO_2 is up again," she explains, which means his lungs aren't exchanging much air.

"I feel so much better when the oxygen is higher," Gene says, close to tears.

■ ■ ■

As soon as I arrive the next morning, Gene announces, "I feel shitty." I kiss away his tears and hold his hand, then ask about his physical symptoms. "I want the oxygen turned up. That would make me feel better."

"No, it's not a good idea," I reply. "We have to trust the doctors' judgments. That's all we've got."

Our doctor in Florida has suggested belladonna for Gene. "It's a poison," the Stony Brook doctor tells us, "but is not given in harmful amounts. It comes in the form of atropine, and works as an anticonstrictor as opposed to a bronchial dilator. There are some risks, but I think they're worth taking." We are ready to try anything.

I take the opportunity to have a private talk with the doctor while the respiratory therapist administers atropine to Gene. Gene has insisted that the doctors talk to him. When a staff member says something to me in his presence about him, Gene rebuffs, "I'm not a him. My name is Gene and I can talk and hear." It embarrasses me a little, yet I find it amusing. I sympathize with his feeling that people treat patients as deaf, dumb, and childlike.

"Gene is still not out of the woods," the doctor confides as we talk in the hall. "The atropine is in many ways the last thing before an inhalator. It's going to upset his stomach," he announces.

"Maybe we shouldn't suggest that to him," I say, and he agrees. It isn't that the doctor tells me much he doesn't tell Gene, it's the way he tells me. There is always hope when he talks to Gene; with me, he admits that Gene still faces imminent death. With Gene, he always has something else to try; with me, he is pessimistic that there is anything, short of an inhalator, that will work.

As soon as Gene inhales the belladonna, he feels better, and the peak-flow meter shoots up from its usual baseline reading. Smiling and optimistic for the first time in days, Gene announces to a surprised doctor, "I have broken through." He is better than I have seen him since I arrived, and he heartily eats lunch.

Gene is still doing well later that evening, although his stomach is upset. I don't suggest that it might be from the new medication. Maybe this is the best we can do.

"I really admire you," he tells me lovingly, "and the way you are handling this."

"Do you really?" I ask, feeling proud.

"Yes, I feel so loved and cared for. And I haven't had to worry about you."

"It's been hard."

"I know. And I want to help you. When I can," he adds cautiously.

"I admire you too and how you're coping. You have everything I have to deal with, and more, and you have the physical discomfort." Gene's eyes brighten. He is pleased too. "I can't believe how much I love you now," I say.

"Me either," he responds. "Your love has gotten me through this. I don't know what I would have done without it. Maybe the worst is over."

"I hope so," I respond. Please god, let this hold, I whisper to myself. Just a little more time.

On Thursday, I sleep late and feel happy as I awake. When I call Gene, he says he is doing OK. I reach a new level of optimism, and I take my time getting to the hospital. This feels manageable now. Yet how horrible this improved level of health would have seemed just two weeks ago.

When Gene says after breakfast that he is not feeling well, I panic, and then recall that often he doesn't feel well after eating a large meal. Now it seems to happen after any food intake. Just as I relax, Gene tells me he has problems with diarrhea. It is always something, I say silently. But I am relieved it is only this. Is this too coming from the atropine? When he is unable to make it to the bathroom in time, he cries out in anger, "I feel like a vegetable." The anger is a good sign. He has not had enough energy to be angry in the last week.

I cry with him. "It's not so bad," I say. "Just a little shit."

"How can you love me?"

"I just do."

"I don't know how, but I'm glad," he says lovingly. I feel good about what I feel and the way he and I are relating. More and more I am able to handle what happens, even though I am scared to death.

■　■　■

"I want to tell you about the discussion I had with your doctor when I was in the San Francisco airport," I say to Gene a few hours later when it seems he is well enough to handle it.

When I mention radical treatment, Gene says, "Radical treatment? You mean they thought about putting me on a respirator? I wasn't that bad."

"You faded in and out," I remind him. Shocked, he refuses to believe me. Then he tries to remember the sequence of events leading to hospitalization, and can't.

Suddenly acknowledging the seriousness of his condition, he says, "We have to make this easier for you. You can retreat from the pain any time you want. I understand."

I like that he is thinking about me, and say, "I don't need to retreat. For some reason, I don't need to hold back my feelings. I want to be here with you. I can stand the pain."

"I want to get well so bad," he says, with tears in his eyes. "I want more time together."

"I miss you physically, especially the cuddling," I say.

"But I don't have the energy."

"I know," I say sadly. "But maybe it'll come back."

Gene feels, in his words, "rotten," the next day. When that sinking, numb feeling threatens to visit me, I think, "Carolyn, put this in perspective. For the last few years he has complained about feeling rotten almost every morning. It is apparent that he is better compared to the first week in the hospital. This is a 'normal' cycle."

The doctors say his CO_2 reading of fifty-nine is much better than they ever hoped to achieve. This level is the same as it was in June, the last time it was measured before coming to New York. They tell us he can go home in five days.

That night I get into bed with Gene, and he has enough energy to hold me for the first time since entering the hospital. "This is the most loving we've ever been," he says. I feel it too. "You thought you were losing me, didn't you?" When I nod yes, I feel tears flow down my cheeks.

"Did you cry on the plane when you were coming here?" When I tell him I did, it brings tears to his eyes. "I don't want to cause you pain."

My sensitive, caring Gene is back. I let go and sob. Nobody can comfort me like Gene. My pain doesn't scare him. It makes him feel loved. What relief.

Now I can return to Tampa.

9

"HI, BABY," Gene says cheerfully as he gets out of his van and grabs the oxygen cannula I bring to him. After a quick embrace, I carry the portable tank while he walks unassisted the ten yards to the front door. I have missed him during the week I have been back in Tampa alone teaching my classes.

"Your smile is great," I say.

"You should see yours," Gene replies. "And the sparkle in your eyes. Let's go out back. I want to feel the sunshine on my body." Unable to stay apart, we keep touching. He is my Gene again.

"You look good," I say. "Except you're skinny."

"I finally weigh less than you," he kids. I shudder as I look at his six-foot, one-inch frame that now carries slightly over 130 pounds.

We have cheese and champagne on our patio as we talk about making the best of this situation. When we relive the crisis, much is still blurry to Gene. As I tell him how I felt in San Francisco, he holds my hand, attentive to every word, feeling my emotion. A sob rises from his throat, "Oh, my darling. How horrible it must have been for you."

"And then I decided I wanted to marry you."

He smiles, "I'm so glad you love me like this. It makes life worth living. You haven't pulled away as I feared; quite the opposite, you have showered me with love."

"I'm not ready to die," Gene says suddenly. "I want more time to experience life and be with you."

We discuss Gene's "new level" of health, which represents a tremendous drop in functioning. "We'll deal with it," I say.

"How did it happen so fast?" he asks, and then he answers. "I suspect the natural deterioration of the lung led to little oxygen being exchanged. Then the buildup of carbon dioxide poisoned my system."

"The doctor said carbon dioxide also came from exhaustion," I say. "You have to be careful not to tire yourself out. And, watch the codeine."

Codeine had taken the place of marijuana as a bronchial dilator, because it didn't yet have bad aftereffects and, in addition to aiding his breathing, it calmed him and temporarily got rid of his many aches. But doctors had warned him to ration it, because the drug also would slow his breathing.

Gene grieves anew for the failure of the "kick-ass" philosophy that has sustained him until now. "It's hard to think that I can't do that anymore. I don't know if I can sit back and be careful."

"I'll help you stay healthy," I assure him. "I want you around as long as possible. We also need to get a nurse when I'm busy."

"I guess, but just someone to go out in the world with me when you're at school, maybe two or three days a week."

"But I need time to work in my office upstairs on the days I'm home."

"I'll be OK then."

My knee problem had caused a major delay in reaching my December 1 deadline on my book. It was already September and, since May, I had completed only two of seven chapters. Wondering how I could be thinking about book deadlines when I could lose Gene any day, I say, "I'm concerned about finishing my manuscript, but I also want to spend time with you."

"We can do both," he replies. "I'll help you edit. The worst that happens is you don't make the deadline."

I suddenly recognize the reality the deadline has taken on. "I guess you're right," I say. "But to motivate me, I'll work as if the deadline is fixed. If I don't make it, I don't make it. Time with you is more important."

"What happens," I continue, changing the subject, "if you get too sick to take care of yourself?"

"When I'm helpless, I want to kill myself," Gene says, echoing the same attitude he has displayed for a few years. "I'll take pills. Will you help if I am unable to get to the pills?"

"Sure," I say. "But I want to make sure I'm protected." When I remind myself that I need to write the Euthanasia Society for legal information, it feels like just one more chore.

"Would you go to a nursing home?" I ask.

"I wonder what it would be like."

"I have this image of coming to see you every night and having loving conversations."

"But there would be only old people and me."

"And everyone would be sick," I add. No, we both agree, we don't want that. "I want you at home," I say, "where I can take care of you."

"Do you really?" His eyes light up.

I picture him in bed at home, reading, with a nurse by his side. When I relieve the nurse, Gene and I hold hands and talk. I never want to put him in a nursing home. What I don't know is that a peaceful death at home will not happen either.

"The steroids have destroyed my muscles," Gene says, pulling the flabby skin on his arm. While in the hospital, his steroids were increased from ten units every other day to sixty units every four hours. Now he takes sixty units a day, which he quickly must reduce.

Gene agrees when I say, "I think it's time to take over the decision making about your medicine. We have enough knowledge, and we are in tune with your body twenty-four hours a day. The doctor's advice can serve as a general guideline."

"I don't want to go back to the hospital," says Gene. "Those doctors will kill me. Look at what they did this time. I got much worse. I'm weak and twenty pounds thinner." I agree, but wonder what would have happened without the doctors.

Looking at the sunset and stars, working out problems and sharing ideas, I feel serene and happy and ignore the voice in my head crying out for help. It is silenced only when Gene and I make love, gentle because of his frailty and our feelings. When we cuddle all night, I have a sense of security that I have not enjoyed for a while.

I do not write in my journal for the next three weeks because I am busy teaching, writing, and caring for Gene. Writing seems less important when our lives are calm. We are amazed at how well Gene is doing. Although he often sleeps until noon, he then reads, watches TV, pays the bills, and attends to his medical records. He delights in editing my chapters and his students' work. We spend quiet evenings at home. Sometimes we buy things for our new home. We socialize some and, although Gene would like more, I enjoy the quiet.

■　■　■

"Mr. Weinstein's pulmonary disorder is best described as 'end-stage' in that he has a one-year prognosis. Over the next year my patient's chronic lung disease will progressively worsen and he will need specialized home-care facilities if we are to limit the number of repeat hospital admissions." Although Dr. Simpson had informed me that Gene probably would not live more than a year, the words in the letter he sends to verify to the insurance company our need for nursing service shock both of us. "A year," Gene asks, "just a year?"

"The doctors can't predict. And," I remind him, "we asked him to do a 'worst case' to give us a chance for reimbursement." Since my rationalizations make us feel better, I ignore the voice that says this prognosis probably is optimistic.

Gene makes arrangements for a nurse four hours a day, three days a week. Mary is cheerful and gets along well with Gene. At least once a week, she accompanies him on errands and to doctor and dental appointments, and she fixes his lunch each day. Gene likes her companionship and getting out of the house. I like the rescue from weekly grocery and drugstore errands.

By end of September, life is less rosy. The insurance company refuses our nursing claim. The services the nurse provides, they argue, could be done by a nurse's aide or companion, which they, of course, don't cover. Although we can afford twelve hours of care a week at $15 per hour, what happens when we need more? Our hesitation to increase nursing hours adds to the growing tension.

■ ■ ■

On September 28, 1984, I write:

> I feel back in the rut again. I felt so much love when he was in the hospital. Now we are fighting. It's over control again. Whenever he has been sick and gets better, we argue. He feels I take over, which I do when he's sick. Then he wants control again when he's better, but it's hard for me to give it back. How do we get out of this pattern?
>
> Just today we had a fight. Gene had planned to buy me weight equipment for my birthday. We had a good time looking at the different options (although I was a little embarrassed to be with a man who had oxygen in his nose). First, Gene got upset because I considered getting equipment that cost $1400 instead of the $400 set he wanted to buy, even though I would pay the difference. He said I wouldn't use it much. I said I would. He said I had robbed him of the pleasure of buying a present for me and that it made him feel like a cheapskate. So I gave in.
>
> He wanted to put the equipment in the garage, instead of the spare bedroom as I had planned. I said no.
>
> He demanded that we have it delivered and set up. Since it would cost over $50, I insisted on doing it myself. When I asked my neighbor to help me carry the equipment into the house, Gene blew up. He said he didn't want that kind of obligation to Bob. I exploded. "This is between Bob and me," I screamed. He said I should have conferred with him before asking Bob. I told him that I was an individual and could make decisions without him.

So what started as a treat ended in argument. I didn't understand it. Only later did I write:

This was a much bigger deal to Gene. This event was a tiny part of my very busy life. It was a large part of his not so busy life. That puts it into perspective for me. I wish it would for him too.

He feels that giving me gifts is a way of doing things for me since he has greater financial resources. I had partly robbed him of that by wanting equipment costing more than he wanted to pay. Gene's male ego was hurt when I asked another man to help me do what he couldn't. He wanted to compensate by paying for the equipment to be delivered and I wouldn't let him.

■ ■ ■

Gene felt good for a couple of weeks and then, suddenly, his condition changed drastically. Except for the time in the hospital, he was worse than ever. Decreasing the massive doses of steroids had left him weak, frail, and unable to move around. After our rising expectations, the drop was a huge disappointment. As usual, we took our time facing the problem. The increased tension and worn-thin patience were most apparent when we tried to leave the house.

Getting ready to go out to dinner has zapped most of our energy: his, to get himself ready; mine, to deal with all the preparations—fill the oxygen tank, make sure the wheelchair battery is charged, find the pill box under the seat, remember the antacid. Oh, no, the oxygen tank won't shut off. Get the hair drier and an extension cord. When we finally are ready to go, Gene spills urine on me from the bottle we carry in the van.

Now, I have another task—clean up the piss. I have taught all day and have looked forward to a nice dinner. "I'm sorry," I say, knowing I appear upset. "I'm not mad at you. I just get tired of the disasters."

He replies sadly, "Yeah, me too. And I always cause them." My heart goes out to him; at the same time, I can't get rid of my anger. I think of all the accidents of the last few days, like yesterday when he backed into a neighbor's car and caused $140 worth of damages.

By the time I calm down, I must deal with getting into the restaurant— the battery on the Amigo is loose; the lift gets snarled up; Gene can't breathe. Finally, my frustration starts to dissolve and Gene tries to be gay. But when the food is served, Gene's shaky hands spill a glass of wine into my plate and over my white pants. The waiter moves us to another table and gets another entrée. "I can't believe you did that," I say to Gene's silence. "This is too hard." I feel sorry for both of us when I realize that any possibility for gaiety has ended, but I need to be angry now. If I cap it, the pain, the frustration, the fear, everything will explode. We realize then that our reprieve is over. Solemnly, we finish dinner, not tasting anything, and come home.

We no longer talk enthusiastically about marriage. Instead, we say, "Well, if you want it or need it, I would do it." I have cold feet, and hope he doesn't pursue it; perhaps Gene is protecting himself or responding to the negative energy between us.

■ ■ ■

My close friend Elva asks me, "Do you feel trapped?"

"Yes, I do, but I get something from him even now. And I made the bargain. I chose this."

"That doesn't mean you don't feel trapped. You had no way of knowing what it would be like."

"Not in my wildest imagination."

What relief I feel that someone understands and doesn't blame me for making the choice, nor Gene for the situation.

A few days later I write: "I am all bottled up. Work and worry. I don't like it. I want to be light and lively again. What to do? Therapy is not the answer. Who or what is? I'll try anything. For now I'll take a good affair. I know why I want outside sex. It is the only way I know to get emotional release."

■ ■ ■

"He's so sick," I tell my friend, Sherry, a physician. "And our battles have gotten worse. When he is irascible, I scream back at him."

Sherry is supportive and encourages me to talk, then hugs me as I cry. "It looks like he'll be around for a while," she says, "so it would be best if the two of you could make this easier."

"I know. I want to. But I'm not sure his living a long time is the best thing." Although I know I have only released a trickle from the dam, I feel relieved. Talking and crying with friends is more helpful than therapy.

"I'd like to talk even though it's midnight," I say to Gene when I arrive home. He immediately turns off the TV, and we move to the kitchen table to discuss our interpretations of recent events. The battle over the weight equipment exemplifies our battle over control. Gene finally acknowledges he is responding to his shrinking world and I admit I am acting out of fear of his deterioration; we understand now that much of the problem stems from our emotional responses to his declining health.

"I'm really needy," I say, going a step further in revealing myself. "And it's difficult to talk to you about it." This conversation shocks and hurts Gene every time it comes up.

"I want you to be able to talk to me about everything."

"You know I love you?" I ask.

"Yes, you know I love you?"

"Yes, but I can't let down with you because I don't see you as being strong now," I say with care.

"But I am."

"No, not always," I respond. "You can't be because of your body."

"I guess I understand," he says sadly, "but I wish it were different. You have to let me try."

When he complains that he has no one to talk to, I reply, "You have Joan."

"But she isn't here, and, anyway, I don't like to talk about you. I have nothing to do, no social life."

"With your health problems, it's difficult to meet people," I say. We discuss his dependence on me and my unavailability because of my job. We ask how we can make his life better. Can he deal with the smoke-filled bridge room again?

We stay up until 2:00 A.M., something I usually won't do because of work. As I fall asleep, I think about how much I organize my life around my job, and it makes me question my values. Shouldn't my relationship be more important than my work? Especially now? I cuddle up close.

This quiet night suddenly contrasts with the last two weeks. Gene usually tosses and turns all night now, even sometimes sitting up in bed. Occasionally his hand involuntarily shoots up and remains suspended, as though the nerves have a mind of their own. Then his body trembles and shakes. To sleep, I have had to move to my side of the bed.

I grieve that night for the loss of my comforter and sleeping companion.

■ ■ ■

"I'm feeling worse than usual," Gene says when I call from school the next day. What is usual anymore, I wonder, as I feel alarmed. "Do you think the sex this morning had an impact?"

"I hope not," I answer, "but there's no way to know."

"It was worth it," he says.

When I come home, Gene's breathing is so labored that talking or eating exhausts him. When he is unable to sleep, I rub his back each time he pumps out. When the sun begins to rise, I am relieved to hear his steady breathing. "Just a bad night," he says when he gets up at 2:00 P.M. At dinner, we talk and laugh, almost like old times.

After a two-hour dentist appointment the next day, Gene's nurse, Mary, writes that he is short-winded and unable to move around, and that this is one of the hardest times he has had. When I get home, Gene is exhausted, but asks to go for a walk on the Amigo. "Being out might be good for me," he says. He perks up from the walk.

Then again he lies awake all night, and, by the next evening, he dozes off in the middle of sentences. When he says he can't eat the Chinese food I bring home, I tell him he just needs rest. His alarm is covered by a dazed look, mine by fear and denial. The periodic hum of the pumper provides background for his grunts and groans and the rattle of the extra pills he shakes from the bottles.

By Saturday morning, Gene is so weak and breathless that he can't answer the phone. Nothing helps—not pounding his back or increasing the steroids and codeine. He nods off while reading a book, yet he can't sleep when he goes to bed. I notice a new symptom; sometimes he says something out of context and then wonders why. We both overlook the CO_2 poisoning that is taking place. I don't recall even thinking about it.

▪ ▪ ▪

"I'm suffocating. Turn the numbers up. Please! Hurry! The oxygen. Oh, god. I can't breathe," Gene yells at 3:00 A.M. from the bathroom. Immediately, my heart pounds, everything else slows down. On automatic now, I rub his back and talk soothingly. "Keep your hand on me," he pleads. "It helps." Soon his breathing returns to near normal. "It's so scary," he says. "I haven't slept at all."

From then on, I sleep several half-hour stretches. Every time I wake, he is babbling, stringing together thoughts from his novel, TV programs, the newspaper, past events, and unrelated current events. Just talking in his sleep, I assure myself.

The first time I admit something is seriously wrong is when I am awakened by his mumbling, "928-6424, 246-6712," as he sits rocking on the side of the bed. "What are you doing?" I ask, softly.

"That's my phone number, isn't it? Isn't that my phone number? And I've got to call Jordan and Jordan's phone number is 246-6712. That's Jordan's phone number, isn't it? I've got to go down and talk to him about some of this stuff. I've got to talk to Jordan!" Jordan is the chair of the Sociology Department at Stony Brook.

I continue talking softly to keep alarm from my voice. "Gene, it's the middle of the night. You aren't making sense. Why are you thinking about phone numbers?" He looks at me as if he doesn't know why either.

"I've got to get some sleep," he says in a panic. "When can I take more theodore or codeine?"

"Not yet," I say, worried that he will overdose. "Lie down. Close your eyes," I say soothingly. Immediately, he springs to the side of the bed and nods off, still babbling.

Soon, denial and shock lure me to sleep. I doze and then wake up to his moaning, then babbling, then pumping sounds. Finally, he just sits wringing his hands, his body shaking. I hold onto him, then massage him. I fall asleep, then wake up and hear him talking. "Why are you talking about a kidnapping?"

"Oh," he says, suddenly having insight. "That's happening in my novel. I got confused." He's OK, I tell myself in false relief as my exhausted body fights to return to sleep. Just a little fuzzy and dreaming.

Occasionally, Gene is lucid enough to figure out what he should do. "If only I could get more oxygen, I could sleep. If I could sleep, I would be better." But taking more medication or turning up the oxygen, we agree, is dangerous because it might increase his CO_2 level.

"Try," I coax. "Just put your head on the pillow." He lies quietly for a while, and then pops up.

"I can't lie down," he says, gulping for air. "I'll drown." I hold my breath to see what it feels like. He has no choice but to hold his. How long can this last?

"I'm exhausted, baby," I say. "It's 4:30, and I haven't slept much the last few nights. I'm going to sleep in the living room."

"Please don't leave," he pleads. "I'm scared."

"I can hear if anything goes wrong and I'll come right in."

It seems like the theater of the absurd to be on the couch trying to sleep while Gene is incoherently carrying on an extended conversation with himself in the next room. How can you do this? I ask myself. I hope for a miracle. I also want to escape and take care of myself.

At 6:00 A.M., Gene yells again. "Help me, baby." Sitting beside him, I watch his movements and listen to his incoherence. When he lucidly talks about taking more medicine, I say, "Gene, you're really sick. This is serious."

"No, it isn't. I just need more sleep." I desperately want to believe him, and since I don't know what to do, I make him lie down and I rub his body. The voices in my head argue about the seriousness of the problem. "He is delirious." "No, just a little confused from exhaustion."

When the sun finally rises, I no longer can deny what is happening. I have never seen him this way. The loneliness I feel at that moment is matched only by the loneliness I will experience at his death. I have lost my best friend. It is my battle now, alone; Gene can't help. Barely able to talk, he constantly mutters endless, senseless babble. "Come on, Gene, you are not making sense," I try to coach him into coherence as he talks about some plot from his novel in which he has become a character, and then mixes in some real life event.

"Gene," I say, crying and pleading, "I think you are really sick. We need to go to the hospital."

The distrust on his face informs me that I am now the enemy. "Absolutely not. You are not taking me there." His voice gets louder and louder, until he is shouting, "You are overreacting. Leave me alone."

Determined, I kneel in front of him, hold both his hands, and say, "Gene, I love you. You need help. I can't handle this alone. Please."

"No, goddamn it," he replies. "They will make me worse. Kill me. I am not going and that's final." Then the babble again.

"Come on, baby," I say, trying to help him up.

"No!" Viciously he frees his arm from me. "Get away from me." Then he lapses into unintelligible phrases. Finally, he sits silently, holding the pumper listlessly in his hand, the expression on his face indicating he is trying to figure out what is going on.

Where is my Gene? I wonder. The one who was so strong and powerful, so rational and in control of his world.

Although I don't realize it then, from that moment on negotiation takes on a different meaning. We no longer are on equal footing; he is not competent to share in decision making. I cannot trust his reasoning. More and more, deception will become a strategy on my part.

"Gene, I'm going to call Sherry. Will you listen to Sherry? She's a doctor."

"OK, call her," he says clearly. "But I am not going to the hospital, and that's final."

By the time I reach Sherry, I'm frightened, shaking, like a little kid, but one with life and death responsibility. When Sherry can make out what I am saying, she instructs, "You have to get him to a hospital."

"His doctor," I say between sobs, "is out of town. What do I do?"

"Let me call the clinic, and I'll call you back."

Sherry's helpfulness calms me. I say softly to Gene, "Honey, Sherry thinks it would be a good idea to go to the hospital, just to have your blood gases checked." The look of uncertainty passing over his face informs me he is no longer quite as adamant about not going.

He softens and says, "I will talk to Townson, nobody else."

"Honey, Dr. Townson is out of town," I say through the streaming tears. "You can't talk to him. There will be another doctor you can talk to."

"Nobody but Townson." Since when has he gotten so loyal to Townson? I wonder.

What do I do? Hyperventilating, I call Donna, a friend and respiratory therapist, while I wait for Sherry's return call. After I describe his situation,

Donna says, "Carolyn, you have to get him to a hospital soon. Just take him to the emergency room."

Sobbing this time, I say to Gene, "Donna thinks you ought to go to the hospital, too." He stares at my eyes as though he is trying to figure out what I am up to. Then he says defiantly, but softly, "No hospital."

Sherry calls back and says, "The doctor on emergency will call you in a few minutes." The phone rings as soon as I hang up. Holding back tears, I tell the doctor a little of Gene's history and describe the current situation. "You have to get him to an emergency room."

When I say that he won't go, the doctor suggests, "We could have the police force him."

"Oh, no," I mutter. The thought of police dragging him away is an unbearable image. Maybe I would rather see him die. I fight that thought from my mind, refusing all thoughts of death.

"He is afraid of being intubated, put on a respirator."

"That'll be his decision," says the doctor. This makes me feel better and will provide ammunition to persuade Gene to go to the hospital. The doctor continues, "Eventually, he'll pass out from lack of oxygen, or at least be unable to resist you. Then bring him in as soon as possible."

"But might he die before that?" I ask, finally putting my unspoken fears into words.

The doctor hesitates, and then says calmly, "No, I don't think so." But I am not reassured. Doctors go through this all the time, I realize. Gene is just another dying patient to him, and some other doctor's responsibility.

Returning to Gene, I kneel in front of him, and say as calmly as possible, "Honey, the doctor feels you should come in to have your blood gases checked. They can give you something to make you feel better."

He listens, and then yells loudly, "I will not go to the hospital. They will want to intubate me and ruin my life."

"No, that will be your decision. Nobody will do it if you don't want them to. The doctor assured me," I say calmly. His face softens as he looks down, his fierce will dissolves. "Just to have your blood gases checked," I say softly. "Don't you think you need to?"

"Yes," he says, and then, looking me straight in the eye, "but no intubation. Just blood gases."

"OK," I assure him, before the babbling starts again. How can he be so coherent one minute and so crazy the next?

Now thinking more clearly, I get the manual wheelchair. Gene's eyes are glassy, and his speech and movements have slowed. Sometimes the muscles of his mouth move of their own accord and no words come out. When he gets into the wheelchair, his passive cooperation surprises me. Please let this complaisance continue. "Wheel me to the table. I want breakfast. Eating might make me feel better."

I speak in a slow and soft voice, hoping not to break the mood. "What do you want, baby?"

"Cookies and milk." After he slowly eats one cookie, he says, "That's all. I can't eat anymore."

The quiet is deafening. His eyes and voice indicate he is far away. I alert the nearest hospital that we are coming. Then I say calmly, "Sweetie, we're going to go check your blood gasses." He nods off in the wheelchair. After filling his portable oxygen tank, I put it on his lap, attach it to his nose, and wheel him into the van. He tries to help by guiding the chair onto the lift.

Although I drive slowly, I have forgotten to lock the wheelchair in place, and Gene rolls to the back of the van. I stop to reposition him, apologizing quietly. In a loving, euphoric voice, he says, "That's OK." He will tell me later that the experience was like being high on psychedelic drugs.

Facing the back of the van, he continually asks me, "Where are we? Where are we going?" I tell him our exact location and explain as many times as he asks that we are going to check his blood gases. Thinking we are shopping, he says, "Hand me the packages and I'll put them back here." I am calm, numb really, and prepared for anything.

When we arrive at the hospital, Gene stops asking questions, and does everything I ask. By the time we are at the admitting desk, he babbles continuously, seeming to have lost all control of his mouth muscles. The gibberish of words and sounds is interrupted occasionally by short phrases of normal conversation. But Gene seems not to know what is going on. Sometimes he hears the receptionist ask me questions, and nodding his head in cooperation, he responds in his most polite voice, trying to repeat my answers. "Yes, Car Car Carolyn El Car Ellis," he says, after saying his own name and before continuing the incomprehensible chatter about his novel. He smiles, seems almost euphoric still. But he can barely say my name.

I fight back tears. Why are we answering these inane questions? Do something. But I am on automatic pilot again. I want to fit into the system and get help. Making trouble might delay Gene's care. These people are the only hope I have.

When the nurse finally wheels Gene to emergency, I go to the phone to call someone. Anyone. Before I can dial, Donna, the respiratory therapist, and Kathy, another friend, walk in. I have never been so glad to see people I know.

In a few more minutes, Sherry arrives. I feel love from and for those people who will hold me and help me make decisions.

Donning a white coat, Sherry goes into the emergency room. I collapse a little, now that I can, embraced by my friends. My mind is on hold. The look on Sherry's face when she returns warns me the news is bad. Putting her arms around me, she says, "Carolyn, they want to intubate him."

There are no tears in my eyes, but my stomach clutches continually as though I am sobbing. "No, not yet," I plead. But what do I know? If it means the difference between life and death, I want it. It has to be better than death, doesn't it? Then I wonder, better for whom? Gene or me? I ask Sherry, "What do you think?"

"Given his CO_2 and O_2 levels and the pH reading, I agree."

"Will he die if we don't?"

"There is a real good chance," she responds.

I start to consent, then ask, "Does he know what's going on?"

"He seems to, although he fades in and out. He said, 'Hi, Sherry,' when I walked in."

"Does he know they want to intubate?"

"Yes, and he keeps saying over and over 'no intubation.'" A pain shoots through my chest.

"What are they doing now?"

"They're getting Farbman on the phone, the doctor covering for Townson. Maybe you can convince Gene, Carolyn."

"You really feel it's necessary?"

"Yes, I do."

"Intubation is temporary, isn't it?" I ask, turning to Donna to be reassured.

"Yes," Donna says. "Many people come to the hospital to get intubated for a few days to give their lungs a rest and then go home." I feel better. These are my friends, and they know.

"OK," I say, taking a deep breath and still praying for a miracle.

I start to cry, but stop when a nurse says I can go into the emergency room. Gene looks better and is more lucid than when we arrived. His eyes are ablaze and his head rocks back and forth as he says, "No intubation, no intubation," over and over. Then he closes his eyes and seems to doze, but quickly awakes and says, again, "No intubation." Other than a nurse taking care of the IV, everyone stands around looking at him. The atmosphere is icy. The resident looks angry. I almost laugh at the picture of this semi-incoherent man, with IVs and oxygen attached, in control of the attention.

I kiss him and say, "I love you."

He says forcefully, "No intubation."

"The doctors think it's necessary."

"No, it will kill me." He looks at me as though I am a traitor.

I cry silently and begin to plead, "Please, Gene, it's all we have to do. I want you to get better. Donna says it's temporary."

Gene appears a little confused and unsure for a moment, and then repeats more forcefully, "No intubation."

A nurse tells me Dr. Farbman is on the phone and has received a description of Gene from the staff. When I explain that Gene doesn't want to be intubated, in a quiet and calm voice, he responds, "I don't think there is a hurry to intubate. We can treat him conservatively and see if he comes out of it. If he doesn't, we can intubate later."

"But might he die now?"

"No, he doesn't seem in immediate danger. I like to do what the patient wants." What a change from the attitude of the resident and staff at this hospital. Dr. Farbman continues, "We will have to transfer him to Florida General, where I can take care of him."

"How do we do that?"

"Tell the staff with you now that we are transferring him and that you need an ambulance. I'll meet you at Florida General."

When I tell the resident what we are doing, he says, "I don't agree with this, and he'll have to sign a release form saying College Hospital has no responsibility and that he refused treatment and left against our advice."

Gene is able to read the form, and he signs it. If I had been a relative, I could have signed it for him. Gene appears to be improving, and I recall that surges of anger always make him better.

Staff members transfer Gene onto a stretcher, and now that he has gotten what he wants, he slides into a daze. A male assistant gets into the back of the ambulance. I climb into the front beside a stern-looking female attendant, who says, "I want you to understand, if he passes out we are obligated under law to intubate him."

"I understand," I say passively. What else can I do? I'm almost glad not to have control. As much as I want to do what Gene wants, I don't want him to die.

We drive in silence. I keep looking through the back window, but I can't tell if they are intubating Gene. What can I do anyway? I wish we would go faster; yet I relax these few minutes to collect my thoughts, but they are silenced now by numbness.

The ambulance attendants take Gene into the intensive-care unit and tell me how to find the waiting room. Donna and Kathy, who have followed in their car, come to meet me. Donna goes into intensive care and then comes to tell me, "You can go in with him." I am surprised and glad to have friends who know the system.

In intensive care, eight beds surround a glassed-in nurses' station. Nurses and residents gather around patients who have tubes and oxygen attached to their bodies. I walk quickly toward Gene. Briefly, he looks glad to see me, but then he is preoccupied. His eyes dart here and there as he tries to focus.

I long to hear Dr. Farbman's quieting voice that makes me feel everything will be all right, but he has not arrived. Staff members in intensive care, who also want to intubate Gene, don't quiet my fears. One young male resident takes me aside and says sternly, "If this were my father, I would certainly want him intubated." I don't correct his misconception. I feel confusion again when he pushes, "Would you as a relative give permission for us to intubate?"

Silence. I finally admit, "I'm not actually a relative."

Immediately, he becomes more formal. I no longer am necessary to his institutionalized medical model of decision making. Since I am unable to give the go ahead for the next medical procedure, I am in the way. The resident says coldly, "Who is his closest relative?"

"His mother," I say, and feel a chill. Gene's mother has no idea he is this sick. What will she do? She will be upset, but she will give permission, of course. Then Gene and I will lose the little control we have, I think, suddenly back in collusion with Gene. Should I call her and tell her what Gene wants? No, I want to leave her out of this. I start to feel that I must take action. These strangers aren't going to make this decision. Especially not before Dr. Farbman, who has become my savior, gets here.

I seek out the resident and say bluntly, "I want to be considered his common-law wife."

The resident coldly replies, "That would take a court decision and we don't have time," then walks away. I feel helpless still, but my fighting spirit returns. These residents are not going to do anything until Dr. Farbman gets here. Without the status of relative, I probably don't have much power, but I feel better thinking these thoughts and planning a course of action than just passively agreeing. It's hard to believe the medical staff can do something that Gene says he doesn't want. Still, I am bothered by that nagging feeling that Dr. Farbman might be wrong. What if Gene dies while we debate intubation? Will I feel it was my fault?

When I return to Gene's bed, the respiratory therapist working on him says to the intern, "I absolutely will not give another breathing treatment until it is ordered by a doctor. I have always been instructed to give these treatments only every four hours. I refuse to take responsibility for this." I don't ask questions, because I realize the slightest wrong move on my part or just calling attention to myself might mean I will be asked to leave. I want to blend into the woodwork and use resistance only in an emergency. I feel small in the face of this powerful bureaucracy.

"No one called to tell me Gene was here," Dr. Farbman says to me as he walks in the door. He is a calming influence. Finding out that Dr. Farbman is head of pulmonary care helps me make sense of the sudden change in demeanor of the staff. The surly resident now is meek as he tells Dr. Farbman he thinks they should intubate. Dr. Farbman listens calmly and then turns to hear what Gene has to say, which remains, "no intubation." Dr. Farbman's reassurance that they will use an intubator only as a last resort calms Gene, who also seems to place confidence in this sensible man.

Dr. Farbman tells the respiratory therapist to use a positive-pressure breathing apparatus, the same one used in Stony Brook, to get rid of CO_2. When he says to treat every fifteen minutes, the therapist looks at him incredulously and says, "As long as I am not responsible. This is not the way I was trained."

Dr. Farbman replies quietly, "Don't worry." He works with Gene, talking to him, and encouraging him to breathe.

Gene holds my hand, but I don't feel he's aware of me. He is more concerned about breathing and about what the doctors are saying. The doctors occasionally joke among themselves. At one point they talk at the foot of Gene's bed about his condition, and Gene yells out, "Hey, I can talk. Ask me." He tries to participate in the conversations about him. Occasionally, the doctors listen; mostly, they frustrate him by ignoring him.

Dr. Farbman wonders aloud about what has changed to cause the sudden decline in Gene's health. Understanding only part of the conversation, Gene says, "I'll tell you what is changed. Passion, that's what." No one responds. Later, I hear Dr. Farbman say that Townson always sends them his worst patients when he is away. The staff laughs. When Gene does not react, I am relieved he didn't hear. This is my honey you are talking about. I am reminded how bad Gene is, and I know Dr. Farbman is probably right. Still, his savior status diminishes.

Gene dozes and is occasionally incoherent, but not nearly as bad as before. After the first hour, his condition improves even more, and Dr. Farbman says that Gene is going to make it. Exhausted, Gene finally falls asleep, and I go to the waiting room. I wipe away the residue of the many tears I have shed the last few hours, thankful this battle is over.

10

"YOU'RE ALLOWED to visit only fifteen minutes," a nurse says when I arrive the next morning.

"How is Gene Weinstein doing?" I ask.

"To get his CO_2 down," she replies, "we decreased his oxygen intake last night. When his oxygen level dropped from sixty to forty—a dangerous low—we increased the oxygen flow hoping it would not bring the CO_2 up with it. He seems better now." I wonder at what level brain damage occurs, but I don't ask.

Gene is alert and happy to see me. We embrace for a long time. I feel like crying, but it's hard to do while smiling.

When we talk about the day before, Gene remembers the discussion of intubation at the first hospital, but he does not know how he got to this hospital. "You probably gave in to the disease once you successfully fought the intubation," I suggest. "We have to get me power of attorney," I say, after describing the trouble I had because I was not his relative.

His response is shocking. "I have considered that, but after yesterday, I don't know. You sided with them when I needed you."

"No, I didn't," I hastily answer. How could he think that?

"You cried and pleaded with me to be intubated," he accuses.

"Only because I thought you'd die without it. But I always wanted to do what you wanted. Please understand. I was confused and you weren't lucid. I didn't know what to do."

Even now, I don't know how to feel about what happened. He doesn't reply, but takes my hand and holds it to his face lovingly. How can I team up with someone who is not lucid?

I tell him his mother knows what happened. "I wish you hadn't told her," he replies. "She doesn't want to know."

"She says she does."

"She only thinks she does. It's too painful for her."

"And who are you," I ask, "to decide what she really wants or needs? It's like the doctors trying to decide for you." I have made my point.

After thinking Gene was going to die, just to have him alive is now enough to make me feel some optimism. When I get home, I write:

> The depression has lifted, the gut bomb is gone, the body tension has stopped, and the freedom from numbness allows me to feel some emotion other than fear and hopelessness. Sometimes when I hear myself telling my story, the despair returns. But I don't let it last long. I quickly find something to do or something else to think about.
>
> It is better that it is all happening gradually. I am adjusting to the idea that he will be on machines, that he will die. I think he is too.
>
> Sleep is a wonderful escape. I don't want to wake up, because THE PROBLEM is still there. Additionally, I have to go to work. How will I ever manage? One step at a time, I answer.

During the next few days, I teach classes, attend to details of my work, and even edit my book manuscript. Gene and I have loving visits at the hospital every evening while he eats his favorite foods, which I bring him. Sometimes we talk; other times we quietly watch TV. He seems weaker than prior to hospitalization, making it more difficult for him to make it to the bathroom on his own now. But his breathing seems to improve every day, helped especially by atropine, the medication that saved him in Stony Brook. Except for the frailty—he now weighs 128 pounds—he does not seem as sick as he did in New York.

∎ ∎ ∎

One night near my birthday, I am surprised when eight friends bring dinner and presents to my house. For a short while, I live a normal life. We laugh, tell jokes, and wash dishes. Then they are gone and I'm alone with my exhaustion, numbness, and fear, which threaten to make me scream until I lose consciousness. But I don't.

∎ ∎ ∎

I am nervous about bringing Gene home in his weak condition, but I miss him, and, as I drive to the hospital, I try to concentrate on how happy I am that he is OK. OK? He isn't OK. We are just postponing the inevitable.

A nurse on Gene's floor tells me that the checkout is in the lobby, but a receptionist there informs me that Gene has to be checked out by a family member. "Can't he do it himself?"

"Yes, of course, if he's able." Trembling with anger, tears flow as I tell Gene we have to stop at the desk to sign him out because I am not a relative. He doesn't say anything. Is it too much for him? Or doesn't he care?

That night we open a bottle of champagne, watch the sunset, and talk about what has happened. Gene is delighted when I ask if I can tape our discussion. As we go through particulars of the experiences that led to hospitalization, we tell each other our interpretations.

What he remembers most about the latest episode are details of the staff wanting to intubate him. In his words:

> I remember the hassle of not wanting to give up control of the therapeutic procedures. . . . They shoved a statement under my nose to sign. It said essentially that I was turning myself over to the care of the hospital. It said among other things, like insurance stuff, that I was accepting whatever the hospital thought was the best care for me and that in the event I was unable to make judgment, that my relatives could make decisions. That's the one that got me. If they decided you were incapable—it's a catch-22 here. If I refused treatment they thought was best for me under the circumstances, that would be glorified evidence I was incapable of making a decision.

I respond, "Yeah, just like in Goffman's [1961] total institutions. If you rebel against being treated as insane, they use it as evidence of insanity. I understand what you're saying. But when we took you to the hospital, it was apparent you weren't capable of making a decision. You didn't know where you were or what was going on."

"When?" asks Gene. "I thought I was slipping in and out. I was just sort of dozing off."

"Wrong. There would be three to five minutes when nothing you said made sense. You couldn't answer my questions. The doctors and I sometimes talked about you in front of you, and you didn't seem to hear us. Other times you could. The first time it clicked for me that something was really wrong was when you were repeating telephone numbers the night before."

After I describe the details of that evening, Gene responds, "It sounds like a dream state."

"It was a dream state, but much scarier."

Gene continues: "I remember not sleeping. I just couldn't sleep. . . . I remember going to the bathroom and not being able to breathe. I remember pumping out and trying to sleep. But it was like I was suffocating. I was afraid I would die in my sleep. . . . I didn't want you to get pissed at me for keeping you up. . . . I remember the trauma of your leaving to sleep in the living room. . . . I remember seeing the sunrise, the pink. And all through the night, no sleep."

"Do you remember discussing going to the hospital?"

"Just that you said, 'Let's go to the hospital,' and I didn't want to go." As I tell him details, he remembers that we talked about having his blood gases checked. Then he recalls being wheeled in the wheelchair and holding his portable oxygen on his lap, but the most confused periods of being transported to both hospitals have escaped him.

When I tell him how he resisted me, he says, "You must have thought I was terrible."

I reply softly, "You were. But you didn't mean to be. You didn't know what you were doing really."

"I remember feeling guilty." When I ask why, he says, "Because I didn't want to throw the whole burden on you."

Until we discuss the first day in intensive care, Gene cannot remember anything about it. Even then, what he actually remembers gets confused with what I tell him happened.

"What have you been thinking about me during this emergency?" I ask, changing the topic, because he becomes frustrated by his lack of memory.

"I don't remember," he says. "I just remember wondering how much control I have over my own course of treatment. Like signing this piece of paper. Not wanting to wake up and find myself with a goddamn tracheotomy."

I push, "My sense was that you never really cared much whether I was there or not, until you got out of intensive care."

"Oh, you mean at the hospital?" he responds. "You have to understand something. I knew that what was happening to me was just a freak-out for you. And you needed to get away."

"No, I'm not referring to after you got better in the hospital. I mean in intensive care and the emergency room. I don't think anything real negative about this. You just weren't very oriented toward me. You were into healing yourself. You didn't cling to me at all or anything. You were just into hiding the disease and making yourself well."

"That's what I had to do. I had this thing in my mind, not to push or demand emotional support and I had a fight to fight. That was the idea. The emotional support was not going to make me any better, and I knew you'd be around. There was nothing you could do anyway."

"Yes, OK, that's understandable. I thought you'd be scared and want me to be there. To tell you the truth, I'm glad you didn't."

"You think I didn't know that? That's OK. You were scared shitless. I knew you wanted me to live. You have no benefits to my going. Well, that's not true. But a different set of benefits [meaning financial ones]."

"I don't have any benefits," I respond adamantly.

"So you know what I did for myself in this? I went around telling myself and everybody else how concerned I was about you."

"You're talking now about during this emergency or the hospitalization in Stony Brook?"

"Both. I said how hard it all was for you. I wanted people to think I was a real considerate person, and to make a little capital off your back," he says with a chuckle.

"You stinker," I say, laughing as I think about how much I enjoy this kind of open honesty, when we reveal even our self-serving motives. I kid him then, "So you really weren't concerned about me? You just wanted to look that way?"

"Well, it was a little bit of both." We laugh.

We talk about the hospital stay. "It was a parade," I say. "There were people around your bed all the time."

"Yeah, I need to get x-rayed, they would say. I need to get weighed. We need urine. We need blood. Time for a treatment. Blood. Treatment. The doctors were coming around. Then another batch of them."

"Could you get into the whole scene while you were in there, or were you well enough to observe?"

"Oh, I looked around some. You have to know what the ranks are. There were head nurses, regular nurses—RNs and LPNs—nurses' aids, orderlies, and cleaning personnel. Some jobs you think cleaning personnel would do, the nurses do. Like changing linen. But nurses have a lot of tolerance and they really do have more sense than anyone about what's going on. Plus, they have a smattering of medical knowledge. I sort of like nurses actually."

Comparing the status systems and the task assignments of the two hospitals Gene has been in reminds me why I am never bored with him. Afterward, we cuddle in bed, thankful for this reprieve.

■ ■ ■

The next day, two friends come to dinner. The visit gives us a sense of being "normal" people doing "normal" things. It is a pleasant occasion until a neighbor calls and asks to use our hot tub. I tell him he can come in through the back gate. When I hang up, Gene accuses me of making a unilateral decision. I am surprised by his response, but since I don't want to argue, I call the neighbor to tell him not to come. I am angry that Gene has attacked me in front of company and that he has burst our bubble of joy for no apparent reason. After our guests leave, we both explode. How quickly we turn from love to anger.

"I didn't deserve that," I accuse.

"Yes, you did. You do that all the time, make decisions without talking them over with me."

"I didn't think this one was that important."

"Well, it was. How dare you not consult me."

"I've had it with you tonight. This is abuse. I'm going to a party."

"What party?"

"One I've been invited to."

Gene's whole demeanor changes as he pleads, "Please don't go. I'm scared to be alone."

I am too angry to give in, but, because I feel guilty and worried, I stay away only an hour. Do I need to be angry now, to unplug my frustration and pain?

When I come home, we don't speak. I lie on the couch in the living room, but I can't sleep. I look in on Gene in bed four times during the first hour. What if I have made him so unhappy that he commits suicide? The possibility of his dying while we are angry convinces me to join him. He says nothing when I walk into the room, just opens his arms wide, inviting me to slide into them. We cuddle closely, knowing that the next day will be time enough for words about control and shrinking worlds.

■ ■ ■

Death permeates the atmosphere now. Sometimes I see death when I look at him, and often we talk about it. "What about life after death?" I ask.

When he says he doesn't believe in it, I respond, "I think it's as ridiculous for you to say there isn't any as for people to say they know there is." When he tries to scientifically explain leaving the body, I retort, "Maybe the process isn't scientific."

"And maybe you're right."

"Don't you want to be reunited with me in death?" I ask. "I better be the one you want to be reunited with," I continue in a kidding tone. In jest, he puts his finger to his tilted head as though deep in serious thought, and names other women he wants to join him.

"Stop that," I say, shaking him gently in mock anger.

Even though the conversation has serious undertones, the joking helps me accept our situation. Perhaps the same thing happens for Gene when he recites over and over to the tune of "Tom Dooley," "Hang down your head, Gene Weinstein, hang down your head and cry. Hang down your head, Gene Weinstein. Poor boy you're bound to die." His rhyme is funny and disconcerting. He often adds, seriously, "I don't want to die yet. I want to live." I believe him.

■ ■ ■

A week after Gene is home from the hospital, he decides to go to a talk at school. It will be good for him to get out of the house and be intellectually stimulated. But, during the talk, I keep constant vigil. His head jerks back continually as though he is falling asleep. Then he shakes it and looks around, his eyes open wide. In a few minutes, he repeats the movement. I hope he is only bored, but I know that something else is causing the nodding off. I fear he will make a comment—he has never been at a talk that he hasn't—and not make sense.

We get through the presentation without Gene saying anything or falling asleep. Since he seems fine then, I accept his explanation that the codeine he took earlier made him sleepy. I grieve for the intellectual Gene I was so proud of.

While we are out of the house, we go to *Places in the Heart,* our first movie in months. Gene rides the Amigo to his seat and I park it in the lobby. When I see that the movie is sad, I say, "Oh, no, I can't stand it."

"You must be kidding." And just as he had responded to the movie *Whose Life Is It Anyway?,* he continues, "You think it can be worse than what we're living?"

This movie is a wrenching tale about loss and suffering. When the widow says, "I miss my husband," Gene and I embrace each other, sobbing. I have not seen Gene let go like this before. "I feel like a leaky faucet," he says. Crying for others' problems in a movie served as a vehicle for crying for his own. That way he didn't have to directly feel sorry for himself.

Afterward, he says, "The movie made me think about how much I'll miss you when I die." Even though we laugh at his statement, he is serious.

I reply, "You won't be sad, you'll be dead. I'll be the sad one."

"How do you know what corpses feel or need?" he retorts quickly, which makes us laugh again.

When I ask, more seriously, "Did the movie make you think about how I will feel when you die?" he hugs me close, as if to protect me from pain.

We cuddle part of the night, but then Gene's body starts to shake. He talks in his sleep and when his arm rigidly extends into the air and trembles, I awake and move away from him. I talk soothingly about relaxing and rub his body, startled by how frail it is. How will I know when he is suffering from too much CO_2?

The next day, Gene and I drive to a restaurant. Then he sits in the car, reluctant to go inside because he feels nauseated. When I push, he struggles into the restaurant. But since he is too sick to eat, I resentfully put the food we ordered into a box. We return home, not saying much.

The next day, Sunday, I note that Gene has not slept for two nights. He did not eat last night and now he cannot eat breakfast. I feel guilty that the outings on Friday and Saturday might have caused the downslide. Why did I push him to go to dinner? It seems we can't go out two nights in a row. Maybe we can't go out at all.

During the morning he stays in bed, but he feels like he is drowning every time he starts to fall asleep, so he gets up and watches TV. He tries to be cheerful, but I see how hard it is to breathe. Then, praying for a false alarm, I question whether he actually is much worse than usual. But when he says his lungs are jammed, I note he is nodding off again. He hasn't been home a week and he's on the verge of being back in the hospital. How are we going to handle this? I'm not sleeping either. I must sleep in a separate bedroom. I have to be able to work. Yet, I want to be there if he needs anything.

Waiting for death is a lonely experience. I feel numb now most of the time. I need relief. I need release. I don't know what to do. Even sex can't fulfill my need for an emotional outlet now. When I finally release, what will I let go of? Now I understand Gene's reluctance to let go. I feel like I'm going crazy, but I can't.

■ ■ ■

On Sunday night, not knowing what else to do, I give Gene two sleeping pills. Although he's still coherent, he's had little sleep. If he doesn't sleep soon, we will make an emergency trip to the hospital. The pills do not help; now he can't keep his head down for five minutes. Lying helpless at his side, I watch him, first up and then down, moaning all the while. When I help him pump out at midnight, his respiration has not changed. "Break through, you bastard breath," I mutter.

An hour later, I go upstairs to sleep. "Can't you sleep on the couch down here?" Gene pleads.

"I really need a few hours of deep sleep. You can call me anytime." I hate to leave him, but I can do no more. Either his body fights it, or it doesn't.

From upstairs, I hear him talking to himself and moving about. Still, I manage to sleep. Then I wake with a start two hours later as reality tumbles back. I go to help him pump out. Although slightly incoherent, he's still able to reflect on his confusion. "What I said didn't make sense did it?" I tell him no and ask what he was thinking about. "I was thinking about the novel I'm reading by Saul Bellow, and that must be why I was talking about deans." Then he explains his unconnected ramblings as "dreaming out loud" and "like there's all this mush in there that just randomly pours out."

Still hoping for more sleep, I stay on the couch in the living room. At dawn, he calls, "I'm scared. And I still haven't slept." I put medication in his pumper, and this time I have to hold the mouthpiece.

"You need to go to the hospital," I say, and am surprised to hear him agree. "I'll call Dr. Townson."

When I suggest an ambulance, he says, "If it's easier for you."

"No, I think I can handle you in the van, as long as you can help." He continues to be agreeable, but now he mumbles incoherently. Meaningless phrases appear interspersed within our sensible dialogue.

When Dr. Townson returns my call, I describe the situation. Then, holding onto the thin thread that we may be overreacting, I tell him, "Maybe we are acting too quickly. He's not as bad as other times we've brought him in."

"You can't mess around with this stuff. You must always bring him in right away."

"When is right away?"

"We have to talk about that and about quality-of-life kinds of things," Townson answers, and my stomach retracts.

Our mood is different this time. Hushed. No panic. No arguments. I feel close to Gene, loving him, as we accept with resignation this fate. As I fill his portable oxygen tank, he says quietly, "I don't want to be intubated."

"What if it's a matter of life or death?"

"I guess in that case, yes, I will."

With help, Gene slides into his wheelchair and I push him onto the van lift. He is exhausted and anxious to get to the hospital. Just as I notice that his speech is rambling, he says, "I can't even talk." Looking through the rearview mirror, I see his face twitching and his mouth moving randomly.

Since the hospital has been forewarned of our arrival, attendants immediately take Gene to emergency. I stop to fill out admission forms. Crying, I tell the receptionist that I am Gene's wife. When she points to the record on the computer screen that lists me as friend, I say, "OK," and give no explanation. What I want to say is, "You asshole bureaucracy, how dare you have a right to control my life?"

The waiting room is filled with Mexicans, Cubans, and African-Americans. From the appearance of their clothing, most of them are poor. They politely look away as I cry and focus on keeping their many children quiet. All of us have problems. Why else would we be here so early on Monday morning? I feel a comradeship.

Listening to their statements to admissions, I learn some are here for real emergencies, such as knifings and shootings, but just as many use the emergency room as their family physician for minor problems. They have no other resources, have no place else to turn, or have discovered that this is the easiest and cheapest way to medical care. My observations of the world outside take my mind off my problems and I am boosted by realizing the social observer in me never stops.

"Come on back. He's pretty bad," Dr. Townson says as he enters the waiting room. "We'll try to treat him conservatively, but I don't know if that will work this time." I note that no one else in the waiting room is invited into the emergency room.

I can't believe Gene's rapid decline. When the nurse shakes him, he opens his eyes wide. Looking startled, his head moves from person to person like a periscope in a Popeye cartoon, and he laughs shrilly like a mad man. His eyes reveal a look of wildness, convincing me that he has no idea what is going on. He says nothing and then falls asleep. Never before have I seen him so disengaged from the outside world.

"Sleeping pills were a bad idea," says Dr. Townson. "Not sleeping built up carbon dioxide. And then when the pills worked, they produced more carbon dioxide."

Our wrong decision about the pills distresses me, but doesn't evoke any guilt. Even without them, he'd probably be here anyway.

"It's now urgent," Dr. Townson says, "that we keep him awake to get rid of carbon dioxide." How ironic. While the nurses manipulating machines and tubes are busy, I slap Gene's face gently to wake him, but then cringe at having hit him. He wakes up giggling and giddy, as though drugged, recognizing no one or anything.

In the midst of this, a nurse asks if I am kin to Gene. Oh, no, not again. I fear she will ask me to leave if I say no, so, proudly, I admit, "Yes, I'm his common-law wife."

"Do you live with him?"

"Yes."

"Does anyone else live with you?"

"No."

Why she asks these questions becomes clear when she acknowledges, "That's funny. A woman outside says she's his girlfriend and lives with him."

"What?" I respond, then wonder if one of my friends is trying to see us.

With a horrified look, the nurse backs away, extending her hands as a barrier and saying, "I'm not getting into this." Seeing that she is serious, I laugh.

"We do not live in a ménage à trois, I swear," I yell to her.

Then, to no one in particular, I say, "I can just hear her mumbling to herself, 'He doesn't look so great to me. He must have a lot of money.'"

Suddenly, aware of rules of etiquette, I look around for reactions to my outbursts and notice the staff is laughing. The tension in the room and in my body is broken momentarily, leaving a new appreciation for medical gallows humor.

The episode turns out to be nothing more than a case of mistaken identity, since the man in the bed next to Gene has a name similar to Weinstein. "Good luck," I say under my breath to the girlfriend, knowing the trouble she will have because she is not his relative. Again, I make a mental note to check on power-of-attorney. So far, I have made most decisions, but I can't be sure I'll be allowed to continue.

When my friend Donna, a respiratory therapist, arrives, I cry heaving sobs and a nurse asks me to leave. Then I hear security call Gene's name over the intercom. I laugh at the administrative absurdity of this. He certainly won't answer. Donna checks and finds that security is threatening to tow my van. I have forgotten that, in my haste, I left the van parked next to the emergency entrance. The intrusion of mundane administrative regulations into my state of mind where life and death are at issue makes me feel I'm in a Woody Allen movie.

Donna moves the van. Then a security guard comes to tell me again they are going to tow my vehicle. "Someone else is moving it," I say, and see in his sad eyes and apologetic manner that he is sorry to have bothered me in my misery. I must be a sight as the tears, increasing now to accompany my feeling of appreciation that the security guard has a human side, stream down my face.

"We have to intubate him. The conservative treatment isn't working," Dr. Townson says quickly, but apologetically, as he walks toward me.

"Might he die?"

"Yes."

"Even if he's intubated?"

"Yes, possibly. But we won't feel guilty about it, not you or me. We are doing everything we can. We'll make it as comfortable as possible. And if he doesn't die now, he will die soon anyway."

"OK," I say, choking down sobs that now heave deep between my chest and gut.

Intubation takes only ten minutes, but it seems like hours. I am resigned, and anxious. When I reenter the emergency room, a tube runs down Gene's nose to his lungs. Only when I see how calmly he breathes with the machine doing most of the work do I realize how hard he had labored before. He appears to be sleeping off and on. But his eyes now focus on things and people, revealing that he has some recognition of the outer world.

Dr. Townson is flippant with Gene, much different from his softer style with me. "Finally, we're going to get an intelligent person's opinion of this thing. It's not as bad as you thought it'd be, is it?" Gene shakes his head, yes, violently, and then falls back to sleep.

All the nurses have moved on to other people, leaving me alone with Gene. Is he sleeping? No, as I move closer, he looks dead. There is no breathing, no life anywhere. I beat on his chest. No reaction. I am paralyzed, in shock, and yet I think how absurd to be pounding on what I assume is a dead man. For the first time, I actually experience the sensation of his death. This is no longer practice.

I am tense and taut. Maybe it's better for him. At least the battle is over, I think during a calm clock second that emotionally seems of infinite duration, but which intellectually I know is only an instant.

I can't understand my peaceful demeanor. Perhaps it results from the thought that "this is it." It feels much like the tranquility in the midst of an automobile accident, a premonition of a release from the burdens of life.

Then my heart pounds, as if trying to explode out of my chest. In that instant, I abstractly sense our entire relationship and I scream, though no noise escapes, "No, I don't want him to die. I want more time. Please."

When he moves, my heartbeat diminishes and leaves me feeling I have crossed a threshold. Even if he is not yet dead, I know he will die and I foresee how I might feel when he does. It terrifies me more than I have ever thought possible. But I also discover I will be alive afterward and coping. I calmly call for the nurse.

Several medical attendants hover over him then, working quickly, so I step back. A resident takes his blood pressure, but cannot get a reading. They shoot him with dopamine to raise the pressure, then adjust the bed so he is almost upside down. Now movement indicates life.

The resident apologizes for not telling me what was going on.

"It's OK. I knew."

"Intubation causes this sometimes."

I sit beside Gene for a while, watching his chalk-colored face, the tubes, the calm sleep, and this time no heaving chest. Thank god, he is at peace. What will he be like when he awakes? I wonder, even though I try not to. Will he be angry about the intubation? I had no choice, I remind myself, and feel at ease with what has been done.

I leave for coffee, but when I return and ask to go into the emergency room, a security guard says, "I can't let you do that. You'll have to ask at the admitting window." The woman there says, "You'll have to ask the head nurse." But people are lined up at her office and she's nowhere to be seen. No wonder so few people go into the emergency area.

Pretending to know what I'm doing, I walk through the door leading into emergency. This technique works for me but, I'm sure, not for the casually dressed African-Americans in the waiting room. I think then how differently I would be treated by medical staff if I were not white, educated, and did not speak their language. The relationship between status and hospital treatment and the prejudices of medical staff help me understood why the people in the waiting room sit passively.

My heart quickens when I see that Gene's bed is now empty. Did he die while I was gone? A nurse tells me he has been moved to the coronary care unit. "There is no room in intensive care, but he'll get the same attention and have his own private room in CCU."

"Can I get in there to see him?"

"Yes, and they might let you stay there longer."

When I find the CCU, Gene is sleeping. I check him occasionally to make sure he is alive.

■ ■ ■

"Are you a relative?" a woman asks as she enters. I suspect she is concerned with money matters, because she is well made-up and dressed in business clothing with high heels and jewelry.

"Yes, I am his common-law wife," I say, as though I've said it many times, and act as if it is an ordinary, and, of course, acceptable, relationship. The phrase comes off my lips easily and feels right.

"Oh, dear," she says, handing me papers and then fretting with her hands. "I need a relative to sign these. I don't know if you can sign or not." I note they are the same ones I was not allowed to sign at the admittance office.

"Well, he sure can't," I say, nodding toward Gene. "And he has no relatives here."

"I guess I will allow you to sign them then, but let me warn you, it might not be valid."

When I read what she is "allowing" me to sign, I laugh because my signature is needed to protect the hospital from malpractice claims. I initial statements that give them permission to release information to insurance companies, to receive money directly, and free them from responsibility for Gene's personal items. But I refuse to sign the section stating I am responsible for debts not covered by insurance. "I'm sorry, but I absolutely can't sign that."

"Oh dear, oh dear," she nervously says again, amid more handwringing. "Well, you can't expect the hospital to be responsible."

"I'm sure the hospital doesn't want to be responsible. But neither do I. After all, I'm not his relative."

Then, because I sympathize that she is just trying to do her job, I reassure her. "It's just a matter of principle. His insurance always pays."

"But we must have a signature," she says desperately. I look at Gene and then shrug my shoulders. In a small way, I have gotten revenge on the system. I do not intend to be his wife when it is convenient for the bureaucracy and no kin the rest of the time.

The hospital operated as a bureaucracy functioning as a modern business. It needed rules to assist its efficient operation and thus to make a profit. This sometimes meant that the medical-legal-administrative system forced its personnel to make decisions counter to needs of patients.

Kinship rules, for example, narrowed the number of people whose concerns hospital personnel had to take into account. Even within an acceptable group of relatives, it provided a hierarchy of power so that spouses had more say than children, parents more than grandparents. Thus, medical personnel did not have to spend time making informed decisions on a case-to-case basis about which person the patient might choose to make decisions for him.

Like most hospital rules, this one preserved bureaucratic rationality and professional impersonalization in the face of the human pain suffered by those who made the medical administrative system necessary in the first place. The system was most obvious when it broke down in situations like ours.

Since I am determined to find a legal way to deal with not being Gene's relative, I ask a patient representative about power-of-attorney. "The patient has to sign it," the representative instructs, "and doctors must verify that he knows what he is signing. Then I can notarize it." I drive to a stationary store for forms, and, while there, I look at a file cabinet for Gene. For a fleeting second, I calculate whether it is worthwhile to spend the money, since he won't be alive long. Horrified by the thought, I remind myself not to treat him like a dead man until he's dead. Then, getting into the spirit of buying presents to celebrate that he is alive, I buy other gifts as well.

When I return to see Gene later that evening, he smiles and mouths, "I love you," and, although I've been told many times about respirators, I am surprised that he can't talk. Then I realize the tube goes through his vocal cords.

"Do you know what happened?" I ask. He shakes his head no. "Do you want to know?" Yes. Sometimes his eyes indicate he understands what I'm saying; other times, he falls asleep as I talk. He writes on a piece of paper, "Call Joan and cancel her visit."

The next morning Gene is sleeping when I arrive. When I wake him, he immediately writes, "What happened?" He doesn't remember anything I told him the night before. When I can't read his lips, he becomes frustrated.

The staff asks me to leave only when they vacuum the mucus gathered around his lungs. "It's too unpleasant to watch the suctioning," they say. Why is seeing the sputum I wipe off his mouth any worse when it is in a tube? Or, is it the excruciating pain they don't want me to see?

Dr. Townson comes in and says he has tried to call me. We start for the door to talk in the hall, and stop ourselves, but not before Gene catches the movement. "I want to know," mouths Gene, angrily, "absolutely everything."

Dr. Townson explains the intubation. Gene shows disappointment when Dr. Townson says the tube must stay in until tomorrow. "I hate the tube," he mouths. "It hurts." He then writes, "I think this happened because I wasn't getting enough oxygen."

"No," says Townson. "Your body can't get rid of CO_2."

With anger and pain in his facial movements and eyes blazing, Gene mouths as a statement and a question, "Then I'm dying." Although there is no sound, the words reverberate around the room, casting a chill.

"You're not dying," says Dr. Townson, with an edge of a chuckle. I catch my breath. Townson isn't being truthful. But Gene already knows he's dying, so why does he ask? Dr. Townson continues, "There are some radical things to try," but he hasn't told me about anything else.

Gene mouths to me, "He's not being straight with me." I feel caught in the middle of a spider web, deception tangled every which way I turn, including inward, and I don't know a way out.

When Dr. Townson leaves, Gene turns his face to the wall. I gently turn it back, and say, "Baby, he doesn't want you to give up hope."

"I just want him to be straight with me."

"It's hard to tell someone he's dying."

"I want the truth."

"Basically he's telling you the truth. They don't know anymore."

He becomes uncommunicative, so I go to school. Between classes, without warning, the dam breaks. While I talk to my department chair, I cry. When I tell him about Gene, he says, "But you had time to prepare for this." Then he adds, "But I guess it's still hard to see him this way." The implication is that I should be coping better because I have had time? Bullshit. I talk about Gene with one other colleague. Nobody else seems to know or care, or else they don't know what to say. I want them to care about what I am going through.

Perhaps I expected too much from those not directly involved in the working out of my life story. Perhaps my story threatened their "vital lie" (Becker 1973), which denied death and mortality.

I usually cry in the company of other people, especially when I expect, need, or feel compassion from them. I cry when I introduce the topic of Gene or if someone else suddenly says something about him. I cry for the attachment I feel to a friend who cares. I cry for the loneliness I experience when I talk about Gene's condition with an acquaintance. Lately, I have been crying loudly and unashamedly for myself while alone.

That night Gene has an upset stomach and a bad headache. His request for an aspirin takes an hour to be approved by his doctor. When I see how frustrated he becomes at not being able to respond verbally to my questions, I say, "Let me tell you what happened and how I feel, and you listen." When he doesn't react, I say, "You do care how I feel, don't you?"

With a startled look, he takes my hand, pulls me down close and mouths, "Oh, yes, darling, I care about how you feel. Please tell me."

My closest friend doesn't even know yet that I have experienced his death. He comforts me as I cry and tell him how scared I was in the emergency room. Describing my feelings serves as a catharsis, and I feel better. Gene is still my buddy, my alter ego. Because I am emotionally open, I sob while driving home and feel alone in a way I have never felt. Who will I talk to when he is gone?

The next morning I don't want to wake up from my deep sleep. My body doesn't want to respond to gut-wrenching emotions anymore. So I exist in the moment. What needs to be done right now? I ask myself, so that my thoughts are swayed from reliving the agony. Or I make what's happening into a rational process—this is what's happening to him now, this is what needs to be done to get him through this one, these are the tasks that must be accomplished. I sever my mind from painful emotions. The void makes me more mentally efficient. My calm, cognitive orientation convinces me that I am as in control as I can be as I solve problems and organize my life. Then I think about how little control I actually have, and I get out of bed to stop the thoughts.

■ ■ ■

"Somebody loves you. I wonder who. I wonder who it could be. It must be Gene. Even though he can't scream. I love you." I barely recognize Gene's hoarse, scratchy voice on the telephone, but I recognize this variation of our favorite poem. "Somebody loves you," he continues. "It must be Gene. Cause you're peachy keen. I love you."

I laugh and cry to hear his voice. He is happy, loving, excited to be alive, and glad he can talk. He is also realistic about what is happening. "We will make it through this one and for a while longer. But we can't go on like this. I guess I'll have to have the tube again. But I hate it."

"Was it really that bad?"

"Worse than I ever imagined. It made my throat hurt. And when they suctioned me, it felt like a vacuum cleaner pulling up pieces of my lung."

He continues, "I don't know what we're going to do. I just know I love you. I don't know what I'd do without you. I felt so bad last night when you said, 'Don't you want to know how I feel?' I want to know and I want to be strong for you like you are for me. I want to take care of you in this. I was so wrapped up in myself that I wasn't thinking much about you." His voice starts to crack. "I want to make this as easy on you as possible. I'll do what you say, whatever you want."

I love him then as much as I ever have, and rejoice that the romance is back. Impulsively, I turn off my computer and go directly to the hospital.

■ ■ ■

Gene and I overhear a conversation about an autopsy and then a woman moans and slumps over a patient in a nearby glass cubicle. The nurses pull the curtain, but there is no mistaking the death cry that comes from deep in her soul. It makes us both turn to thoughts of his dying and our feelings about it.

"Who should know the seriousness of your illness?" I ask.

He answers with a question, "Do people in Stony Brook know?"

"Yes," I reply, "although I give few details and let them conclude what they want."

"I don't like everyone there knowing. There is nothing they can do."

"They can and want to offer you support."

"But they want to be reassured I'm OK, and I have to perform."

"But you owe it to them to let them have a part in this. And I need them to support me, especially Joan. That's why I tell her everything."

Dying is social. Who wants only the official actors, the doctors and medical staff, involved? I have openly discussed what has happened in the last few months with close friends, more than I admit to Gene. Sometimes I feel disloyal, like I'm revealing to people that Gene is not in control.

I feel better when Gene says lovingly, "I understand. How are you doing anyway?"

He is trying so hard to be in a good mood and to be supportive, even though he is light-headed and has a headache. Although I feel he shouldn't expend energy, I greedily suck in his concern, and tell him, "I'm scared, down in the dumps, and horribly lonely."

"Oh, baby, I want to live for you."

"I'm glad," I say. "I don't want you to die. I guess living for me is as good a reason as any." I do not know then that I will change my mind.

"Intubation is terrorizing. I don't want it again. But I will if you want me to," he adds quickly.

"If you were going to die without intubation, then I would want you to try it again. Unless you make the decision not to," I add, backing off.

I feel better driving home. Our souls have touched through conversation. I am not in this alone. Gene will help make decisions, for now anyway. Feeling better frees me to work on my manuscript.

■   ■   ■

Dr. Townson calls as I work. "I want to know everything," I tell him. "I can handle it."

"Yes, I think you can. And it's good you're being realistic."

"How long do you think he has?"

"We don't really know, but data show that someone who has been intubated usually has about a year. And since Gene has not been doing well, it's safe to say he has less than that."

I recall that, two months prior, the doctor in Stony Brook also had predicted a year or less. "I see. So we're talking weeks or months."

"Yes," he says kindly. I am numb through the rest of the conversation. "What will happen?" I ask. "Will his lungs just stop working?"

"No, he'll get weaker and weaker and we'll have to intubate him again."

"What happens when intubation doesn't work?"

"We can give him a tracheotomy to connect him directly to a respirator."

"Can he come home?"

"Yes," the doctor says; then he adds, "but would you want him to?"

"No, I don't think so," I say, without knowing what I want. "And I don't think he would either," I continue, to make me feel better. He doesn't even want to be intubated again; surely he won't want to live attached to a machine. "So what do you do then?" I ask.

"At some point," he says, a little nervously, "we just don't intubate him. And I'll make sure it's all comfortable," he hurries to assure me.

"I think Gene wants to know all this."

"I feel that intellectually Gene wants to know everything, but deep inside he doesn't," Dr. Townson responds.

I have assumed Gene wanted to know, but will he want to hear what I just heard? "I'm not sure he wants to hear that there is no hope," I say.

"Exactly," Dr. Townson responds in relief. Did I let him lead me to this conclusion? Do I know what Gene wants? Does Townson? How could he?

Then Dr. Townson says, "I'm going to try some experimental drug that might leach CO_2." I feel renewed hope. Is he just placating me? "But it will make his stomach worse and might negatively affect his breathing."

His pessimism assures me he is telling the truth. There really is no hope. All we can do is prolong the dying process. I write later that day: "How does one handle the hell of no hope? By fantasizing hope. There is no other way—that works. I don't want Gene to be without hope. Yet I want always to be truthful with him. What a dilemma."

■ ■ ■

"I don't know what my prognosis is, but I have an idea you do," Gene says the next day when I visit. When I say nothing, he states in the tone of a question, "I know anyway. I think probably less than a year?"

"I'll tell you what the doctor told me?" I respond in the same tone. When he nods, I continue, "The prognosis for someone who has been intubated is about a year. Since you had problems, you probably have less than that. It depends on your body."

In a sad but matter-of-fact voice, Gene responds, "I wanted to have a year left or at least live until my birthday in June."

"Maybe you will."

"I want to die at home. But that will be too hard on you."

"No, it won't, baby."

"Maybe we could go to the beach, or I would go alone."

"You won't be in shape to do that," I remind him. "When we have talked in the past about a romantic death, we didn't realize the pain you would be in or that the CO_2 would make you incoherent." My experience has helped me to "cut through the myths about dying," particularly the romantic ones (see Lerner 1978, p. 212).

"Maybe it will be better for you to die in the hospital, where I'll have help," I continue. "Staff will know what to do and can ease your discomfort.

One of the hardest things in all this is that in a crisis you can't help me because you lose touch with reality. I never expected that."

"Neither did I. What if I'm on a respirator?"

"Dr. Townson says you could live at home like that," I say hesitantly.

"Well, if I still could talk maybe I could tolerate lying in bed, but I don't want to live attached to a machine. And, I would have to feel decent. Now I feel horrible, short of breath, headachy, and speedy." I share Gene's vacillation; I don't want him to die, but I also can't imagine his living for an extended time on a respirator.

"I know I don't want to be intubated anymore."

"And that is like being on a respirator. Certainly I'll respect your wish, but think about the respirator some more."

"What do you want?" he suddenly asks.

"I guess for you to be intubated one more time if you're willing. I want to feel we still have something left to try," I say, echoing Gene's usual refrain. "I don't want to think that the next time you are hospitalized could be it."

"That sounds reasonable. But if I'm back in the hospital in a week, then what's the use of being intubated one more time?"

I agree, but then say optimistically, "But maybe you'll have a long reprieve. Then the intubation will be worthwhile. And it might give us that much time again." Gene agrees, and I'm glad we see the situation in the same way. "You don't have to live for me; yet I want you to live as long as possible."

"I understand that," he says, "and if ever you decide you've had enough, just tell me."

"Thank you, darling, but I want you around for a while."

"This conversation makes me feel good," Gene offers. "I feel less torn about being obligated to live for you even when the pain gets to be too much. You are making this easier."

He continues, "You seem to be accepting my death and yet not putting up a wall between us. That means so much. In the past when my health has gotten worse, you've protected yourself. Now you're so open and loving. You know I might not really want to die."

"I don't think you do."

"Maybe I'll fight this thing," he says, changing strategy. "Anyway, it's not over till the fat lady sings."

I agree and say, "We haven't lived like you're dying in the past, and I don't want to do it now."

"Me either. It doesn't make sense."

"Do you want to write a statement about not wanting to be attached to a machine?" I ask.

"I guess I should. I wonder how it works."

"Can you just refuse to be intubated?" When he says he doesn't know, I make a note to get information.

"We have an amazing love," he says tenderly. Then, "How do you feel about marriage now?"

"I want it just because I want it. Not because you're dying. Not because you want it. But because of the way I feel about you. I no longer want to hold back anything! No matter the pain."

"I love hearing you say that," Gene says, with an impish grin, not needing to deconstruct the meaning of my every word and motive.

As I help him shave and dress, I notice how weak and shaky he has become. Dying threatens to take on a new reality.

■ ■ ■

"I told the doctor that he and I needed to talk," Gene says on the telephone from the hospital.

"What did he say?"

"He said he had an open talk with you. And I said, but you haven't had one with me. When he asked what I wanted to know, I asked again if I were dying and he said no, that there were things to try."

Does Gene want Dr. Townson to admit he is dying? Should I tell the doctor to be open with Gene? Or maybe the three of us should talk. Or does Gene need someone to be mad at?

"I feel awful now," Gene says. "My head hurts and my lungs are raw." When I start to cry, Gene tries to stop me.

"No, baby, I need to cry," I say.

"I understand. I can't do that. I choke it down, because it is crying for myself."

"But it might make you feel better. I cry for myself and my loss of you. And sometimes I cry directly for the pain you're feeling."

"Don't give up," Gene says, trying to sound cheerful. "I might even have some fight left. But it's hard."

"I haven't given up," I say and then switch to a more immediate topic. "We still haven't called your mother."

Gene responds, "I don't want to call her until after the weekend. They don't need to think about my dying while they're celebrating at my brother's wedding. There will be time to tell them next week. I want to send a telegram, though. To wish Jerry a happy second marriage."

"You think it up, and I'll make sure it gets sent."

After talking to Gene, I note a calm feeling. Whatever happens is all right, I tell myself. My thoughts now echo the doctor's words, "We are doing the best we can." Then I feel nauseated. He's going to die. "I can't stand it," the voice inside screams. So, I go back to work.

11

"I, EUGENE WEINSTEIN, do not wish to be kept alive through attachment to machines," reads the living will we take, along with power-of-attorney forms, to the notary's office on the way home from the hospital.

"You sit on the patio," I tell Gene at home, "while I grade papers; then we'll start our party." After reading one paragraph, I put the papers aside, "Let the party begin. This time is too valuable."

"In fact," I continue, "I've been thinking of telling my publisher that I won't make my December 1 deadline. It's more important that I spend time with you."

Gene is silent, and then says, "You couldn't have given me a better gift. Are you saying this is my time now?"

"Yes, all yours for whatever you want to do with it."

"I feel so loved," he says, tears forming in his eyes.

We open the bottle of Mouton Rothschild we have saved for a special occasion. What is more special than cheating death one more time? I broil steak, while Gene cuts up vegetables, just like old times. We watch the sun set and the stars appear. Each moment seems like eternity, but it is not long enough.

We talk about topics we have not approached before. "I don't want a funeral," Gene says. "I want my body sent to a medical school."

"What about donating organs?"

"Yes, if I can do both. My mother might want a funeral."

"I don't want a funeral, but I'm willing to do anything that anybody wants."

"What will you do right after I die?" Gene asks. "You have to start thinking about that."

"I have been," I tell him. "I plan to go to New York to be with our friends and to Miami to be with your family. It's easier to move me than everyone else. My presence will help legitimate the occasion for mourning."

"That's a good idea."

"Sherry said I might not be strong enough for all this. But I think I will be. It might even be nice to get away for a while."

"I'll give you a list of people to get in touch with when I die," Gene says. "Should I let people know I'm dying? What is the proper etiquette? It feels funny to call and say 'I'm dying.' And why should I?"

"No reason, unless you want to."

"How does one do this time well? I'm doing it like a task, because I don't know any other way."

"There are no models," I say. "Anyway, we want to do it our way. We're doing pretty well. You know, I thought you died in the emergency room."

"The 'icicle' touched your heart, didn't it?"

"That's exactly the way I would describe it. How did you know?"

"I can imagine it," he says. Does he remember what he felt when his son died? Or has he experienced his own imagined death? "But at least you lived though it, and you know you can stand my dying."

"Yes, but I don't know if I can stand your being dead."

"Does this experience remind you of your own mortality?"

"Yes, but that makes me feel better, not worse. To be reminded that all of us will go through some version of this makes it seem less unjust."

Sensitive and attentive to my feelings, Gene wants to help me work through my thoughts. I am reminded of a part of him I love and often miss now—his ability to experience the world from my point of view. How many hundreds of hours we had spent over the last nine years with my telling him every detail of something that had happened or some thought I had had. Through our interaction, I came to know a part of myself that would have been hidden from me otherwise. He got the same from me. "You give good listening," he often said.

I write in my journal: "Sharing in Gene's death is a beautiful experience. To say all the things we want to say, to hold back nothing."

What an intense relationship we have. And we will have an intense death.

■ ■ ■

Gene doesn't sleep well the first night home, and when finally I drift off, I dream that "it" has come again and we are going to the hospital. When I awake in a panic, Gene is pumping out. "Are you OK?" I ask, touching him.

"Yeah, don't worry, go to sleep," he says, nonchalantly, kissing my hand. "This is a preventive measure."

"Have you been sleeping?"

"Yeah, some," he says. "But my lungs are jammed." Jammed? The word makes my heart race. "Not real bad," he reassures me, patting his chest. "You know, like usual."

How closely now I listen to Gene's every word. I dread his losing touch again. But I can't live waiting for "it" to come. Exhausted, I fall asleep. Living on the edge of dying takes a lot of energy.

A few days later, Joan visits. When I come home from school, the atmosphere is warm and Gene is perky, making jokes, and laughing. We feast on Beluga caviar and delight in our extravagance.

While Gene enjoys the new stimulation the next few days, I have time to work without worrying. I feel unpossessive and want him to get the most out of his life. I enjoy having a friend around who is concerned about how I am doing as well. I'm getting closer to all of Gene's best friends now. When did we begin having friendships about Gene, yet apart from him?

I listen as Gene talks frequently on the phone. With acquaintances, he plays down his illness. He tells those closest to him the details of his illness, acknowledging that he probably won't live long, but then ends upbeat, "At least Carolyn and I are close and loving," or "But I seem to be feeling much better now."

Some people continued to respond superficially to Gene's admissions, "You'll be OK. Hang in there." Many still were unable to deal with his illness, or chose not to, and turned to me with their important questions. Some tried to stay in control of feelings. Some cried quietly; others sobbed and asked for support and counseling. Are they crying for themselves and their loss? Or for Gene?

"This is a good-bye call," Gene says dramatically a few times. After one of these, the recipient calls me back, hysterical. "I don't know what to do. I can't stand the thought of Gene dying." I comfort her, but I feel put upon.

When I tell Gene, he says, "I don't want to be overly dramatic. Or leave the problem to you. But I want to be real."

"It's hard to know how to act," I respond, "for us and our friends."

"It's hard to support others," Gene says. "But sometimes I feel loved when someone breaks down. And being the comforter makes me feel strong."

I, too, spend much time talking to people about our situation. "How is he?" people ask. When I say Gene is doing better, people say good and usually act relieved. OK, that's taken care of, I have done my part by asking. But, he isn't good, I want to scream. He's dying. Better than what? I wonder. I am reminded of a passage in *Heartsounds*, a book I am reading, written by Martha Lear about her husband's death from cancer: "Friends say, 'Well?' and I tell them he is better, and they say, 'Wonderful!' and I cannot explain how it is both wonderful and not. I cannot explain that he is recovering in order to die" (1980, p. 439). After a while I change my response to, "Holding steady." Then, "It's just temporary." And then, "He is going downhill rapidly." The benchmark against which I judge his state gets worse.

If I am silent about the deterioration, I do not get my due sympathy, and I live alone in the world of terminal illness; if I claim too much sympathy, I fear I will overdraw my sympathy account (see Clark 1987, pp. 303–308). But Gene is about the only topic I talk about now. Sometimes I realize that I know little about what is going on in my friends' lives, and then I make a concerted attempt to ask about their problems. But my heart isn't in the effort.

Just being able to tell people what is going on helps. A network of friends in Tampa make themselves available and constantly keep in touch about my situation. "We would talk and catch each other up on what was happening," one of them told me later. "If we didn't know, one of us made sure to call you. Or, if we found out you were in an emergency, we worked out who would do what when. It was informal." Just when I needed it, someone phoned or took me for a drink, and gave me positive feedback about how well I was coping, or provided a new insight. "He is lucky to have you to experience this with. Most of us will be old when we die, and go through it alone," a friend says. A chill of recognition goes through me when another, whose brother had died from cancer, admits, "Making living wills, signing POA forms, paying for cremation, all sometimes made me feel I was contributing to his death."

■ ■ ■

"Is there imminent danger?" Gene's mother asks, when I call to catch her up on Gene's condition.

"He seems to be holding steady now," I say, "but the situation could deteriorate again anytime."

"Maybe he isn't getting the best care."

"Yes, he is. This is the natural progression of the disease. It can't be halted."

"I keep wondering if you are hiding anything. But you aren't telling me things are OK. In fact, you're telling me the situation is pretty horrible, so I have to believe you."

■ ■ ■

During the week Gene has been home, we are ecstatic that his health has been so much better than we had hoped. "I didn't expect this," Gene says, when we make love.

"Me either," I say. All the disharmony disappears for the moment. Although the sex cannot be adventurous, feelings of love, attachment, and impending loss make it one of our most loving experiences. His usual irritability and my impatience are smothered by our love and concern about each other's feelings. I write that "there is nothing we hide." Then I add, "Except I hide my depression, my stress, and my impatience."

The lull is interrupted when we go to dinner at our favorite Thai restaurant. When Gene tries to get up to leave, he falls back into the chair. As I help him, I have a sinking feeling we are close to the next plateau, perhaps the final one.

■ ■ ■

"This is hard to believe," the doctor says at our appointment a few days later. "Your CO_2 is down to forty, lower than it's been in years, while the oxygen level is normal. I put your name on medical alert last week, sure you'd be in the hospital before I got back into town," Dr. Townson says flippantly.

Usually Gene likes to hear he is doing much better than he "should" be doing, but today he is angry that the doctor doesn't answer his questions. "Instead, he makes jokes," Gene complains, as we walk to the car.

"But most of your questions—how long do I have? what happens next?—have no answers," I say, feeling empathy with the doctor's position.

"But he doesn't even give me time to formulate questions; he just rushes through." These five-minute appointments do contrast with the unlimited time we had with our New York doctor. But this is a clinic with many patients to see. And Dr. Townson is not hand-holding Dr. Silverman.

■ ■ ■

"I just can't face your condition," Gene's brother, Jerry, says on the phone. "That's why I haven't called you before." Then he suggests things Gene should try.

Exasperated, Gene finally responds, "Give me a break, Jerry. There's nothing we haven't done. Trust me. This is the natural progression of the disease."

"But isn't there still a respirator? Mom said you could try a respirator. You must try," Jerry pleads.

"Jerry, a respirator doesn't make you better. It just prolongs the misery. Besides, it's painful. How would you like to live attached to a machine?"

"Oh," says Jerry. "Let me talk to Mom."

When Gene's mother, who is visiting, gets off the telephone, she says, "Jerry was a little choked up. He couldn't talk anymore. He said to tell you he loved you, because he couldn't say it."

■ ■ ■

"I think a Lazy-Boy chair would help you sleep, especially when you feel you can't lie down," I say.

"I guess," Gene replies, "but I don't know if I have the strength to look at them today."

"Let's try while we're out shopping," I say, "and if you don't, we'll just go home. You're in charge." It doesn't cross my mind then that buying this chair will be the end of sleeping together.

In the store, I try to help Gene push a chair into reclining position as he sits. Shaking his clenched hands, he is exasperated as he says, "You don't understand. I don't have the strength."

Although I recognize that his anger symbolizes his general frustration and I feel sorry for him, I also resent his public outburst. We manage to buy a chair, and Gene apologizes. But when he adds, "Sometimes you cause it by interfering too much or thinking you have the answer," my anger is renewed, and then just as quickly inhibited by thoughts about the patterns of my responses to Gene and how I can make the situation better. When I get home, I write: "I can't express my anger. I am scared he will die while we are angry. I couldn't stand that. Yet I have to do something with my anger. He is unfair. I am only trying to help. And his mind often is slow. Sometimes we have problems because I am way ahead of him in my thoughts and actions."

Why was it so important that Gene not die while we were angry? Because it would have caused me pain and would have made me question whether I had "done dying well." I feared living the rest of my life burdened by guilt and regret.

■ ■ ■

Toward evening, Gene becomes groggy, and he is irritated as soon as something isn't done the way he wants it. "You didn't bring my codeine," he yells when I get his pills. "I told you I need water," he says again when I don't come right away.

"I have already lost my best friend," I write that day, and I experience this feeling now with more certainty. I am glad his mother is visiting so that little direct interaction occurs between us. Yet I feel alone and lonely. That evening, I seek solace in Lear's (1980) *Heartsounds*. I am engrossed by the parallels to my situation. Reading it is like talking to a friend.

Gene and his mother think it strange that I read "death" books. "Don't you get enough of it in your real life?" asks Gene.

"I might learn from others' experiences," I reply. Anyway, death and deterioration are all I'm interested in now. And, it makes me feel better to know others have survived this. Besides, you know how I like to immerse myself. Like eating pizza three days in a row."

Later that evening I write: "Sometimes, like the woman in *Heartsounds,* I wonder if I don't want him to die to get this over. I feel like we are waiting for something to happen. This is 'living like a dying person.' Something we were able to avoid for so long. It is now upon us. So quickly it came."

■ ■ ■

"Look at this pamphlet," Gene's mother says. "There's surgery to arrest emphysema."

"No, Ma," Gene replies, "it's too late. I'm going to die, Ma." Then, "I don't know why I rub your nose in it. I guess so I have to face it. It keeps my emotional muscles strong."

The next day I write:

> Sometimes I want to scream, "Shut up, I don't want to hear anymore." Yesterday, I felt on the edge. The tightness is back full-force. I am choking. My stomach is in knots, although now I am eating instead of dieting. I must get back to that control. It makes me feel good. Food makes the knot feel bigger.
>
> There is a curtain between me and life. Detached, I watch it all go by. I identify with the woman in *Heartsounds,* who says, "When his spirit soars, it is hardest to think of losing him. When querulous, demanding, then it is easiest to accept" (Lear 1980, p. 453). I go through the same ups and downs, except I don't feel the abstract anger she describes. I feel anger only when Gene is unreasonable. Even when I know he can't help it. But sometimes I think he can.
>
> When he feels better, I feel better. How long can I go on feeling this tense? I haven't cried for a long time, although I know there are people who would take care of me if I did. But it seems so useless. Why don't I want to break down? For one thing, I don't want to overburden my friends.

Sunday morning I dream Gene has died. First I feel a release, then I sob as I realize my loss. Although I am in a crowd, nobody notices. When I awake and tell Gene, he says matter-of-factly, "You will feel relieved, you know."

Gene is unable to sleep that night. He says phrases, which, while they are coherent, have no context. Aware that something is wrong, he is concerned about his failing condition. I say repeatedly to myself, "I can't stand this." Then the numbness sets in and I know I can. The next morning, we call Dr. Townson for advice and to alert him that Gene might be returning to the hospital. "Increase your steroids to sixty milligrams a day," Dr. Townson recommends, "and stay in touch."

I reach a new level of exhaustion the next day. When I call from school, Gene's attempt to be gay falls flat. I feel like a walking zombie with heightened emotions. It is almost too much when I find out the department evaluation committee might not approve my application for early promotion to associate professor. Maybe Sherry was right when she asked, "Why are you putting yourself under this pressure now?"

"Because now is when it's happening," I replied.

"Please don't leave me again," Gene pleads when I go home between classes. But when I tell him I will cancel my evening class, he says, "No, go. I don't want to go to the hospital and be intubated."

The nurse's notes from that day confirm my fears: "Extremely lethargic . . . tired but trying desperately to be cheerful. . . . Fell asleep during lunch. . . . As usual concerned about others. . . . This man is a fighter who tries not to complain."

I ask my friends Kathy and Donna to stay with Gene while I go to class. Since Donna gives Gene constant breathing treatments, he is better and sleeping when I arrive home. His pulse has decreased from 128 to 98. "I think he'll make it," Donna says. "If he had gone to the hospital, he probably wouldn't have been intubated, but he would have been given IV-medication. His CO_2 level was up when we came, but it's down now." I am delighted to have company and find our conversation and laughter wonderfully therapeutic. When Karen and Donna leave, I pace, nervous now to be alone with Gene.

For the first time, Gene sleeps in his chair all night. I get up three times to help with breathing treatments. By Wednesday, I am so fatigued that nothing, except taking care of Gene and writing up notes, seems important.

I write: "I wouldn't want Gene to know this, but I felt almost disappointed that he didn't go to the hospital. No not really. I just wanted to get rid of the responsibility. It would be blissful not to think about him all night long."

Sometimes I fantasize that he dies. Then I feel guilty and lonely.

■   ■   ■

"Hi, Dr. Townson, this is Carolyn. Gene seems some better. I've been giving him breathing treatments every half hour."

"You know you'll have to bring him in soon anyway. Don't feel guilty," he repeats. "None of us will."

"Are we doing harm by not bringing him in now?"

"No," he replies. "There isn't much we can do."

"We have a living will," I say, "to be used after one more intubation."

"Don't show it to anyone," he instructs. "We'll take care of it. Don't worry."

I get up with Gene several times the next night. Now that he sleeps in the living room, I have to be more awake when I help him. I think he is going to the hospital, and that he will die soon. Later he will tell me that he had similar thoughts.

On Thursday morning, I wash and dress him, get his medications, and give him breathing treatments. In addition to his regular medications, he now takes potassium and lasix to prevent water retention. When the nurse arrives at 11:00 A.M., Gene is ready to go back to sleep and I barely have enough time to make it to school for my first class. This is not working.

That evening, Gene insists on accompanying me to the airport to pick up Jim, his closest friend. Gene continually nods off in the car while we wait. During the wait, I call a colleague to find out what has happened in my promotion case. "Two out of the four votes are negative," George says, and I cry. "The promotion problem is a catalyst for all the agony inside me," I explain.

"Gene, my promotion vote was split," I say at the car window, unable to keep the information to myself.

His head jerks up, and tears form as he says, "Oh, baby, I wanted you to get promoted before I died." Agony shoots through my gut, and then suddenly Jim appears.

Although Gene perks up from being with Jim, his energy lasts only for thirty to forty-five minute intervals before he falls asleep. Jim gets into the rhythm. When Gene is alert, they talk sociology; when Gene sleeps, Jim reads or talks to me.

Since Jim is around to take care of Gene, I make an appointment to see Rose Andrews, a massage therapist, on Friday. Although several people have recommended her, I am afraid to hope that massage will help. The knot in my stomach is about to explode. I have been on the verge of tears since Tuesday, crying often when alone. Although I cry violently, my tears are only raindrops falling into the ocean compared to the tornado in my heart that wants to explode. With Rose, I find a safe place to let go.

Rose is an attractive middle-aged woman who exudes warmth. As I lie on her table covered with hot packs and warm towels, soothing new-age music plays. Rose holds and gently massages my head. I feel loved already. "Forget everyone you're taking care of," she instructs. "Women almost never get to be taken care of. This is your time. Forget all your obligations and responsibilities. Start to breathe deeply. Let your body relax."

The explosion roars toward the surface. "I'll cry if I relax," I say, and pray she doesn't reject me. Without hesitation, Rose flings off the towels and hot packs. Undaunted by my naked body, she holds me in her arms. "Let it go," she says, "all of it."

I will never forget her angelic face, her maternal embrace. Totally accepting, she absorbs the pain and agony from the volcanic sobs that have been camping in my body. Then she climbs on the table, kneels, and rocks me against her. I travel far inside myself as my internal barriers implode. What I experience is reminiscent of the relief I used to get in Gene's arms, and probably much like a wailing baby being comforted. And, finally, what I had sought in "casual" sex came, spurred on by understanding and total acceptance.

The crying slows as I become self-conscious of my loss of control. Intuitively, Rose says, "Don't stop until you're ready. I'm here for you." With this permission, the sobs pour out again and again. After twenty minutes, the crying finally slows of its own accord, and Rose says, "Talk if you want, or be quiet, or cry some more."

"I'm in such pain," I mutter, and the renewed crying comes more from cognitively feeling sorry for myself than from the physiological and spiritual release of before.

When the crying subsides this time, Rose quietly replaces the hot packs and towels and massages me with long, slow, firm yet gentle strokes. One after another, each muscle relaxes. "You look like a little girl now," she says after working on my face. I like the image. "If you want to cry again, don't hold back." But now the tears are gone, and I enjoy the physical touch. How long it seems since I have been touched!

Rose appears to be in no hurry. Doesn't she have another client? Then, too soon, she whispers, "I'll be back in a few minutes. Just rest."

When she returns, she holds me again for another half hour as I tell her about Gene. Rational advice alternates with her philosophy of healing. She tells me how to touch Gene and send energy to his lungs. She instructs me to take many showers and to sit by fountains to get rid of negative ions. Two hours before, I might have found this absurd. Now I listen closely to what she says and think how showers make me feel. Maybe the good feelings come from more than the restfulness of the water and getting away from the illness. "Anything, I will try anything," I say. For that moment she is my guru, performing miracles, holding my hand and looking into my eyes with concern and intensity. I won't reject anything she says. She is the most pure love imaginable.

"I don't know," she says, "if this is in your belief system, but I want to share some other things with you."

"My belief system is rationality."

"That's a hard one," she responds. "But if it's right for you, then OK."

"But I'm open to other ideas," I say quickly. "Much of it seems to make as much sense as rationality, which doesn't seem to be working now."

"The first twenty days after Gene's death will be an important time," she says. "You and others should pray for his journey."

My body tenses. This sounds too much like the religion I have rejected. "Carry crystals for good ions," she continues.

"I have trouble with some of these ideas," I say gently, but I have such respect that I continue to listen.

"That's OK," she replies, nondefensively. "Take what you can use." I want to believe everything she says. Crystals, crosses, good-luck charms, rationality—what is the difference? Gene will die, no matter what.

■ ■ ■

"Gene, I have to tell you what happened," I say when I bounce through the door.

After my description of Rose, Gene responds, "I'm so happy you found her," and I see love in his eyes. "I can feel the difference," and I realize that I too have contributed to our tension.

For the first time in a while, the world feels manageable. I can think and feel past the moment at hand without necessarily moving to Gene's death. Although I know the problem still exists, within a range I have some freedom.

"You look so peaceful," my friend Susan says when she arrives.

"My life seems more continuous, flowing, and integrated," I respond.

"Yes," she says, "I've had the sense that you had it all categorized—now is the time to jog, now is the time for Gene, now is the time to work." I am amazed at my energy. How much I needed a break from disciplined, controlled routines.

When Susan and I go to a concert, the lightness continues. I feel like a normal person, participating in normal activities. When we come home, Gene is silly, giggly, in a way he hasn't been in a long time. "Jim and I ate marijuana brownies," he says, his eyes crinkling in laughter. "I'm high. I love it."

I smile, appreciating that the fun-loving little boy and lover of life isn't done yet. Then I wonder how much he will suffer when he comes down. It has been several months since he has smoked marijuana. I ask Jim how it has gone, and he says, "Well, there was a time after eating the brownies when we weren't so sure we should have because Gene got a little panicky."

"But now I feel good," Gene says. "And that's what's important." What fun we have laughing. How long will it last?

After a while, I ask Gene if he wants to cuddle in bed. His eyes sparkle, "Yes, you bet." I long to be physically close to him, not for sex, but for emotional connection. We make love and I have an emotional orgasm, once again crying as Gene holds and comforts me. I am sad when he goes to his chair to sleep. But when I awake in the morning, Gene has returned to bed, and we spend the morning cuddling.

■ ■ ■

"Why didn't you turn left there?" Gene asks angrily.

"Gene, it takes the same amount of time going this way," I respond calmly, refusing to react, knowing how hard it is for him to relinquish control of driving. After three hours of showing Jim around, he is tired.

"I want to go home right now. Don't do anything else. Don't even stop at the dry cleaners."

As I fight the traffic past the dry cleaners, Gene says, "Turn in there, why didn't you stop?"

"I can't anticipate that you want something you say you don't."

"But I didn't know you were going to drive right by the cleaners."

Why has he ruined a nice day? Why does he take his frustration out on me? I resent that my anger must be contained and that he doesn't have control over his irascibility anymore. I'll have to swallow my anger from now on.

"That was a lot of self-control," Jim whispers as we get out of the van.

Gene dozes in the Lazy-Boy chair through most of the evening. I take off his shoes and cover him without waking him. He seems so vulnerable. Maternal love wells up in my chest. Yes, he was a bad child today. But I understand.

"I'm worried about you," Gene says later when he awakes. I sit on his lap, glad to be held.

On Sunday Gene feels better, but the irascibility continues. When he asks me to bring pants, I say OK but continue with what I'm doing. "I want my pants," he yells. "You say you're going to do something and then you don't. I don't ask for much."

I say quietly, "You're going to feel real bad about what you're saying." By his look, I can tell he already does. I am learning not to react to his irritability, to view it as part of his disease. Instead of feeling morally outraged at his unfairness, I just want to get through it.

On the way back from taking Jim to the airport, I shop for Christmas gifts while Gene waits in the car. When I come to show Gene possible purchases, he is irritated about being kept waiting. "I don't feel well," he says, "and I want to go home."

"All right, but you said it was OK to shop."

"I know, but now I feel awful. And you were so long."

"I was only twenty minutes," I say, then I calmly apologize, feeling tight and tense. He is irritable again about the route I take home. When we stop at Home Depot, he immediately says, "Why didn't you park over there?"

Finally, I respond, "Be quiet. I can't deal with you and the traffic and the world too." He is silent.

I am tired of being patient. This juxtaposition of frustration and closeness drives me crazy. I never know when Gene will be upset over something minor. Or take out his physical pain on me with verbal aggression. How should I handle this? I can't let this keep happening.

When we are settled at home, I say, "Gene, let's talk through some of the day's events. I want you to see how patient you demand I be."

"OK," he says, happy to do some problem-solving. Gently describing his irascibility relieves my anger and makes me feel better. "I'm sorry," he responds. "It's just so hard. I can't do anything to help you. And I feel bad all the time now."

"I understand," I reply, "but don't take it out on me. I'm your partner."

"I'll try, baby. I will."

12

"YOU ADVERTISE 'an affordable burial,' and I'm calling for rates," I say to the funeral-home director. "This is for arterial embalming and transportation only."

"Five hundred and fifty dollars? The last place wanted only four hundred ninety-two dollars." We talk about charges for loaded mileage, local pickup, embalming, use of facility, and filling out documents. I handle it like a game, and laugh about the absurdity of looking for the cheapest burial.

"This director says we have to have a relative's signature, and that my power of attorney is inadequate. How about your mother?" I ask Gene after putting my hand over the receiver.

"No, tell them I'll sign," Gene says.

The director tells me Gene's signature isn't good enough. "You must be joking," I respond. Apparently, burial is not for the dead. The living have to approve.

"Call another," Gene commands. The next director tells me they can take Gene's signature, but he'd have to come in to sign the papers.

Taking the phone, Gene yells, "I'm a sick man. I can't come there." After much discussion, we found no real reason to sign in person, other than that it was routine. Finally, the director consented to mailing the forms. The problem was that I was not a relative.

■ ■ ■

"Why don't you take Mary's car," I suggest when Gene and his nurse Mary go on errands.

"No, I want to drive," Gene says. "It makes me feel like a whole person."

"But Dr. Townson told you not to drive."

"He said it was OK in the neighborhood."

"Yeah, after you insisted," I think. Gene already has caused several

213

fender benders and his reflexes are not good. I will have to do something soon about his driving. The narrowing of my world brought on by his not being able to drive scared me, but not as much as how he would deal with this added loss of control.

■ ■ ■

"Damn traffic light," I say. When I continue to complain, I sound like Gene when he directs his anger at the environment. I wonder if I learned it from him.

"Why are you so irritable?" Gene asks.

"Because you're well enough for me to be."

■ ■ ■

"Oh, god, no, I can't get up," Gene says, and falls back into his chair. "I don't have the balance or strength. I have to be able to get up," he says over and over, out of breath as he tries unsuccessfully to rise from the chair. I first stare silently and then give him a hand. He is so wobbly when he walks that I worry he will fall.

"I can't stand the disease anymore," Gene says.

"Do you really mean that?"

"No, I still want to be a fighter," he responds quickly, relieving my fear about ending the agony—his and mine.

Since Gene is having trouble standing on his own, I suggest the next day, Thanksgiving Day, that we take the manual wheelchair to dinner at George and Sharon's. "No, I want to walk," he insists.

I try to lead him into using the chair, since this strategy always works better than demanding things be done my way. "Do you think you ought to walk? It might be cold tonight and it's a long walk."

"Is it supposed to be cold?"

"I think so. Why don't you save your energy for dinner? You know how you always feel after a big meal. What do you think?"

He replies, "To be on the safe side, I guess we should take the wheelchair."

"Yes, good idea," I say. "Do you want to ride it to the car now?"

"Why not?" he replies.

Dinner is lively. The food is excellent. All of a sudden, with no warning, Gene decides we must leave immediately. He is impatient as Sharon makes us a care package. When he has to wait outside for her to place our food into the van, he yells, "Hurry up. What's taking so long?" I try, but fail, to cover his outburst with conversation. Embarrassed, I shudder to think what the situation would have been like *sans* wheelchair.

"Listen to yourself," I say. "Do you hear the irascibility?"

He says yes and calms down. In the car, he is defensive, "I was only irritable for a few minutes."

"You always measure irritability by time. I measure it by the bad atmosphere it casts over the occasion. Your aggravation saps me of my strength and compassion."

"I know," he says. "I'm sorry. I don't want to be like that. But when you're scared of life, irritability comes easy."

"Are you scared?"

"No, not really, it's just all so uncertain." I reach out for his hand and he holds on tightly.

On Friday, he again has more trouble than usual breathing. "I have no strength," he says. We agree he is worse now after every excursion. I spend most of the day helping him with his nebulizer treatments. During the evening, I jog and then go to my office to work and make phone calls. It is a relief to be away and to be working. Even so, I call him several times.

Saturday morning I work while he watches television. Then he and I go Christmas shopping. "I want to go," he says, "but it's scary now even on the Amigo."

"I know," I reply. "But listen, I can deal with anything, anything but irritability."

"I'll try, baby, I'll try."

After one store, he is ready to quit. I ask him if he feels like having dinner next door, since he is already out of the car. When he tries it for me, he is miserable, and the food tastes like sandpaper.

"I know our outing was not much fun," he apologizes when we get home. "I'm sorry. I am Ivan Illich—no fun," he says wistfully, his head hanging down. I respond distantly, not wanting to feel the pain.

"Just didn't want you to feel alone," I say, when I get up during the night because I hear Gene groaning. I miss him and wonder if sleeping alone is preparing me for parting.

"Thank you," he weakly smiles, taking the water I offer.

■ ■ ■

"Absolutely not, Beth," Gene yells into the phone. "You will not be a member of the wedding while I die. I want to be with Carolyn." I flinch at his harshness, knowing that Beth must have suggested coming to live with us.

"I will protect our time," Gene says, when he hangs up. "Beth has quit her job to come here. She just visited a few weeks ago. This is special time for me and I hope for you too. I assume you feel you'll have plenty of time alone to do other things when I'm dead."

"Of course it's special time for me, but I need help. Maybe Beth should come for a while," I hesitantly suggest. There are close moments that happen only when Gene and I are alone. Yet we've said everything now we need to. And it would be comforting to have someone with whom to share the burden. Beth loves Gene and is good with him. "It should mean something to you that she wants to be here."

"Let's ask her to visit during Christmas, but not to come to live," Gene suggests, and I agree. "Christmas is only a few weeks away."

. . .

I wait now for something to happen. Normally, when I feel like this, I want the event to occur and be over. But I experience my current dilemma as a nightmare in which my situation can only get worse.

Martha, in *Heartsounds,* says that she didn't realize that after her husband died, she would long for these times when he was an invalid, those times she dreaded so much when they were happening (Lear 1980). "Remember that," I tell myself. "Savor these moments, in spite of their imperfection. Be here with him now. Be happy for this time, no matter how bad it is. It won't last forever."

Is there a difference in perspective after loss? Are things remembered as better than they were? Do we cry for what we had, or for the presence of the other in some more idealized way?

. . .

"It feels weird to think about being alive," says Gene. "But it would be weirder to think about being dead." He grins.

When he says more seriously, "This is a strange, unreal time," I know what he means. It is as if Gene has reached a liminal space between life and death. "There are two realities here," he explains. "One is that I think I could die anytime. Then I get better and have to orient myself to living."

"I live in the same duality," I reply, surviving and dying—two halves of the circle (Lerner 1976, p. 183).

. . .

The first week of December feels like the calm before the storm. What will happen next, and when? Sometimes I get lulled into thinking that things will be better. Then, when the storm hits, and it is inevitable that it will (I know that, don't I?), it is even more of a jolt.

Our orientation has changed to planning for the future now, instead of assuming Gene will die any minute. We can't live all the time as though he is dying.

We stay home most of the week. Teaching classes and working on my manuscript provide breaks from the stress of crisis. Gene comments on my writing, but I am growing more confident about my own ability and need less from him now. It is a good thing, because he has less to give.

Gene seems better, but what does that mean? He rarely gets up from his chair now. It was only a few days ago that he first fell back into the Lazy-Boy chair, but his identity changed to that of an invalid after that event. This scares me. Him too. He mentioned it, but we didn't talk about it. What is there to say? How do we make something positive out of this? We don't, we just cope with the new level. We have stopped talking in the ways we had before.

"You aren't very introspective about all this," I tell Gene.

"Yes, I am, but I try to maintain expressive control. I think one can't be too introspective and do dying well." Is he right? Am I too introspective? Doesn't matter, I can't be any different. Maybe he can't be more introspective because his head is preoccupied with what goes on in his body.

■   ■   ■

"He and I were good for each other," I tell Rose during one of my weekly massages. "I wouldn't have lived this part of my life any other way. Look, I'm speaking in the past tense."

"I've heard you do it several times."

I write that week: "There is a way in which I am now ready for the rest of my life. I feel almost guilty writing this."

■   ■   ■

"Is your life worthwhile?" I ask Gene.

"There have been some good times lately. It's still worth it because we're together. Is it all too much for you? If so, I could just turn up the oxygen and quit taking medication and go out on CO_2." Although he speaks calmly, he is asking if I still want him around.

"No, not yet," I say, and mean it. Will I ever be able to say, "It's time now." I can't imagine life without him. I also can't imagine life continuing very long like this. I am glad I don't have control over the choice. Do I?

We are peaceful now and often share silence and tender looks of love and understanding. Gene seems to have lost some of his fight. So have I. Sometimes I am fine with the eerie calm that has settled; other times, I miss our talks and sharing our anxieties.

Life seems fragile. I feel some financial insecurity; I feel a lot of emotional insecurity. These feelings show in my dreams. In one, I sell our house; in a second, our house burns down.

Everyday I spend several hours on Gene's routines, made more difficult now because he rarely stands. The urine bottle must be emptied, he must have liquid, his pills, his meals, he must be washed. Although I complain to myself, I like this time with him. My patience and kindness are my way to show love now; his is by being appreciative. There is little more to communicate now.

Gene's son, Paul, calls to say he is coming for a week. "Stay only a few days," Gene commands. "I don't want company for more than that." And to me he says, "It'll tire me out. Anyway I want to be with you. You keep me going." I smile at the sentiment, then wonder why we need time alone since we only watch TV.

When I ask Gene again to read my death books to open up conversations about what is happening to us, he refuses. Then he says, "I don't think of this thing in terms of norms or values—of sociology."

"Sociological concepts are pretty useless now, aren't they?" I respond, a little angry at how removed from life experience our chosen discipline seems to be. "But these books are different. They have stories about others going through this experience," I argue. Then I realize it takes all Gene's energy just to cope physically. There is nothing more for him to analyze or compare. He is dying.

When Gene gets a yeast infection on his tongue from some of the medication, Sherry, our physician friend, writes him a prescription. She suggests support stockings for his edema and a change in antacid to help his constipation. Sherry saw things that were important for someone in Gene's condition but that weren't caught by a doctor who saw him once a month.

I realize how well Gene has been doing the past few weeks when on Wednesday his speech again becomes slow and disjointed. I no longer can ignore the inevitability when he says, "I'm on the edge of another attack." For several hours I put cold packs on his head and neck. "Please don't leave me," he pleads. I feel hemmed in, worried about my work and scared that he is going into carbon-dioxide poisoning again.

As I take care of Gene, sometimes I feel love, but mostly I am an efficient robot who wakes him each time he falls asleep. How can I feel nothing? Because I pretend this is not real. Yet a part of me waits for the situation to get worse. The wait is bad enough that I almost welcome what is to come. How many more times can I go through this? Then love escapes from my heart when I pay attention to how hard Gene is trying to keep breathing—the heaving chest, the wide-open mouth. I close off feeling. Because his body hurts, I can't hold him, and I can't get held myself. Both of us feel the loneliness of being in pain separately.

I am only slightly relieved when Gene's condition finally improves.

The next morning, Gene falls into my arms for support when he stands.

For that brief second, his body feels good against mine and I like holding him.

"Soon you might not be able to walk to the bathroom," I say.

"People also deal with that," he replies.

He's right, of course. We reinvent the wheel daily as we figure out how to cope. I want more nursing services, but we still aren't sure insurance will pay.

When I say, "A walker might help support you," he doesn't respond.

By afternoon Gene is again incoherent and nodding off. When I get ready for my dentist appointment, both Gene and Paul, who has arrived, beg me not to leave. What a life I have. I can't even go to the dentist. I block out my petty thoughts and cancel my appointment, glad Gene wants me with him.

"I think I want to cash it in," Gene mumbles.

Paul says, "I vote no on that."

I say nothing and then Gene changes his mind, "No, I want to fight it."

I don't know how I feel then, but Paul is relieved. "You have been there during the important times for me," Paul says, waking Gene from dozing. "I wish I had been more receptive. I wish we had been closer." I wasn't sure Gene understood, but he later would tell me that this was the best time he ever had with his son.

Several times I cry in the bathroom, since I don't want to upset Gene. I think he needs to go to the hospital again. Since Gene is past the point of making decisions, the resolution is in my hands. The knot in my gut wells up. I feel tense and calm, full of energy yet tired. I pour myself a scotch.

"I don't want to go to the hospital," Gene says from his fog.

"Even if you don't have to get intubated?" I ask.

"No, not even then."

"I want to keep you home," I say.

"I like that. It makes me feel loved."

"It makes me feel loving. No cold tubes for my honey."

I inform Dr. Townson of Gene's condition. "He's probably in respiratory failure again," Townson says. "You know he might die this time?" I tell him I do. "How are you doing? That's just as important now."

"Hanging in there. I want to keep him home."

"That's great, but you know if you need the hospital, we can admit him."

"He's decided against intubation," I say, "but he doesn't want to die either."

"I will tell Cloaker, the doctor on duty, not to intubate unless you or Gene say to."

"I want Gene to make the decision."

"By the time he gets here he can't always make it. I'll make it."

"No, I can make it," I continue. "Gene asked me to find out if he might die if he went to sleep."

Dr. Townson laughs nervously, "Well, that wouldn't be so bad, would it? Let him sleep. Turn up his oxygen to one and one-half. If you can't arouse him from sleep, don't be alarmed."

"How many treatments should I give him?" I ask, refusing to hear what the doctor is saying.

"Do whatever you think best. We're in no-man's land now. We can't do things by the book."

From the other room, Gene says, "Don't I get to talk to my doctor?" I hand him a phone, and listen in. He is more coherent now and the doctor speaks optimistically, "There are still things to try." I am glad when his optimism gives Gene hope. "It's OK to sleep," the doctor tells him, and Gene is reassured. Such multiple realities—from sure death to something to try; from sleep as rest to sleep as death. Unfortunately, I know one is taking over the other.

"I am keeping him home and letting him sleep, knowing that there is a possibility he won't wake up," I say to a friend who calls. I am unable to stop crying. I am ready for him to die, and yet, a part of me won't let him.

"I know you're doing what you think is right," she says. "You think you'll form some rational basis on which to make these decisions so it will be easier next time. But it never is."

When I hang up, I suddenly swing into action, making Gene take medicine and treatments, and instructing Paul to keep cold washcloths on his head.

Gene improves quickly, and his appreciation ("You and Paul saved my life") touches my heart, especially when I think that I almost let him die.

Next day, I go to school after Gene's nurse comes. I call home several times and get no answer. I teach my class, even though I feel sure he is at the hospital. How many classes can I miss? When a colleague comes to my class to get me for Gene's call, at least I know he isn't dead.

"I couldn't shit," Gene says, "so I stayed in the bathroom while the nurse went to get suppositories. I couldn't get to the phone." I am relieved to hear his voice and don't understand that this is the beginning of yet another decline.

I stay in my office for a while, to think about what is going on.

Respiratory failure? The doctor's phrase gives me something tangible to tell people. "The doctor says he is in respiratory failure," I will say. See I'm not crying wolf. Do I want more sympathy credit?

I think of all the dreams I have had lately about moving out of our house, death, and funerals. I dreamed one night of telling Gene he had died. In the dream, he says, "But I don't feel it, I don't feel anything."

"You may never," I reply. I remember I had this same dream when my brother died, and I felt the same responsibility of bearing bad news.

I call Gene again and he asks me to come home. "Aren't you OK, baby?" I ask. When he says yes, I tell him, "Then I want to stay here a while." He feels he makes no demands, but he does.

"OK," he says quietly.

"Do you want me to come home?" I ask again.

"Not if you don't want to." I hang up and go home.

I think about what I have to look forward to. "Put it away," I tell myself. When Gene is glad to see me, my spirits lift. I exercise and cook dinner. Then, to create a nice atmosphere, I make a fire in our fireplace. Immediately he worries that the fire clogs his lungs.

I feel sorry for myself. All the happiness and pleasure have been removed from my life. While I sit watching the fire, Gene sends me for things he needs—water, medicine, emptying his pee bottle. He tells me he has to shit now, but isn't sure he can. I want to scream, but try to be gentle. Not really succeeding, I say, "Could I relax for a while without hearing about a problem?"

"You're right," he says sheepishly, and, of course, my heart melts.

"I wish we had more nursing services," I say. "Other than the twelve hours a week Mary comes, I'm on duty constantly."

"You are not," he says, his voice rising. "You're upstairs working a lot of time."

"Even then," I say, "I'm still on call." These discussions go nowhere and make us both feel taken for granted.

When he says, "I do appreciate you," I respond, "Me you too," and smile.

"Would you put the fire out?" he asks softly.

"Of course," I say, and get up, deceiving my tired body, to which I have promised rest.

■ ■ ■

Events are relatively calm during the second week of December. But, my definition of "calm" has changed, since during this week Gene becomes weaker and weaker, until one evening he falls to the floor when he tries to stand. His breathing becomes shallower and the confusion, though less acute, occupies more time. I unsuccessfully try to ignore it.

The next day Gene wants a shower. Since taking a shower has become a relationship problem involving control, this time I take a different approach. "What if you let me decide how to do it, but you have instant veto power about anything you don't like? Or, if you suggest alternatives, I promise to stop what I'm doing immediately and follow them."

When he agrees, a process usually filled with conflict relaxes into one where we work smoothly together. It is important not to fight each other and for me to share control as much as possible.

Later that day, in front of friends, Gene lets me help him from the Lazy-Boy chair to the table. He clasps his arms around my neck as I bend over him. Standing straight pulls him up. I am pleased that they see how well we cooperate. Gene enjoys the sociability and is a wonderful conversationalist.

By that night Gene can't sleep, and I am up with him several times in spite of my two-day virus. Next morning he calls into the bedroom for me to help him get in bed. "Were you missing me?" I ask as I snuggle up to his tiny body.

"Yes," he says, "and I feel alone." Later, when I help him back to his chair, he falls to the floor. He looks up at me like a frightened child. "I'm scared to be so weak," he says calmly, after I help him into the chair.

"I know, baby. I'm scared too. I'm here to help you."

"I love you."

He can't defecate or shower by himself, and now he can't walk. How many more stages are there before death? I wonder as I fall asleep. That night I dream a gang of boys try to kill me. I hide in my childhood house, knowing they can get in and I have no protection. I wake up feeling vulnerable, wanting to call Gene to comfort me, but I know it is better not to upset him.

Instead, when I get up, Gene tells me, "I'm scared. I think I'm losing it." Afraid he's right, I grade papers beside him, and we both are nervous when I leave for a meeting.

It is hard being at school. I feel on the verge of tears. When a colleague asks how Gene is doing, I indicate so-so with my hands, and then go into the bathroom to sob. This episode suggests another reason my colleagues normally don't ask about Gene. Perhaps they suspect that their questions will bring forth my emotion, and they and I will have to deal with its display.

When I arrive home, Gene says, "I don't think we're doing everything we can. I need cold cloths on my head."

"But, baby, I'm so tired."

"Then we need to take me to the hospital or get help. I didn't know you couldn't handle it," he responds angrily.

Although I get the cold cloths then, I already sense it is too late. Even with the cloths and pumping out, he starts babbling about the TV program *Dallas,* as he nods in and out. He still is able to tell me what he is talking about. But then he starts talking back to the TV. When a woman on a program asks a man if he wants to have sex, Gene responds, "No, baby, I can't."

"Don't I turn you on?" the woman asks.

Gene replies, "Yes, you turn me on. It's just that I don't have the strength."

Then he tells me he is playing in a bridge tournament. "Are you serious?"

"Yes, right now I'm playing." Then he names famous bridge players who are playing with him. "It's a simple tournament," he says.

"Baby, listen. You are real sick and you should go to the hospital."

"OK," he readily agrees. After leaving a message with the doctor and obtaining Gene's approval, I call an ambulance. Several men in a fire truck arrive. Why are they here? One says the rescue squad will be here soon. "Who are you?" he asks.

"His common-law wife."

"Oh," replies the man, and then proceeds to ask more questions. "How old is he?" "What medicines does he take?" What difference does it make? I would be asked these questions two other times that same night. Almost in tears, Gene asks me why all these men are around while he is trying to pee.

Because they do not understand how weak he is or how much his body hurts, the men have problems getting him out of the chair. They also don't know how to deal with his oxygen. Eight strange men in the way—it played like a tragic comedy. Why had I let this part of the medical orthodoxy invade my house?

Here I am riding in an ambulance to the emergency room. The sirens roar at stoplights. This must be a movie, or a dream.

At the hospital, I am told Gene's CO_2 level is in the 80s, which is not so bad, but his oxygen is dangerously low at 30. His pH, a measure I don't understand, is 7.24, which the doctor tells me is horrible.

Drs. Townson and Cloaker both arrive from a party. Dr. Townson comes out of the emergency room and says in a kind voice, "His numbers aren't as bad as we thought. We have increased his oxygen to three. We won't intubate. His body is deteriorating from steroids and lack of movement. He's not going to get any better. He might make it through this one or he might die during this hospital stay. But he won't get better."

"Do you think he caught my flu?" I ask, still trying to find a cause.

"No, he didn't catch your flu. He has been building up to this one for a while, probably a few weeks."

When I go in to see Gene, he says, "I can't pee, and I just want to sleep." He is restless, uncomfortable, and weak. "I might die. It's getting close. But I don't think so. I have to get stronger here. This is what I need, a rest." I say nothing, just stroke his brow.

I go home to an empty house, glad to have my dog Poogie curl up beside me. Gene's empty chair looms in a way it never has before. I get up to check one more time that the doors are locked.

When I call Gene the next day, the nurse says he is sleeping and has opened his eyes once but didn't say anything. His CO_2 level is now much worse, up to 111, and his O_2 is 97. I am angry that he hasn't been better monitored during the night, but, after all, we have decided not to use extraordinary means, haven't we? Perhaps staff thought he might die in his sleep from too much CO_2. It would have been nice. My god, it would have been devastating! What do I want?

When I call the hospital at one o'clock, I hear the nurse say, "Do you want to talk to your wife, Mr. Weinstein?"

"He just woke up," she explains to me.

In a frantic voice, Gene says, "I don't know what happened. I'm so scared. And the dreams."

"Do you want me to come there?"

"Yes, oh yes. Please come."

"I'll be there as soon as I can. Try to calm down. We brought you into the hospital last night. You're going to be OK now."

He says, "Yeah, the fire truck came. I have to pee," Gene says, "and I need a washcloth."

"Tell the nurse. What else do you need?"

"An orange sherbet Haagen Dazs milkshake and some fresh-squeezed orange juice." What a strange request.

"Do you want me to live to get out of the hospital?" he suddenly asks.

"Oh, yes," I say, and know that I mean it.

"I don't think I'm going to die. But it's close." I can tell he is trying to process what is going on, to be optimistic and, at the same time, realistic about his chances.

When I arrive, Gene sits on a portable potty in his room. "I can't shit," he says, almost in tears. "And look, I have a catheter in my penis. God, I'm glad you're here."

"The suppositories are in the top drawer. Find them," he commands.

"No, honey, they're at home. You're at the hospital now, and the nurses are unable to give you suppositories because the doctor hasn't ordered them."

A nurse says we have to move him to another room. When the aides try to get him from the bed into the wheelchair, he tells me how he wants it done. Based on past experience of what works, I try to tell the aids what he wants. One of them says nastily to him, "Will you just give us time to get something done?" He apologizes and she says nothing. This angers me; yet I realize she probably hates her job and needs to be detached. All the aides are that way. Yet they are friendly to each other.

Just as we leave the room, Gene says, "The pot. We must take the pot. They're hard to get and I must have one."

"The portable potty can't go off this floor," the nurse interjects.

"There will be one upstairs," I say. Gene looks panicked, but by this time the nurses are rolling him down the hall. I feel motherly, like I must take care of my child's concerns.

Just getting to our destination with all the tubes and poles intact exhausts him. When he chastises me for not bringing his comb from the other room, I explain, "Your comb is at home."

"No, it isn't," he insists. "It was in the other room."

"That was a hospital comb," I say patiently.

"No."

"I brought you here. You had only shorts and a shirt. Nothing else."

"I guess you're right. You know better." He is helpless now, not able to trust his mind. This incident reminds me that lately he relies on my mind more than on his. I recall that even at home this had happened. Parts of his brain seem to blank out sometimes. Then he can't figure out reality, but, at the same time, he proudly works out the answers to TV game-show puzzles faster than contestants.

Gene tells me the dietitian came in while his penis was uncovered. "Nobody bothered to cover me up," he says. "And the tube was sticking in it." Hospital personnel become so desensitized, it's hard for a patient to have dignity. I do not question my premise that dignity and being covered are synonymous. Seven years later, when my dying aunt insists on uncovering herself, justifying her lack of modesty by saying, "This is how I came into the world, this is how I'll go out," I realize that being covered is not inherently dignified, only a social construction.

"I'm so sorry that happened. I won't let that happen again," I say and wonder how I will keep my promise.

When it became apparent that Gene had gotten lost in the cracks of the bureaucracy, I realized how little control I had to make anything happen. Moving from one room to another during a shift change meant Gene was on nobody's list. Thus, he had no nebulizer treatments all day and nothing to drink, the bed wasn't made, and he couldn't wash because he had no washcloth. Unable to pull himself up in bed, he now had open bedsores. The RN who had just come on duty said she couldn't put antiseptic on the infection on his nose because it wasn't on his orders. Another nurse put it on anyway. At some point in this nightmare, I was horrified to think that we might need a nursing home sometime soon.

After the details are finally in place, I ask Gene about a dream he has mentioned continually since I arrived. He says: "I had a big dream and a little dream. The big dream was life. I had trouble breathing and had to pee. The little dream was a multiple dream, where I could dream anything I wanted. I had total control. It scared me."

"Why?" I ask. "Was it a death dream?"

At first he says no. Then, "I decided to have an average dream. Now what is an average dream, I asked myself. So I dreamed about the sunny weather in Florida and people were out. We were at a friend's house."

"Why did you dream an average dream?"

"Because I felt I should."

"Why did this scare you?"

"Because I had all the control."

"Why did that scare you?"

"I didn't like having all the control."

"Why?"

"Because I wasn't supposed to be dreaming at all."

"Why?"

"Because I was gone."

"Dead, you mean?"

"Yeah," he says quietly, almost reverently. "I had the power to die. That's what frightened me. But I knew I wasn't going to die. I want to die with dignity."

"Why do you think prolonging life as long as possible is dying with dignity?"

"It just is. It isn't right not to fight it. People should be able to suffer."

"That sounds awfully Jewish," I say.

"It is," he admits. Then he adds, "Death was coming to Tampa in the form of a dream."

"I think you do have control over your dying unless you get hit with a serious infection. This is a change from my feeling that death just happens."

Surprisingly, he and I have a beautiful evening. "What a love we have had and are having," he says, and I agree. I lie beside him in bed and I cry for how much I have missed our closeness. There is no need for talk now.

"I wouldn't give up this moment for anything," I say as I feed him dinner because he lacks the strength to feed himself. When I'm not with him, sometimes I think I can't bear this tragedy any longer and it would be better for him to die. But then when I see him and we communicate, I can't tolerate the prospect of his death.

13

"I HAVE TO APOLOGIZE to you and Gene," Gene's brother, Jerry, says on the phone. "But I'm not good at handling situations like this. I make business decisions for people every day. I support my mother. But I want to make everything better for my brother and I can't, so I avoid it. But if he died before I saw him, I'd never forgive myself."

"Then you better come now," I reply.

"But what will I say to him?"

"Just hold his hand. The words will come."

"I'll be there tomorrow."

"Remember, Jerry, you can cry."

"In front of him?" he asks incredulously.

"Especially in front of him. It'll let him know you care. Just take a cab to the hospital. I'll work on my classes while you visit Gene."

"But don't you want to be there?"

"Jerry, I see him all the time. It'll be good for the two of you to be alone."

"But I won't know what to say."

"Yes, you will."

"Well, OK, yes, you don't have to meet me. But I'll check outside the airport just in case you decide to come."

Gene is ecstatic when I tell him about the visit. "Great, I can't wait to see him. I was afraid that he didn't want to miss work or he had something else he wanted to do."

"No, that's not it," I say. "He's been afraid to face your condition."

■ ■ ■

"I fed him," Jerry says proudly when I call the next day to see how the visit is going. "I told him when I came in that I was taking care of him. I've never done anything for my brother, and he's never let me, either."

When I go to the hospital in late afternoon, Gene and Jerry are watching

228

football. When Gene has to urinate, Jerry proudly shows me "the best way to get Gene out of bed." I like the closeness between them, but I object to Jerry thinking he now can do things better than I.

"Gene and I managed a bath last week. You should have been there then," I say casually. After that, whenever Jerry starts to tell me about how he solved some problem Gene was having, he adds, "But I don't have to tell you."

"I love you," Gene says to me, as Jerry and I leave to go to dinner. Then he takes Jerry's hand and says, "I love you, too."

Pronouncing Gene's name in pig latin, Jerry says, "I love you, too, Enejay."

At dinner, Jerry says to me, "I don't know how you're doing all this. Gene says it doesn't bother you. That you do it because you care. He wants to believe that you still get something from him."

"It does bother me, Jerry. It's horrible. But the rest is true."

"I understand that," he says. "The whole family does. I'm a selfish person. I wanted to go skiing with my sons and it was inconvenient to come here," he says to explain why he hasn't visited before. Although I appreciate his honesty, I am struck by how different from Gene he is. "But," he continues, "it doesn't mean I love Gene any less. I'm proud of the close relationship he and I have always had."

"Well, I'm not going to try to convince you to change if you're OK being that way. But Gene started questioning your feelings for him."

"I know I was wrong," Jerry says, "and I didn't make a wise decision, but that's just the way I am."

These words remind me of a conversation I had had with Jerry several years before. "I blow up quickly," he had said about his temper. "I can't help it. That's the way we Weinstein men are. If my wife is patient and calm, it blows over in a hurry."

"I know what you mean," I had said. "I'm similar. If Gene blows up at me, then I get angry and scream back. If he will just be patient with me, I'll calm down quickly. That's just the way I am."

"I'm thinking of marrying him," I say suddenly, returning to the present, and am surprised when I don't feel a warning twinge.

"That would be neat," Jerry says. "It's something you want to do for him and he said he wants to do it for you. You know you're at a disadvantage now in your relationship. You can't be pissed off at him. And he knows that."

"I know. It drives me crazy," I say, surprised by his quick insight.

"In some ways Gene handles this similarly to how I think I would. I'd fight it and not let it control me. But I wouldn't be so realistic to think I was going to die. Gene's fighting it and yet he knows death will get him."

Gene's early morning call the next day reflects the conversation he had with Jerry. "Is this still worth it to you?" When I say yes, he asks, "Is it still net plus to have me alive?"

"Yes. And you know how I know it? Because of how I feel in this empty house without you."

"Do I still fill up the spaces for you?"

"You bet. Hey, want to get married?" I ask.

"Do you mean it?"

"Sure do."

"Let's do it."

．　．　．

"The doctor wants to release Gene soon," Jerry says, when he calls from the hospital. "Since the IVs are out, there is nothing more they can do."

"But he's not ready yet," I say. "I'll call Townson."

"He's no longer an acute-care case," Dr. Townson tells me. "The hospital is pushing to release him."

"This is going to be a trip," I say. "He can't walk now."

"I know," says Dr. Townson. "How will you manage?"

"We'll manage," I respond, and then tell Dr. Townson that Gene and I are getting married.

"Good," he says, "it might make things easier."

"Maybe," I respond, "but that's not why we're doing it. We're doing it for the fun of it."

"I hope you don't kill him on your honeymoon."

"Unfortunately, this marriage may never be consummated," I say, and then wish I had taken the bait and said instead, "I hope I do."

．　．　．

"Do you really want to get married?" Gene asks when I arrive to take Jerry to the airport.

When I say yes, he replies, "If that's what you want, then that's what I want. But I don't want it as a gift."

"Oh, I want it, but only if you want it," I say, playing our game.

"Oh, I do," Gene says, his smile covering his face, and I melt from seeing him find pleasure in life even now.

I know now that I want to be Gene's wife; after he dies, I want to have been his wife. The relationship should have the importance and respect in the eyes of the world that it had for me. I want to tell people later about my "husband." I have lost my husband, not just a friend. Take it seriously. Categories such as husband and wife give people clues about the qualities of relationships. Now Gene and I are "category discrepant"; we are not spouses, but we are not just friends.

I want to give this relationship its due before I close the door. I want to have no regrets. I just want it! What fun to plan a wedding, and see Gene's eyes sparkle. Everyone should have a party before death.

"I'm surprised you're coming home so soon," I say.

"Dr. Cloaker said the only reason they kept me this long was to give both of us a break."

On the way back to the airport, Jerry says, "I'm glad I came. I don't think Gene will live much longer. I don't know how you're going to handle him at home."

"Nor do I," I admit, and feel close to Jerry. "I've ordered a hospital bed, potty chair, and tray table."

When I return to visit Gene, I am suddenly aware of how much care he now requires—to sit up, feed himself, and urinate. I thought I could hire people to take care of him, but it isn't working out that way. I'm glad I never imagined how bad it would be.

"Lie down with me," Gene requests. "Are we really getting married?"

"You bet. I'll get blood-test forms this week," I say. "You can get your blood test here in the hospital. How about December twenty-eighth, the day after I return from my parents?"

"Sounds great. And Beth will be here. I'll pay her to cater it."

"This is so romantic," I giggle.

"One thing though. I want a promise of monogamy," Gene says.

"Up to six months," I respond, smiling at the absurdity of the conversation. "Then let's renegotiate."

"Deal," he says.

I leave Gene a copy of the last chapter of my manuscript. "If this book is going to be dedicated to you, you have to approve it," I announce.

"I like feeling I can still do something for you," he says. Even in his condition, he caught some typos and changed a paragraph.

"You know what I'm going to say in the dedication? 'For Gene, of course.' " He smiles.

■   ■   ■

Tuesday I put final touches on my manuscript and turn in semester grades. I talk to the funeral home I have chosen to make sure they have received the local obituary that Gene and I have written. I go to a lab for a blood test. The official birth of my manuscript, Gene's death, and our wedding are dealt with in the same day.

I call an ambulance service to bring Gene home and then decide not to spend the $100 it will cost. When the hospital bed I ordered is delivered, it creates an intruding presence in the middle of our living room.

Finally, I drive to the airport to pick up Beth, who will stay with Gene while I make a quick trip to visit my parents in Virginia. Catching her up on Gene's condition, I tell her how much I need her now. She says she is not angry at Gene for refusing to let her live with us. "I'm prepared to take care of him for as long as I can," she says, "but I feel apprehensive. I haven't gotten my return ticket yet."

"Let's just play that by ear. You don't have to tell Gene you don't have it." She and I now are on the same side.

On Wednesday I write a letter to my editor to enclose with my finished manuscript. "I hope you have not minded my revelations about my situation," I write, "but it is impossible or at least impractical to separate my various roles right now." Afterward, I think that, in a way, they are separate. The person writing this manuscript is different from the person caring for Gene. It is part of my two-track life—one that focuses on taking care of Gene and one that concentrates on keeping up the life that will continue after he dies.

A nurse calls from the hospital to tell me they are ready to release Gene. I rush to the clinic to pick up my blood test form, but it has not been signed by the doctor. Then I go to the courthouse for a marriage form to take to the hospital for Gene's notarized signature. When I get to the hospital, Gene is ready, but he still does not have his blood-test results. "It will take another hour," the lab says.

Gene has requested that Dr. Cloaker notify the hospital notary of his competence, but when I go to the notary, it hasn't been done. "The bureaucracies don't work here," I say to the notary.

I know," she says calmly. I am appalled that Gene can't sign forms without a doctor's OK. At first, Gene also resents it, but now he takes it in stride. I am glad because I have battle fatigue. The notary explains that this is standard procedure for anybody in the hospital. In other words, it does not imply incompetence, it is only a formality.

Beth and I put Gene into bed immediately upon arriving home. Even there, he is uncomfortable. When I get up at four o'clock to help with Gene's treatment, I note that his sheets have been changed. I help him to the portable potty beside his bed. He tells me that Beth changed the sheets when he got on the potty.

He wakes me at 6:30 yelling for help. "I have to shit." I help him to the potty and he sits there thirty minutes before anything happens. When I give him pills, he says over and over, "Thank you."

When I can't get his pill box closed, I am cranky. I apologize and say, "Sometimes I'll be grumpy, but I'll get over it fast. Like when you're irritable."

"That's OK," he says.

Later that morning Beth explains that she changed the sheets during the night when Gene wet the bed without realizing it. Will incontinence and confusion occupy the next stage?

"I stayed up with him until three," Beth says. "He loved it when I rubbed his back."

"I'm glad you're here," I say, feeling close to her.

"You're wonderful," she replies. "I would have been nuts doing this as long as you have."

"Don't ever get killed," she continues. "If you did, he would die in two hours."

I call the notary who will perform our wedding and confirm the December 28 date, the day after my return from Virginia. I ask her to make a symbolic change in the ceremony, to say, "I pronounce you wife and husband."

Gene and I have a conversation about marriage. I don't want to be a wife," I say. "But I want to be married to you."

He replies, "I understand. You want to be family with me."

"That's it, exactly."

"For me, too," he agrees.

"You forgot to get in bed with me last night," Gene reminds, when we finish making up a twenty-person guest list for our wedding. "You said you would."

Although it is time to leave for the airport for my trip to Virginia, I slow down, jump in beside him right then, and tell him how well he is doing, how wonderful he is, and how much I respect him. "I need to hear that," he says. "It helps keep me alive."

I am sad to be leaving, but I haven't seen my parents for a long time. And, being away might renew me, I rationalize, which will be especially important if Gene stays alive a long time. I hope death comes soon, just not while I am away. The closer death comes, the harder it is to believe that death will mean no more Gene. I have convinced myself now to believe that his spirit will continue. My heart feels hollow as I think that I may never see him alive again. I assure myself that I will. Still, my feelings threaten to overwhelm me.

"I'll miss you," Gene says, and I wonder if he also is thinking that this might be our last time together.

"I'm able to leave only because I know you have control over your death and you'll wait until I return," I say.

"I will," he says. "I wouldn't do that to you. Unless I can't help it."

"I love you with all my heart," I say, making contact with Gene one more time from the airport.

"Alive 'til eighty-five, that's my motto," he replies.

■ ■ ■

When I arrive at my parents' house on Friday, I call Gene. "Beth is doing fine," Gene says in a weak voice, "but she has trouble watching me suffer. She and I have planned all the food for the wedding. We'll have spinach pie and champagne and some surprises."

"Beth picked up the marriage certificate. It makes me so happy that you want to marry me at this time instead of wishing I would die."

"Yeah, you betcha', baby. I want you to live." I mostly mean it.

"I'm groggy," he continues, "but Beth says I'm coherent."

Sensing that he is tired, I say, "I'll call often, but we'll have short calls." When I ask to talk to Beth, he continues talking a while before giving the phone to her.

"He took a codeine," Beth explains in a tired voice, "and is groggy, but that's all. I got a nurse for him this afternoon, so that I could do errands. He enjoyed helping me plan the food for your wedding. It's really going to happen, Carolyn. I also got him a bell, so he can ring it when he needs me."

"Try turning his oxygen up to one and one-quarter," I advise. "If he gets worse, turn it down. If he's better, leave it up for a while."

■ ■ ■

"I'm going to marry Gene, if he doesn't die before I get home," I tell my brother Art on Friday night.

"He'll make it," Art says. "I agree with your decision not to tell Mom and Dad now. They don't know about your nine-year relationship, so all this will be hard for them to understand."

"Yeah, they only know he's a good friend, that he's real sick, and I'm taking care of him, though I assume they suspect more."

■ ■ ■

When I call Gene Saturday evening, Beth answers and says, "Gene is totally out of it." I hear yelling and groaning in the background. "He laughs sometimes and sometimes yells 'help me.' "

It's the codeine, we agree. "Does he ask for me?"

"No," Beth answers quietly, thinking I will be disappointed.

"Good," I say, glad not to feel guilty.

"He confused us a couple of times and yelled for you, then me. He has said very little that is coherent since this afternoon. The last thing that made sense was when Sherry came, he said, 'Hi, Sherry,' and then went out of it. At one point, he said, 'I'm trying to break through, but I can't.' "

"Sherry tried to give him a treatment, but he kept falling asleep. Having an hour to relax while she was here was a relief," Beth continues.

"Keep me posted," I say, as I hang up.

Beth calls later to tell me an ambulance has taken Gene to the hospital. "When Gene heard the ambulance," she says, "the only coherent thing he said was, 'no intubation.' He said it about twenty times."

"Don't let them do it then," I say, wishing I was there.

"Gene clawed himself in the stomach and legs in the emergency room," Beth says the next morning. "He says he's trying to stay in touch with his body. His heart was going crazy, up and down. They put in a catheter and gave him an antispasmatic. He calmed down then and slept."

Similar to the last hospitalization, by the morning Gene's CO_2 level had gone up from 99 to 111 after an increased oxygen flow from 1.0 to 1.5, although this time his oxygen level was higher at 70.

"I'm going to breakfast at a friend's house," Beth says, "but I'll keep in touch with the hospital. The nurses say he hasn't responded to anyone so far. I don't like being in the house alone and staring at the empty hospital bed. I worry about you rattling around here alone."

"Yeah, I'm always checking doors."

"I can understand that."

"I guess there's nothing for me to rush back for."

"Doesn't look like it."

When I phone Joan, she says, "I just talked to Gene yesterday morning. He was coherent then."

"Beth said he was alert until he took a codeine. Then he lost it."

"Are you going there now?"

"Only if he comes out of this. What use is my being there otherwise?"

When I call to ask about Gene's condition, the nurse says he is "nonresponsive." "What does that mean?"

"I'll get the head nurse."

The head nurse repeats, "Mr. Weinstein is nonresponsive."

"I'm his wife," I say. "I'm in Virginia and I need to decide whether to come. Is he sleeping or unconscious?"

Reluctantly, the nurse says, "You'd better come now. He's in a coma."

"Well, actually I'd be in more of a hurry if I thought he would come out of it."

"It doesn't look like it," she says. "No, it doesn't look like it."

"Thank you," I say as I hang up and cry.

In spite of the bad news, or maybe because of it, I call to get a flight that day, December 23, one of the two busiest flying days in the year. The only one available is a standby at 6:30 P.M.

"I decided to go even if he died. I want to see his body," I say when I call Joan again.

"Do they know that's important to you?"

"I didn't tell anybody, but Beth will know."

When my parents return from church, I tell them Gene is in a coma, and my brother volunteers to take me to Washington. I am touched when my mother offers to ride to National Airport with us, a place she has refused to go near since my brother's death. "I ought to come to Tampa with you," she continues.

"No, I have lots of people to help me there."

I call my friend Kathy and ask her to pick me up in Tampa. "Oh, yes, please come. I don't think he's going to make it."

"Does he know anyone?"

"He opened his eyes and said, 'Hello, Donna,' when she was there." Now I am even more eager to see him.

On the way to the airport, Art and I talk about my history with Gene. "Guess I'm not getting married after all."

"Oh, I still think you will."

I now have a confirmed flight leaving at 6:30 P.M., arriving at 10:00, for $268. When I find that Eastern has one for $179 leaving at 8:00, arriving at 11:00, I take it, and question my thinking about money even at a time like this. How will I feel if he dies between 10:00 and 11:00? I console myself that since this flight is direct I have less chance of being late.

When I call Beth with new flight information, she says, "Gene comes in and out now, and he knows me. When I told him what happened, he looked me in the eye and said, 'I died last night.' He said it very clearly many times. I reassured him he was still alive. When I told him you were coming, he said he understood."

"Oh, god, I can't wait to get there."

■ ■ ■

When I walk into his room, Gene opens his eyes, they light up, and he hungrily kisses my mouth again and again. Then he goes away. Sometimes his eyes are shut, not sleeping really, but his body moves up and down slowly as if organs are at half-speed. Or, if his eyes are open, they stare blankly. When everyone leaves the room, I talk to him in his unaware condition. "Please do what you need to do. Have a good journey. Come back to us if it's right or relax and go with it if it's time. I love you," I say, and am surprised when he responds softly with, "I love you."

I hold his hand and rub his body. When I say, "Your fiancée is here," he smiles. "It's going to be OK. You'll find peace. You're so brave." Then I tell of the people who send love. I wait calmly without crying.

I am glad to see him and to sense that he knows I'm here. During the next few hours, Gene is not conscious most of the time. But when he occasionally looks at me, I know he's aware of my presence. Other times his eyes are hollow or half-shut with only the whites showing. Since he jumps when the phone rings and becomes alert when he hears voices, I sense that he can hear.

When Kathy, Donna, and Beth return, we hang on to his every word. If this were a movie, this scene would be tragic comedy. Gene says "Ah" and we rush to his side, looking over him like in a Renoir painting. Whenever a new person enters the room, Gene brightens up, smiles, says hello, and sometimes utters the person's name before returning to his inner world. A few times, he looks around the room at the many women gathered there and smiles. I think that to be surrounded by adoring women fulfills his fantasy.

At 2:45 A.M., I settle down to sleep in a chair. Gene cries out when the mucus clumps and chokes him. Sometimes he mutters over and over, "Oh, god," other times "oh, boy," and his head moves quickly from side to side. Each time, I go to him, and say, "It's OK. I'm here. Relax," and he usually calms down. Since the pumper has been left in the room, I give him several treatments. Finally, I sleep from 4:30 to 6:30.

At breakfast I feed him a doughnut and milk. Although he eats it without talking, he smiles often. "Honey," he says finally, "pull me up in bed." Then, "I want a Coke." After I get a Coke, he says, "I'm high," and then mutters, "I died," before returning to his inner world.

At 10:00 A.M., a nurse addresses him as Weinstein, pronouncing a long *e* in the last syllable of his name. "No, it's Weinstein," he says, emphasizing a long *i*. I am shocked to hear him speak again. When he continues talking, I write down his words as though I am a passive observer looking in on the human condition.

Shortly after 10:00 A.M. he says, "Vey is meir." (He says this over and over.) Then, "My stomach and lungs are a ball of fire. I hurt–stomach. I want to work at the controls. I hear voices."

Then Gene says several times, the last time vehemently, "I think I died. I'm not wavering a bit."

When Beth calls, I put Gene on the phone, and he says, "Hello. It's a miracle I'm alive now." He listens for a while and hands the phone to me.

He goes back into his inner world for the next few hours, mumbling incoherently.

At 1:40, he again says that he died.

"What is being dead like?" I ask.

Gene answers seriously, "A bath in chicken ála king."

"Was it fun?"

Gene replies loudly, "No."

"You'll be OK."

"No, I won't," says Gene angrily.

I'm immediately sorry I said that. I have tried to be as truthful as possible. He babbles and only occasionally is he coherent. Then he asks for food. He mentions a big miracle and little miracle.

"I was so cute," he says. "Wasn't supposed to be in control. But I was. It was a godless night." Then, "Do you cater?" I assume he is thinking about our wedding. Soon he falls asleep.

At 2:13, he awakes and says, "My mother will want to take pictures. I want to be in an affair. A marriage."

He seems happy, smiling almost constantly, and mumbling. Once he says, "I'm a sculptor." Much of the time now he is awake and fairly alert.

At 3:00, he says, "First magic words are I love you." He also mumbles the word "transliterated," which means to represent or spell in characters of another alphabet.

When Beth comes at 4:30, I go home to jog. Then I clean house and do wash, rushing back to the hospital to relieve Beth, who will pick up Gene's mother and brother from the airport.

Gene wakes up when I come into the room. The nurse says that he has not eaten or had a treatment since I left because he has been sleeping. He eats the soup I give him as though he is famished, and then devours cookies and milk.

"I can't process information," he says painfully. "Every time I say something, it resonates through me. I keep hearing it."

"Can you understand me?" I ask.

"Yes," he answers.

"It's the CO_2."

"CO_2," he says over and over. "I can't fight it."

"Just hang in there, baby."

Then he says "vital life functions" over and over and periodically calls himself the "miracle man."

I show him our rings, simple coral and turquoise bands. "They came," he says, his face brightening.

"You want to wear them now?"

"Yes," he says and holds up his finger.

I say, "I pronounce us wife and husband. See, we are doing this—just you and me."

"Just you and me," he repeats and smiles.

This is the most coherent he has been. I feel optimistic again, and I appreciate the thirty minutes of closeness we have before the crowd arrives.

The crowd brings mass chaos. I am delighted that Gene is glad to see everyone, until I notice that he is involved in and frustrated by the debate about who should stay the night with him. Everybody—his mother, brother, and daughter—volunteers to stay. I propose going for a walk to decide the matter. Since Beth knows the ropes, I suggest she stays. Everyone agrees, but when we tell Gene, he disagrees.

"Oh, do you want me to be with you?" I ask, happy yet exhausted by the prospect.

"No. My mother," he announces. Then Beth and I decide that she also should stay, and I would take Jerry home with me. Alert and responsive now, Gene talks pig latin to his brother.

When the therapist comes in to give him a treatment, Gene says, "Hi, I'm the miracle man."

When Jerry wants to check on the notary who will marry us, Gene says, "No, Jerry, I don't want to get married."

Surprised, I ask why. "Is it because your head is confused?"

"That's one of the reasons," he says, and doesn't continue.

When I tell Gene to sleep, he says, "Do you think that's a good idea?"

"Are you afraid you might die?" When he shakes his head yes, I reassure him, "No, we won't let you. We'll wake you up."

When I call the hospital at 9:00 A.M. on Christmas Day, Gene's mother answers, "Gene wants you to bring his cuchino shirt, a pair of pants, and a file to manicure his fingernails."

"You think he wants to get married?"

"Of course, silly, why else would he need a good shirt?" she responds affectionately.

"OK, let me think of what I have to do, and I'll call you back." Is he alert enough to get married? Does he have the energy? He didn't last night. I guess he must.

It's finally going to happen. I desperately want the wedding, although I feel overwhelmed. I am glad for the endorphins surging through my body, the extra protection that calmly, yet energetically, has kept me going for months. What a way to plan a wedding. What will I wear? What an absurd thing to worry about. My kimono, which I had planned to wear at our wedding, is at the cleaners. The two dresses I have are both black. I call Gene's mother.

"Oh, no," she says, "don't wear black." Then, trying to accommodate—we all are—she continues, "Or at least you'll put something white around your neck. Or wear pants, that's better. You're modern."

She's right; black is too symbolic. In my closet, I find a white outfit I have never worn. Since Gene likes to help choose my clothes, I call for his approval. We don't talk about getting married. What is there to say? It is something we want, and we both recognize the need to hurry. Gene says, "Bring a glass to break. It's part of the Jewish tradition."

Then I ask Beth to check if there is a notary in the hospital. If not, where will I find one on Christmas Day? Thank goodness we already have our marriage license. When I hang up, Robin, a friend, calls to see if she can visit Gene or help in some way. "Gene is real sick, dying actually," I explain. "But we're getting married today. I have to hang up because I'm looking for a notary."

"I know one," she says, "and I bet he'll marry you."

"That would be wonderful."

She calls back to say her friend Fred will be our notary. "Would you come too?" I ask.

"I'd be delighted," she says. "Honored. Would you like a little music?" I think of Robin's beautiful voice and tell her yes, not believing my good luck. "Do you have a favorite song?" she inquires.

I think quickly. "No, but do you know a song with the refrain, 'Somebody Loves Me' in it?" I sing, "Somebody loves me. I wish I knew. I wish I knew who it could be."

"No, but I'll see what I can do."

"Thanks, Robin," I say in tears.

"I've been wanting to do something special to help you and this is a wonderful opportunity."

"There could be nothing better. What time can you be there?" We decide on 12:30.

I call Sherry because she is Gene's closest friend in Tampa. When George, my colleague, calls, I tell him about the wedding and he says he and his wife will come. There are many other people I want to invite, but since it is already 10:30, there is no time. I put some champagne in a cooler. As Jerry and I leave, I think about flowers, a corsage maybe, but no stores are open.

"See if you can borrow those poinsettias," I say to Gene's brother as we pass through the hospital lobby.

Gene looks happy, yet so old, sick, and tired. "Clean my nails," he commands, after everyone leaves so we can be alone.

"I want to be married," I say to him as I clean.

"I almost called it off because I'm too weak to go through with it," he responds, his shaky, strained voice demonstrating his point. So that was what he meant last night.

"Don't worry, you won't have to do anything other than let me wash you and put on your shirt."

Surprising me by his competence, he says, "I arranged an extra breathing treatment at noon." Then, "I died yesterday," he announces proudly, telling about the experience while I take notes. "I discovered verifiability of spirituality. It's circular. Cognition goes into spirituality which goes into cognition. We can't deny cognition; it's part of spirituality."

"Was it pleasant?" I ask.

"No. It was stomach wrenching."

"Because you were scared?"

"Maybe so. There were no lights. Another time, I died. A little guy came from other place. He kept popping back."

"In the form of a person?"

"Yes."

"Is there a heaven and hell?"

"No. And I don't believe in any of that Bible shit."

"If you could live your life over, would you believe in God?"

"Yes, I guess so. That's hard for me to say."

Since he seems tired, I don't push, but my mind is whirling with questions. "Do you mind that I write down what you say?"

"No, not at all," he answers, actually appearing delighted.

"I love you," I say, looking into his eyes.

"Me you too."

"I'll miss you so much," I say, the words coming from deep in my throat. "My heart aches." Sobbing, I get into his bed for a minute. He hugs me, a resolved, contented look on his face. Even now he offers support. I have never felt more love between us.

Sherry arrives at noon, bringing an orchid corsage sent from another friend who has snipped it from her mother's Christmas plant. Saran Wrap and a rubber band hold it together.

"Somebody in the elevator asked me if I was going to the wedding," Sherry says. What a way to cheer up a hospital on Christmas. Someone jokes that this is one of those weddings where the minister doesn't show.

"That really only happens in a small portion of weddings," another person responds.

"We've been among the small portion a lot lately," I say.

Finally, the notary and musician arrive bringing champagne and food. We take pictures. Our favorite respiratory therapist brings a box of Kleenex. I look at the potted plants we have borrowed and think that I have everything. And all in three hours.

Making nervous jokes about the low cost of the wedding, we wait expectantly for the ceremony to start. Then Gene breaks the silence by saying, "Look, I'm still here. And I died before. I am miracle man." He beams, like it is the biggest accomplishment of his life. I hide my face on his shoulder and we all sob. The realization hits hard this time; my Gene has been dead. Looking at his frail body and happy eyes wrings every bit of love to the surface. It is a beautiful moment, broken finally with a muttered "Oh, my" and nervous laughter from one of the guests.

"This is going to be an emotional ceremony," I say, "and that's OK."

The notary presents us with four services from the Unitarian Church. I look at two and say, "No, I don't think so."

Gene reads the other two. "What do you think?" he asks.

"You're the one who's found spirituality. I'll go along with you. I just want to be sure Fred says 'wife and husband.' " Gene picks the simpler one.

"Do you take this woman to love and care for her?"

"I do," says Gene.

"Do you take this man to love and care for him?"

"I do."

The notary reads: "By the power invested in me by the State of Florida, I now pronounce you husband and wife." I feel wonderful, in spite of the obvious mistake. Who cares? We kiss. Everyone cries except Gene and me. We melt into each other's eyes.

When Robin sings the song she had written, I barely hear the refrain that goes:

> Somebody loves you darling
> Somebody loves you I know.
> Somebody loves you darling
> Somebody loves you so.

I will never forget the peaceful, happy, little-boy look that camouflaged Gene's aged, tired face as he listened.

"Now is the time to break the glass," Gene says when the song is over. Since Gene doesn't have the strength, I announce, "I'll break the glass. That will be my symbol of equality."

Gene giggles, "Great idea. The woman's breaking the glass." Then his relatives say a Jewish prayer. Love, congratulations, hugs, and tears flow freely, punctuated by laughter. We raise our champagne glasses and toast to happiness.

Robin sings "Turn, Turn, Turn," "The Rose," and then our song again. I finally hear our love message in the refrain of the song. It is a perfect wedding.

When Gene and I are left alone, I climb into his bed. "I'm so tired," he says. "I don't know what you want now."

I smile at the implication. "Just to be close." I cuddle in quietly. "It's all done now. You can let go if you want. Whatever is all right."

"I'm so close to dying."

"I know you are."

"It's so hard."

"I know. Do whatever you need to do."

Quickly reality tumbles in. "I have to shit," he says, "now!" Because I can no longer get him out of bed by myself, we ring for the nurse.

14

~~~

I WRITE in my journal:

> The last few days, I have been working at maximum efficiency. The engine is cranking, slow, sure, steady. Decisions. All the time. Mind working. A, then b, then c, which branches 1, 2, 3, 4. Pick a, then off to d, now back to a. Get an overall picture. What has to be done? Priorities, in case everything can't be done. Don't forget to tend to any detail. And know that the most elaborate scheme might be blown by an emergency or a glitch in hospital bureaucracy or Gene's needs.
>
> Don't collapse. Don't overdo. Listen to your body. The endorphins have been in control for some time. Just like at Rex's death. The numbness, the peace—they are my friends, the endorphins. Much like tranquilizers, only better because you don't come down in four hours. I feel like a machine—processing all the time.
>
> I want to awake from the nightmare. But there is no waking. I must stay tuned into Gene's every need.

■ ■ ■

Tangible signs now signal that the end is near. The van title must be changed to Beth's name, my name added to Gene's bank account, and everything notarized. I am amazed at how easily I accomplish things as Gene's wife, and I wonder if everything would have worked out as smoothly without being married.

Dealing the next day with Gene, who feels well enough to be out of sorts, and with Beth, who is exhausted from taking care of Gene for two nights, is more than I can handle. The three of us argue about how forms should be filled out. To add to the stress, Gene has diarrhea three times during the morning, and Beth and I together can barely lift him out of bed.

When Beth leaves, Gene and I discuss his giving $600 to Beth for helping. "I don't think you have to do that," I say. "You've given her your van."

"I don't want her to spend her money while she's here. And I'm loaning her money to fix the van. I told you I want to give my children money when I want."

"But she and I have already agreed that you and I would pay one-half the repairs and she'll pay the other half."

"Why are you negotiating with her?" Why, indeed, I think, as he continues. "That's my responsibility."

At the moment we're paying $15 an hour for nursing services that the insurance company may not reimburse, but what can I do? It's his money.

Changing the subject, Gene and I talk about the last few days. "I remember your coming back from Virginia."

"What were you thinking?" I ask.

"About how loyal you were."

When we talk about whether he was conscious or not, his answer is not definitive. "Sometimes consciousness was sharper and sometimes it narrowed," he acknowledges, "and sometimes I lost it."

"What about your near-death experience? May I record what you say?"

"Sure. In death yin goes into yang and yang into yin. The spiritual person took over. I didn't like that. I didn't know what it was like to be spiritual. Go away. I don't want to think about you, so I'm blocking you out."

"Was it a human being?" I ask.

"Yes."

"A man?"

"Yes."

"What did he look like?"

"Amorphous."

"Did you experience any connection to Bobby [his dead son]?

"No."

"Was spirituality death?"

"Yes."

"How do you know you didn't just dream that?"

"Don't." (Another time in a short conversation he had answered that question with, "When it happens, you just know.") "After knowing the inconsistencies, it's totally inconsistent. Yet the two have to be merged and accommodated. It is binary. 1, 2, 1, 2. That's the way cognition works. Fire, no fire. Spirituality is binary too. But smoother, more coherent in its own way. It really is God."

"One god or many?" I ask.

"One god. God is a person."

"How do you know?"

"Don't. A coherent entity anyway . . . that partakes of human essence."

"Do you think your consciousness will stay intact after death?"

"Yes, that's what death is."

"Would you worship God if you could live?"

"No."

"You don't think it would make any difference?"

"No."

"So you don't think it matters whether you live a good or bad life?"

"No, because I don't know what that means."

"Like hurting versus helping others."

"I'm tired now."

"I have a sense there's a plan," I say. "That even accidents are planned. That everything happening to me is making me into who I'm supposed to be."

"Karma?" he asks.

"I guess."

■ ■ ■

I spend the night at the hospital curled in a chair watching Gene sleep restlessly. His body shakes constantly, but now his lungs no longer work well enough to produce clumps, nor does he have the energy to cough them up. When he asks, I get in bed with him, and then, on my own, join him again later in the night.

Beth spends the next night with him, and, on Friday, she calls to tell me the doctors are willing to release Gene, who wants to come home. When I arrive to pick him up, Beth insists on driving my car while I drive Gene home in her van. "I just want out," she says. "I've had it with caretaking."

When Beth arrives home, I tell her I have to do a few errands, implying that I want her to stay with Gene. She replies, "I'm leaving for a few days. If you do errands, I'll be stuck with caring for him again."

Although I'm aggravated, I tell her to go and recall that she has offered me a day off several times. She has been working consistently hard for eight days, and tends to give her all in these situations. She doesn't pace herself like I try to do. Maybe it will do her good. Maybe I will like being alone with Gene. Maybe I envy her being able to go when I can't.

When she tells Gene she is leaving, he asks, "Do you need to get away from me?"

"No, I need to get away from caretaking."

"I understand," he says. "Go, have a good time."

When Gene and I have a peaceful and loving evening, I realize we have not been alone nearly enough lately. Later, when he brings up his pension,

I suggest watching football, since I don't feel like talking about what will happen after his death.

At 2:00 A.M., Gene is still awake. I give him a treatment; then I hold his hand until he falls asleep, and I appreciate why Beth is so tired.

■ ■ ■

A visiting nurse sent by the hospital explains that there is a movement to return sick people to their homes so families can take care of them. She has one patient on IVs at home, she says, and a nurse visits every six hours. "I will routinely come to your home if you have questions about medications, or whatever." We talk through how to use a bedpan, change sheets while Gene is in bed, and get Gene up, but I already have learned these things from trial and error.

"What I really need," I say, "is someone to stay with Gene."

"That we can't help with, although someone from RESPITE can relieve you for eight dollars an hour."

"But the insurance definitely won't pay for that."

"No, it won't," she agrees. "Do you need me to come back?"

"Not, really, unless he has to be on IVs or a respirator."

The nurse writes in her notes, "The companion seems knowledgeable."

Since Gene is alert, I go over our insurance bills with him. Until a few weeks ago, Gene had taken care of them, even though they had frustrated him. The time has come for me to take on this chore. "You don't understand how complicated they are," he says. And he's right. Some of the bills are paid directly to providers from Blue Cross, while others are paid to us from Major Medical, and parts of some bills are paid by both. Hospitals and doctors mistakenly have sent many of the bills to Florida Blue Cross, instead of New York Blue Cross, which adds to the maze. I am glad for this transition time and Gene's help.

By 2:00 P.M. Gene is mumbling in his sleep, "Turkey just called about nickels and dimes. He called about getting together this weekend." Then he talks about money.

By the time a new nurse, Bonnie, comes, Gene is lethargic and has turned a chalky gray color. The nurse asks how long he has been this bad and what to do if he takes a turn for the worse. Confused, he says, "I don't understand why she's here and you're leaving me." I explain again that I'm doing errands and having dinner. I am surprised that he has forgotten. "Don't be gone long, OK?"

"I won't," I say, "and I'll keep in touch." When I call to tell him I am on my way home, I am relieved to hear Beth has come home early.

Gene sleeps continuously through the evening. "Will we take him to the hospital if he gets worse?" Beth asks.

"I don't know. I haven't had a chance to ask him." When he wakes up and wants to watch a movie, I ask, "Do you want to go back to the hospital if you get worse?"

He thinks for a minute and says, "There's no point now. In a few more days maybe."

"I would rather keep you here."

"You're so lucky to be healthy," he replies.

After the movie, I get in his bed. "I like this," he says. Just give him some peace for a while, I plead silently.

Refreshed, Beth says she will take care of Gene during the night. I hear her get up three different times.

The next day Gene is lethargic and nauseated again. We manipulate his medicine, and, though his ankles are swollen, we stop giving Lasix for water retention because it weakens him. We cut Motrin for pain from 600 to 400 milligrams in case it is affects his stomach.

Since Beth and I have decided to alternate night care, tonight I take over and am up four times. Sometimes he rings his bell so lightly or hollers "help" in such a weak voice, I barely hear. What happened to his booming voice?

■ ■ ■

After Beth leaves the next afternoon, Gene and I have a wonderful talk. Perhaps Beth is correct when she complains, "He only talks to you."

He says he wants a codeine. "But you know what it might do," I respond. "I'll get it if that's what you want."

"I don't want to commit suicide. I just want to feel better."

"Well, it will be risky."

"How long do you think I'll live without taking codeine?"

"Maybe as long as a month," I say, stretching the truth.

"A month?" He has an "oh, no" expression on his face.

"But probably only a few days or a week," I say, wanting to be truthful.

"And if I take codeine?"

"I think you have a fifty percent shot of it getting you now."

"Call Townson," he commands. "I want to know what'll make me feel better."

I call, but it is 4:30 on New Year's Eve, and the clinic has closed. "This is not a question to ask the person covering for Townson," I say.

"I don't want to commit suicide," Gene says again.

"What do you think about during the day when you're so quiet?" I ask, to take his mind off his pain.

"Not much. I can't process information because my body symptoms overpower everything. The only other thing I do is love you. I feel it so strongly."

Holding hands, I say, "I love you so much, I can't believe it." When I see tears in his eyes, I cry. "This is so romantic, a higher moment than flying in the Himalayas."

"Oh, baby, it is," he agrees.

"Do you remember our marriage ceremony?"

"Yes, it was wonderful."

"Somebody said we should have done it a year ago, but I disagreed. This was the best."

"I agree. Will you be OK after I'm gone?"

"Yes, but there'll be a big hole in my life. You've been such a part for so long, my romance for nine years."

"Don't make me a Rex," he says. "Send off my body as soon as I die. Clean the house. Forget me."

"Yeah, sure."

"I mean it."

"I'll be OK, but I'll never forget you, nor do I want to. But I won't spend my life grieving. My life is all I've got."

"At least you'll be OK financially, with a third of my pension."

"Yes, thank you for that. Are you afraid of death?"

"No, I just don't want it. I wish I felt better. I would like to laugh like Mr. McGoo and make you happy."

"Oh, Genie. Genie. Genie," I cry.

■ ■ ■

When Beth comes home, she reads to Gene, and I think how incredible she can be. We watch *Raiders of the Lost Ark* on video and then get ready for New Year's Eve. It will be our last. At midnight, we kiss and open champagne.

"Alive 'til eighty-five. I made it," Gene toasts. But the celebration is shortlived, since his upset stomach prevents him from drinking or carrying on a conversation.

Tonight is Beth's turn to care for Gene. I fall into bed at 12:30 A.M. and am awakened by Gene's bell at 1:30. When Beth doesn't respond, I help him urinate. I wake up again at 4:30 and give him a treatment. He asks me to move his aching legs, which he can no longer move on his own. I am up again at 7:00. Where is Beth? Although I don't like getting up, I am used to it, and I'm glad she's sleeping. Every time I am up, Gene asks me to get into bed with him. I say, "Later, I need good sleep now."

But I feel guilty when I don't. Each time I think that this might be his last request. I'm afraid he might die and I will not have done something for him or been kind to him.

In the morning, I get into his bed. First he must urinate, then spit, then he asks me three times to move his legs. Finally, we fall asleep for a while. When Beth gets up to take care of morning routines, I go back to bed since I will take care of him all day and night.

An hour later, all hell breaks loose. Gene has to defecate, but when I get him onto the portable potty, he can't. I insert some suppositories, and Beth, who is stronger than I, lifts him back into bed. When she hurts his back, I take over. Since I am taller than she, it is easier to stand with his arms clasped around my neck. Then he asks for the bedpan, then to get off, then back on, then for Metamucil, and still nothing. "I can't stand this," Beth says, breaking down. "I was supposed to have left two hours ago for the beach." Please don't leave now, I plead silently. When Beth starts to cry frantically, I understand. If I didn't feel I held this situation together, I would cry too.

We gently roll Gene over and give him an enema. Then he is on the bedpan, then off, then on again. Beth offers to stay, but I tell her to go.

The bathroom saga continues until after 6:00 P.M. The enema makes Gene feel he has to defecate when he doesn't. I call Sherry who says that we should use a water enema to stimulate the bowel.

Gene worries that he disrupted Beth's plans. "I'm not just being difficult," he says.

"I know you aren't, baby," I say. "I understand." Feeling for his agony, I try to be loving even though I am going crazy. When I lift him from the potty into bed, he holds on for a long time.

When I express hope that I make it through this, Gene says, "I should just die."

"No, baby," I say then, "we'll get through this and then things will be better. You have to let me blow off steam too." I don't want him to think he should die. No, no, no.

"I know," he says. "I appreciate you. Thank you." I feel better then and am proud of how well I am coping.

I call the nursing service and find that, because of the holiday, it will cost time and a half for a nurse tonight. Since that's almost $25 an hour, I decide I can handle the situation. But, panicked about what is to come, I call Joan in New York. "Please come," I plead. "I need help."

"I'll be there tomorrow," she says.

That evening Gene and I agree that this has been the most difficult day of all, "and the worst day of my life," Gene adds. "It's too hard. I want to die. I want codeine." When he doesn't insist, I don't respond. Instead, I assure him it is OK to let the water run out of his butt on to the absorbent mats under him.

When Beth gets back at 8:00 P.M., I ask her if she can manage one more night until we get a nurse. She says she feels refreshed after being with her friends for five hours. We agree to four-hour shifts, so we both can get some sleep. When I continually wake up during her time from midnight to four, I feel something isn't right, but when I ask her, she tells me to go back to bed.

At 3:15 I hear Beth sobbing hysterically. "Come into the bedroom," I say gently.

"He's all yours," she says. "I'm through. I'm not doing this at night any more. I can't. I just yelled at him. I can't stand taking care of him now." I feel for her pain and try to comfort her. She pulls away and says, "Every time I do something for him and get back in bed, he rings the bell again." I know what she means. "I can't help it. I yelled at him."

When I go out to take care of Gene, he says in a soft, scared voice, "I don't know what happened. I don't mean to be difficult."

"I know," I say. "Beth's exhausted. That's all. I'll take care of you." I clean the feces off his butt, help him pump out, and rub and move his legs. Then I say gently but firmly, "Now you're going to sleep and I'm going to sleep. OK?" He agrees. "OK." I hear Beth sobbing in the back room as I fall asleep.

Although Gene rang several more times during the night, I managed to sleep a few hours. When I woke up, I was glad Joan was arriving. Beth started to take care of Gene's morning routines so that I could pick up Joan, but suddenly she was sobbing again.

"It's not you," she replies, when Gene asks what happened last night. "You can't help it. It's just that I've gotten no sleep and I can't handle it."

"You just got seven hours of sleep," I say angrily.

"Yes, but I cried myself to sleep and had nightmares."

I am exhausted, not only from the stress of taking care of Gene, but also from dealing with the contradictory emotions I feel toward Beth. From that moment on, I would offer little support.

As soon as Joan and I arrive home, Beth sobs and flees upstairs. Joan follows and explains later, "Beth is exhausted, but she's also jealous of you. She feels used and thinks that if you and Gene didn't need her, you wouldn't want her here."

"We didn't want her to live here. And it's true that when Gene feels well, he turns to me."

"It's akin to sibling rivalry," Joan says.

"I feel for her, but I have no energy for sympathy, Joan."

Joan takes care of Gene while I organize our lives for the next phase, and Beth runs errands. Beth's presence now disturbs my inner peace and makes me tense, so I'm glad when she's out of the house. Since Gene has open sores on his back and buttocks, I order an alternating pressure mattress, moleskin bandages, and an egg-crate ring to sit on.

The head nurse from a new nursing service that I called arrives. She roughly pulls off tape to look at his bedsores. "Our nurses will give medications only as listed on the prescription, no more or less," she states adamantly. "Any change must come from a doctor's order."

"That won't work," I explain, "because already he's not taking medicines as listed on original prescriptions. But I worked closely with the doctor in changing them, and he allows me to manipulate them as I see fit. I don't want to deal with a doctor every time we make a change."

"We simply can't allow that," she says.

"OK," I say, "you do what you have to. I'll work it out with your nurses."

"No," she continues, "they will do only what's ordered by a doctor."

"Look, I don't want to fight your nurses. I have enough problems. I guess we can't use you." Then I call the more expensive nursing service I have been using to arrange for nurses every night.

■ ■ ■

Ada, the night nurse, is a middle-aged woman who tells me she is an ordained metaphysical minister who does astrology and reflexology. Metaphysical to her means "outside the universe." She informs me that she believes in talking to people who are dead, or "over there," as she puts it. I like the peacefulness of the new-age tapes she plays. I tell her that we have given Gene a Fleet enema. Now brown liquid is continuously leaking from his butt and he has cramping and pain. "The doctor doesn't think it's an impaction, but if it was, he said we'd have to bring Gene in. That's absurd, the trip would kill him." The defecation problem doesn't seem to bother Ada, and I sense Gene is in good hands.

I fall into a Valium-induced sleep from midnight until 6:30, when Ada wakes me, "I'm sorry to bother you, but we have a serious problem. Gene has an impacted bowel."

"What do we do?"

"He needs another enema and then when his stool softens it needs to be pulled out."

"By hand?" I ask, glad I have Ada.

"Yes," she responds. "And we'll need plastic gloves."

"Where can I get this stuff now?"

"It doesn't matter because I can't do any of this without a doctor's order."

Disappointed, but realizing that now is not the time to fight this battle, I ask, "What if I try to remove it and you direct me?"

"That might work," she says. The thought of pulling out shit with my bare fingers is disgusting. But Gene is in such pain, I have no choice. Thankful for the barrier of cellophane Ada wraps around my finger, I gently reach up in his rectum and finally, little by little, I am able to loosen enough fecal matter in an hour to give Gene relief. I am proud of my accomplishment.

The next day I phone Dr. Townson to get an order for an enema. "The nurse can do it without an order," he says, and now I am not so sure about nurse Ada. "But call me anytime."

"I don't want to wake you at night."

"That's the way the system works. I go right back to sleep. I'm used to being up and down at night."

"Maybe you could come and sit with Gene since you're up anyway," I joke.

"No, I like waking up in my own bed. What a mess."

"Yes, if you have any magical solutions, be sure to let me know."

"If I did, I would have told you. Things aren't going to get any better, you know."

"I know. But Gene wants to fight as long as possible."

"How far? Do you mean machines and all?"

"No, only as long as his natural body holds out."

"That sounds reasonable," he says.

"I support that," I say. "I got the impaction out last night."

"You're unbelievable," he says, and I am glad he thinks so.

It takes all three of us—Beth, Joan, and me—to take care of Gene the next day. Periodically, I remove more impaction, we clean off the liquid that continues to ooze, move his legs, fix the bed, and put new covering on the sore on his back side. We place guards on the open sores on his heels and ankles. Gene talks only about his pain, not about the impaction or what we're doing to him. He refuses to be helped out of bed.

I hire Betsy Brown from a newspaper ad as day nurse for $8 an hour. I show her what needs to be done and tell her we do not plan to take Gene back to the hospital. Now I have coverage from 11:00 P.M. until 7:00 A.M.

every night and from 7:00 A.M. until 3:00 P.M. five days a week. Beth and I agree to take turns the rest of the time.

■ ■ ■

"Gene, do you mind if I tell Beth to limit calls to thirty minutes? She talks long distance every day, and she's been on the phone now over an hour."

"Beth," he says weakly, and when she comes into the room, he continues, "it's time to get off the phone." How petty I feel to have gotten him involved.

We have new nurses the next two nights. Energetic and caring caregivers, they move Gene's body around and massage his legs to help him sleep. One assumes I am Gene's daughter. "That's OK. It's not immediately apparent," I say.

I spend the morning jogging with friends. What wonderful freedom. I am sorry I had not gotten nurses before, no matter the cost. When Beth leaves to spend time with friends, I enjoy the quiet. I work for awhile, then fix macaroni and cheese for Gene. Since he feels better, we turn off the TV and talk.

"Do you know what's been going on the last few days?" I ask.

"I know you've been upset, probably because of how bad I am," he says.

"That," I say, "but also because of Beth."

"I know that too. I know Beth's version and Joan's version, but I don't know yours." So I tell him, concluding with, "I've worked hard to create a positive, loving atmosphere, and she's ruining it."

"If it costs $500 on phone calls to get through this, don't worry. This is a problem that has always gone on. She feels my women come first." What does getting through this mean? It means until his death, of course, and then I feel worse about complaining to him. Why can't I let go of my anger at Beth. Why are the phone calls so important to me?

"Because this is so difficult and you're being so great," Gene continues, "I want to give you a present. Let me pay someone to index your book."

"Thank you," I say appreciatively, but my sense of reality is confused— Gene won't be around when I construct an index, and then his money will belong to me and his children.

Soon I fall asleep in the chair beside his bed. I had forgotten the peace and love I often experience when we are alone. I want Beth to leave. But, of course, I am not being realistic. The situation won't continue being this calm, and I wouldn't have wanted to be alone with him these last few days. Beth gets only the bad times, and doesn't share in these tranquil periods of nourishment.

"Go to bed," Gene says softly. "You're tired." I barely hear the nurse let herself in at 11:00. I sleep until 6:40, when I help her position Gene in bed, and then I sleep until 9:30, finally long enough to dream. In my dream, Gene is at a sociology meeting in a hospital bed.

∎ ∎ ∎

On Sunday I work all day while the nurse takes care of Gene. Sitting in his chair, Gene watches football during the afternoon. He is well enough to worry that I have not been getting my allergy shots.

Finally, I have time to think. My situation is different from that of most people facing death of a spouse in that I have to plan for a long life afterward. The result is that I hold down two careers now in my two-tracked life. In one, I am Gene's devoted caretaker. In the other, I work to create a life that will go on after Gene—finish my manuscript, keep my career together, maintain my friendships, take care of my health. More and more, I am concentrating on the second. Who will I be? What will I do? Will I have another intimate relationship?

∎ ∎ ∎

"Why are you checking each figure? It's a waste of time," Gene says on Wednesday as I work on insurance bills.

"When you're doing them, you can decide how," I reply, resenting his intrusion and desire to regain control. "When I'm doing them, I want to make decisions." Then, more softly, I add, "If you have suggestions for improvement, I'll listen. But I refuse to be less careful, because I've already caught a one-hundred seventy-five dollar mistake on a nursing bill." After that, he accepts that I am in charge of bills.

Gene has trouble keeping people and events straight. "Thank you for getting me a drink," he said to me yesterday, after Beth brought him water. Then he asked Beth about her father in Luray. When she said, "You are my father," he replied, "No, I mean your grandfather." He realized there was a category problem—my father was in Luray, not Beth's—but then he changed the wrong category—from father to grandfather.

"Are you aware you mix up people?" I ask him.

"Yes, especially in the morning."

"It is worse in the morning," I agree, and then, because I think that if I give him a reason, it will be easier to take, I say, "Probably you don't get enough oxygen to your brain after your shallow breathing at night." To make him feel better, I continue, "It's easy to confuse nurses because you deal with so many," but he doesn't respond.

Gene had always remembered anything that was important to him, though occasionally he forgot to do routine things, like zip his pants. Now, aware that he forgets, he asks the nurse to write down what he wants to say on the phone. My growing fears about his mental acuity are relieved when I hear him talk to a student, "Make it falsifiable. . . . Call the chair at Michigan and use my name." I wonder if I have been overreacting.

. . .

"Hi, Dr. Townson, I need a letter sent to the insurance company saying Gene needs twenty-four-hour-a-day coverage." Then, "You wouldn't believe how well he is doing."

"I hear him talking loudly in the background," he says, as Gene tries to convince me the letter should come to him. "I can't believe he's that strong. Y'all are amazing."

"Gene wants to know how low the prednisone must be to stop physical deterioration. He's on fifty-five units a day now."

"Twenty should do it."

"He wants to do isometrics to walk again," I continue. "Unfortunately, he hasn't been up since last Sunday, when we hurt his back."

The doctor reminds me, "Look, he's not going to get better. He'll never walk again."

"But we don't have to tell him that," I say quietly, walking into another room so Gene can't overhear.

"No, we don't."

"He is optimistic that he will use the Amigo again, so he doesn't want Beth to take his van yet. I like his attitude."

Gene asks to speak with Dr. Townson and then describes his accomplishments of the last few days. When he gets off, he says, "That telephone call was worth it."

. . .

A package arrives from Gene's friend Mark, a colleague at Stony Brook. "You are the 'leader of the band,' " Mark writes to Gene. We cry together as we listen to the song entitled "Leader of the Band" on the Dan Fogelberg album he sent. The song is about an aging leader who has had a powerful impact on the author. The author writes this song to acknowledge to the old man how important and kind he has been, to thank him for all he has done, and to tell him "I love you."

"That's all I ever really wanted," Gene says, "was for people to see me that way. I wanted to put more into the world than I took out. I've tried to live an authentic life. I know I've been fake, but I tried."

I tell him then about a conversation I had while he was in the hospital with a friend of his from his tenure at Vanderbilt. "Lou said you were a godsend at Vanderbilt, the socio-emotional leader. He said you gave so much, always challenged the faculty and got them working, as well as taught them. He said he learned more around your kitchen table than he ever learned in classes." Gene beams at the compliments.

Soon after, his good feeling dissolves quickly into anger when my friend David calls and doesn't ask to talk to him. "I'm writing him a letter telling him I hate him. And," he continues, "I don't want you to be friends with him."

"Gene, I can't believe you want to hurt someone after all the love that's coming in and how loving you've been. Don't do this."

As a compromise, he tears up the letter of recommendation he had on file for this former student, who had not asked for letters from Gene for years.

■ ■ ■

Sometimes I stare at Gene, wondering how we got to this point. He has a yeast infection in his mouth from steroids, lesions on his lip and nose that refuse to heal, and a sore on his ear. The fecal impaction is almost constant, but now the bedsores on his back side and ankles create the biggest problems. The worst is the two-inch open wound around his tail bone that oozes constantly. Every day we slowly pull off old Duoderm— second-skin bandages—and apply new ones as he holds onto the bed railing, moaning.

Because he eats little now, we supplement with Ensure, a high calorie and protein drink. He gets breathing treatments at least every four hours. We wash him, brush his teeth, and shave him. And give him medicines, always medicines. Riopan for his stomach, Lasix for water retention, and all the other pills—we change around like we're playing musical chairs.

It takes two of us to reposition him in bed every few hours. When he sinks down until his chin is tucked into his chest and his almost-motionless feet protrude over the edge, we extend our arms under his shoulders—the nurse on one side and I on the other—and, on the count of three, pull up firmly yet gently, now without Gene's help. When that is painful, Gene instructs over and over, "Only quarter inches at a time," and then it sometimes takes ten minutes to get him positioned. Once there, he insists we continue holding onto his body, because letting go too quickly hurts. Several times a day, we turn him to his side and help him defecate on absorbent pads. At least once an hour we turn him for comfort and to combat the bedsores. We move and massage his legs when they ache.

My notes alert me that the last time we helped him out of bed was January 6, four days ago. His body hurts too much now to be moved; he aches even while he lies in bed. The Motrin he takes for pain no longer works. Other painkillers would slow his respiration, maybe kill him. So? I shake my head free of this thought.

He is a torso with a head that rolls from side to side and two moving arms that tremor so much that he can barely get the nebulizer to his mouth. When someone asks now, we say he is doing OK, and let it go at that.

I still try, but it is more difficult, to have meaningful conversations with Gene. Snatches of good dialogue are abbreviated by shortness of breath, abdominal pain, or his hurting lungs. I show him an article I've been able to complete now that the nurses come regularly, but I don't take his suggestions for revision. When I tell him where I might send the paper for publication, he yells, "Just send it to *Qualitative Sociology*," and I resent that he still wants to have influence over my work.

Yet, sometimes I get into bed with him and feel loving as I cuddle with him. And I appreciate that he continues to want to help me and others. When one of our nurses tells me she is having personal problems, and I offer advice, Gene tells me, "I'm counseling her. I'll handle my clients and you handle yours."

■ ■ ■

Sunday, January 13, is the anniversary of my brother's death. Since Gene's nurse, Betsy, is with him all day, I go jogging, then for a massage. Mostly Gene sleeps, but when he is awake often he is confused and irritated, especially at Beth. The nurse writes that at 10:30 A.M. he was "becoming agitated and provocative when speaking with daughter. Encouraged him to be calm, relax. Appears frustrated due to inability to participate in all activities."

Gene talks continuously about the Super Bowl party he has decided to have. While I was delighted when he first mentioned it, now it has become just one more problem. He orders people around nonstop, demanding that we make Super Bowl party lists, lists that already have been made time and again. When we complain, he apologizes.

The night nurse notes that mostly he is confused. He spends most of the night watching television, dozing, then reading magazines, often sleeping only thirty minutes at a stretch. Every time the nurse manually removes his stool, he states he feels 100 percent better.

On Monday, Gene is more confused and angry than usual. When we are informed that insurance will cover all but the first forty-eight hours per calendar year of nursing care, Gene demands, "Call Total Care, and tell them to bill the insurance company directly."

"No, let's wait since I have bills ready to go out to the insurance company."

"Give me the phone," he says angrily. He calls Total Care and tells them that Linda, who is in charge of billing, is supposed to come out to talk to him about the bills. When I call later, I am told that Linda has not spoken to Gene.

He tells Beth to go to her room. "I want to talk to you in private," he says to me. The conversation makes little sense.

"I have a concept for you," he says, and I assume he is talking about my life after he dies.

"Fowler is your husband," he says several times, smiling. The only Fowler I know is the street near our house.

"But you are my husband."

"No, Fowler is your husband."

He says something about the romance in our relationship, and then mentions the jealousy paper we have written.

"I have money stashed away," he says. Then, "My number-one value is to get points for being a strong fighter and a good person."

He continues talking in fragments about death. "I want to die." "I want you and me to die." "Everybody but you and me to die." "No, I want you and me." "Everybody but Junior." "Everybody but Burt Reynolds; no, I want him to die too."

"I feel no pain," he says repeatedly, which I assume indicates his CO_2 is up.

"He has been this way most of the day," Beth says later, when I tell her of our conversation. "He talked a lot about wanting to be considered a good person, and other things I couldn't understand."

"Sometimes he is unable to get a sentence out," I reply. Beth suggests increasing his medication, but I choose to wait. More steroids will just do more damage.

"I don't know how to think about this," Beth says, expressing my own ambivalence. "I want him to live as long as possible, and yet I'm ready for him to die."

When I increase his oxygen to 1.25, he becomes more clearheaded immediately. This makes me think that he was not getting enough oxygen to his brain.

■ ■ ■

On Wednesday, Gene goes on a rampage, insisting on calling Total Care because he has decided to pay nurses $2 more an hour. The night nurses receive $8 out of the $15 we pay Total Care, and we have increased the day nurse to $10.

"I want to pay my team more because they are a team," he says. "They cover for each other, and they care for me."

I reply, "You have had six or more nurses lately and most have come only once or twice. Do you think they are part of a team? We pay Total Care seven dollars per hour already to organize this team." Two dollars more per hour meant $32 more per day out of our pockets.

"You aren't going to control me like this," Gene screams. "This is my decision and I don't care if it costs a thousand dollars a month, I want to do it." Finally, because I don't have the energy to do anything else, I listen quietly.

When a friend we have invited to the Super Bowl party calls to say she has a slight cold and may not be able to come to the party, it sets him off again. "She absolutely cannot come," he screams. "Don't you care about my condition? I can't risk catching her cold."

I make a conscious decision that it is time to yell back. The behavior of the last few days has gone on long enough. He has turned into a screamer, much like his father had been described to me. His behavior represents a microcosm of Gene at his worst.

To try to extinguish the behavior, I stay mad for a while, even when he makes gestures to make up, such as reaching out or looking as though he will cry. It is a struggle not to give in.

Later that afternoon, I say, "Gene, sometimes you are confused about what's going on."

"So you're telling me I'm a vegetable?"

"No, just confused. I like that you are a spunky fighter. But you don't always take others' needs into account. There have been times when you couldn't organize your life and we have had to do it. Now suddenly you want to reorganize everything, but you don't realize that you mess up all the systems already in place."

When he starts to cry, I say, "I love you and I'm your friend. Why don't you remember that, instead of making me your enemy?"

"Oh, I do," he says. Then he turns immediately to talking about the party, which has become the center of his existence. Plan, plan, plan, he demands, even insisting I draw up floor plans for arranging the chairs. I do what he wants.

Suddenly he talks about death. He says, "I was dead, but I probably hallucinated it all."

"Do you still believe in God?" I ask.

"No, in spirit," he says emphatically. "It's the opposite of cognition, but it includes it. I couldn't believe I was thinking. I wasn't supposed to be thinking because I was dead. Did I say I believed in God?"

"Yes, you did."

"Good grief," he replies.

A nurse came for the evening so Beth and I could go to a Thai restaurant for dinner. I was feeling much closer to her. She was trying hard, and it would have been impossible to do all this without her. Beth was the only person in the world who shared both my love for Gene and the tremendous frustration I felt; the only other person who was scared he would die, yet wished for his death.

When we brought dinner back for Gene, he ate hungrily. "I'm having a party," he says, "because it tastes so good. Feed me."

"Maybe you should feed yourself to keep your muscles working," I say, although I enjoy feeding him. I am a mother, but one who moves from anger to a melting heart almost every day now.

■ ■ ■

On Thursday we have another fight. We always fight in the morning, when he is more confused and presents the schemes he has thought up through the night. He tells me again that he is going to pay nurses $2 extra per hour. Money, rarely a problem in our relationship, would be the theme of the next few days.

"You're causing this problem," I scream.

"No, this time it's you."

I leave the house for school and tell him I have evening plans and that he can make his own arrangements. "I've lost my best friend," he cries as I go out the door, but I keep walking. I want him to let go of paying the nurses more money and I want him off my back about how I do things. His nurse said he sobbed after I left, and complained that I always think I am right and won't back off.

I was mad at him for making me mad. This wasn't doing dying well. Am I being self-serving and stingy? Do I just want the money myself after he dies? Should we pay the nurses more? Will there be enough money?

I go through the day feeling detached from what I am doing. As soon as I get out of my afternoon class, I call Gene. "Baby, I love you and I want to talk to you."

Crying, he says, "I love you so much." I cancel my plans for the evening and go home instead. "We need to talk at night when we have more time and not in the morning when I'm in a hurry to get to school," I suggest.

"But then you're too tired."

"I won't be. I promise."

I feel goodwill between us, but later, when the topic of paying the nurses comes up, we fight again. "What do you care?" he shouts. "You're getting money from my pension. Why are you worried?"

"Because I am. And you're leaving more to your two children than to me." Although I feel petty, disgusting, and self-indulgent, I continue. "I'm last on your list, somewhere after the nurses."

He says, "That isn't true. You are first in my life and I want to give you a lot of money. I'll get a grant or do some consulting."

Suddenly, I listen to what he is saying and I realize that I am arguing with someone without all his marbles. That realization makes it easier to make up, but five minutes later he is talking about paying the nurses again. As obsessed as he is with doing it, I am just as obsessed with stopping him.

"But we need the money," I say. "Who knows how long we'll have to pay nurses. We already are responsible for twenty percent of their cost. And what if your major medical reaches its limit?"

"I have a lot of money," he says.

"Oh you do?" I ask. When I show him the $1,000 balance written in his checkbook, he talks about not having enough to bet at his Super Bowl party.

"You have nine thousand dollars in savings," I respond. "You don't have to worry about betting at the party."

"I don't know if you're bullheaded or just confused," I say, as I go to bed, trying one more time to shake him back to my reality.

15

GENE OFTEN lives now in a fantasy world. Sometimes he is crazy; then, seconds later, rational. This stage will be the hardest, for with it Gene loses his status as "person." I write in my notes: "He has been irascible, confused, and obsessive. He spends his days and nights planning, administering, and repeating himself. This acute delirium is harder than the physical deterioration. He is not my loving Gene anymore, except for a few rare moments. I live for those. And I dread the day they are gone forever. Even writing this scares me shitless."

"The night nurse said Gene was working on insurance forms at five-thirty A.M.," Betsy, the day nurse, whispers when I awake on Friday. "He slept only forty-five minutes the entire night, and he has been making phone calls since seven-fifteen this morning about his Super Bowl party."

"Who have you called?" I ask, turning to Gene, who seems happy but hyperactive and tense.

"I invited Mark to the party. I'll pay his plane fare. I also invited Jim and my brother, but they can't come. I dictated a letter of recommendation for Mark. It was a good letter. Now I want to call Total Care to make sure they're OK with my paying the nurses more money."

"You cannot pay the nurses more money," I say, and leave the room abruptly before I explode.

Late that night, I suggest that Ada go upstairs so that Gene and I might talk. I get into bed with Gene. "I love you, baby."

"Oh, I'm glad," he says. "I love you too."

"Please let's not fight anymore about money," I say. "Let me try to explain again why I don't want to pay the nurses more. I'm worried we will run out of money, and I think we pay the nurses enough. But, on the other hand, I love that you want to spend money for things to bring you joy, like flying people down for the party."

"I'm glad you feel that way," he says, and, thinking we finally agree, I am pleased with my strategy.

"Don't leave yet," Gene pleads, and we cuddle a while.

"Ada said I had to make sure it's OK with you that she take the twenty dollars extra I gave her last night," Gene says when I get up the next morning.

"I don't approve," I say angrily, then decide to be strategic, "unless you want to give each nurse a twenty dollar gift instead of extra wages."

"I want to give them a gift and pay more," he says. I sigh and shake my head, having no idea what to do.

"I want Beth to go," Gene announces. "She's demanding and tries to control me. She doesn't respect my privacy and tells the nurses too much. She told Betsy about my personal life."

"Maybe she might want to go to Miami for a few days while you have company," I say, trying to make peace. I don't want Beth to leave, because I need her and because I see how much she wants to care for him. "She's really been trying," I say, aware of the sudden role reversal between Gene and me.

Gene is impossible all day—demanding, planning, even sending Betsy to the store for a light bulb we don't need. I go to a double-feature movie for relief, but come home before the ending.

I get up when I hear the night nurse going up and down the stairs at 2:00 A.M. Gene has asked her to look for papers that had come from the social-security office. I massage him and talk calmly when he tries to administer bureaucratic details. When I remind him that he needs to rest to get ready for the Super Bowl party, he finally relaxes and sleeps for two hours. When he awakes, he asks the nurse to peel shrimp for the party. Then he requests that she make phone calls for him, since he has trouble dialing with his shaky hands.

When he tells me angrily the next morning that the nurse has a bad attitude, I respond, "If a nurse refuses to do something you ask for, it may be because she thinks I can accomplish the task more easily. Or maybe it isn't a good time. You should listen to her reasoning. You're confusing night and day. Calls can't be made in the middle of the night. Do you understand?" He says he does.

■ ■ ■

Gene continues to be confused on Super Bowl Sunday. When I turn up his oxygen, he gets better immediately. But after breakfast, he tries to tell me about his "managerial school." Then he says, "Get George on the phone. I want to tell him how to handle your promotion."

"Tell me," I say, "and I can tell him. That will be better, because I will have your helpful input yet I can have the satisfaction of doing it myself." Gene agrees. Thinking up logic that he will accept in his fantasy state exhausts me.

Later, he still wants to make the phone call, but when I remind him of our agreement, he says, "Oh, that's right," and lets it drop. I finally am learning to handle this stage, which seems to have its own brand of logic.

When Mark arrives from New York for the Super Bowl, I notice that he talks to me instead of Gene. Finally, I tell him, "This is your last chance to be with Gene. Even if you can't verbally communicate with him, touch him and be close to him."

"That's hard," Mark responds. "We always had a verbal relationship." Later I see him holding Gene's hand.

Although Gene had planned for two weeks for the Super Bowl, now, as the guests arrive, he is so disoriented he can barely utter a sentence. When he does, it usually makes no sense.

People try to relate, but soon they stop paying attention to him, which, given his condition, is the best strategy. About an hour into the game, back pain causes him to moan and yell out for about half the game. I try to make him more comfortable, while others pretend to watch football.

When the game is three-quarters over, Gene improves. But he still can't figure out who is winning or which team is which. After the game he insists the betting pot is $70, which it isn't, and he thinks he has won, which he hasn't. He is frustrated, but mostly so confused that he doesn't know anything is wrong. After everyone leaves, he sleeps. When he awakes and doesn't remember what happened, I tell him how much fun he had.

He is still confused and in pain when his night nurse, Dana, comes. "Is this the beginning of respiratory failure?" she asks. "I have never seen him this lethargic."

Afraid he will die, I stay up until 1:30. "We don't want to take him to the hospital," I tell Dana, choking back tears. How will I stand it when he dies? We talk about having IVs at home, a safer conversation that is oriented to the future.

In bed I remember that the first thing Gene told Mark was how romantic it was to be married and monogamous. The other topic he talked about continuously was calling my colleague about my career. Even in his craziness, I sometimes can see his chain of associations. Mark thinks that the purpose of some of what he does is to block out pain; for example, when he counts students in my classes. Also, he focuses in on a detail and then, even if the circumstances change, that detail keeps coming to the surface. For example, he had decided that each person at the Super Bowl party would bet $10, which would have totaled $70. That number stayed in his mind even though they bet only $5 each.

On Monday, I am up at 6:30 to check Dana's notes. Gene has dozed only occasionally through the night, and Dana writes that he "was demanding, often became irritated, and talked to himself out loud. . . . He wakes up periodically, needing to be reoriented to place and time, then drifts back to sleep." When she offered him a treatment, he asked not to be pushed. He moaned and complained of severe back pain.

When Dana takes Mark to the airport and before the day nurse comes, I crawl in bed with Gene. "You seem better this morning," I say.

"I think so. I'm sorry Mark left so soon. I wanted to talk to him some more about going back with his wife."

"Mark knows how you feel about that."

We have a forty-five-minute cuddle, even though his back hurts. "You know, I love to enjoy. That's one of my best characteristics. God, it's beautiful," he says about the sunrise streaming through the window.

"I want someone to take pictures of us in the sun," he continues, "hugging and kissing. I want a mirror to see myself and to reflect sun from the front of the house." Realizing how long it's been since he's seen his face, I bring him a little pocket mirror.

"No, a big one," he says, and I promise to buy a mirror and also to take lots of pictures.

"Let's turn your bed around," I suggest. Then you can see flowers all the time." He loves the idea.

"I want to give you a gift," he says, "but I need to talk about it because it will be some trouble."

"What is it?" I ask anxiously.

"Another dog. Something to love after I'm gone." We cry together and I am touched by his thoughtfulness. "I don't want you to be lonely."

I love him at that moment with both a mother's and a lover's heart. "I want you to tell everyone we got married. It's important to me," Gene continues, and I know he is thinking of my parents. To appease him, I say I will, but, since I can't risk additional pressure now, I decide to tell them after he dies.

After Gene drinks his protein milkshake, he starts talking in confused phrases again. Does he get less oxygen to his brain when his body digests food?

When I call the doctor later to ask about back pain, he says, "Give him a codeine if you have to."

"But he's already confused."

"Then don't give it to him. Do whatever you have to. It's a collapsed vertebra, from the steroids. There's nothing that can be done."

■ ■ ■

During the next week, Gene moves from being weak and unable to breathe at one liter of oxygen to being hyperactive and confused at 1.25. When he has too little oxygen, he wants to sleep all the time and, even when awake, is sometimes unresponsive. When he is confused, he has two states. In the one, he is a belligerent, senile old man demanding unreasonable things from those around him. In the other, he is a weeping, emotional little boy who is loving and vulnerable. In both, he can be rational one minute and hallucinating the next.

Little that Gene said on Wednesday and Thursday made any sense. When he was coherent by Thursday night, he refused to believe he had been confused for those few days, although he didn't remember anything that had happened then. "Only when I wake up in the morning," he says.

"No, it's more," I say, and we cycle through the conversation again. Then I wonder why it matters. It matters because he is demanding when he is high on carbon dioxide. All his discussion centers on money and power. He is high as if on drugs. Although confused, he rarely forgets anything he plans, and the planning never stops. He calls the nursing service when there is no need and makes arrangements for pest controllers to spray when chemicals would kill him. Beth and I lie now to control him; we tell him he already has made a phone call he wants to make or that lines are busy.

When he is unresponsive I long for him to be better. Sometimes when he gets better but is confused, I think of how peaceful it was when he was unresponsive. When he is high on CO_2, sometimes he is loving. When levels are right, mostly he feels pain. Sometimes he gets demanding because of pain, and sometimes he is stoic. Gene the complainer fluctuates with Gene the fighter.

I write that week about my own feelings: "I am on a roller coaster. There is no happiness in my life. That's not quite true. When he and I touch, when he is loving, I feel wonderful. And, in spite of all this, I don't like to leave him although I need to sometimes. I want to be around for those good moments, like the puppy discussion. And I still think of how empty my life will be when he dies."

■ ■ ■

"He has gone absolutely nuts," Beth writes in a letter she leaves behind when she goes to the beach. "He's talking on the phone to Joan about getting grants, driving the van, and god knows what. He wants me to go to

Miami to see his mother, but he wants me to take your car so he can have the van when his back is magically cured so he can amigo at the minimum and probably drive himself. And now he's called the exterminator to come."

Gene also tells me he has called Missouri and Texas about getting a toy fox terrier puppy. Then, quickly, he moves to buying a new car. "I want a Chrysler Charger. I want to buy an American car." Then, "I had a discussion with Jack Jones," who is a psychology professor at my university. "We discussed whether same/different is hard-wired and the role of language and Chomsky." He gets angry when I question whether he has actually had the conversation. "Call him," he insists, "if you don't believe me."

Instead I ask when the conversation took place. "Yesterday," he replies. Then, "No, I had lunch with him a few days before. I can't remember when, but I know I talked to him and I think it was today."

■ ■ ■

On Monday night I show Gene pictures from our around-the-world trip. I am surprised when he can name all the places and buildings, especially since he has faded in and out of reality all day. When I can't remember some of the names, he says," "Who's crazy here? You or me? I trust my memory more than yours." I smile and enjoy his mastery. He lovingly recalls some of our good times. Then he becomes more interested in organizing the pictures than actually looking at them.

■ ■ ■

"It's going to be hard for you to let him go," nurse Ada says, when she arrives that night, "and you'll have to do a lot of soul searching. But it won't be fair to hold on."

"It's going to be harder for him to let go than for me."

"At some point," she continues, "he won't have a choice and then it will be up to you. I believe he will go to another reality."

I listen quietly, as she continues, "I've dealt with situations like this before and you have to help him not be afraid. Just make his physical body more comfortable."

Maybe I can learn from her experiences. Or is she a kook? "I don't think he's afraid of death," I say, "and I don't think that he really wants to continue living."

"I have helped people let go," she says. "You can keep him alive by holding on."

■ ■ ■

"Fuck it," he says over and over when he gets an erection as I play with his penis. Although it withers as soon as there is penetration, Gene is delighted and says repeatedly, "I'm not impotent. It felt so good. I want to do it some more." The next day he would say uninhibitedly in front of his nurse that he "wanted to fuck again."

Later Wednesday night he turns blue and we increase his oxygen to 1.25. At 5:30 A.M., Dana wakes me to say he is belligerent. Assuming his CO_2 is up, we decrease his oxygen. "He insists I make phone calls in the night," she says, "and I can't talk him out of it." I calm him by getting him to close his eyes. Every time he starts to plan, I stop his thought processes with soothing talk. When he falls asleep, his vulnerability tears at my heart.

Often Gene hallucinates now about being famous or "filthy rich." He tells me he wants to be president of Northwestern University, where he got his Ph.D. "I'll hire Jonathan Black," he says, who is a well-known sociologist. "He'll be chair at Stony Brook," Gene continues. "Even if I die, Black can take over as president. I need someone with money to back me."

"Who?" I ask, now getting into the fantasy.

He names the father-in-law of a sociologist, who probably has financial resources but is someone Gene has never met.

Then he talks incessantly about the "diamond worth hundreds of millions" he gave his first wife. "My in-laws have it and I want it back." Then we have to prevent him from phoning them.

I wonder if our arguments about paying the nurses have contributed to his obsessiveness about money. Then before taking too much credit, I remind myself that he also hallucinates about the TV program *Dallas*.

■ ■ ■

On Friday, January 25, I take the day off to exercise. Beth says Gene has been hallucinating all day. The nurse writes that he is unable to relate date, month, or year. We turn his oxygen down to one in early afternoon, and by seven o'clock he is totally coherent but in a bad mood. "You turned down my oxygen too much. I'm suffocating," he accuses.

Angry, I say, "You can have it where you want it, but you hallucinate when it's up."

Refusing to believe me, he constantly queries, "Am I hallucinating now because I took so long getting that sentence out? How about now?"

"No, Gene," I patiently answer, deciding that there is nothing to gain by convincing him he has been out of it. He is angry when I try to move him, and he blows up when I leave him to get into the hot tub for ten minutes. "I'm in pain," he yells, referring to his constant back muscle spasms.

When I go upstairs to talk on the phone to a former student of his, Gene says, "I feel paranoid when you do that."

"But it's easier to be honest with people about your condition if I don't have an audience, even you," I say. "I'll tell you everything I say," I lie, thinking that most paranoia has some basis in fact. Most of the time he hasn't been aware when I left the room to talk to people. Now, he insists on knowing immediately to whom I am talking.

The former student asks questions about Gene's condition and I answer honestly. Then he calls back to ask, "Is Gene dying?" I say yes. "Any chance of his getting better?" I respond no. "I had a stormy relationship with him, but there were a lot of things I never got to say to him."

"A number of people seem to have had ambivalent relationships with Gene and now feel the need to tell him how much he meant to them. Unfortunately, he may not be able to understand."

"Does it bother you to talk about him dying?" he asks.

"Not at all, I do it all the time."

■　■　■

On Saturday, I go by myself to see *The River*. This movie about human struggle makes tears well up again and again, but I fear if I let go, I will never stop. I feel as though Gene is already dead. Being in the theater reminds me of how much fun Gene and I used to have together. I want him here. He would like the photography and we would enjoy critiquing the movie. I can't wait to get home and tell him about it. But he won't be interested or even able to follow. Instead, he will want to plan how to get money or engage me in another of his obsessive thoughts. I live in two different realities with no intersubjective connection.

■　■　■

The emotional roller coaster continues the next few days. Gene is depressed when he hurts, then ecstatic when he thinks he has won *Dialing for Dollars* on TV, then angry at me for hurting him when I move him, and angrier still when I tell him he hasn't won *Dialing for Dollars*.

"You'll have to reimburse me if I lose the money I won," he threatens. "Call and make sure."

"You haven't sent in your name. You don't have a chance." He looks confused; I feel hopeless.

He loves to anticipate, but then loses interest quickly. I make arrangements for Rose to give Gene a massage. He can't wait until she comes, but after a few minutes of massage, he turns on the TV.

He insists that the nurse give him the extension when I am on the phone. When she refuses, he says, "You care more for Carolyn than me, and I pay you," a line he uses often now. "He's after your ass," Gene says about a friend who visits. "I don't want him here. I'm going to call him and tell him we're on our honeymoon and he should leave my wife alone."

"You can't do that," I plead, understanding that Gene has no self-monitors now. When he continues, I say, "I'll tell him not to come to our house," and with that he seems placated and able to move on to another obsession.

He is relentless about calling his old girlfriend, Joyce, to apologize for having hurt her in the past. "It is not a good idea to call now," I say.

Gene screams in response, "Stay out of my business."

Because I'm fairly sure he has the wrong number, I let him dial over and over. What will I do if he insists on calling information? I don't want her to hurt him, nor do I want him to make a fool of himself. He rehearses the call so many times that eventually he thinks he has actually talked to her. I even make up her response then, "Yeah, remember, she accepted your apology and was glad you called."

"She definitely doesn't want to talk to him," a mutual friend tells me. "When I told her his condition, she said it sounded like an exaggerated version of what Gene was always like."

I resist that thought, and then my guts churn at the truth I haven't wanted to face. He was always irascible, controlling, insistent, and demanding. Yet, I remind myself, he also was sensitive, charming, warm, giving, and loving.

Gene decides finally to call Joyce at work. While dialing, he asks me to go to the basement where it is warm—my house doesn't have a basement—so I can't hear the conversation. From my bedroom, I hear him leave a message, but she never calls back. Although he mentions her a few more times, he finally seems satisfied with my explanation that he has already talked to her.

My reality is shaken again on Wednesday when I tell Sherry, my physician friend, what's going on with Gene. "I think it's brain damage," I say.

"No, this is just the trip he's pulling on everybody," she responds. I feel relieved, then irritated at Gene, and then at Sherry for saying this about Gene. Then I decide that the reason for his behavior is unimportant.

■ ■ ■

"I can't get in the hot tub. The water's hot enough to burn me," Gene's son Paul, who is visiting, says. Why do I have to take care of everybody? But when I check, the water is close to boiling, and when I turn off the water circulation, the heater near the house bursts into flames. Stopping myself from talking to Gene about what to do, I call the fire department. When the fire truck arrives, neighbors come to see what is happening. "Don't worry," I yell, "it's only a fire." It plays like a scene out of *The Three Stooges* and is indicative of what my life has become. I miss Beth, who's away for a few days.

■ ■ ■

"Something real good happened today," I say to Gene when I call him from school on Tuesday. "You want to guess?"

"We got the grant," he says, referring to his latest fantasy.

"No," I say, "my promotion went through and I'm an associate professor."

"That's great, baby." Although I'm not certain he understands, he congratulates me when I arrive home, and the next morning, when he opens his eyes, with a twinkle, the first thing he says is, "Hi, associate professor." Then he has the nurse help him do isometric exercises, "so I can walk," he tells me.

When Ada comes to take care of Gene that night, she again tells me that I will have to decide to do something about pain. "When he can't stand it, then I'll give him something for pain and face the consequences," I reply. "He hasn't said he can't stand it yet."

"I'm not trying to rush you. I just want you to be aware and know it's going to be your decision." I am glad she is honest but resent her sounding like a broken record.

The next night, we have what Gene calls "our wedding party" with Joan, who has come to visit and to "work on the grant." All day Gene is excited about the bottle of Chateau Lafite Rothschild and the Beluga caviar and fresh sturgeon Joan has brought from New York. For a few hours I forget he is mentally confused. We laugh as we take turns feeding him, and cry when we listen to "The Leader of the Band."

Still, even when he seems normal, he talks about the car he will buy and the ring he will get from his in-laws. Although we convince him to wait until after the party, he insists I call Beth and tell her to ask her grandfather for the engagement ring he had given to his first wife. "They should want to give it to me," he says, "because I got Paul off drugs this trip."

Gene sometimes thinks he has the ring, then he thinks Beth has the ring. Then he thinks Beth is going to sell the van and give him the money.

I am exhausted. He is relentless. I am beat down. Yet I keep working on my manuscript. And, I keep being loving and understanding. How am I able to feel this? "He can't help it," I tell myself over and over. "This isn't really him. Don't take it personally."

That night Gene asks his nurse to get a certified check for all but $10 from his bank account. Then he calls his brother and asks to borrow $30,000 to buy a car. When Gene starts talking about the car and ring as soon as I get up on Thursday, I am glad to leave for school.

He and Joan "work on the grant." He plans a simple budget, talks superficially about methodology, and says the topic will be "the meaning of situations." "Now type it up," he demands. When Joan says she doesn't know what to write, he accuses her of playing dumb.

When I call home, he tells me how much money he has gotten me with the grant. "You couldn't have gotten that money," he informs me, "because you don't have a name in the field. Look what I'm doing for you and then you won't even let me buy a car."

"He insisted that I dial Total Care all day and he talks constantly about paying nurses more money," Joan tells me when I return home. "I told him the line was busy. Then he wanted to call about a car. Now he wants to call his mother."

"We have to let him," I say. Joan intercepts his mother's return call in the bedroom and tells her Gene wants to borrow $30,000 for a new car. "We don't have money for that kind of foolishness," she says.

When I take Joan to the airport that afternoon, she says, "There is nothing more I can do for him. He won't talk to me because I tried to talk him out of the car. How can I help you?" she asks.

"What is this with the car? It doesn't make sense."

Joan replies, "Maybe it does. What did he do after his son died?"

"He bought a car."

"And why did he buy his last car?"

"To make me happy after my brother died."

"Maybe this is the way he responds to tragedy."

"So this car will be for his own death."

When I arrive home, Betsy, the nurse, says, "While you were gone, Gene insisted on calling the Dodge dealership to put a car on hold. He got so frustrated that I let him get through. He was real excited when he got a salesman. They had the kind of car he wanted and he told them to save it for him." Until now we had told him repeatedly that there was no answer or that the phone was busy.

Betsy tells me he also has talked to his mother. "We have to be firm with him," his mother says when I call. "I have known others to whom this has happened. Maybe the doctor can do something."

"Wait for the car, just until you can ride on the Amigo," I say to Gene.

"You aren't being my friend," he responds angrily. "I feel all alone, and I have to beg to spend my own money."

"That's not true," I say. "I know it seems like it to you, but your mind is confused from the disease. It doesn't make sense to buy a car now."

"We just have different values and you say it's Alzheimer's whenever I disagree with you."

"I only said that once," I reply.

He demands that I call his brother again. When Jerry tells him he will loan the money, I take the phone from Gene. Not caring that Gene will overhear the conversation, I say, "Jerry, play it straight. This isn't working. Otherwise, Gene will try to go through with buying the car, and it will make my life more difficult."

When Jerry tells Gene he can't loan him the money, Gene says, "Mom bought you your apartment and I didn't get anything." This was so different from the Gene I knew, who never asked for anything, who always was appreciative of what his mother gave him, and often even refused her gifts of money.

Jerry keeps saying, "Don't hang up on me Enejay," but Gene finally yells, "You've betrayed me, Jerry," and hangs up.

Jerry calls back, "Enejay, I will buy you that car myself when you can get out of bed, and you won't owe me a thing."

"But I want this one right now. It's just what I want. Don't you understand? It would make me happy. No one understands that," Gene whines, dropping the phone.

"Don't take it personally, Jerry," I say. "We're all getting this."

Gene says I have betrayed him by telling his brother and mother not to loan him money. He refuses to eat. "Maybe we can rent a car and just let it sit in the driveway," Beth suggests.

At first I think this is a brilliant idea. "But he can't even see it from his bed," I say. "And if we manage this, what will be next? Somehow we have to stop this fantasy. If we give in now, there will be another one." I am too tired to continue playing the game, and too tired to stop it.

■ ■ ■

On Friday, I call Dr. Townson to discuss Gene's obsessiveness. "It might be CO_2," he says, "or steroids, or just being confined. People almost never live this long in his condition, so this is all unusual, although not unheard of. Take away control," he instructs. "You have to. Call the bank."

"What about his back?" I ask. "It is unbearable for him even with moist heat. We can't move him or change his bed."

"Maybe a Tens Electrical Stimulation Machine would help."

"I'm ready for this to be over," I say quietly.

"I knew it," he replies, sounding almost triumphant. "Don't feel guilty about feeling this way."

"I don't," I say, though putting my thoughts into words sends a pang of guilt up my spine.

"It's quite a situation," he says. "Sorry I can't do more."

"Thanks for being supportive."

■ ■ ■

I call the car agency and tell the owner our situation. Although he doesn't want to be bothered, he agrees to call Gene and tell him the Charger they discussed has been sold, which is actually true. When he doesn't call, I let Gene call him. Gene is close to tears when he hears the car is no longer available. I am not prepared when he says to the employee, "Order me one, then," and I realize that although part of his mind is gone, what is left is devious and sharp. The employee says it will take four weeks. Is he really going to order one? After I leave for school, Gene calls the agency four times to describe the particulars he wants on the car.

When I phone home, the nurse says Gene is extremely agitated. While watching *Dialing for Dollars,* he yells at the TV because they aren't calling him. Since Beth recently had sent his name in, he is even more insistent that he will win.

Gene is anxious for me to come home and upset that my friend Susan is coming to visit. "I want time alone with you," he explains, "and you made a unilateral decision, but it's OK." We have a nice time nevertheless and make cheese tyropitas and his favorite chocolate-chip cookies. We drink the left-over wine and eat caviar. Gene says he likes the "party."

When the night nurse has to leave at 5:30 A.M., Gene doesn't call for me. When I get up at 8:00, he says he has tried not to wake me. He could still be sweet, in spite of being crazy.

The strange thing is that, other than his back and his mind, his health has been good this past week. That day, I write:

> I don't want to write today, except that I do want to purge myself of all this horrible stuff. He has been so awful. I am so controlled about it, but I feel on the brink. I seriously need a vacation from it all. In actuality, I want him to die. There I said it. I am fucking ready for him to die. Die, you bastard. This is horrible. I could have done without this phase. It is horrible. He is horrible. He is a monster. All of his worst characteristics are coming to the forefront.

> And we just ran out of oxygen. As long as he didn't know it, he was fine. As soon as I suggested it was a problem, he started to have trouble breathing. Then when I told him the oxygen was OK, even though it wasn't, he was fine. I called the company for an emergency delivery. In my mood, I feel it would be a good way to die. But I don't really mean any of this. Except that I do, sort of. I had no idea how bad things would get.

By the time I get up on Saturday, Gene has instructed Betsy to write down a list of instructions:

Go to bank, take check book, certify as much money as possible without going over amount for free checking and top bank interest. Take to Robert Morris Dodge, get GMAC financing for one year for remainder. If insurance required, get from Allstate at University Mall, Faye Boston is agent, get serial # of new car and put on binder. See if can get new rate—now married. Carolyn Ellis will be principal driver.

Carolyn should not be able to screw this up.

Pick up brochure from dealer. Sign and fill out forms, etc.

Power package windows locks and seats if they can do it.

Ask if they can shave the head and still retain emission controls.

Betsy had written in her notes that "he seems elated about buying new car and prospects of driving it." "He wanted me to go to the bank before you got up," she tells me. "He said he could stay alone for an hour. But I stalled until now."

"It's Saturday," I say to Gene. "You can't get a certified check today. Let's talk about the car, like partners. I want to help choose it. When you are well enough we can go out together and get it." I am back into supporting the fantasy.

"No way," he warns, "you stay out of this. Leave it alone, Carolyn."

"No, I won't," I reply, not knowing what else to do or say. When I come near him, like an animal, he bites at me and says, "Sometimes I hate you." Then he turns to Betsy and says, "Leave the house. I pay you and you listen to Carolyn." Then back to me, "You are not my friend. You take advantage of my helplessness. You just want my money."

"I am your friend, " I say quietly, surprised that I feel so little. "And I love you."

I beg Betsy not to quit. "If Betsy leaves," I say, "you will be alone for several hours a day."

"That's OK," he says. "I'll hire other nurses or go to a nursing home or hospital."

When I say, "Fine. I'll help you make the arrangements," he stops threatening.

Since Beth has returned, I go to dinner at a friend's house. I know things must be bad when Beth calls. "He insisted on calling the doctor," she says, "and he can't even remember the doctor's name. When he got a doctor on call, he asked him to pick up car forms and bring them to him. Then he wanted to call a lawyer to charge me with a kidnapping felony and I finally had to take the phone away. As long as he was abusive, I refused to do anything for him. When he finally calmed down, I fed him. He says he's going to cut us out of his will."

"I'll be home in a few minutes," I say, after listening silently. "I understand."

■ ■ ■

"Go away," Gene screams every time Beth comes near. "Don't touch me."

"He hasn't peed all evening," Beth says. So I help him urinate and move his legs, hoping to soothe him.

"Beth kidnapped me," he says, "and took my phone away."

An old friend, who has not been in touch, calls long distance. I wonder about his reaction when Gene instructs him to call the doctor and tell him he is being held hostage. "You don't want me to have any pleasure," he says to me and Beth. He accuses me of leaving him alone without a phone, and then tells Beth he will rent a condo and hire his own nurses, who will be loyal to him.

That night a new nurse writes: "He is exhibiting hostile attitude towards family. He says, 'They're taking away my ability to function . . . taking advantage of my condition.' He requested me to 'go clean out his car—now!' When he slept, he sweated and continued talking in an agitated manner."

By 6:00 A.M. he is lucid, concerned about how he has talked to the nurse during the night. But by 7:30, she writes that he is "hostile. Verbally abusive. Making requests that this nurse cannot carry out." At 8:00 A.M. she writes that the "patient is awake and screaming at nurses and family." The nurse said he cursed us all while he slept, but then when she mistakenly turned up the volume on the television, he complained that she was waking me up.

The situation gets worse. The morning nurse writes that Gene is "aggressive when approached" and has "requested family and nurse to 'get out of my sight.' He is making false accusations to everyone."

When I get up at 8:30, I learn that Gene has refused to take anything from Betsy, no pills, bath, nothing. He says over and over, "I want Betsy gone," and he will not talk to anyone. Finally, we stop directing conversation to him. I suggest Betsy stay in my bedroom. "OK," she agrees. "He wouldn't even go to the bathroom. But I left a Motrin on his tray and he took that."

"Do what you can," I say quietly, as Beth goes to visit friends and I go jogging.

There is no communication between Gene and Betsy until an hour and a half later when he asks her to call Joan. "They're driving me crazy here," he says, and Joan tries to calm him.

When I return, I bring him a brochure on his fantasy Charger, and his eyes light up for a minute before he becomes belligerent again. Then he asks to talk to Dr. Townson. I listen only to his side of the conversation. "I appreciate your keeping me alive, Doc. . . . Yeah, and everything everybody is doing. But Carolyn and I don't always agree on values. I need someone to represent my interests. . . . No, she doesn't always do that. You need to call Larry [who is, as far as I know, a fantasized lawyer]. . . . Please." Frustrated, Gene hands me the phone after Dr. Townson asks to talk to me.

"Yes, he does sound crazy. I'm prescribing an antipsychotic for him. It is mild and won't hurt him as much as codeine. But it still might do him in," he cautions. My heart twists. "But at this point we have to calculate what will happen if he stays like he is without eating and taking medications." I agree.

In spite of my urgings, Gene refuses food, but he takes his pills and his treatment after I leave them beside his bed. He says he is angry about our taking the phone away. "You can call anyone you want except people like police and lawyers," I say.

"You get joy out of taking away my control," he accuses.

"I love you," I repeat over and over. "I'm sorry for what's happening. But I want you to remember how happy we have been for nine years."

"Yeah, and now your strong will is ruining that."

"No, yours is, Gene." His eyes fill with tears when I talk about our relationship. Once, he lets me kiss him. Then he retreats and I can't reach him no matter how hard I try.

Most of the day, he lies in a fetal-like position and is noncommunicative. But when I tell him Betsy will stay with him for a few hours, he says, "You shouldn't leave me with her, because she will probably be arrested." Although he seems calmer with me than with Betsy, I need some time away, and go to see *Beverly Hills Cop,* hoping Eddie Murphy will provide a laugh.

Gene continues yelling and swearing for Betsy to leave the house and attempts to hit her when she approaches. He dozes on and off, sometimes moaning for "endorphins." Betsy sets up a breathing treatment, which he later takes, and when he won't eat or let her do anything else for him, she spends the rest of the time in the bedroom.

When I walk into the house, Gene tells me to "get the fuck out of my house." Then he tells Susan, who has come to visit, to get out. I say to him in a quiet but strong manner, "This is my house too, and I won't get out." I tell Susan, "Just stay out of his way."

"I just want a phone," Gene screams, "and to be able to run my own life." I try to hug him but he is stiff, shutting his mouth tight when my lips come near. "You left me without a phone," he screams, "and no way to reach anyone in an emergency."

I hand him a phone. "This one doesn't work," he screams.

"Yes it does," I say, letting him listen to the dial tone. He grips the phone tightly to his chest with both hands. I hope that at this point he will not be able to operate it.

He refuses food and pills. When I coax him and then try to put pills into his mouth, he spits them at me and tries to bite me. He has moved from a vegetable to an animal.

"Will you talk to anyone?" I ask.

"Joan," he volunteers. When she isn't home, I call Jim from the bedroom, tell him the situation, and, thinking it will cheer Gene, ask him to call.

I am not sure it is a wise move when Gene opens the conversation with, "You would never do me this way, take advantage of my condition. I made Carolyn. Without me, she would never have gotten her Ph.D., and now she is trying to take my money."

I cringe, feeling each of his words like a lash to my heart. I feel defensive, but tell myself over and over, "This is not him." I wonder if this is what he really thinks, now that his thoughts are unmonitored. Is there any truth to what he says? Would I not have made it without him? Or is it just my turn to be the target of his belligerence? I feel at that moment that his assistance through the years has cost a lot, perhaps my self-confidence. I listen closely, a pattern developed over the years when one of us critiqued the other, trying to understand and improve ourselves from the other's insight.

I pick up the phone to hear both sides of his conversation with Jim. Jim tries reality therapy. "You didn't make her, she made herself. I was there."

Jim tries to reason with him, but Gene continues his tirade against me. "Carolyn is abusing me in this condition. All she wants is my money. This isn't love." Maybe I am money-grubbing and concerned about myself. Maybe we should buy him a car. Stop, Carolyn: *Gene is crazy now.* Finally, the horrible truth sinks into my soul. We aren't on the same side anymore; we are enemies. I want him dead; he wants to live. This is the final negotiation for control. Why should dying be different from living?

"Jim, I need your help. You have to get my insurance policies to me, so I can cut Beth and Carolyn out of my money." Beth and I look at each other. No way, our looks say to each other. Jim objects, trying to talk sense into Gene in both the literal and figurative sense of the word. "I need you to send me money," Gene pleads with Jim. Finally, he yells at Jim, "You just don't understand." When he doesn't get the response he wants, he hangs up.

My sympathy for Gene is mixed with my own pain, which makes me want to lash out at him. Sympathy wins out. As I wonder whether reality therapy is best now, Jim calls back, concerned for me.

Wanting to try anybody who might calm him, I call Joan and ask her to phone Gene. Gene starts in with the same conversation: "Get the insurance forms so I can change my beneficiaries. . . . call my nurse Dana and tell her to call the cops." Joan plays along, then calls me back to say she thinks she should pretend to help to keep some channel of communication open. "Try anything you want," I say.

Joan calls again to tell Gene she can't get Dana. By the time he says to her, "I know you would never do me this way, take advantage of my illness like this," I am too aware of how crazy he is to respond.

After each conversation, Gene says to me, "You know I'm not lying."

Joan phones back and asks about the antipsychotic. "I haven't picked it up yet," I say. "I guess I was being optimistic that he would come out of this. I didn't really want to give it to him, since it might kill him."

"How much warning will you have before you crack?" Joan asks.

"I don't know. I've never cracked before. I don't have a comparison."

I drink a scotch. How many more stages can there be?

16

"ADA, YOU'RE FIRED," Gene says when she walks in Sunday night. "You wouldn't let me have the phone," he accuses.

I describe Gene's condition to her, then go to bed. According to her notes, he refuses to let her do anything for him. At first, he dozes for short intervals and calls for "Charlotte" in his sleep, probably referring to the head of Total Care Nursing Services. At 1:00 A.M. he awakes and, when Ada approaches him, says, "Get the fuck out of here. All you do is make me suffer." He turns on his breathing machine, but continues to be "verbally hostile" and refuse medication. At 2:00 A.M. he yells for an attorney, then for "bottle, bottle."

"Do you need to urinate?" Ada asks, as I watch silently from a few feet away. He nods his head yes. Then he moans and curses in half-sleep, asking constantly for endorphins, then "Larry, help."

I doze lightly for the short intervals between his outbursts, and get up when I can take it no longer. Each time I approach him, he shouts, "Get away from me, you bitch." Feeling helpless, I return to bed.

At 4:00 A.M. Gene begins screaming loudly and continuously, "Police, help. I've been kidnapped." I wonder if the neighbors can hear, but I worry more about my own sanity and exhaustion. Where is he getting the energy? He drifts in and out of sleep, screaming as he awakes. Then he gives himself a breathing treatment, yelling between breaths. Ada writes, "At this time, he seems more withdrawn from reality."

At 5:15 he drinks a can of Ensure and takes a sip of antacid. He screams again for police, then Dr. Townson, then he adds Ellen and David, and I wonder who they are.

Determined to do something, I get up again. When I talk soothingly, he hisses as me. "You have to give him something. Get him to sleep," Ada commands. "You can't hang on." I resent her then, since I would like nothing better at this moment than for him to die, but I don't know what to do. Anything would be better than this situation, wouldn't it? Desperate, I get two Valium from the medicine cabinet and hide them in my palm. "Will you take your pills?" I ask, getting his regular pills out of bottles in front of him. "These will make you feel better," I say softly, feeling like a cross between an angel of mercy and the wicked witch.

"Get away from me, you bitch," he hisses. I try to open his mouth and force the Valium down his throat, but he spits at me and bites at my hand. I cannot believe this is happening. I keep the Valium in my hand, place his routine medications on his tray table, and say, "They're here if you want them."

Gene continues yelling, now with his eyes closed, and I return to bed, placing the Valium on my nightstand in easy reach. Occasionally he drifts to sleep, and as soon as I relax, he yells. I hate him.

When Betsy comes at 8:00 A.M., I get up. Screams for police, then endorphins, then "I'm being kidnapped" are punctuated by periods of silence. Searching for anything to try, I ask him if he wants me to call Dr. Townson. "Yes," he responds, "he can get me out of here."

Before I give the phone to Gene, I talk to the doctor in private. After my description, Dr. Townson says, "Do you want to put him in the hospital?"

"I guess so. I had wanted him to die here. But I can't let this continue. He wants to talk to you. He thinks I'm kidnapping him." Townson laughs.

Listening in on the extension, I am surprised at how rational Gene sounds. "I've got to get out of here, Doc," he says. "They're abusing me. I've got to get help."

"Carolyn wouldn't abuse you."

"Yes, she is, Doc. I've got to get out of here."

"Let's put you in the hospital. We can do more for you there."

"Like do the physical therapy?" Gene says, with hope in his voice. For the first time in a while, my heart melts. My god, he's still trying. When the doctor says yes, Gene continues, "OK, but someone has to call the ambulance."

"Carolyn will."

"No, she won't. You don't understand the situation here."

"If she doesn't, then we'll take care of it. Don't worry."

I shower first, taking time to feel the hot water running over my tired body. Then I call the ambulance.

While we wait, Gene says over and over, "No one has called the ambulance."

"Yes, we have," I reply calmly each time. There is nothing more to do.

"You won't call the ambulance. Help, police," he screams again at the top of his lungs.

I have described the situation on the phone to the ambulance service. "It's not an emergency," I say, unable to stand the thought of sirens and fire trucks and people who do not know what to do invading my house. This trip should be calm. One screaming maniac is enough. "But he needs to go to the hospital," I add. "He's incoherent, bedridden, and in pain. It will be difficult to move him."

When they arrive, they hesitate to take him. "We don't have resuscitation equipment if he goes into respiratory failure," the attendant says. I panic. Please don't leave him here with me now.

"It doesn't matter," I say, "because we have a living will."

"Oh, a no-code? Oh, that's fine then."

The ambulance driver says, "Are you the nurse?"

"No, I'm his wife."

"You're too young to be the wife. You're supposed to be old, gray, and slumped over."

"Yeah, it's not like in the movies, is it?"

Listening to Gene explain that we have kidnapped him, the young attendant says, "I don't understand what's going on here."

Looking at the nurse and then me, the driver says, "I wouldn't mind being kidnapped here." Gene is angry at the joke. Not understanding Gene's direction of "quarter inches at a time," the men move him quickly. "You're bastards," he yells, "you're hurting me on purpose." And, they, too, become part of his plot.

Although I feel I have to accompany Gene to the hospital, I am detached from it all now that Gene is angry and there's nothing I can do for him. Yet, silently, I still plead, "Don't let him die like this. Let him love me again." On the way to the hospital, I want the driver to quit talking to me. Don't come on to me. Not now.

At the hospital I meet Beth, who has been staying with friends, and we have breakfast while Gene is admitted. Then I enter the emergency room and ask to talk to Dr. Colter, who is on rotation. Dr. Townson has assured me that Dr. Colter will know not to resuscitate. I have never met Dr. Colter before, and introduce myself, "Hello, I'm Gene Weinstein's wife."

"I'm Dr. Colter," he says, and then immediately, "How long have you been married?"

"Since Christmas. But we were together nine years," I add.

"I was just telling these guys that this kind of thing happens in San

Francisco or New York," he says, pointing to the other residents. "But not in Tampa."

"It's true," I say casually, "that I haven't had much support for my life-style from this hospital. Is he giving you trouble?" I ask, pretending to be nonchalant.

"Oh, no," he replies.

"Well, let me go in there and then you'll get to see some anger."

"Angry? Who, him?" For a second, I think Gene has calmed down. Then I realize Dr. Colter is being facetious.

"Oh, well, there didn't seem to be much I could do," I say to justify having brought him in.

"We don't know what's causing this, but we'll give him an antipsychotic, probably Haldol, and get a psychiatrist to see him."

"Well, I'm glad he's yours now. Good luck. I give him to you," I say, with a sweep of my hand. I leave without even seeing Gene, who is a nonperson to us all now.

Ironically, I go to a talk I have set up at school on patient-doctor communication, of all things, but the presentation is sterile and uninteresting. Social scientists who study tapes know so little about the intimate intricacies of patient-doctor communication, I conclude. What about how it feels? The nonverbals? What's not said? The conspiracies of avoidance and deception?

■　■　■

Beth calls me at school and says, "A psychiatrist called our house and asked all kinds of personal history, family questions. He said he thinks Gene's problem is genetic."

I freeze. For a second, I wonder about my own definition of reality. Have I been living with a crazy man all these years without knowing it? Is that why . . . ? Nonsense, stop reinterpreting the past. This is hogwash. Anybody in Gene's current condition would be psychotic!

Then she says, "Gene called here."

"He did?" I ask, not believing my ears.

"Yes, and he said in a quiet voice, 'Bethie, will you come see me. I want to talk.' I'm going there," she says excitedly.

Gene doesn't answer his phone when I call, but his nurse says he is stable. "What does that mean?" I ask.

"He's stable," she repeats.

Soon Beth calls from the hospital and hands the phone to Gene, who says, "I want you to come. I think we can work this out and save our marriage. I want to try anyway. But you have to promise that you'll never

take away control again or take the phone from me. I made Beth promise too."

"I promise."

"Please come," he pleads softly.

"OK," I say, though I am exhausted from lack of sleep and feel I can't
deal with him now. "Put Beth back on the phone."

"Beth, call me from the lobby. I need to talk to you."

"How is he?" I ask when she calls.

"He's still crazy. But calm, from the Haldol, probably. He thinks you
and I spent the night in jail. He still thinks we kidnapped him, although he
said he would try to forgive us." We giggle.

"I don't want to see him now," I say. "I need to be away for a while."

"I understand," she says, "but he really wants you to come."

"I'll tell him I'm sick."

"Whatever you have to do," Beth says. "I'll stay with him tonight."

"Make sure he doesn't make phone calls."

"The nurse says so far he hasn't tried to make any."

I call Gene and, in a weak voice, tell him I am throwing up in the
bathroom. "That's horrible," he says. "You should stay home and take care
of yourself." The concern in his voice makes me feel guilty.

"I hate this. But I'll come tomorrow. I promise."

I call Sherry, my physician friend, to talk about what the psychiatrist said.
"That's a silly diagnosis," she says. "What can he know after one visit?"

"I know," I respond, glad to have my view validated. "And Beth said the
psychiatrist wasn't aware that Gene was terminal until she told him."

"The psychiatrist says we have to deal with reality and can't play along
with Gene's fantasy," Beth says when she arrives home the next day. "He
wants to talk to you too."

When I call him, he tells me, "The problem has always been there. It's
just been waiting to come out." I listen politely as the psychiatrist talks
about how this illness ran in Gene's family, and I realize his diagnosis comes
from Beth's brief family history. I do not have to remind myself now that
this is absurd.

"If I started shouting in the hospital, it would probably be more proof
that it 'runs in the family' and they might lock me up too," I say when I get
off the phone, and my comments make Beth laugh.

Then I call Dr. Townson. "When did you start giving the Haldol?" I ask.

"In the emergency room."

"Will it bother his respiration?"

"It shouldn't. But who knows. We're not usually working with anyone this far along in the disease. If the Haldol does slow it down, that might be the best thing that could happen."

"I agree. As far as I'm concerned, Gene Weinstein is dead and that's just a shell there."

"Unfortunately, that's true," Dr. Townson says almost wistfully. I swallow with difficulty.

■ ■ ■

When I call Gene, he asks me to bring him a bottle of champagne and hacked chicken, one of his favorite Chinese dishes. When I can't figure out where to get the chicken, I make it and take it, along with brownies, soup, and champagne, to the hospital.

"You spent the night in jail," Gene says immediately as he gasps for breath.

"No, I didn't."

"I called Larry, my lawyer. He had you locked up. You and Beth."

"No one spent a night in jail."

"Yes, you did."

"Well then, how do you feel about putting me in jail?"

"Ambivalent. You made me be in jail, and I wanted you to see how it felt."

"But if I were in jail, I wouldn't have been able to come see you."

"But you deserved to be. I could sue you for big money for violating my civil rights. I could sue Jerry Falwell too, and then you would be in jail together. But I love you so much, I want to work it out."

"We will," I respond.

"I love you," he says again, almost in tears, and, at last, the love is back.

Gene voraciously eats the food I have brought. "Beth said the champagne will interact with the Haldol," he says.

"Who knows. Drink it if you want," I say, but he decides to forego it.

For the first time in weeks, my appetite returns. Gene's mouth continuously opens for another piece of chicken, and he watches me suspiciously if I feed myself more than him. "Keep it coming into my mouth," he demands. "I don't want to lose the taste." And neither did I.

"That's Big Nurse. She's rough. I call her Nurse Wretched," Gene says loud enough for Nurse Wretched to hear.

"Why don't you like her?" I ask, thinking this is part of his hallucination.

"She wouldn't even touch the Kleenex that wiped off my penis. And she locks my bed straight up, and makes me feed myself. It hurts. I won't let her come near me."

Since I know Gene has been difficult, I apologize to the other nurses, who say they understand, but I don't try to talk to Big Nurse since, after I see her, I have the same feeling about her as Gene does. Although he gave the other nurses a hard time initially, he now says, "The others are nice. Don't cause any trouble with them or make anybody feel bad." Is he getting back to himself?

Gene asks for a Motrin. "It's hard to get medication or a treatment here," he says.

"Yeah, it was better at home. I don't have any," I lie, and then, wondering why I am being so cautious, give him one from my purse. "Now don't take the one the nurse gives you in an hour."

He says he won't, but then he does. As I tell Joan about it on the phone, I say, "But what the hell, we're hoping the antipsychotic drug kills him. What difference does an extra Motrin make?"

■ ■ ■

On Wednesday, I call Gene to tell him I will visit later in the afternoon. "Please come now," he pleads. "My chest hurts. I feel horrible. I need you." So I do, and I enter into the middle of the worst experience of my life.

"It's killing me," Gene pleads, turning to me with a wild look in his eyes. "The Haldol is killing me."

Dr. Colter, whom I barely know, accompanied by a doctor I have never met, commands, "You must take your Haldol, Mr. Weinstein."

"See how short of breath I am. They're trying to kill me," Gene continues, his eyes asking me to do something. My heart fills with tears as I look at this vulnerable and scared little man who used to be my Gene.

I step into the hall to talk to Dr. Colter. "I don't see Haldol making any difference in his breathing," the doctor says coldly. "Without it, he's going to be back where he was when you brought him in here."

"God, I don't want that."

"He has a genetic condition. The Haldol is helping."

"I disagree with that diagnosis."

When the doctor doesn't respond, I feel angry and frustrated. First the psychiatrist diagnoses Gene after a ten-minute visit. Now this doctor, who has known Gene for only a few days, agrees. I don't like him. But I need him.

I ask, "Can you give him Valium or codeine or something to calm him down if he won't take Haldol? He needs something to help get rid of the tremendous breathing pain he has. He says his chest hurts."

"Does his daughter feel that way too?"

When I respond yes, my voice is calm, but there is a roar churning, like

I have plunged into ocean waves right before a hurricane. Then it goes away, and what I am saying has little impact on me.

"Townson is in the hospital. I'll have him paged," Dr. Colter says. When he returns, he says, "I'm going to go in and make Gene take the Haldol, unless you object. You can stay out here if it would be easier."

"No, I want to be there," I say, following him. The play I'm in seems to be in fast forward. Is this the right thing to do? I can't have him the way he was without the Haldol. Should I stop the doctor?

"Mr. Weinstein," the doctor says in a loud voice, as if he is talking to a recalcitrant child or a hearing-impaired person, "here is your Haldol."

"I don't want it. It's killing me," Gene insists, turning his mouth away.

"If you don't take it, I'm going to stick you with it," the doctor says, holding the pill next to Gene's puckered mouth. A glass of water threatens in his other hand. I see the doctor as a large face with distorted features, like in a cartoon where the bad guy expands to occupy the whole screen. I am screaming, but no sound comes out.

Gene pleads, "Please don't. You said you wouldn't. You bastard." I try to make a sound, but when I see Gene is about to give in, I hold back and let the drama unfold in front of me.

"I didn't say I wouldn't."

"Stop," the sound escapes. "This is awful." I cry out the words, but softly, hoping the doctor won't hear and will continue in his mission. I am suffocating, as I try to wake up from this nightmare. Instead, I wake up in it, holding my breath during the worst moment of my life.

Knowing he has broken Gene, Colter keeps going. I am surprised when Gene opens his mouth, whimpering softly. Colter holds the water glass for him while he drinks. It is done.

I hate Colter.

"Dr. Townson is coming, baby," I say to Gene, my voice breaking, after Colter leaves, "and we can talk to him about all this."

"Is he coming now?" Gene asks.

"Yes." What a system. Here we are, Gene close to death, and we have to deal with some doctor we hardly know. Dr. Townson would not have forced Gene to take the Haldol. But how can I complain? I want to give him Valium, which will probably kill him. Whose side am I on, anyway?

I describe the forced Haldol to Dr. Townson, who listens thoughtfully outside Gene's door. "It was awful. Can't we give him Valium or something to calm him and ease his pain? He thinks the Haldol is killing him."

"You know what the Valium will probably do?"

"I know."

"What a situation," he says. "He's living from sheer will. The planning keeps him alive."

After Dr. Townson talks to Colter on the phone, he says, "I think it's best not to give Gene anything else right now. It's unclear whether he is competent and has the right to refuse Haldol. Until the therapist says he isn't, he can refuse it. To add something to this now would complicate matters. Let's just deal with the Haldol and see what happens. We can talk about other things later."

"OK," I say, disappointed and relieved. "One more thing," I say, as he is leaving. "Could you order the physical therapy, if only for a placebo effect?"

"Sure." He smiles empathetically.

"And would you talk to him again? He feels better talking to you."

He turns and goes into Gene's room. "The Haldol is killing me," Gene says softly.

"I don't think it's affecting your breathing," Dr. Townson reassures. "And it seems to be keeping you calm." Gene doesn't move or say anything. When Dr. Townson tells Gene about the physical therapy, he perks up slightly. I thank the doctor with my eyes and a nod of my head.

When Dr. Townson leaves, Gene lies slumped down in bed, broken. My child. "He made me take it," he says quietly.

Draping myself over him, I shroud my face in his still broad and hairy chest. I hug him, careful not to exert too much pressure. My body heaves from buried sobs. "You don't have to take it again if you don't want to, ever," I declare, my voice coming from deep in my gut. "I'm sorry I let that happen, baby. It won't again." I would see to it. I would protect him. Those bastards. I feel brainwashed. What have we done to him? That spirit, so wonderful and irascible, I felt it leave the room when he swallowed the Haldol. It is no longer a part of his face. Gene the fighter is gone.

I am surprised when rather nonchalantly Gene says, "Well, they think it's helping and I want to cooperate." A childlike expression replaces the agony of before.

What? Just as I am ready to fight? The anger drains quickly from my body. I don't say anything. OK, maybe this is better. At least easier. What do I want anyway? To have him treated like a human being. That's all. Where is dying with dignity?

■ ■ ■

Gene organizes his days around breathing treatments even though he doesn't complete half of them and they don't seem to do any good when he does. The first two days in the hospital, he showed an amazing breathing capacity, but now he is weak. Is it the Haldol? I shake the question from my mind.

I am in love with him again. Although there is little verbal communication, the feeling moves back and forth between us. I love taking care of him and can't do enough.

Since Gene is mostly operating in my reality now, I think the Haldol must be working, and I'm glad he takes it without complaining.

"Have you called about getting the new puppy?" he asks, with a gleam in his eye. This was a topic I thought he had forgotten.

"I'm not sure this is a good time to get a new dog."

"Yes, it is."

"But you're in the hospital."

"You can have it trained by the time I get home. And bring pictures and just tell me all about what it's doing, playing and all." Gene's eyes twinkle. Love and sadness break open my heart, interrupted by his insistence that I call Missouri about the dog.

"I'll call when I get home," I lie.

"Do it now," he commands. I ask why, and he responds, "I just want to hear you make the calls."

So I call Missouri and then follow a lead to Texas and back to Missouri. Finally, I track down a toy fox terrier puppy. "Now you can go to Missouri and pick up little Likker," Gene says, remembering the name I have decided to call my next dog.

"I don't think Poogie [my twelve-year-old terrier] needs another dog in the house now."

"She'll like it," he says. "They can play."

"But it's snowing in Missouri. It might be dangerous to fly there." My argument has no impact.

Beth arrives and Gene changes the topic to his car, asking Beth to get a certified check. Then he remembers, "Oh, yeah, Betsy is supposed to do it." Then he demands that Beth take notes about his car. "It should be a crystal-red Charger with red-cloth upholstery and a custom turbo. The deposit should be paid for with a cashier's check for whatever is in my account minus one thousand dollars. Get it from Bob Wilson Dodge. Make sure it has automatic transmission, good radio, and factory air. Find out about T-roofs, insurance, and GMAC financing." Beth writes this down and then we divert his attention with a breathing treatment.

Then he brings up calling Joyce, his old girlfriend, again. "I can't remember if I called her or not."

"Well, you told me you did," I say.

"Then I must have done it."

. . .

Fearing that this time I will have to put Gene in a nursing home, I call the hospital social worker from home to talk about health care. I leave a message for the social worker not to talk to Gene about this. When I call Beth at the hospital, she tells me the social worker came to Gene's room and said, "I'm here to talk about health care after the hospital." When Beth asks him to step out into the hall, he tells her that nursing-home care is expensive. "And they are selective. They don't take problem patients; they won't mess with problematic insurance."

"What a nightmare," I say. I can't, and don't want to put him in a nursing home anyway. Earlier that day, Gene had said to me, as though reading my mind, "I am still worried that we might have a difference of values and that you might send me off to a nursing home."

"I won't do that," I said, my heart breaking at the same time I wished he would just die. I am over my limit.

. . .

I shower and dress casually. A knock comes almost immediately at the door. A wave of excitement flows through my body. "You must be Robert, Susan's friend," I say, and he nods. He is dressed conservatively and neatly in a sports jacket and matching pants. His hair is short. It's not what I expected.

"Come in." I point to the hospital bed in the living room and say, "You understand my situation."

"Yes, I do."

"You're OK with it?"

"Yes, I want to be here."

He follows me into the bedroom. The sex is easy, almost familiar. I block out my life and feel no guilt. I don't dare let go of my emotions. But the physical release is welcome. Nothing exists but the sensations.

Afterward, I say, "I would feel better if you'd leave now."

"OK, if that's what you want."

"Thank you," I say.

"Thank you," he replies. "I hope to see you again, when things are easier for you."

This vivid fantasy provides escape from the harsh reality I live!

. . .

On Thursday, I spend the day at school, while Beth stays with Gene. "You and Carolyn are all Gened out," he says to her when she arrives.

"No, we aren't," Beth responds, and Gene's face brightens, but then saddens when he says, "I'm all Gened out."

During my class in deviance I feel like I will pass out, but I talk until the feeling disappears. My only female colleague comes to my office after class and asks how I am doing. She holds me when I sob.

"You don't have to keep teaching," she says. "You can miss some classes. Or I'll take the next one."

"No, I don't want to get behind. I know I'll miss some when Gene dies. But I don't even know what I'm going to talk about in my next class. It's Emotions, so maybe I'll talk about depression."

I call Joan and cry some more. "I felt I was plotting his murder with the doctors," I say as I tell her about the Haldol.

"But," she says, "you've said several times lately that there is so little between the way he is now and death. There's no quality."

"But I've never faced the difference between something—anything— and nothing. There's a lot between those two."

I break down continuously during the day and feel on the edge in a way I haven't before. Everything feels hopeless—this situation and life in general. I fear I might not be able to cope.

When I call Gene, he says in a barely audible voice, "I love you." When he hands the phone to Beth, she says he is too weak to talk.

After classes I talk to students and then, preparing for Gene's death, make up an exam I will need next week. It feels good to get some work out of the way.

■ ■ ■

"Thank god you're here," Gene says when I arrive at the hospital at eight o'clock to relieve Beth. After I kiss him, I walk down the hall with Beth. "He's suffering a lot," she says quietly. "I think we ought to get some Valium from the doctor, just in case."

"I have some," I say, "always in my pocketbook. But it's his decision."

Gene cannot lift his head off the pillow. His respiration is labored and heavy, not shallow as before. "My stomach is too upset," he says, to explain why he has not eaten all day. He is soft and expressive. "I love you," he says over and over. "Kiss me," he asks occasionally, and I comply.

We talk little. I feed him Ensure and he sips Coke. At midnight he eats some walnut horn cookies Beth and I made and drinks a pint of milk. He is appreciative when I massage and move his legs. In between, he moans with each breath.

"Do you want something for your pain?" I ask after midnight.

"No, it might depress my respiration."

"Even if you know you'll never feel any better than right now, do you still want to live?"

"Yes," he replies without hesitation. I assume he is rational and knows the meaning of the question. A burden is lifted. I stop worrying about whether I should assist in his death. I want to fight along with him until the last second. If he can bear the pain, so can I. I am glad to be with him. While he dozes off and on, I watch a TV movie about a mother who gives her daughter an overdose of sleeping pills. My life flashes before me.

Gene asks for a breathing treatment. Since the machine is in the room permanently now, I set it up for him. "The saline hurts my lungs," he says.

"Are you afraid to die?" I ask, as I watch the struggle.

"Yes," he says. "I can't get my breathing to catch up."

I call Beth. "I think we're close to death. But then we've thought this many times. It feels like something is about to happen. It is so calm here, in spite of how restless he is."

"He talked about his fears today. He said that for the first time he felt he might die," Beth tells me.

"He said that he still wants to live, so I no longer feel guilty that I should be helping him die."

"I feel released too," Beth says.

"I want to help with his battle, not try to kill him for my convenience." When Beth agrees, I think that we are a good team.

"I want the TV to be in order. It's too hard to take it in," Gene mumbles. But then he is coherent. He is in so much pain that I pray for the hallucinatory, oblivious phase of high CO_2.

I settle down for the night in the fake leather chair with worn-out springs and popcorn-feeling seat cushion. I feel calm, resigned, and ready for whatever will happen. My heart, however, feels constricted, like it is slowly being split into two pieces by a thick rubber band squeezing tighter each time I try to inflate my lungs. Gene dozes for a while and then calls for me as though he fears I have left.

"I'm here. Don't worry. Are you afraid you might die?" I ask.

When he replies yes, I say, "Don't worry, I won't leave you."

"Thank you, baby. I'm glad."

"I'm afraid he'll die if I go," I write as I watch his struggle for every breath. "But what if he continues to live? I can't do this every night." I wish he were home, where we have nurses and I have my own bed. Then I write: "Don't give up now. Stay with him. You are almost at the end."

At 1:00 A.M., he says suddenly, "You can go now. I'm OK."

"What made the difference?" I ask.

"Oh, Herschel Walker and Doug Flutie are here."

Realizing they are football players, I ask, "Are you having a party with them?"

"No, but you know, there's a lot of activity. Don't worry, I'll be fine."

Delighted he is happy in his fantasy, I kiss him and say, "You have a good time. And I'll see you tomorrow." Feeling like I shouldn't leave and that I don't want to, but that I must, I escape home to sleep.

■ ■ ■

Friday, February 8, 1985. When I awake, I call Gene's nurse, who says he is pretty much like the night before. "Does he seem to be in pain?" I ask.

"He moans a lot when he's awake," she answers.

I think about making the half-hour trip there and then decide to go first to my department meeting and then to lunch with my colleagues. Afterward, on the way to the hospital, I consider going shopping but then feel pulled to the hospital. When I walk into Gene's room at 2:15, he is sleeping on his side, an unusual position for him now. His breathing is light and easy. I am relieved, then frightened as I hurry around the bed. His eyes are shut and I am startled by the lack of heaving chest. When I watch his tongue tumble around in his mouth, I am sure that death is coming.

"Has Mr. Weinstein's doctor been in today?" I ask, approaching a nurse.

With a worried look, the nurse says, "Let me get his nurse." Her demeanor further validates how bad things are.

"Mr. Weinstein started going downhill around noon," Gene's nurse informs me, speaking quickly, "and he's been going down rapidly ever since."

"He doesn't respond now," I say quietly.

She hurries to his room although her movement seems to be in slow motion. She pinches him. No response. She hits on his chest. Nothing. She looks at me sadly. I cry quietly. "Is he dying?" I ask, and when she shakes her head yes, I say, "I want to be alone with him."

"Of course," she says. "If you need anything. . . ."

"Thanks," I say, appreciating the kindness.

Shutting the door, I stand next to him. "Let go, baby. It's time. The journey will be OK. You're going to feel much better now. You've fought a valiant fight." I watch closely as his tongue continues to roll back and forth. "I love you so much. My life will never be the same without you. Let go. Don't be scared. I'm with you."

Suddenly, I rush to the phone and call Beth at her friends' house. She will want to be here. But there is no answer there or at home.

When I return to his side, his eyes are open. They don't blink. I feel close as I hold his hand, now almost lifeless, and I continue encouraging him. The breathing stops momentarily and then he makes a gurgling, swallowing sound. His tongue lies flat, no longer moving in circles. Still no breath. Only silence. Five seconds. Then another raspy, gargling sound. Then no breath for ten seconds. This happens several times, and each time the silence increases before the gasp. I hold my breath to let it out with his.

He looks like an old man. His pulse is faint, but I still hear and feel life. Although I have no idea if he can hear, I continue telling him I love him and urging him to let go of life. His breathing stops again, this time for a longer period. It doesn't return. I watch for a while. I hold the hand that is now lifeless. Nothing has arrived. There is no clear demarcation between life and death. It looks like there is still spirit in the body. I think I feel it, I want to feel it. But I'm not sure. I don't see it leave.

But when I see him later at the funeral home, I will know the difference. Gene will be a body then.

With a short, quick nod of my head, I indicate to the nurse in the hall that it is over. She listens to his heart. "No," she says.

"No, he's not dead?" I ask, praying that he is, daring not to hope for a miracle of life, knowing there is none at this point.

"Yes, he's dead," and I breath now with relief.

Another nurse enters and together they turn Gene on his back and pull him up in bed. I cringe and almost cry out to stop them before I realize that it won't hurt now. When they tidy the blanket, I think that yes, this is a more appropriate position for a dead person. I feel little emotion—some relief, some agony. The nurse puts her hand on my shoulder as I cry quietly. "Do you want to come to our office?" she asks. "Have some juice?"

I consider it. "No, I'm fine. I want to be with him."

"Of course. As long as you like."

I cry quietly by his bed side. I know emptiness. Aloneness keeps me company. I fight it away and then it washes back through me. I touch his body, smell his skin—it is sweaty, stale, almost putrid. I talk to him and now I think I feel his spirit. Even though his body starts to get cold immediately and he looks so tired, he still looks like Gene and he still has color. Suddenly, remembering what Rose has told me, I say out loud, "I don't want to be sad. It's important to be happy for you and your journey." I feel better then, but I am not happy. I take in the details, knowing I will write about them later. The thought seems ludicrous, yet having a purpose contributes to my sanity.

I walk around the room, aimless, moans escaping easily from my throat, occasionally glancing back at the dead body on the bed. Dr. Colter arrives, nods quickly, listens for a heartbeat, and then leaves to sign the death certificate.

When Susan is not at home, I call George at school. "He died," I say quietly.

"Thank goodness," he replies. "Are you OK?"

"Yeah, I'm fine. Just wanted to connect with someone."

Dr. Townson calls and asks if I have any questions. Any questions? What questions? "If you do, call me. Don't feel guilty. In this state of the disease, this was the best thing."

"Thank you. You've been wonderful. You know he was such a tough fucker that he waited until I got here," I say. I believe it then, that he was not already dead when I arrived, and I feel Gene's approval of the message I give Dr. Townson.

"He did hang on," says Dr. Townson. "Now give yourself some time and then move on with your life."

"Yeah, thanks."

When I get off the phone, a feminine-looking young man dressed in a polyester gray suit carrying a clipboard appears. "Is this Eugene Weinstein?" he asks, officiously, pointing to the bed. Intuitively, I know he is the hospital social worker.

"Yes, he just died."

"Just now?" he replies, as though he doesn't believe me, looking hard at Gene, and then holding his clipboard out in front of him for protection as he backs toward the door.

"Yeah," I say nonchalantly, perversely enjoying the scene.

"Have you told them?" he asks, his index finger extended as far as possible toward the nurses in the hall. I nod. "Can I do something?" he asks, lowering the clipboard as he suddenly takes on a professional demeanor.

Although I say no, he stands in place, immobile, once again unsure of his role. Enough. I lean down and hug Gene, and the social worker is gone when I look up.

I hesitate and then throw Gene's glasses into the trash can and the rest of his things into a paper bag. His sweater smells strongly of him and of sweat and sickness. I can't wait to wash it, but then I hold it under my nose and breathe in, realizing that this is the last smell. I look at him once more, and, since I can think of nothing more to do, I leave. To make his death real. To release the body. To release myself. Otherwise, this feels like the next step in the deterioration. OK, now, how do I negotiate this stage? What happens next? No, no, this is death. There is nothing else.

"I am leaving," I say to the nurse.

"Do you want a patient rep to take you to the door?"

"No, I'm fine." What will that do? I'll still be alone when I go outside. Why do they offer? Because that is all they have.

"Should we call somebody for you?"

"No, I'll be OK."

Walking to the parking lot, I keep my head down so that I do not see people. Now tears flow. I breathe the fresh air, ridding my nostrils of the stench of death, but hold on to the paper sack from whence escapes his body odor.

I should have gone there, earlier, been with him when death first appeared. It would have been easier for him with me there. Did he need me? Was he scared? In pain? I crave the details. I'll ask the nurse. What were the last hours like? But I never do. What can she say? Perhaps he had to be alone to let go of life. The thought calms me.

As I drive out of the parking garage, I think of saying to the parking attendant, "Do you get a discount if the patient dies?" I laugh, hysterically almost, but I say nothing.

■ ■ ■

From that moment the screaming began that continued for three days, and was so terrible that one could not hear it through two closed doors without horror. . . . For three whole days, during which time did not exist for him, he struggled in that black sack into which he was being thrust by an invisible, resistless force. He struggled as a man condemned to death struggles in the hands of the executioner, knowing that he cannot save himself. And every moment he felt that despite all his efforts he was drawing nearer and nearer to what terrified him. He felt that his agony was due to his being thrust into that black hole and still more to his not being able to get right into it. . . . Suddenly some force struck him in the chest and side, making it still harder to breathe, and he fell through the hole and there at the bottom was a light. . . . And suddenly it grew clear to him that what had been oppressing him and would not leave him was all dropping away at once from two sides, from ten sides, and from all sides. . . . "And the pain?" he asked himself. "What has become of it? Where are you, pain? . . . And death . . . where is it?" He sought his former accustomed fear of death and did not find it. "Where is it? What death?" There was no fear because there was no death.

In place of death there was light.

"So that's what it is!" he suddenly exclaimed aloud. "What joy!"

To him all this happened in a single instant, and the meaning of that instant did not change. For those present his agony continued for another two hours. Something rattled in his throat, his emaciated body twitched, then the gasping and rattle became less and less frequent.

"It is finished!" said someone near him.

He heard these words and repeated them in his soul.

"Death is finished," he said to himself. "It is no more!"

He drew in a breath, stopped in the midst of a sigh, stretched out, and died.
(Tolstoy 1886/1960, pp. 154–156)

■   ■   ■

February 8, 1985: The final negotiation. It is done.

Living a self-conscious life, under the pressure of time, I work with the consciousness of death at my shoulder, not constantly, but often enough to leave a mark upon all my life's decisions and actions. And it does not matter whether this death comes next week or thirty years from now; this consciousness gives my life another breadth. It helps shape the words I speak, the way I love, my politic of action, the strength of my vision and purpose, the depth of my appreciation of life.

Audre Lorde, *The Cancer Journals*

PART V

Negotiating the Story

The social science model of writing, in effect, requires researchers to suppress the story of their own research, the human processes through which the work was constituted over time. . . . Narrative is the best way to understand the human experience, because it is the way humans understand their own lives. . . . If we wish to understand the deepest and most universal of human experiences, if we wish our work to be faithful to the lived experiences of people, if we wish for a union between poetics and science, if we wish to reach a variety of readers, or if we wish to use our privileges and skills to empower the people we study, then we need to *foreground,* not suppress, the narrative within the human sciences. How and for whom we write lives matters.

Laurel Richardson, *Writing Strategies*

IN THIS CHAPTER, I return to the writing chronicle I began in the introduction. Over the nine years of writing and rewriting the story, I moved from conceiving of my project as science to viewing it as interpretive human studies, transforming the process of writing the text from realist ethnography to a narrative, and my primary goal from representation to evocation. Here I discuss the details of this transformation.

My interest in examining my own writing experience as an example of the reflexive and inductive processes involved more generally in writing autobiographical sociology has been inspired by the deconstruction of writing conventions advanced by postmodernist writers. These authors have shown that "all disciplines have their own set of literary devices and rhetorical appeals" (Richardson 1994, pp. 10, 11; see also Agger 1989; Brown 1987; Clifford 1986; Clough 1992; Maines 1993; McCloskey 1990; Nelson, Megill, and McCloskey 1987; Rose 1990; Simons 1990). Literary and scientific genres of writing thus are situated within historical and linguistic practices (Clifford 1986, p. 2) that hide ideological interests and largely determine what will count as a legitimate contribution to knowledge. One important effect of this "rhetoric of inquiry" project has been to promote a more self-critical attitude about one's own embeddedness within institutional practices and conventions. Adding my voice to this important endeavor, now I invite readers to take a rarely shared personal tour through the concrete details of my writing process.

From Science . . .

> How do you chart the incoming tide, the rhythmic pattern of wave upon wave, the slight increases in peaks and troughs, the imperceptible advance of tide's edge? What scale of measurement is appropriate to the wearing away of rock by drops of water, the erosion of land by rushing brooks, the hollowing out of rock by falling water?
>
> Gerda Lerner, *A Death of One's Own*

Shortly after Gene's death, I designed an empirical study of grief. I intended to follow and compare survivors who joined grief groups with survivors who received individual counseling and with those who had no intervention. After writing a grant proposal, I had second thoughts when I considered how this work would construct my life. If successful, for the next five years I would manage a large social science project in a bureaucratic setting. I concluded that this was not how I wanted to spend my time, nor the best use of my talents. Besides, I knew I was interested in writing from the inside, about the bigger picture of the process of loss, a goal not achievable in an outcome study.

Returning to the field notes I had kept on my relationship with Gene, I decided to analyze my own experience of loss. As I considered modes of constructing these materials into a scholarly project, I developed two sections of notes into a story. In the first, an emotional tale about our attempt to deal with Gene's inevitable death, I bared our vulnerabilities and anxieties. In the second, I told about dealing with Gene's deterioration in our trips to a doctor's office.

Content with the narrative form and emotionality captured in these two excerpts, I sent them to friends and colleagues. From people in the helping professions and several sociologists, I received glowing evaluations about how well-written and emotionally expressive these stories were. But other friends in the academy admitted not knowing what to say, feeling "uneasy reading these materials," embarrassed by my "emotional nakedness," as though they had peered into a dimension of my personal life they were not supposed to see. Even colleagues active in the movement to include emotions in sociology showed concern. One reader asked, "How does what you are saying tell me anything about my own experience? How can this be generalized?"

As a young scholar trying to find her "place," I felt disappointed by these questioning reactions, though I understood that, from an orthodox sociological point of view, they expressed legitimate concerns. Yet, I also believed this project represented some of the best sociology I had ever written, a belief validated by other readers. One colleague, for example, acknowledged after reading my excerpts: "I can never remember being so deeply and emotionally affected by something, time and again. Each time I read about your experiences I am blown away, amazed by how you were able to cope, and in deep admiration of your ability to love and care. . . . You are correct in doggedly sticking to your guns, ignoring the chastising of your colleagues and respected 'scholars,' because you have something so much more powerful, so much more moving, so much more important."

The intense responses to my work, even the critical ones, signaled that I was on to something important. I decided to pursue this risky venture rather than produce work that did little more than add items to my vita. My vulnerabilities were overshadowed by the challenge of convincing the academic world that introspective ethnography should be included in sociology and could meet the criteria of rigorous inquiry. I stopped working on this book and spent a year researching introspection as a method.

The first paper I wrote discussed introspection as a "scientific" approach and used narrative excerpts from my unfinished manuscript to demonstrate its value. I sent this paper to a few sociologists whom I thought would be sympathetic. The first response I received read: "the greatest gift that we can give, is the gift of our dispassionate analysis, our coolness, our marginality. We can bracket our experiences." This person continued: "[Your writing] reminds one a bit of the poems that some write while on drugs. I kept asking myself what is the significance to a sociological reader of your encounter with Gene's doctor. Does a reader *really* care?"

When I gave this paper at a national meeting, the discussant wrote: "My major emotion in response to your paper was horror. I kept thinking to myself: How could anyone use such an experience for sociological purposes? . . . This experience is much too important to demean it . . . with sociological methodology. It should be presented as an experience without all of the sociological trappings."

Life is not significant enough for sociology! Life is too important for sociology! My experience was too vital to be applicable to sociology or sociology was too mundane to be relevant to my experience. Either way, I was horrified by these well-meaning responses signifying that in sociology the vulnerable dimensions of lived emotional experience were stamped "off limits."

In response, I wrote and rewrote this paper, never sure of my audience, simultaneously addressing it to interpretive and mainstream sociologists alike. To make my work more traditionally sociological, I replaced the autobiographical case materials with interviews about others' emotional experiences. Then, hesitantly, I added myself as one of the subjects.

"Develop the 'introspection as science part,'" instructed a special-issue editor at a mainstream sociology journal, "and then we might be able to publish it." After two sets of reviews, the journal editors suggested they would consider my paper for a later issue if I would revise and speak more directly to the "weaknesses" of introspection as a scientific method.

Several of the reviewers argued that my paper should be more scientific and analytic. One spoke in terms of "sample size," suggesting "we need other data to confirm feelings" and "experimental bias," fearing that since we know our own hypotheses, we might "shape reports of emotions to make a point." Another said: "I often have a good sense of what the author means, much as I know what a poem means, but that doesn't make it good science. I respect the author's literary ability—she writes like a dream when it comes to describing emotions—but that is not a substitute for the kind of conceptual analysis that is required to elucidate the kinds of issues she has chosen to address."

The review that got most of my attention included the following:

> This is an important (major) contribution to the sociology of emotions, but it is flawed at present because of its heavy commitment to a positivistic, verifiable, generalizable (pre) postpositivist view of theory, data and empirical research. Like William James the author is caught between two camps—hard psychological (sociological) science, and interpretive, imaginative, humanistic, phenomenological inquiry. You can't have it both ways and this is why introspection fell from favor around James' time. American psychologists couldn't scientifically validate introspective findings. The manuscript is schizophrenic; it makes a plea for the method, and then turns hard science against it and ends up limply defending its case.

My "schizophrenia" had been identified. Being an integrationist, I fought the label. Being careerminded, I finally gave in, revised the paper again, omitting the focus on science, and sent it to *Symbolic Interaction*. The article was accepted with minor revisions (see Ellis 1991a).

... To Interpretation

> Each day seen by itself was an island, existing in its own space and time, longer than any known day because it was irreplaceable. Against the dead walls of doomed time ahead, each day was perfect within itself ... the minutes precious in those golden moments when acceptance brought silence and rest. Yet each day was convulsive, torn with useless thrashing, with resistance and effort, with frantic struggle of will against fate, will against body, soul against nature. ... There is no better way to learn about process than by living beside the dying.
>
> Gerda Lerner, *A Death of One's Own*

The acceptance of my article began a transition. Maybe I was talking to the wrong audience, and maybe trying to open a space for detailed, lived experience within orthodox social science was the wrong strategy. So I turned to an examination of what could be learned from my project about how meaning is attached to human experience. Although some mainstream sociologists—especially women—were receptive to my work, I stopped trying to talk to orthodox social scientists on their terms and began to seek out scholars who might be interested in taking an interpretive stance toward sociology. For the most part, they were symbolic interactionists, qualitative methodologists, feminist theorists, and sociologists studying emotions. They would be hard enough to convince.

Now I was ready to return to writing the narrative in *Final Negotiations*. At times, I still wondered what I was doing. Why am I writing a kind of sociology for which there are no models? Is this sociology or literature? Fiction or fact? Did I want to write literature and work in the tradition of humanities or be a scientist and try to follow rigorous rules for doing social science? Though still unsure, I put aside the questions and just wrote. What came out was more chronological narrative. Ironically, feeling then that I didn't really "fit" in science or humanities freed me (or forced me) to begin to develop my own quasi-humanities, quasi-science link (Zald 1991).

I stopped working on my narrative again a few months later to begin a second article, "Emotional Sociology," precipitated by the process of writing my story. I advocated examining emotions emotionally (rather than reducing them to cognitive processes), viewing our own emotional experiences as objects of study, and focusing on how we feel as researchers.

"Your writing is still too defensive," Art Bochner, a seasoned academic writer and communication professor complains when he reads a draft of this article. "Don't spend time talking about what others don't do. Or why what you do is valuable. Assume it is and convince your audience through your prose and exemplars."

"But this is the way I was taught to make an argument." As I speak, I realize that Art is on to something. Suddenly, what he says seems obvious.

Art became my romantic and academic partner in February 1990. Although educated in different disciplines, he and I were interested in the same topics—close relationships and the social construction of knowledge. His critical stance toward social science and my attempt to use experimental forms to link social science and humanities joined hands and hearts. My relationship with him, our conversations, his critique and encouragement of creativity, and support for interpretive research magnified my desire to tell a personal and emotional story about attachment and loss.

Now, instead of trying to convince others of the scientific value of my work, I dropped my defensive posture and began to approach emotion as a subject of interest in its own right and on its own terms—emotionally. I wrote for social scientists likely to be receptive to this approach and published "Emotional Sociology" in *Studies in Symbolic Interaction* (Ellis 1991b).

When I returned again to my book manuscript, however, I wondered anew if "all I was doing" was self-therapy, the other critical response sociologists had offered over and over. For example, one sociologist had written: "The problem is that there are some things which are good to write, but not to read. That is, your writing is primarily therapeutic, not didactic." It took a while to realize that this was yet another dichotomy I had accepted uncritically. Of course, my writing was therapeutic. Isn't most useful research "therapeutic"? Because my research was helpful didn't mean it lacked intellectual substance. What I had learned from my own struggles for meaning was unique enough to be interesting, yet typical enough to help others understand important aspects of their lives (Abrahams 1986). Don't we all need to know we are not suffering alone? Neither the therapeutic and scholarly nor the particular and universal are mutually exclusive.

Once again I questioned the discipline in which I had been socialized. The treatment of therapy as an illegitimate motive for research, the sense that to be scholarly our work should be impersonal, the denial of the emotionality of the researcher, the call for separation of subject and researcher, and the rejection of addressing emotional experience, did not conform to my values or my interests. Couldn't feeling and thinking come together in sociology?

By this time I knew I did not want to write a traditional academic book and that I wanted to write a book that would speak therapeutically to a mass audience and sociologically to an academic one. But, I feared there were too many stories to tell to too many people, especially since publishers and reviewers normally demand one point and one audience. What kind of book would I write? Would I tell my story, or use it as grist for sociological analysis? Would it be a scholarly or trade book? Would I write to social scientists or a mass audience? If social scientists, would it be all sociologists or some sympathetic section of them, such as symbolic interactionists, those to whom I had addressed my papers? Would it be a self-help book or a contribution to the sociological literature?

These issues arose as I was going through intense grief. The losses of Gene (1985) and my brother (1982) were renewed when first my dog of fourteen years died (1986), and then my father passed away (1987). Any questioning reaction to my work presented more threat of loss—loss of identity—and I often felt defensive and judgmental in response to criticism. Similar to irresolvable grief that often results from ambiguous feelings felt toward a loved one who dies (Parkes and Weiss 1983), negative criticism coupled with indications that my work was important made it more difficult for me to resolve how to accomplish this project. My response was to purse my lips, clench my fists, tighten my jaws, and become more determined.

I couldn't stop writing because working on a book that might help me and others understand and cope with loss provided day-to-day meaning and continuity. Sometimes I felt I was fighting to make my work meaningful in order to rekindle the deeper meanings of my life—a life now superficially safe, afloat in a rowboat, yet threatened by a sea of continuously challenging waves of response no matter where I placed my oars. In which direction would I go? Or did the strength and unpredictability of the waves make direction a mute concern? Finally, I pulled in my oars and set off on my own adventure, eager to see where it would lead me.

From Realist Ethnography . . .

> I could not live in any of the worlds offered to me. . . . I believe one writes because one has to create a world in which one can live. . . . I had to create a world of my own . . . in which I could breathe, reign, and recreate myself when destroyed by living.
>
> Anaïs Nin, *In Favor of the Sensitive Man*

I wrote many versions of narrative text. Initially I approached my task as an ethnographer, defining what I was doing as self-ethnography. If one could do participant observation with others, why not with the self as subject? At various times throughout the writing of the manuscript, I referred to my project as an ethnographic novel (Jackson 1989), experimental ethnography (Marcus and Cushman 1982), autoethnography (Hayano 1979), self-ethnography, introspective ethnography, interpretive ethnography, or impressionistic tale (Van Maanen 1988).

I reconstructed events that occurred prior to taking field notes and wrote about them chronologically. Once events were recorded, they became field notes, much like those I kept during the last eight months of Gene's life. But because these notes were constructed long after events they described had taken place, I had difficulty capturing the level of detail of the day-to-day field notes. Even more than in my daily notes, these stories concentrated on epiphanies. My descriptions resembled a family picture album, depicting life as composed of vacations, social gatherings, and transitions. However, understanding that lived experience is commonplace (Henry 1971) as well as epiphanic (Denzin 1989a), I pushed hard to recollect the mundane and everyday as well. Especially helpful for this purpose were the day-to-day calendars and letters I had kept.

In writing from both introspective and reconstructed field notes, I used a process of "emotional recall," similar to the "method acting" of Lee Strasberg at the Actors' Studio (Bruner 1986a, p. 28). To give a convincing and authentic performance, the actor relives in detail a situation in which she previously felt the emotion to be enacted. I placed myself back into situations, conjuring up details until I was immersed in the event emotionally. Because recall increases when the emotional content at the time of retrieval resembles that of the experience to be retrieved (Bower 1981; Ellis and Weinstein 1986), this process stimulated memory of more details.

My first draft attempted to stay as close to the reconstructed events, field notes, and emotional memory as possible. I wrote from an autobiographical and subjective point of view, incorporating all the ethnographic detail and feelings I could remember. I tried to describe the complexity of experiencing contradictory and ambiguous thoughts and feelings at the same time, and across times, as well as the lone, loud voice screaming inside my head or the raw fear gnarling within my gut. I wrote down, whenever I could, what many competing voices in my head were saying. The experience was similar to a conference call in which I interacted with many speakers at one time.

I told what happened chronologically, sometimes generalizing about events that happened often, such as trips to a doctor's office. Generalizing allowed me to handle many repetitious events quickly and to show sociological patterns. Occasionally, when scenes were described in detail in my field notes or on tape or I had a particularly vivid remembrance, I used dialogue and described specific scenes.

While writing the manuscript, I checked for consistency. Did my description and interpretation of this event cohere with other similar events I described? Was the order of events accurate? Did I describe my feelings differently here than in other related situations? If so, why?

This process resulted in a 700-page draft that I showed to several friends who had been present during the time Gene and I were together. They sometimes questioned my recollections and interpretation of events, and they encouraged me to recall painfully the anger and ambivalence I had felt toward Gene. This was difficult because, for a time, I, like most survivors, needed to reconstruct our love as "pure" (Kearl 1989). Responding to these criticisms, hard as it was, contributed to my goal of making my account as close to the lived experience as possible.

Thus, I began as an ethnographer concerned with issues of validity, bias, and accurate representation. But already my manuscript differed in important ways from most ethnography. I was both the author/researcher and the subject. The work was organized chronologically, not topically or conceptually. It described what happened and did not follow the ethnographic model of filtering out experience by interpreting field data with conceptual apparatus, which then required examples of personal narrative to be inserted to make accounts real, interesting, and alive (Bruner 1986a, p. 9; Peacock 1984). I was consciously and decidedly emotionally connected to my project. I cried when I read my "data" and worried later, when I read it without emotion, that I had moved too far away from my experience to capture emotional intensity.

Although I was committed to autobiographical and emotional narration, within that frame I struggled to connect my experimental work more closely to analytical sociology. When I tried summarizing portions of the story with conceptual and thematic analysis set off from the rest of the text, much of the response—including my own—was similar to this sociologist's: "When I first got your letter, I immediately grabbed up the sections of book manuscript. Reading them was a very emotional experience. Strangely, it wasn't so much saddening as somehow cathartic. . . . You mentioned when we talked that many of your sociological friends confessed skipping over the 'sociological' part and jumping to the 'story.' Add me to the list of offenders. . . . I skimmed the abstract analysis as quickly as possible, and poured over the actual events time and time again." When I tried integrating within the story my involved narrative voice and my all-knowing sociological voice commenting from afar, the results were forced and unintelligible.

Still, I wanted to blend analysis into the narrative. I persevered because it was important to me that others define my project as sociological and, more compelling, because the sociological imagination had been such an important part of coping during the experience. Wasn't there a kind of analysis, different from distantly and abstractly interpreting what happened for readers, that would assist, rather than detract from, my desire to show lived experience as it happened? Couldn't analysis occur as part of the story and be shown in conversations and reflections on the experience?

As I pondered this question, I continued writing and reflecting on the medley of encouragement and criticism from readers. A literary agent who read several narrative chapters and liked my emotional descriptions instructed me to eschew all sociology and to tell a story for a mass audience. "You must move readers ahead in the story. They will not wait for you to go back to do analysis," she said. She suggested I use literary techniques to show instead of tell or teach, which talks down to readers, and make the material more dramatic and vivid. When I put myself into the role of reader, I knew the literary agent had a point. But following her suggestions felt too much like writing fiction—making it up—and not obeying the canons for doing rigorous, realist ethnography.

During the next few years, a number of reviewers for academic presses asked that I organize the material under a limited number of themes and tell the reader "in sociological terms" what they read. Realizing I was continuing to be schizophrenic, but rationalizing that I was trying to keep options open while I experimented with finding my voice, I wrote various abstract social-science introductions to my work that promised both more analysis in the text and a chapter at the end that would theorize my experience. In the meantime, I followed the literary agent's advice to enliven the text through dramatic presentation.

One reviewer reminded me then that I still had not dealt with readers' discomfort, a response I got more often as the text became more emotionally engaging. Insisting that emotional writing should be cleansed of any potential discomfort, the reviewer wrote: "It isn't the actual material [that] . . . was making me embarrassed. . . . It's her treatment. To do this kind of 'survivor' writing . . . you not only have to have been somewhere awful, you have to give the reader a sense that you have reflected on it, come to grips with it, and moved beyond it. The writer's calm has to quiet the reader's embarrassment."

This response provided another significant turning point. While I considered this reviewer's embarrassment a legitimate emotional response to my story, I began to wonder if "quieting" it should be one of my major goals. Since emotions as lived experience often are uncomfortable, I started to realize that it could be useful, and even desirable, for readers to feel some discomfort when reading my work, instead of the boredom and passivity more commonly expressed in response to social-science prose (Pratt 1986; Richardson 1992). Perhaps signs of readers' discomforts would be "evidence of my study's success" (Krieger 1984, p. 283) at bringing readers into the emotional complexity of my experience.

... To Storytelling

'All sorrows can be borne if you put them into a story or tell a story about them.' The story reveals the meaning of what otherwise would remain an unbearable sequence of sheer happenings.

Hannah Arendt, *Men in Dark Times*

I spent the next few years writing and rewriting narrative, experimenting with form, trying out dialogue, and setting scenes. As the narrative changed and developed, I recorded the shifts in my writing style, and my reactions to them. How one turns ethnographic "data" into a meaningful story was the question that inspired this part of the project.

In initial drafts, I often told what happened. Now I concentrated on showing interaction so that the reader might participate more fully in the emotional process, not merely observe the resolution. This meant moving from generalizing about a kind of event, such as doctors' visits, to showing one visit in particular, a strategy that demanded more specific scenes and dialogue.

Now I tried to construct conversations Gene and I might have had, conversations that made a point, animated the description, and enhanced analytic understanding. Although I could reconstruct what I might have said, I found it difficult to capture the rich texture of Gene's conversation. I listened to tapes of his voice. Then I read notes from his classes and articles he had written, keeping in mind that written speech is not the same as spoken speech. I read conversations out loud to myself and others, took turns playing each part, always listening for the ring of authenticity. I considered my motives in each presentation. Was I trying to make myself look smart? Kind? Had I really been that way? Had Gene? Did this conversation cohere with others I had recorded? With the way I remembered Gene?

Converting general description into conversation showed the reader succinctly and vividly what had taken place. Often, three lines of dialogue captured two pages of descriptive narrative and demonstrated how we talked to each other and how we analyzed our experience. With each version of the manuscript, dialogue increasingly replaced third-person description.

Dialogue and scenes also helped to capture emotion. Trying to convey emotion by saying "I felt [insert emotion word]" had not worked. This construction was passive, without tension. Emotion words were too general, connoting too many different meanings for readers (Davitz 1969). Readers did not feel my anger, nor their own, just because I said I was angry. Thus, after several drafts, I replaced many emotion words with scenes that showed the emotions I felt.

To keep the reader involved in the story, I referred to sociological sources sparingly, usually only when my notes indicated they had influenced me near the time of the event I described. This strategy eliminated the interruption of citing every reference on each topic I addressed and acknowledged that I wrote from relational and emotional experience, not from citations (Allen Shelton, personal communication).

The resulting narrative paralleled the way I had lived the experience with Gene: Committed to experiencing life to its fullest, we took part in as much living as we could; committed to the sociological imagination, we worked to understand and cope with love and despair through talking analytically, descriptively, and emotionally; committed to understanding and coping with my own life and its context, I paid close attention to my emotional and cognitive reflections, sometimes examining them alone, other times in interaction with other people.

As I continued with the demanding chores of shortening and enlivening the narrative, I was drawn to biographical novels, "true stories" (for example, Roth 1991), which helped me realize that my prose did not have to tell a continuous story nor connect scene to scene. As the narrative became more focused on the story and less on layers of awareness, authority, and authorship, the sign posts that had denoted metalevel shifts disappeared.

I edited the manuscript to eliminate as much material as possible without destroying the story and then developed more fully the episodes that remained. I tried to remove repetition. Relationship patterns repeat. Episodes recur. We have the same arguments in the same ways over the same issues. And, because readers of chronological narratives expect to be moved ahead in the story, it is not always appropriate to detour into the different thoughts and feelings associated with each experience. This means that experience, although it may be exciting and varied when it happens, may become boring in repetitive retellings. By describing similar scenes over and over to "show everything precisely" as it happened, I had produced stories already grasped by the reader, dulling their engagement with the text.

A good example was my many descriptions of frustration in earlier drafts. In ethnography, one can say that frustration happened many times and then describe a "typical" case, talk about the pattern, count the number of times it occurred, or develop categories of frustration. Telling an enlivened story chronologically eliminated these strategies.

So I began to condense into one scene several events that happened close together. Sometimes, I connected everything about one topic, even when not chronologically near (for example, our discussions of suicide or examples of frustrating interactions). Now, instead of telling about general patterns of events, as I did initially, I showed a single episode. I felt this evocative composite would be powerful enough that readers would put themselves into the experience and know intuitively that similar scenes and feelings happened repeatedly. Now I was no longer trying to "capture reality" exactly as it happened or duplicate sequence precisely. At the same time, I did not give up chronological telling for static categories.

We do not live life linearly, I reminded myself. Thoughts and feelings circle around us, play back, then forward (see Ronai 1992). Life is "lived through the subject's eye, and that eye, like a camera's, is always reflexive, nonlinear, subjective, filled with flashbacks, after-images, dream sequences, faces merging into one another, masks dropping, and new masks being put on" (Denzin 1992, p. 27). In real life, the topical is woven with the chronological. An experience reminds us of similar events that have occurred and prompts us to think about what happened right before and what might happen right after the event. Ironically, by playing down linear representation, I moved closer to presenting life as I thought I had lived it.

I began to concentrate more on being true to the feelings that seemed to apply in each situation I described than to getting all the facts in the exact order. Even utterances that had been recorded in field notes or on tape were now edited with the goal of making them clear, focused, and concise, since the unnecessary words, pauses, and hesitations in spoken speech give a muddled quality to written texts. More and more I was moving away from trying to make my tale a mirror representation of chronologically ordered events and toward telling a good story, where the events and feelings cohered, where questions of meaning and interpretation were emphasized, and where readers could grasp the main points. I became less concerned with "historical truth" and more involved with "narrative truth," which Spence describes as "the criterion we use to decide when a certain experience has been captured to our satisfaction. . . . Narrative truth is what we have in mind when we say that such and such is a good story, that a given explanation carries conviction, that one solution to a mystery must be true" (1982, p. 28).

Still, on another level, I continued to grapple with chronological representation—what I "know now" and what I "knew then." In traditional ethnography, it is taken for granted that events happened then, the author observed, categorized, and analyzed them, then told the reader about them from her current, distanced perspective, which, presumably, does not affect the telling. Time is more complexly enmeshed in personal, chronological storytelling, where it is hard to ignore that the narrator and subject merge (Polkinghorne 1988), and that each telling affects the teller, which, in turn, affects the next telling.

I tried at first to represent the difference between how I saw events then and how I see events now by mixing past and present tense, then I moved back and forth between first and third person, all with little success. Finally, I admitted this was not a problem that could be resolved. Even in "real" life we don't always know when we know things since life is lived forward and understood backward (Crites 1986; Kierkegaard 1959). My solution was to use present tense to describe scenes and hold conversations, and past tense to describe what happened more generally between specific scenes and to comment on what occurred. Present tense served to bring the reader into the action and feeling that took place, while past tense helped to give the reader relief from heightened emotionality.

My failed attempt to disentangle what I knew at each point confronted me with how much my current situation influenced each telling of the story. Sometimes I took out whole scenes that once had seemed vital to my story. For example, Gene's relationship with my colleagues, which initially occupied ten or more pages, was reduced to a brief passage. As my identity, relationships, and purposes changed, these scenes became unnecessary for the point of the story.

Thus, the reality being depicted was transformed. But stories always transform experience (Bateson 1972; Denzin 1991; Derrida 1978). "There may be some truth in that story . . . but there is no reliability in the telling of it" (LeGuin 1981, p. 195). As soon as experience, whether mundane or epiphanic, is put into words, it is shaped by language and cultural understandings as well as orientation to an "other." The experience is always more than can be put into the text (Denzin 1991), and less than the text tries to tell (Goodman 1994). And, the telling of it always involves circular emotional and cognitive understanding and processes of interpretation that in everyday life blur and intertwine (Denzin 1984).

How then does this text differ from fiction (Krieger 1984)? My story was based on my experience. Certainly fiction usually originates in personal experiences of the author. "Both fiction and autobiography attempt to impose order on the only life the writer really knows, his own" (*New York Times Book Review,* April 12, 1992, p. 35). But, where fiction may start with a story that uses personal experience, the author is free to manipulate and change it in any way. On the other hand, I worked from an assumption of "truth" rather than an assumption of "fiction" (Webster 1982) and told a story that was restricted by the details of personal experience, my notes, and recollections of others (Krieger 1984). The end result is an effort to tell a meaningful story that is "faithful to the facts," and stays close to what happened (Richardson 1992).

Yet, this distinction overstates the difference between my text and fiction. Sometimes I collapsed events, invented conversations, said or omitted statements to protect peoples' privacy. Names and, occasionally, some details were changed to camouflage participants other than family members. I de-emphasized the nature and frequency of activities that might have drawn away from the main point—in our case, that we were two people trying to create meaning in a situation that challenged all our reserves. What was this but "fictionalized truth"? On the other hand, this was exactly how I wrote *Fisher Folk* and what most astute ethnographers do to persuade readers (Clifford 1986, pp. 6–7; Geertz 1973; Krieger 1984; Warner and Lunt 1941).

Still, I struggled to transcend the sociological ideal of getting lived experience precisely "right." Conversations with Art helped to clarify what I wanted for my work and for sociology in general.

Art: It's still difficult for you to give up the idea that your depictions have some direct correspondence with reality, isn't it?

Carolyn: Well, that's the way I was trained as a social scientist. I was told that what made sociology significant as a discipline was that if we listened hard enough (and, of course, used the right methodology), we would hear reality speaking its truth, and the only way to do that was to keep your distance, not let your own feelings and beliefs intrude. I know now that reality doesn't speak, but I still don't find it easy to give up the goal of representing reality or telling it the way it really is.

Art: I know what you mean. I share the same impulses. Most of us with orthodox social-science educations never though deeply about what "telling it like it really is" meant. We emphasized the reality part, not the telling part.

Carolyn: My struggle as a writer and as a social scientist is precisely about that. No matter how provoked I am by reality, I end up having to put the lived experiences into sentences. In that respect, reality is always being mediated by language and by intrusions of the writer's life history.

Art: Yes, that is precisely why social science knowledge should be considered "made," not "found." When you have to write sentences, you're always fashioning the product.

Carolyn: And as the fashioner, I'm always part of the materials of reality that I'm trying to represent. Why can't social scientists see this as liberating?

Art: Because we want to see what we do not only as different, but also as better than what other storytellers do. "Accuracy," "correspondence," "progress," "truth"—these are the terms and the rules of the social-science knowledge game.

Carolyn: The new ethnographers aren't playing that game. We don't want to separate the existence of our work from empirical reality, but we also know that reality doesn't write our books, we do. I want to be true to life. I want all sociologists to be true to life. But what is different, and more important to me, is creating the effect of reality, making what I've seen and what I say about it part of other people's worlds in a way that they can feel its truth and resonate with its meanings.

Art: So you want to make sociology more responsive to its audiences?

Carolyn: Yes, but more than that. I want sociologists to think about what people do with what we write—to view sociological knowledge as a form of social encounter in itself, and to see this endeavor as a respectable, legitimate way of doing sociology.

. . . And Evocation

There are many interpretations of a good story, and it isn't a question of which one is right or wrong but of what you do with what you've read.

Robert Coles, *The Call of Stories*

My attention to responses of readers (Barthes 1986, p. 30) has led to, and resulted from, my emphasis on evocation as a goal of this manuscript. Evocation is a means of knowing (Marcus 1986; Tyler 1986). In evocative storytelling, the story's "validity" can be judged by whether it evokes in you, the reader, a feeling that the experience described is authentic, that it is believable and possible; the story's generalizability can be judged by whether it speaks to you, the reader, about your experiences. As Parry says,

"A story works to the degree that it grasps the hearer or reader, pulls her into its world and persuades her that she is in the reality of the story" (1991, p. 42). The reader's part, as James says, is to willingly "lend himself, to project himself and steep himself, to feel and feel till he understands and to understand so well that he can say, to have perception at the pitch of passion and expression as embracing as the air, to be infinitely curious and incorrigibly patient" (1891/1981, p. 136).

Did my story engender conversational response toward the text as you read? Did the story illustrate particular patterns and connections between events (Richardson 1990a)? Did you want to give the story to others to read because you think it speaks to their situation (Frank 1991)? How useful would this story be as a guide if you encountered a similar experience in your life (Birth 1990)?

What text did you, the reader, create of my story? Did this narrative make you think about or shed light on events in your own life? Would you have acted differently than we did? Would you have told this story the way I told it? Did the words I wrote elicit from you an emotional response to examine? What did you learn about yourself and your relationships through your responses to my text?

Reader response is an integral part of narrative texts, such as the one in this book, that strive to open up rather than close down conversation (Bochner and Waugh, in press). The text I presented here does not have absolute meaning but is dependent on political, cultural, and ideological contexts (Barthes 1967), on the location and time in which it is written and read (Derrida 1978, 1981), and on the experiences and interpretations of readers (Fish 1980; Polkinghorne 1988; Tompkins 1980).

The texts we read give us hypothetical situations to try out in our minds and hearts. They call up our own experiences, making them available for examination. In our interpretations as readers, we can learn about our own lives, "experience things that no longer exist," and "understand things that are totally unfamiliar" (Iser 1978, p. 19). Norman Holland says that "interpretation [of a text] is a function of identity" (1980, p. 122). He believes that people deal with literary texts much like they deal with life experiences. The text is filtered through the reader's usual patterns of defense and fantasies, then translated into an acceptable form. Fish explains how reader response works: "Essentially what the method does is *slow* down the reading experience so that 'events' one does not notice in normal time . . . are brought before our analytical attention. . . . The value of such a procedure is predicated on the idea of *meaning as an event*, something that is happening between the words and in the reader's mind

. . . which can be made visible (or at least palpable) by the regular introduction of a 'searching' question (what does this do?)" (1980, pp. 74–75). Readers, then, are like artists who connect the two-dimensional dots on the page, and, in experiencing the work, create a three-dimensional image with their gaze and response (Giancola 1992, p. 7).

Thus, just as authors and texts construct readers, positioning and constraining their interpretations and reactions, readers construct texts as they read them (Denzin 1989a; Steig 1982). "Sometimes the truths we see in personal narratives jar us from our complacent security as interpreters 'outside' the story and make us aware that our own place in the world plays a part in our interpretation and shapes the meanings we derive from them" (Personal Narratives Group 1989, p. 261). Additionally, readers' responses can function to construct authors of texts.

In my case, formal reviewers' responses significantly affected how this story was told. Responses from readers continue to impact me and lead me to anticipate similar reactions once the manuscript is published. For example, some readers of earlier drafts of my work worried about my presentation of self, especially my naïveté at the beginning of the story. Upon reading the manuscript, one friend called in alarm, "You must change the beginning. You look too naive." Another said, "Readers will want to know that there is a mature, knowing person guiding them through the story." Others echoed these sentiments, arguing that I would lose readers who didn't want to be told a story by a naive, young woman.

"But I was naive at the beginning of my relationship with Gene," I responded. "I was twenty-three-years-old and not that experienced in the ways of the world. That's the image I want to get across." Then I added hesitantly, "But I don't want to lose readers."

My solution to this problem was to write an introduction that placed me in context to make the reader feel properly guided. The "Beginning" served to remind readers they were privy to the "wisdom" of a middle-aged, educated ethnographer who had survived this experience and now was writing about it.

Readers wanted to figure out my "character." "Unlikable," said one. "Not interesting enough."

"A hero."

"No, a martyr."

"Yes, I think, a good person."

"No, not hard enough on herself—she hasn't come to grips with driving forces within her!"

"Too simple."

"No, simply human—ambiguous, contradictory, and complex."

Similarly, "Gene is unlikable in your story. You present him as manipulative," a mutual friend said.

"He was manipulative," I replied. While I was receptive to "errors" that people thought I had made, I held firm to presenting us as I thought we had been.

Still, some will say it doesn't portray Gene accurately, or that this is not the Gene they knew.

"He was worse."

"No, better."

"More controlling."

"More lovable."

"A real ogre."

"No, a mensch."

I wonder now who will read this book after it is published. How many will choose not to take this journey through the details of the human condition? A few already have refused. "I feel I would be too touched by it to be a very good reader," said one person. What will pull readers to this book and how will they react? Some may read it because they have disabilities or care for or work with those who do. Some will read it to experience the details of a relationship or to learn about the processes of attachment and loss. Others will be attracted because they know some of the participants. They will look to find themselves or others they recognize. Many may try to determine if the story represents "reality." "It wasn't really like that. Couldn't have been." "Yes, I know someone who was there."

Some readers will want to distinguish the "good" people from the "bad." Some will decide we lived in a "dyadic morality," caring only about ourselves and our relationship; others, that we had no morality; and, still others, that this was a highly moral relationship, a testing ground of human sacrifice, commitment, and caring.

Some academics will read this story because it is about our own, like a David Lodge (1984) novel ("Ah, so that's what was going on"). Others, because they are nostalgic about "those days" ("I remember them well"). Some will read out of prurient interest, to peer into a relationship that was status, health, religion, class, and age discrepant.

Some will wonder about the meaning of a liaison between a professor and student; their impressions will be colored by the definitions of sexual appropriateness and harassment in today's world. They will have forgotten that in the 1970s status-discrepant relationships were more commonplace and acceptable to many in the academy, and "political correctness" and even feminism had different meanings then. (Will feminist colleagues be upset by the perceived power dynamics in our relationship and dismiss it as exploitative or, worse, reprimand me for being unremorseful?)

How will I deal with responses from discrepant audiences? "How will moral conservatives react?" I asked a friend who is an editor. "If you wrote this book for conservatives, you wrote the wrong book!" he wisely proclaimed. At the moment, I am confronted with how often we/I tell different versions of a story to different audiences and assume they all are true. But now, as the account that is published, this is the one for which I am accountable to all readers, and it takes on a "truth" other written and spoken accounts have not had to bear.

Some readers will be more interested in what I camouflaged. How much sex? With whom? What kind of drugs? How often? Others will be concerned that I revealed too much. "What about your career? After all, it is the conservative nineties."

Some will say Gene would have been unhappy with this project; that it is my story, not his. Some will see it as unnecessarily egotistical and characterize the author as self-absorbed. Others will say I exploited an intimate relationship for my personal gain, as this colleague cautions: "Finally, I must tell you that while I am enormously supportive of this project, I am also uneasy about the possible consequences for you of the book's publication. I'm sure it has occurred to you that some people are going to accuse you of exploiting what 'should' remain personal and private for professional purposes. Of course, were you a novelist or a poet or a filmmaker, such exploitation would be viewed as appropriate. But you know perfectly well that for many people, the transformation of emotionally laden experience into the stuff of sociology seems downright sacrilegious."

Some will see this work as my therapy and use that as a reason to belittle it. Others will see its therapeutic value as a reason to celebrate it. Some will read it as a soap opera, others as a thick description of chronic illness and loss. Still others will call it a memoir and then ask, "Can a memoir be sociology?"

Some will question how I am able to treat feeling as data. Others will wonder why I don't treat feeling more as data.

Many will want more of sociology's authorial voice, and, just as many, less. Reviewers will relish mentioning what is left out of the story and the analysis. Where are her sociological themes? Why doesn't she categorize them? Be more explicit. Guide us. Tell us what it means.

"This is only her experience."

"Just another death and dying book."

"Not sociology—not by any stretch of the imagination."
"Too raw."
"Too much body—sputum, shit, gasping."
"Too much of the author."
"A methodological nightmare."
"Too much interpretation."
"Not enough theory."
"Too involved."
"Not objective."
"Too objective."
Conversely:
"Transformative."
"Gripping."
"Beyond labeling."
"Courageous."
"Pioneering."
"Real life, yes, real life!"
(I, on the other hand, wonder how my mother will respond.)

■　■　■

Gene used to wear a jacket, on the back of which was embroidered: "The meaning is in the response."

PART VI

Endings

December 5, 1984
    "Gene, would you help me frame this manuscript I will do on our relationship." This was a task he usually relished.
    "I don't know how it will end," he said with a grin.

Author's field notes

NOW I MUST take stock of these two stories, come to a close, and construct a self beyond yet inclusive of living and writing about my relationship with Gene. As I do, I find myself resisting both the social-science impulse to "wrap it all up neatly" in categories, explanations, and resolutions, and the humanities impulse simply to tell you to read the story again. I resist the social-science mandate to abandon the particular for the general, but I also resist the psychoanalytical impulse to view self-understanding as the only goal worth pursuing. Thus, I end as I began, attempting to bring together social, narrative, and personal understanding and, in the process, construct a self with whom I can live.

As my story draws to a close, I find myself embroiled in the "central predicament of contemporary ethnography," which is the "dialectics of ethnographic approaches" (Webster 1982, pp. 198, 200). Marcus and Cushman explain: "As a problem of writing practice, there is thus the possible clash of two kinds of rhetoric in any experimental ethnography—that which attempts to close off an account neatly with a satisfying, self-contained explanation, and that which leaves the world observed as open-ended, ambiguous and in flux" (1982, pp. 45–46). Which path do I take?

I am tempted to write several endings, as did Lerner, who notes: "The ending I have just written is not untrue, nor is it quite true. As everything memory serves up, it is a slice of the truth, a layer, a segment. . . . There is another ending, the nightmare version. . . . This is no more true or untrue than the first version. Everything happened sometime. There is yet another ending—untidy, without heroes" (1978, pp. 267–269; see also Fowles 1969). But several endings would confuse the ordered coherence and integration I have tried to bring to my text and to my life by organizing the fragments into one story line. Writing has served to put all the "little incidents" into a bigger picture of recognizable patterns that contradicts to some extent the sense of "disorientation and disintegration" that threatened me when I lived this story. These patterns give the impression, quite groundless, of control and rationality, which as Mairs says, "may save one's sanity even though it can't save one's own or anyone else's life" (1993, p. 25). This order and coherence, while different from the "disjointed and fragmented sense" I had of the experience while it took place, nevertheless seems to be an important part of coping with this experience and of conveying to readers how it was and what it felt like (Ellis and Bochner 1992, p. 98).

At first, I tried to end *Final Negotiations* by giving readers analytic closure in the tradition of Whyte's *Street Corner Society* (1943), moving from the relationship story to a traditional conceptual analysis of the relationship. But whenever I started to summarize and analyze the relationship processes, I was disappointed. Do I now emphasize the coordination and love in my relationship with Gene and the peacefulness of his death, I wondered, or the conflict and anger we experienced in our gut-wrenching struggle against control and death? Knowing I could not discuss one without the other, I considered setting up a typology of dialectics in relationships, much like Rawlins' (1992) dialectical tensions in friendship, in which I would identify the major sociological abstractions to be drawn from this work. But what could I say about the pull of dependence and independence that would capture the intricacies of making the decision to stay with Gene? What could I say about identity maintenance that would tell readers more than the complexity of scenes showing Gene trying to camouflage his illness by carrying on conversations as he choked? What could I say about stigma that would better invite readers to feel the embarrassment I felt when coping mechanisms broke down in public? "Castrating bitch" now brings back whole scenes and feelings about stigma; categories, like stigma, seem bland, unemotional, and static, until they are given a particular and concrete embodiment. I could not get around the sense that categorizing muted the evocative power and openness of the narrative.

Much later, after pressure from orthodox reviewers, I thought of writing a traditional social-science ending that interpreted what readers should take away from my story about relationship negotiation. At times, the temptation to give in and be "finished" with this story and to reach and persuade those for whom writing analytically in the traditional way is the only conceivable form of rational inquiry, seemed irresistible.

But I feared that in the process of doing this, narrative details would then be viewed as grist for the analytic mill, a mill of knowledge assumed to be transcendent and to reveal "what the narrative 'really' exemplified" (Parry 1991, p. 40); that the particular would be subsumed by the general; and the story about my lived experience would be consumed by emphasis on causal patterns of relationships (Bochner 1994). Since this whole text is an attempt to tell my story in my own voice and connect my authorial self to my suffering self (Mairs 1993), I could not now find a reasonable excuse to renege and treat the two as separate, risking that the authorial voice would explain away the suffering one.

So I resisted. By this time I had located my work within the interpretive/ narrative turn in social sciences (Marcus and Cushman 1982; Mitchell 1981) that was contesting issues of authority, representation, voice, and method, and advancing connections between social science and literature (Bochner and Ellis 1992; Ellis 1991a, 1991b, 1993, 1994; Ellis and Flaherty 1992). Postmodernist, poststructural, and feminist writers had created a space for texts, such as *Final Negotiations* that introduce new forms for expressing lived experience within the domain of human sciences. Marcus and Cushman (1982), for example, called for experimental ethnographies; Zola (1982b) wrote short stories about his experience; Bochner (1985, 1994), after Rorty (1982), suggested social scientists seek ways of "coping with" rather than "representing" lived experience, and emphasize stories over theories; Richardson (1990b, 1994) called for valuing the narrative in sociology, looked at writing as a method of inquiry, and applauded experimental representations; Maines (1993) showed that sociology always has been narrative; Denzin (1989b) proposed studying lived experience through the biographical method; Jackson (1989) endorsed making ourselves experimental subjects and treating our experiences as primary data; and Krieger (1991) argued for bringing the self back into social science.

Caught up in postmodern sensibilities, I increasingly was tempted to end this unorthodox text in an experimental format. I considered and dismissed several possibilities. One option was to have a conversation with Art, my current partner, or, alternatively, to record a group of social scientists conversing about the meaning of my story. While I liked the mode of conversation for leaving open the questions raised and emphasizing the ambiguous and unresolved nature and multi-interpretations of the text (see Schneider 1991; Tyler 1986), this approach felt like I was asking for analytic rescue.

Subsequently, I thought of ending this manuscript with a conversation between me and Gene, who would "return from death" to talk to me about what these texts mean. I thought this frame would allow, similar to the relationship story, the best of both worlds—experimental form and analysis in dialogue. Secretly, I hoped Gene's ghost would take the details I knew so well, and make them conceptually palatable for a conventional social-science audience.

But Gene couldn't come back, and pretending he could only added a fantasy aspect to my narrative (and life) that I was not ready to embrace (Adams 1990; Krieger 1991). There also were more serious problems with this ending. Similar to the relationship story, I would have had to struggle to fill in Gene's side of the dialogue, which meant I would have needed to write partly from what I perceive to have been Gene's way of thinking and experiencing. This would have been even more difficult than in the relationship text because Gene had not been around the last nine years to see or interact with the postmodern influence on social science. Did I want to do analysis from a perspective of nine years ago? Did I really need to depend on Gene now? The answer to both questions was a resounding, "No."

Although Gene's voice greatly influenced how I told the story in the first version I wrote shortly after his death, his voice gradually receded into the background during the years following his death. This process paralleled what happened in our relationship: As his illness worsened, we had fewer and fewer conversations about his dying, I sought out others to talk to, spent more time listening to the voices in my own head, and escaped into reading. Although I continued to have imagined dialogues in my head with Gene throughout the writing of the relationship story, his voice was not as present in the final versions as in earlier ones. Now, as I negotiated less with Gene and more with contingencies in my current life, this final version provided a text of my experience more than it did of our experience. Although this work started as our story, it ended as my story. I became the main character (Parry 1991) and the primary listener (James 1908, p. viii). This feels like the way it ought to have "turned out" (Richardson 1992).

Integrating the Stories

The whole point of stories is not "solutions" or "resolutions" but a broadening and even a heightening of our struggles.

Robert Coles, *The Call of Stories*

As I reflect on what I have written here, I see similarities in my two stories that lead me to consider my life now from a distance. I find myself confronted by the multiple ways my two narrative texts relate to each other. Intertextual analysis (Bakhtin 1981; Kristeva 1980; Rosenau 1992; Staiger 1992) allows me to focus on connections between my relationship story and its narrative telling, instead of, as in orthodox sociology, on theoretical concepts that reduce my experience to data or, as Parry complains about family therapy, on "the degree to which [my life story] exemplified a particular discrepancy from a norm described by a theory" (1991, p. 40).

I realize now that telling concrete stories and comparing the stories represent the communicative practices by which I understood my life during the time I lived it with Gene. Often he and I examined closely the details of our situation; just as often we compared the particular situation we were in to situations that had occurred before for us or that had occurred for other people in similar or dissimilar circumstances. In this way, we were able to see our lives in a larger context, as a case among cases (Bochner and Ellis 1992; Geertz 1983), and work through change. When Gene was unable to participate in this process any longer, I compared our situation to that of others who wrote about the dying of a loved one, or I sought out stories of other people with common experiences. Intertextual analysis continues this attempt to understand life as lived.

The relationship story and writing about the relationship story occupied eighteen years of my life. When I note how much these two texts have in common, I come face-to-face with recurring processes in my life and some of my demons. When I see myself in both spheres—relating and writing— going through similar struggles, I am confronted by something about myself and the world I live in that reframes my received stories and provides potential for change. This is one way this text continues to shape me as I rewrite my story (Linden 1993; Parry 1991).

In both stories, I was passionate about the undertaking, yet frustrated by the complexity of the task, sometimes unsure and scared, other times spellbound by the mystery, relishing the unknown and challenge of figuring it all out. In writing about the relationship, I acted similarly to the way I acted in the relationship. I was involved, then detached, withdrew, said I couldn't handle it. But I always knew I would finish, for these projects consumed me. The world was "right" only when I was with Gene; I was doing my "real" work only when I was writing this manuscript. The work took on the same passion as the relationship, and brought out the same fear that this time I might not make it through. Sometimes I wondered why I hadn't picked easier projects, projects with models, since there are few models for performing death or for writing this kind of text. Why am I always crossing boundaries in my relationships and work? Why do I pick such difficult, non-traditional projects as part of my story line and refuse to give up even when they seem impossible?

Both stories reveal a partial answer to these questions in my continuing fascination with demystification, the reason I pursued training in sociology in the first place. The relationship story shows my attempt to demystify our relationship, yet at the same time it uncovers how we "remystified" it through denial and other illusions to make it work. The writing story results from my disillusion with a sociology that too often fails to demystify social processes and through orthodox practices ironically sometimes mystifies them further. For the most part, the sociological literature on relationships mystifies by simplifying human behavior into research propositions that have little to do with complex processes of relating (Bochner 1990; Shotter 1987); academics mystify their own work procedures by failing to criticize their own institutional practices (Rose 1990) and by revealing only their successes in writing. Most sociology does not allow for human agency in contemporary actors' attempts to remystify their worlds, a goal that calls for examining "meaning in the minds and hearts" of individuals who make up the social world (Sherwood, Smith, and Alexander 1993, p. 375), such as in the project I have attempted here.

Finally, I now have some understanding of the pull to tell the two stories. These stories represent my major struggles during the last eighteen years, and the struggles of many academics who must merge private relationships and public professional lives. It became as important to experience, understand, and confront the power that social science wielded over my writing as it did to experience, understand, and confront Gene's power and desire to control in relation to me (Ronai, *in press;* Laurel Richardson, personal communication). These two tasks became goals I had to complete, conquer, and unravel. I had to examine my love for and my need to attract, challenge, and resist, yet ultimately please, the authority of both Gene (men) and sociology (orthodox social-science discourse).

Only now am I able to recognize and admit a pattern that had begun in my relationship with Gene—my attempt to live and write within someone else's scheme, for their approval. I choose now to mention this pattern—there are many others—because this one is the hardest to talk about and the most difficult to deal with and understand. This probably means that it's the one that most needs telling and reading. Although I recognize that many other people—in particular, women and minorities—have had similar experiences, still I don't like acknowledging this vulnerability. I wonder if my admission might change how others see me. Then I wonder why it matters, and why this particular characteristic seems potentially more damaging than all the others I reveal more easily in this manuscript.

I want to return for a minute to a scene that occurred just prior to Gene's death. Crazed from drugs, lack of oxygen, and loss of control during the last stage of his disease, Gene yells, "I made Carolyn. Without me, she never would have gotten her Ph.D." I have pretended until now that these words had no effect on me. After all, Gene was "not himself" then. Yet, if we think of "self" as the unmonitored self, he perhaps was more himself in dying than at any other time. I shudder now at how costly his approval had been; at the same time, I appreciate the contribution our interactions with and feelings for each other made to the person I have become. My relationship with Gene in some ways symbolizes my relationship with the orthodoxy in social science, an elite who have determined how and what I write (Richardson 1990b).

In this context, now I understand that I must author my own ending to this story. Just as I realized at some point as Gene was dying that no one could do dying for him, and, later, that no one could take away my feelings of grief, I understand now that I have to tell my own story in my own voice, as partial and incomplete as it may be. I must take charge of my life/story, a story that now is primarily between me and my readers.

I laugh. Even as I write the above, I recognize that taking charge is an illusion, albeit one necessary for making it through day-to-day lived experience. I already know that when one enters a relationship, she loses some control to the unit; I already know that when one writes an evocative text, she relinquishes control over what it evokes in readers. I also realize that all thoughts, selves, and books are social products; that most work is "collaborative"; that Gene and others have influenced my argument in beneficial ways; that my story is connected to my relationship story and to many larger stories (Parry 1991); that there may be no such thing as a self without an other (Bakhtin 1981), or an individual to be known apart from relationships (Bateson 1984). Even as I assert my independence in my writing, as in my relationship with Gene, I realize that I also assert my dependence. Just as I understood the strength of Gene's need for dominance only by fighting against him, I understand the strength of the oppression of social-science conventions only by railing against them. Without the opposing forces, I would not be able to see the need for the oppositional response. I write to get free of social-science authority. But in my writing, I continue to reveal ways I am contained by it. In the same way I was interdependent in my relationship with Gene, I am interdependent with social science. Perhaps in the final analysis, interdependence and dialectics reign in relationships and in writing. The contradictions of living in a world of others are not oppositions to be settled, only ambivalences to be lived with (Rorty 1982).

Renegotiating Meaning and Identity

> There is something about telling a tale again and again that in and of itself gives shape and meaning to experience.
>
> Diane Cole, *After Great Pain*

Now I must end this project. Some people have said I have not wanted to finish this book because I have not been ready to let go of the past. Indeed, for some time, the opposite has been true. I have "recovered" from grief in Marris's sense that recovery depends on "restoring a sense that the lost attachment can still give meaning to the present." I have "let go" of my past, and I still feel the continuity of self in which I have detached the "familiar meanings of life from the relationship in which they were embodied" and reestablished them independently of it (1975, pp. 159, 37). I have built a relationship with another academic partner interested in meaning and intimate bonds. It is no surprise that our interaction has had a profound influence on the telling of this story.

For the last few years, any fear of letting go I had came from my fear that this book would not be "good enough" to have justified the many years I worked at finishing it—a problem that grew more serious as time moved on—or that it would never get a respectable publisher. Or, if it did, that the book would sit on a shelf somewhere; that is, my life would sit on a shelf. How do I do this well? I wondered, much as I had with death, and the dilemma I faced sometimes seemed almost as ambiguous, unknowable, and overwhelming. As in Gene's death, I feared and, at the same time, craved to be done.

In writing my stories, I have not wanted to complain or call attention to the specialness of my personal disaster since I know from this experience, if from no other source, that there is nothing "exceptional" about my life or my tragedies (Mairs 1993). What I have hoped for is insight, companionship, and comfort during my grief (Hauerwas 1990). The process of writing and the anticipation of an involved audience have provided that. Personally, I hoped you, the audience, would identify with my plight and gain a heightened emotional sense of what it felt like to live this experience, as well as an intellectual understanding of the contradictions and dialectical processes that occurred. In return, I have wanted to offer comfort and "companionship in a common venture" when your time for personal tragedy comes (Mairs 1993, p. 25), and provide a point of comparison for your life story.

Telling both the relationship and the writing stories has been part of my project to make life more meaningful. I found meaning in my relationship with Gene and in being a part of his living and dying. That we worked so hard to create meaning reveals that meaning was always in danger of falling apart. But when death approached and I needed Gene most to help me frame this experience in a way to make it meaningful, he was unable to talk to me about my loss of him, my self, and meaning—a dilemma produced ironically because I had come to depend on him and "us." Nor did I have the safety of our relationship to provide continuity and security to my life when I needed to redefine who I was and what it all meant.

Thus it makes sense that I took on writing this text as an identity- and meaning-making project. Each telling of my story created new meaning in my experience and contributed to personal identity (Polkinghorne 1988). From writing this, I understand in a profound way that meaning is not permanent, "narratives change, all stories are partial, all meanings incomplete. There is no fixed meaning in the past, for with each new telling the context varies, the audience differs, the story is modified" (Bruner 1986b, p. 153).

For most drafts of this book, the "Endings" reflected my struggle to find meaning in relationships. Now I focus instead on meaning-making in my academic work. As I rewrite myself in this way, I am confronted once again with how much of the way we view our lives in the past is contextualized by what is going on in the present.

This project has given me a way to think and talk about close relationships and knowledge that I did not have when I started. In crossing disciplinary boundaries to join humanities and social sciences, this discourse connects human experience as lived to research on emotions and intimate bonds, permitting my "heart and head [to] go hand and hand" (Bochner 1981, p. 70). As this discourse becomes a part of sociological perspective, my life and work are coming together in meaningful ways. The result is a sociology that connects life experience to the pursuit of knowledge. This view makes the activity of doing sociology personally meaningful and anticipates for sociology what Turner once said about anthropology, that it can become "something more than a cognitive game played in our heads and inscribed in—let's face it—somewhat tedious journals" (1982, p. 97).

By contributing to a larger, collective project that seeks to humanize sociology, create a space for experimental texts, and encourage writing stories that have meaning and make a difference in peoples' lives, I have created for myself the same kind of excitement—only more intense—I felt when I first picked up Goffman's *The Presentation of Self in Everyday Life* (1959) and decided to study sociology. It is not only learning about myself that excites me. Additionally, the excitement comes from seeing others through the new lens created by this understanding. And, finally, the excitement comes from demystifying and remystifying social processes involved in work and relationships.

As I wrestle with (and enjoy) the ambiguity, complexity, and contradiction in lived experience, sometimes now I feel I know a great deal about living in relationships and writing narratives; other times, I'm sure I know almost nothing, even about the most basic process. Thus, there is no simple, tidy ending to this book; there is merely a practical one that honors the messiness of living (Marcus 1994).

■ ■ ■

June 15, 1991 (Gene's birthday, six years after his death)

I wake up, emotionally exhausted, in the middle of a nightmare. I dream I am about to read a part of this book to a large audience. It is finally perfect. When I open my folder at the podium, my only copy of the final draft with my handwritten corrections is missing. I ruffle through the earlier drafts that are there. I feel the anticipation of the large, waiting crowd. I crawl under the podium, frantically searching. "I can't find it," I exclaim. "I have lost it, and it was perfect."

"Can't you read an earlier draft?" the moderator asks.

I break down and sob, experiencing the same kind of explosion of the ball of grief as when Gene was dying.

When I tell Art about the dream, he says it is time to be finished with the book, and I agree.

Author's field notes

But, like Gene's death, the writing of this book lingered for a long time after the dream. Gene refused to die; this book refused to be born. Once again, I was immersed in the dialectics of control in relation to the major project in my life. Even now, in 1994, as I add the finishing touches, I do not feel "finished" with the relationship or the book. As Anderson (1968) writes: "Death ends a life, but it does not end the relationship which struggles on in the survivor's mind towards some final resolution, some clear meaning, which it perhaps never finds" (1968, p. 281). Writing privileges one version of a story, but memories of untold details and alternate story lines still linger.

All this said, I finally am ready to put both the relationship and the book on a shelf, relinquishing as I do the responsibility to resolve the "real" ending.

■ ■ ■

Negotiations. Are they ever final?

References

Index

REFERENCES

Abrahams, R. 1986. "Ordinary and Extraordinary Experience." Pp. 45–72 in *The Anthropology of Experience*, edited by V. Turner and E. Bruner. Urbana, Ill.: University of Illinois Press.

Adams, Timothy. 1990. *Telling Lies in Modern American Autobiography.* Chapel Hill: University of North Carolina Press.

Agger, Ben. 1989. *Reading Science: A Literary, Political and Sociological Analysis.* Dix Hills, N.Y.: General Hall.

Anderson, Robert. 1968. "I Never Sang for My Father." Pp. 277–298 in *The Best Plays of 1967–1968*, edited by Otis L. Guernsey, Jr. New York: Dodd, Mead, and Company.

Arendt, Hannah. 1968. "Isak Dinesen: 1885–1962." Pp. 95–109 in *Men in Dark Times.* New York: Harcourt, Brace and World.

Bakhtin, M. M. 1981. *The Dialogic Imagination: Four Essays*, translated by Caryl Emerson and Michael Holquist. Austin: University of Texas Press.

Barthes, Roland. 1967. *Elements of Semiology.* New York: Hill and Wang.

———. 1986. *The Rustle of Language*, translated by Richard Howard. Berkeley: University of California Press.

Bateson, Gregory. 1972. *Steps to an Ecology of Mind.* New York: Ballantine Books.

Bateson, Mary Catherine. 1984. *With a Daughter's Eye: A Memoir of Margaret Mead and Gregory Bateson.* New York: William Morrow and Company.

———. 1989. *Composing a Life.* New York: Atlantic Monthly Press.

Becker, Ernest. 1973. Denial of Death. New York: Free Press.

Benson, Paul, ed. 1993. *Anthropology and Literature.* Urbana: University of Illinois Press.

Berger, Bennett, ed. 1990. *Authors of Their Own Lives: Intellectual Autobiographies by Twenty American Sociologists.* Berkeley: University of California Press.

Bernard, Jessie. 1972. *The Future of Marriage.* New York: Bantam.

Birth, Kevin. 1990. "Reading and the Righting of Writing Ethnographies." *American Ethnologist* 17:549–557.

Bochner, Arthur. 1981. "Forming Warm Ideas." Pp. 65–81 in *Rigor and Imagination: Essays from the Legacy of Gregory Bateson*, edited by C. Wilder-Mott and John H. Weakland. New York: Praeger.

341

———. 1984. "The Functions of Human Communication in Interpersonal Bonding." Pp. 544–621 in *Handbook of Rhetorical and Communication Theory*, edited by C. Arnold and J. Bowers. Boston: Allyn and Bacon.

———. 1985. "Perspectives on Inquiry: Representation, Conversation, and Reflection." Pp. 27–58 in *Handbook of Interpersonal Communication*, edited by Mark L. Knapp and Gerald R. Miller. Beverly Hills, Calif.: Sage.

———. 1990. "Embracing Contingencies of Lived Experience in the Study of Close Relationships." Keynote Lecture to the International Conference on Personal Relationships, Oxford University.

———. 1994. "Perspectives on Inquiry II: Theories and Stories." Pp. 21–41 in *Handbook of Interpersonal Communication*, 2d ed., edited by Mark Knapp and Gerald Miller. Newbury Park, Calif.: Sage.

Bochner, Arthur, and Carolyn Ellis. 1992. "Personal Narrative as a Social Approach to Interpersonal Communication." *Communication Theory* 2:165–172.

Bochner, Arthur, and Joanne Waugh. In press. "Talking-With as a Model for Writing-About: Implications of Rortian Pragmatism for Communication Theory." In *Recovering Pragmatism's Voice: The Classical Tradition, Rorty and the Philosophy of Communication*, edited by Lenore Langsdorf and Andrew Smith. Albany: SUNY Press.

Bower, G. H. 1981. "Mood and Memory." *American Psychologist* 36:129–148.

Brown, Richard H. 1987. *Society as Text*. Chicago: University of Chicago Press.

Broyard, Anatole. 1992. *Intoxicated by My Illness*. New York: Clarkson Potter.

Bruner, Edward. 1986a. "Experience and Its Expressions." Pp. 3–30 in *The Anthropology of Experience*, edited by Victor Turner and Edward Bruner. Urbana: University of Illinois Press.

———. 1986b. "Ethnography as Narrative." Pp. 139–155 in *The Anthropology of Experience*, edited by Victor Turner and Edward Bruner. Urbana: University of Illinois Press.

Bruner, Jerome. 1990. *Acts of Meaning*. Cambridge: Harvard University Press.

Butler, Sandra, and Barbara Rosenblum. 1991. *Cancer in Two Voices*. San Francisco: Spinsters Book Company.

Clark, Candace. 1987. "Sympathy Biography and Sympathy Margin." *American Journal of Sociology* 93:290–321.

Clifford, James. 1986. "Introduction: Partial Truths." Pp. 1–26 in *Writing Culture: The Poetics and Politics of Ethnography*, edited by James Clifford and George Marcus. Berkeley: University of California Press.

Clough, Patricia. 1992. *The End(s) of Ethnography: From Realism to Social Criticism*. Newbury Park, Calif.: Sage.

Cole, Diane. 1992. *After Great Pain: A New Life Emerges*. New York: Simon and Schuster.

Coles, Robert. 1989. *The Call of Stories: Teaching and the Moral Imagination*. Boston: Houghton Mifflin Company.

Crites, Stephen. 1986. "Storytime: Recollecting the Past and Projecting the Future." Pp. 152–173 in *Narrative Psychology: The Storied Nature of Human Conduct,* edited by Theodore Sarbin. New York: Praeger.

Davitz, Joel. 1969. *The Language of Emotion.* New York: Academic Press.

Denzin, Norman K. 1984. *On Understanding Emotion.* San Francisco: Jossey-Bass.

———. 1989a. *Interpretive Interactionism.* Newbury Park, Calif.: Sage.

———. 1989b. *Interpretive Biography.* Newbury Park, Calif.: Sage.

———. 1991. "Representing Lived Experiences in Ethnographic Texts." Pp. 59–70 in *Studies in Symbolic Interaction,* vol. 12, edited by Norman Denzin. Greenwich, Conn.: JAI Press.

———. 1992. "The Many Faces of Emotionality: Reading *Persona.*" Pp. 17–30 in *Investigating Subjectivity: Research on Lived Experience,* edited by Carolyn Ellis and Michael Flaherty. Newbury Park, Calif.: Sage.

Derrida, Jacques. 1978. *Writing and Difference.* Chicago: University of Chicago Press.

———. 1981. *Dissemination.* Chicago: University of Chicago Press.

Dewey, John. 1980. *The Quest for Certainty: A Study of the Relation of Knowledge and Action.* New York: Perigree Books.

Ellis, Carolyn. 1986. *Fisher Folk: Two Communities on Chesapeake Bay.* Lexington: University Press of Kentucky.

———. 1991a. "Sociological Introspection and Emotional Experience." *Symbolic Interaction* 14:23–50.

———. 1991b. "Emotional Sociology." Pp. 123–145 in *Studies in Symbolic Interaction,* vol. 12, edited by Norman Denzin. Greenwich, Conn.: JAI Press.

———. 1993. " 'There Are Survivors': Telling a Story of Sudden Death." *Sociological Quarterly* 34:711–730.

———. 1994. "Between Science and Literature: What Are Our Options?" Review of *Friendship Matters: Communication, Dialectics, and the Life Course,* by William Rawlins. *Symbolic Interaction* 17:325–330.

———. In press. "Speaking of AIDS: An Ethnographic Short Story." *Symbolic Interaction* 18.

Ellis, Carolyn, and Arthur Bochner. 1992. "Telling and Performing Personal Stories: The Constraints of Choice in Abortion." Pp. 79–101 in *Investigating Subjectivity: Research on Lived Experience,* edited by Carolyn Ellis and Michael Flaherty. Newbury Park, Calif.: Sage.

Ellis, Carolyn, and Michael Flaherty, eds. 1992. *Investigating Subjectivity: Research on Lived Experience.* Newbury Park, Calif.: Sage.

Ellis, Carolyn, and Eugene Weinstein. 1986. "Jealousy and the Social Psychology of Emotional Experience." *Journal of Social and Personal Relationships* 3:337–357.

Fish, Stanley. 1980. *Is There a Text in This Class?* Cambridge: Harvard University Press.

Fowles, John. 1969. *The French Lieutenant's Woman.* Little, Brown, and Company.

Frank, Arthur. 1991. *At the Will of the Body: Reflections on Illness.* Boston: Houghton Mifflin.

Friedman, Norman. 1990. "Autobiographical Sociology." *American Sociologist* 21:60–66.

Geertz, Clifford. 1973. *The Interpretation of Cultures: Selected Essays.* New York: Basic Books.

———. 1983. *Local Knowledge: Further Essays in Interpretive Anthropology.* New York: Basic Books.

Gergen, Mary, and Kenneth Gergen. 1993. "Narratives of the Gendered Body in Popular Autobiography." *Narrative Study of Lives* 1:191–218.

Giancola, John. 1992. "Multi-Representation Techniques in Research: The Rise and Descent of the Rain Dance Video Collective 1968–1973." Paper presented at the Southern Sociological Society, New Orleans, La.

Goetting, Ann, and Sarah Fenstermaker, eds. 1995. *Individual Voices, Collective Visions: Fifty Years of Women in Sociology.* Philadelphia: Temple University Press.

Goffman, Erving. 1959. *The Presentation of Self in Everyday Life.* Garden City, N.Y.: Doubleday.

———. 1961. *Asylums: Essays on the Social Situation of Mental Patients and Other Inmates.* Garden City, N.Y.: Anchor Books.

———. 1963. *Stigma.* Englewood Cliffs, N.J.: Prentice-Hall.

———. 1971. *Relations in Public: Microstudies of the Public Order.* New York: Basic Books.

Goodman, Walter. 1994. "Television, Meet Life. Life, Meet TV." *New York Times,* June 19, Section 4, pp. 1, 6.

Haskell, Molly. 1990. *Love and Other Infectious Diseases: A Memoir.* New York: William Morrow.

Hauerwas, Stanley. 1990. *Naming the Silences: God, Medicine, and the Problem of Suffering.* Grand Rapids, Mich.: William B. Eerdmans.

Hayano, David. 1979. "Auto-Ethnography: Paradigms, Problems, and Prospects." *Human Organization* 38:99–104.

Heilbrun, Carolyn. 1988. *Writing a Woman's Life.* New York: W. W. Norton and Company.

Henry, Jules. 1971. *Pathways to Madness.* New York: Vintage Books.

Higgins, Paul, and John Johnson, eds. 1988. *Personal Sociology.* New York: Praeger.

Holland, Norman. 1980. "Unity Identity Text Self." Pp. 118–133 in *Reader-Response Criticism: From Formalism to Post-Structuralism,* edited by Jane Tompkins. Baltimore: Johns Hopkins University Press.

Iser, Wolfgang. 1978. *The Act of Reading: A Theory of Aesthetic Response.* Baltimore: Johns Hopkins University Press.

Jackson, Michael. 1989. *Paths toward a Clearing: Radical Empiricism and Ethnographic Inquiry.* Bloomington: Indiana University Press.

James, Henry. 1908. *The Novels and Tales of Henry James: The New York Edition, Princess Casamassima,* vol. 5. New York: Scribners.

———. 1891/1981. "Criticism." Pp. 133–137 in *Selected Literary Criticism,* edited by M. Shapiro. Cambridge, England: Cambridge University Press.

Josselson, Ruthellen, and Amia Lieblich, eds. 1993. *The Narrative Study of Lives.* Newbury Park, Calif.: Sage.

Kearl, Michael. 1989. *Endings: A Sociology of Death and Dying.* New York: Oxford University Press.

Keleman, Stanley. 1974. *Living Your Dying.* New York: Random House/Bookworks.

Kierkegaard, Sören. 1959. *Either/Or,* vol. 1, translated by D. Swenson and L. Swenson, with revisions and a foreword by H. Johnson. Princeton: Princeton University Press.

Kleinman, Arthur. 1988. *The Illness Narratives: Suffering, Healing, and the Human Condition.* New York: Basic Books.

Kreiswirth, Martin. 1992. "Trusting the Tale: The Narrativist Turn in the Human Sciences. *New Literary History* 23:629–657.

Krieger, Susan. 1984. "Fiction and Social Science." Pp. 269–287 in *Studies in Symbolic Interaction,* vol. 5, edited by Norman Denzin. Greenwich, Conn.: JAI Press.

———. 1991. *Social Science and the Self: Personal Essays on an Art Form.* New Brunswick, N.J.: Rutgers University Press.

Kristeva, Julia. 1980. *Desire in Language.* Oxford: Basil Blackwell.

Lear, Martha. 1980. *Heartsounds.* New York: Simon and Schuster.

LeGuin, Ursula. 1981. "It Was a Dark and Stormy Night; or, Why Are We Huddling about the Campfire?" Pp. 187–195 in *On Narrative,* edited by W.J.T. Mitchell. Chicago: University of Chicago Press.

Lerner, Gerda. 1978. *A Death of One's Own.* New York: Simon and Schuster.

Linden, R. Ruth. 1993. *Making Stories, Making Selves: Feminist Reflections on the Holocaust.* Columbus, Ohio: Ohio State University Press.

Lodge, David. 1984. *Small World: An Academic Romance.* London: Secker and Warburg.

Lorde, Audre. 1980. *The Cancer Journals.* San Francisco: Spinsters.

McCabe, A., ed. 1993. *Journal of Narrative and Life History.* Hillsdale, N.J.: Lawrence Erlbaum.

McCloskey, Donald. 1990. "Formalism in the Social Sciences, Rhetorically Speaking." *American Sociologist* 21:3–19.

Maines, David. 1993. "Narrative's Moment and Sociology's Phenomena: Toward a Narrative Sociology." *Sociological Quarterly* 34:17–38.

Mairs, Nancy. 1989. *Remembering the Bone House: An Erotics of Place and Space.* New York: Harper and Row.

———. 1993. "When Bad Things Happen to Good Writers." *New York Times Book Review,* February 21, pp. 1, 25–27.

Marcus, George. 1986. "Contemporary Problems of Ethnography in the Modern World System." Pp. 165–193 in *Writing Culture,* edited by James Clifford and George Marcus. Berkeley: University of California Press.

———. 1994. "What Comes (Just) After 'Post'? The Case of Ethnography." Pp. 563–574 in *Handbook of Qualitative Research,* edited by Norman Denzin and Yvonne Lincoln. Thousand Oaks, Calif.: Sage.

Marcus, George, and Dick Cushman. 1982. "Ethnographies as Text." *Annual Review of Anthropology* 11:25–69.

Marcus, George, and Michael Fischer. 1986. *Anthropology as Cultural Critique: An Experimental Moment in the Human Sciences.* Chicago: University of Chicago Press.

Marris, Peter. 1975. *Loss and Change.* Garden City, N.Y.: Anchor Press Doubleday.

Merton, Robert K. 1988. "Some Thoughts on the Concept of Sociological Autobiography." Pp. 17–21 in *Sociological Lives: Social Change and the Life Course,* vol. 2, edited by Matilda White Riley. Newbury Park, Calif.: Sage.

Mitchell, W.J.T. 1981. *On Narrative.* Chicago: University of Chicago Press.

Murphy, Robert. 1987. *The Body Silent.* New York: Henry Holt.

Nelson, J. L., A. Megill, and D. N. McCloskey, eds. 1987. *The Rhetoric of the Human Sciences: Language and Argument in Scholarship and Human Affairs.* Madison: University of Wisconsin Press.

New York Times Book Review. 1992. "Fiction's True Art" April 12, p. 35.

Nin, Anaïs. 1976. *In Favor of the Sensitive Man and Other Essays.* New York: Harcourt Brace Jovanovich.

Okely, Judith, and Helen Callaway, eds. 1992. *Anthropology and Autobiography.* London: Routledge.

Paget, Marianne A. Edited by Marjorie L. DeVault. 1993. *A Complex Sorrow: Reflections on Cancer and an Abbreviated Life.* Philadelphia: Temple University Press.

Parkes, C. M., and R. S. Weiss. 1983. *Recovery from Bereavement.* New York: Basic Books.

Parry, Alan. 1991. "A Universe of Stories." *Family Process* 30:37–54.

Peacock, James L. 1984. "Religion and Life History: An Exploration in Cultural Psychology." Pp. 94–116 in *Text, Play, and Story: The Construction and Reconstruction of Self and Society,* edited by Edward Bruner. Proceedings of the 1983 annual meeting, American Ethnological Society, Washington, D.C.

Personal Narratives Group, eds. 1989. *Interpreting Women's Lives: Feminist Theory and Personal Narratives.* Bloomington: Indiana University Press.

Polkinghorne, Donald. 1988. *Narrative Knowing and the Human Sciences.* Albany: State University of New York Press.

Pratt, Mary Louise. 1986. "Fieldwork in Common Places." Pp. 27–50 in *Writing Culture: The Poetics and Politics of Ethnography.* Berkeley: University of California Press.

Quinney, Richard. 1991. *Journey to a Far Place: Autobiographical Reflections.* Philadelphia: Temple University Press.

Rawlins, William K. 1992. *Friendship Matters: Communication, Dialectics, and the Life Course.* New York: Aldine De Gruyter.

Richardson, Laurel. 1990a. "Narrative and Sociology." *Journal of Contemporary Ethnography* 19:116–135.

———. 1990b. *Writing Strategies: Reaching Diverse Audiences.* Newbury Park, Calif.: Sage.

———. 1992. "The Consequences of Poetic Representation: Writing the Other,

Rewriting the Self." Pp. 125–137 in *Investigating Subjectivity: Research on Lived Experience*, edited by Carolyn Ellis and Michael Flaherty. Newbury Park, Calif.: Sage.

———. 1994. "Writing as a Method of Inquiry." Pp. 516–529 in *Handbook of Qualitative Research*, edited by Norman Denzin and Yvonne Lincoln. Thousand Oaks, Calif.: Sage.

Riessman, Catherine Kohler. 1993. *Narrative Analysis*. Newbury Park, Calif.: Sage.

Ronai, Carol Rambo. 1992. "The Reflexive Self through Narrative: A Night in the Life of an Erotic Dancer/Researcher." Pp. 102–124 in *Investigating Subjectivity: Research on Lived Experience*, edited by Carolyn Ellis and Michael Flaherty. Newbury Park, Calif.: Sage.

———. In press. "Multiple Reflections of Child Sex Abuse: An Argument for a Layered Account." *Journal of Contemporary Ethnography*.

Rorty, Richard. 1982. *Consequences of Pragmatism (Essays: 1972–1980)*. Minneapolis: University of Minnesota Press.

Rose, Dan. 1990. *Living the Ethnographic Life*. Newbury Park, Calif.: Sage.

Rosenau, Pauline Marie. 1992. *Post-Modernism and the Social Sciences: Insights, Inroads, and Intrusions*. Princeton: Princeton University Press.

Rosenwald, George, and Richard Ochberg, eds. 1992. *Storied Lives: The Cultural Politics of Self-Understanding*. New Haven: Yale University Press.

Roth, Philip. 1991. *Patrimony: A True Story*. New York: Simon and Schuster.

Sarbin, Theodore, ed. 1986. *Narrative Psychology: The Storied Nature of Human Conduct*. New York: Praeger.

Schneider, Joseph. 1991. "Troubles with Textual Authority in Sociology." *Symbolic Interaction* 14:295–319.

Sherwood, Steven, Philip Smith, and Jeffrey Alexander. 1993. "The British Are Coming . . . Again! The Hidden Agenda of 'Cultural Studies.' " *Contemporary Sociology* 22:370–375.

Shotter, John. 1987. "The Social Construction of an (Us): Problems of Accountability and Narratology." Pp. 225–247 in *Accounting for Relationships*, edited by Rosalie Burnett, Patrick McGee, and David Clarke. London: Methuen.

Simons, Herbert. 1990. *Rhetoric in the Human Sciences*. London: Sage.

Spence, Donald. 1982. *Narrative Truth and Historical Truth: Meaning and Interpretation in Psychoanalysis*. New York: W. W. Norton and Company.

Staiger, Janet. 1992. *Interpreting Films: Studies in the Historical Reception of American Cinema*. Princeton: Princeton University Press.

Stanley, Liz, and David Morgan, eds. 1993. "Special Issue: Biography and Autobiography." *Sociology* 27:1–197.

Steedman, Carolyn. 1986. *Landscape for a Good Woman: A Story of Two Lives*. New Brunswick, N.J.: Rutgers University Press.

Steig, Michael. 1982. "Review: Reading and Meaning." *College English* 44:182–189.

Tolstoy, Leo. 1886/1960. *The Death of Ivan Ilych and Other Stories*. New York: New American Library.

Tompkins, Jane. 1980. "An Introduction to Reader-Response Criticism." Pp. ix-xxvi in *Reader-Response Criticism: From Formalism to Post-Structuralism,* edited by Jane Tompkins. Baltimore: Johns Hopkins University Press.

Turner, Victor. 1982. "Dramatic Ritual/Ritual Drama: Performative and Reflexive Anthropology." Pp. 83–97 in *A Crack in the Mirror: Reflexive Perspectives in Anthropology,* edited by Jay Ruby. Philadelphia: University of Pennsylvania Press.

Turner, Victor, and Edward Bruner. 1986. *The Anthropology of Experience.* Urbana: University of Illinois Press.

Tyler, Steven. 1986. "Post-Modern Ethnography: From Document of the Occult to Occult Document." Pp. 122–140 in *Writing Culture,* edited by James Clifford and George Marcus. Berkeley: University of California Press.

Van Maanen, John. 1988. *Tales of the Field: On Writing Ethnography.* Chicago: University of Chicago Press.

Warner, W. L., and P. Lunt. 1941. *The Social Life of a Modern Community.* New Haven: Yale University Press.

Webster, Steven. 1982. "Dialogue and Fiction in Ethnography." *Dialectical Anthropology* 7:91–114.

Weinstein, Eugene. 1966. "Toward a Theory of Interpersonal Tactics." Pp. 394–398 in *Problems in Social Psychology,* edited by P. Secord and C. Backman. New York: McGraw Hill.

Whyte, William F. 1943. *Street Corner Society: The Social Structure of an Italian Slum.* Chicago: University of Chicago Press.

Williams, Patricia. 1991. *The Alchemy of Race and Rights: Diary of a Law Professor.* Cambridge, Mass.: Harvard University Press.

Women's Studies International Forum. 1987. "Personal Chronicles: Women's Autobiographical Writings," vol. 10.

Yalom, Irvin. 1989. *Love's Executioner: And Other Tales of Psychotherapy.* New York: Basic Books.

Zald, Mayer. 1991. "Sociology as a Discipline: Quasi-Science, Quasi-Humanities." *American Sociologist* 22:165–187.

Zola, Irving Kenneth. 1982a. *Missing Pieces: A Chronicle of Living with a Disability.* Philadelphia: Temple University Press.

———, ed. 1982b. *Ordinary Lives: Voices of Disability and Disease.* Cambridge: Apple-wood Books.

INDEX